WITHDRAWN

CARING
—FOR OUR—
BUILT
HERITAGE

Other titles from E & FN Spon

Building Conservation Contracts and Grant Aid
A practical guide
K. Davey

The Maintenance of Brick and Stone Masonry Structures
A.M. Sowden

Old Waterfront Walls
Management, maintenance and rehabilitation
R.N. Bray and P.F.B. Tatham

Planning and the Heritage
Policy and procedures
M. Ross

Defects and Deterioration in Buildings
B.A. Richardson

The Construction of New Buildings Behind Historic Facades
D. Highfield

Rehabilitation and Re-use of Old Buildings
D. Highfield

The Architect's Remodeling, Renovation and Restoration Handbook
H.L. Simmons

Housing Defects Reference Manual
The Building Research Establishment Defect Action Sheets
Building Research Establishment

The Idea of Building
S. Groák

Getting Rid of Graffiti
A practical guide to graffiti removal and anti-graffiti protection
M.J. Whitford

Building Construction Illustrated
2nd Edition
F.D.K. Ching and C. Adams

Altering, Extending and Converting Houses
An owner's guide to procedure
G. Di Leo

For more information about these and other titles published by us, please contact:
The Promotion Department, E & FN Spon, 2–6 Boundary Row, London, SE1 8HN.

CARING
— FOR OUR —
BUILT
HERITAGE
Conservation in Practice

—— *Edited by* ——
Tony Haskell

A review of conservation schemes carried out by County Councils and National Park Authorities in England and Wales in association with District Councils and other agencies.

E & FN SPON

An Imprint of Chapman & Hall

London · Glasgow · New York · Tokyo · Melbourne · Madras

Published by E & FN Spon, an imprint of Chapman & Hall,
2–6 Boundary Row, London SE1 8HN

Chapman & Hall, 2–6 Boundary Row, London SE1 8HN, UK

Blackie Academic & Professional, Wester Cleddens Road, Bishopbriggs, Glasgow G64 2NZ, UK

Van Nostrand Reinhold Inc., 115 5th Avenue, New York NY10003, USA

Chapman & Hall Japan, Thomson Publishing Japan, Hirakawacho Nemoto Building, 6F, 1-7-11 Hirakawa-cho, Chiyoda-ku, Tokyo 102, Japan

Chapman & Hall Australia, Thomas Nelson Australia, 102 Dodds Street, South Melbourne, Victoria 3205, Australia

Chapman & Hall India, R. Seshadri, 32 Second Main Road, CIT East, Madras 600 035, India

First edition 1993

© 1993 County Planning Officers' Society

Typeset in 10/12 pt Palatino by Excel Typesetters Company, Hong Kong
Printed and bound in Hong Kong

ISBN 0 419 17580 6   0 442 31547 3 (USA)

A catalogue record for this book is available from the British Library

Library of Congress Cataloging-in-Publication data
Caring for Our built heritage: conservation schemes carried out by
   county councils in England and Wales in association with district
   councils and other agencies / edited by Tony Haskell.
      p.   cm.
   Includes index.
   ISBN 0-442-31547-3
   1. Historic buildings—England—Conservation and restoration.
   2. Architecture—England—Conservation and restoration.
   3. Historic buildings—Wales—Conservation and restoration.
   4. Architecture—Wales—Conservation and restoration.   I. Haskell,
Tony.
   NA109.G7C37   1992
   363.6'9'0942—dc20
                                                    92-24192
                                                        CIP

CONTENTS

PREFACE

During 1989, the County Councils of England and Wales celebrated one hundred years of local government. This was a significant landmark because over those years the role of local government had been continually adapted to meet new and changing demands placed upon it. The number of County Councils also changed over this period, as did some of their boundaries.

In England and Wales, as a result of the 1972 Local Government Act, a reorganization of Local Government was effected in 1974, which reduced a number of the old Counties and created several new ones. Prior to 1974, there were 58 County Councils, together with ten National Park Authorities. Today there are 47 County Councils – eight being in Wales. The number of National Parks has not altered.

For many years, the County Planning Officers' Society has been advising the Association of County Councils not only on matters connected with town and country planning, but also on draft Government legislation and preparing reports on matters of current planning concern.

To commemorate this centenary the County Planning Officers' Society decided to publish a book bringing together some of the latest schemes that both County Councils and National Park Authorities had carried out in conserving of the built heritage. It is a companion piece to an earlier booking, prepared by the County Planning Officers' Society in 1989, *Caring for Our Countryside*[1] and includes examples of restored historic buildings, the conservation of archaeological sites and industrial archaeological structures, the protection of historic parks and gardens, and a range of enhancement and town schemes.

Finding an appropriate word that covers this complex and often varied range of work has been elusive, but the words 'built heritage', whilst rather clumsy, certainly emphasizes the breadth of this conservation work and adds a further dimension to the natural landscape heritage upon which County Councils and National Park Authorities have been active for many years now. This book is not intended to be an authoritative text book on the technical aspects of conservation, but rather a review of current work which County Councils and National Parks are undertaking in conserving this 'built heritage'. Above all, it illustrates the degree of professional scholarship that has been brought to bear on a range of schemes involving restoration, research and recording that would have been quite unthinkable a hundred years ago. By any stretch of the imagination, caring for this heritage is a formidable undertaking, and today accounts for a sizeable workload and commitment by local authorities and others.

The response for material has been overwhelming, and the number and range of schemes undertaken has meant that only the briefest information can be given on each. However, enough is included to indicate the possibilities, as well as the problems and pitfalls that were encountered before satisfactory restoration was achieved. The level of commitment, patience, professionalism and skill that is shown by these examples is certainly most encouraging, especially when many schemes have been carried out at a time when money was scarce and the budgets of local authorities restricted.

Often the initiative to undertake a particular project stems from the keenness, determination and single-mindedness of just one person, or group of persons, who have been persuaded as to the merits of a particular scheme, and have been at the forefront in getting the finances raised and the work undertaken. Some of the schemes illustrated in this book might not have got off the ground at all without the co-operation of the District Councils colleagues, who have been willing to assist with both staff expertise and finance. The advice and financial support given by the Historic Buildings and Monuments Commission for England (English Heritage) and the

Welsh Historic Monuments (Cadw) has been, without doubt, crucial to the success of these schemes.

The role played by private individuals, local preservation groups, local industry and others is certainly acknowledged for without their help and financial contributions, many of the schemes could not have been undertaken. The involvement of the Manpower Services Commission's Community Programmes should not be overlooked either. A glance at many of the schemes illustrated, shows the involvement of the Commission and the varied opportunities that there were for young men and women to acquire work skills. Although the Community Programme is no longer available, many of those who took part have been able to learn trades which will be invaluable to them in future employment.

Each of the six chapters of this book deals with a separate aspect of heritage conservation with a final chapter devoted to perhaps the most important matter of all – the publicity and promotional work that many County Councils have undertaken and which is essential in ensuring that the efforts made, and the lessons learned, are available to as wide an audience as possible. The introductions to each chapter represent my own personal view, but the texts that accompany each scheme have largely been written by the officers of the respective Council concerned. Individual enquiries about any particular aspect of a scheme, or a request for some technical information, should be made direct to the county involved.

ACKNOWLEDGEMENTS

I am indebted to a great number of my colleagues in County Planning Departments and National Park Authorities for the considerable help they have given me in compiling this book, for it represents a lot of extra work at a time when their normal workload is heavy enough! Without their help this book could not have materialized. I would like to express my thanks to those County Council officers who have helped me with the introductory texts: John Champness of Lancashire; Jon James of Clwyd; Barry Joyce of Derbyshire; Peter Masters of East Sussex; Eleanor Lloyd of West Glamorgan, and Russell Lillford and Bob Croft of Somerset, for their comments have been invaluable. I am also indebted to Russ Craig, of the Design and Conservation Consultancy, advising the Hertfordshire Preservation Trust, and to Basil Merrick of the Hereford and Worcester Building Preservation Trust for providing information about the work of their respective Trusts. The chapter on Historic Parks and Gardens – an increasingly important aspect of conservation which local authorities are facing up to – has been prepared mainly by David Richardson of Devon County Council to whom I am grateful. My thanks go also to Peter Robshaw for giving me much information regarding the Civic Trust, especially in its earlier days; to Jim Duvall, of the Association of County Councils for making available the many 'centenary celebration' books prepared by County Councils during 1989, and which have provided me with much information for this book; and to Mrs Christine Palmer for transferring handwritten notes into a neat typescript.

I should also like to express my gratitude to those County Councils who have been prepared to contribute to the costs of colour reproduction in this book. Whilst the earlier intention was to confine the illustrations to monotone there is no doubt that a few colour plates add enormously to the recording of a particular project. Many of my colleagues have made great efforts to provide photographs, whilst others spent time searching archives for historical scenes. I am indebted to Matthew Alexander, Curator of the Guildford Museum, for the picture of the cottages in Farnham Road, Guildford; and to Gill Rushton, the County Archivist at the Hampshire Record Office, for the picture of the cottages at Enham, Andover. Also to Rod Lugg and Ian Goodman of Durham and Northumberland County Councils, respectively, Peter Richards, of Essex County Council, Mrs Ruth Harris of Suffolk County Council, and Miss Sandra Caine, of East Sussex County Council, who, amongst many others, took a lot of trouble to ensure some good photographs were available. My thanks also go to Geoff Dudman, of Rother District Council, for supplying me with the aerial photograph of Brickwalls in East Sussex, to Colin Wilkins, for assistance over the picture of Bridgwater Dock, and to John Reynolds of Hampshire County Council whose delightful working drawings accompany the account of the restoration of the windmill at Bursledon.

My personal thanks go to Richard Townley, County Planning Officer for Dorset, and, this year, President to the County Planning Officers' Society, who provided me with much encourage-

ment to write this book, and to Madeleine Metcalfe
of E & FN Spon for her patience and guidance
during its preparation for publication. As a result
of all the efforts of so many people who have
provided me with information about the work
they have been doing I believe we have a fascinating and encouraging story of which to be proud
and which needs to be told.

Tony Haskell
July 1992

REFERENCE

1. County Planners Officers' Society (1989) *Caring
   for Our Countryside*, County Planners Officers'
   Society.

FOREWORD

DEPARTMENT OF NATIONAL HERITAGE
Horse Guards Road, London SW1P 3AL
Telephone: 071-270 5925
Facsimile: 071-270 6026

From the Secretary of State for National Heritage
THE RT. HON. PETER BROOKE MP

The recent creation of the Department of National Heritage is a clear indication of the importance which the Government attaches to our heritage, and caring for the historic environment is an important part of my responsibilities. No generation exists in a vacuum, and an understanding of how previous generations lived and of the continuity of the present with the past can enrich and inform our lives, especially in an era of rapid change.

This book, prepared by the County Planning Officers' Society, bears witness to the wide range of conservation schemes carried out by County Councils in recent years. Each scheme has faced its own particular problems and the way in which these have been surmounted should provide useful lessons for the future.

What has particularly impressed me has been the extent of the achievement in a time of strong pressure on resources. Financial contributions have come from the private sector as well as from County Council and District Council budgets; there has been support from Government Departments' programmes, from English Heritage, and from other public bodies. It has been very much a joint enterprise.

I am happy to pay tribute to the enthusiasm and determination which lies behind these schemes and to recommend this book to all those who are interested in practical conservation work.

Peter Brooke

PETER BROOKE

INTRODUCTION

THE EARLY YEARS

In order to place today's conservation efforts in some sort of historical perspective, it is, perhaps, helpful to look back at the situation as it existed a hundred or more years ago, and to try to understand the attitudes that were prevalent at the time, on environmental matters in general and for caring for our heritage in particular. How did this appreciation of the value of our built heritage come about and was there any particular ground swell of public opinion that set it all in motion? We are talking, of course, of the days when private ownership and wealth were the bastions of late Victorian and Edwardian England. So it is intriguing to contemplate why it was that some public authorities of the day became involved in safeguarding historic sites and structures.

Many are familiar with the words of William Morris, spoken in 1889 on the occasion of the Annual Meeting of the Society for the Protection of Ancient Buildings:

> these old buildings do not belong to us only: that they belonged to our forefathers and they will belong to our descendants unless we play them false. They are not in any sense our property to do as we like with them. We are only trustees for those that come after us.[1]

useful quote

Apart from the private efforts of amateur archaeologists and historians at the time, there was little to suggest an awakening conscience to protect our old buildings. The earliest 'environmental' duty placed upon Counties at the time would appear to be those exercised by the 'Highways and Bridges' committees of the day, where the officer in charge was often styled the 'County Surveyor and Bridgemaster'. In 1890, traffic conditions were so completely different from those of today that it is quite impossible for us to visualize their problem. In Norfolk, for example, in 1889, the County Council 'inherited a network of inadequate and neglected highways, and numerous bridges that had also been badly neglected – a problem that was to be greatly exacerbated by the increased use of heavy traction engines and steam wagons'.[1]

When the County Councils began their work there were no motor cars and general traffic was very light. 'In their early days several County Councils had no full-time officers in their employ. The Clerk of the Peace was frequently a solicitor in private practice, the County Treasurer the manager of a local bank, and the County Surveyor an engineer who gave only a small part of his time to the service of the Council.'[2]

Towards the end of the nineteenth century, the size of cities and towns grew rapidly due to an unprecedented growth in the population, coupled with the need for industrial expansion. With increased traffic using, in the main, narrow medieval streets, it was imperative that a co-ordinated and regulated approach be adopted to ensure that future development could assimilate these pressures, and bring a degree of efficiency, quality and pleasantness to the urban scene.

Social reformers, like Ebenezer Howard, were already proposing the Garden City as an answer to the dreadful urban housing conditions of the time, and, indeed, it was the need to provide for an improvement in urban housing that brought about the first piece of town planning legislation, The Housing, Town Planning, etc., Act, 1909. It was introduced as a Bill in the following terms which, some eighty years later, reads as distinctly Utopian: 'to provide a domestic condition for the people in which their physical health, their morals, their character and their whole physical condition can be improved by what we hope to secure in this Bill. It aims in broad outline to secure the home healthy, the house beautiful, the town pleasant, the city dignified, and the suburb salubrious'.[3]

The final years of the nineteenth century and the first decade of the twentieth saw the first developments in what we now call the conser-

2–10 Farnham Road, Guildford. A group of medieval cottages which as early as 1910 was threatened with demolition for road widening. Local determination was instrumental in securing their retention 'on historic grounds'.[4] However, by the middle of the 1950s, they were considered unfit for habitation and were demolished in 1957. There is little doubt that, in today's conservation climate, such fine houses would have been carefully restored and would be continuing to make their contribution to the local streetscape. (Reproduced with kind permission of Guildford Museum.)

vation movement. This was a time when issues affecting our 'heritage' became the concern of a growing number of the public and away from the preserve of the scholar versed in the study of antiquities. Both the Society for the Protection of Ancient Building (SPAB), founded in 1877, and the National Trust, founded in 1895, were established after considerable public disquiet over the fate of particular historic buildings. Today both bodies are still playing an important role in conservation; the National Trust has become one of Britain's largest charitable institutions, and is the largest private landowner with countless historic buildings and landmarks accessible to the public.

The Victoria County Histories was established in 1904, and to this day still represents a valuable repository of historical information of considerable 'heritage' value. This was also the period that saw the blossoming of interest in County Archaeological Societies, whose work over the following decades was often to be a source of considerable assistance to the County Councils in their work. The setting up of the Royal Commission on the Historical Monuments of England in 1908 was an indication of the considerable interest placed at the time upon the need to evaluate and survey the extent of the historic buildings and monuments in England, and in 1914, the (Royal) Town Planning Institute was founded.

It is noticeable that early legislation was concerned principally with Ancient Monuments and ensuring that major archaeological structures such as castles and prehistoric features were recorded. The first Ancient Monuments Protection Act became law in 1882, followed in 1913 by a Consolidation and Amendment Act which introduced the concept of Preservation Orders as a legal tool to assist in the protection of the monuments. Whilst it is possible to chart with some accuracy the development of an archaeological awareness, during these years, it is harder to detect the same degree of concern for the numerous historic buildings in the land, which had to wait until after the Second World War for legislation to introduce the concept of 'listing'. In the introduction to *Britain's Historic Buildings – A Policy for Their Future Use*[5] it is stated: Early efforts at preservation naturally concentrated on the oldest and rarest buildings and structures, on prehistoric and Roman remains, ruinous abbeys and castles, cathedrals and parish churches. From the late 1930s, this was followed by an increasing concern at the state of great houses, reflected in the introduction of the National Trust's Country House Scheme in 1937.

The centres of most of our towns and villages have deep historical roots and can trace their origins back over many centuries, evolving slowly in a way which reflected the gradual growth of an economy based on agriculture. However, the rate of growth of settlements was to increase rapidly with the coming of the Industrial Revolution when many new manufacturing centres were created and buildings erected. This growth in construction work has been unprecedented, particularly at a time when there was a limited amount of skilled building manpower available, and the transport of the heavy machinery and materials required was both arduous and time consuming.

However, not only were handsome structures erected to house the new industrial processes, but the scale of the undertakings can still surprise us today. No wonder these monuments to our early industrial past are a source of considerable public interest today, very valuable components to our built heritage.

Overcrowding, the lack of basic sanitary facilities, and generally poor housing in many of the towns and cities were the principal shortcomings which led to the identification of many buildings as being unfit for human habitation. Successive Public Health Acts since the turn of the century would appear to have had little regard for what we would today consider to be environmental or conservation issues. Unless the remedial works were relatively inexpensive and simple, there was often no alternative but to demolish such defective buildings. With hindsight, it is now possible to see that whilst some buildings which were subsequently demolished may well have been of little historic interest, others were cleared away that would still be a credit to our streets today. It is certain that in the present conservation climate, strenuous efforts would now be made to both repair and rehabilitate such buildings. Some of the schemes illustrated in this book show that structures that would once have been considered beyond repair can be rescued and restored to enjoy a new lease of life and by so doing continue to make a contribution to the quality of our surroundings.

The first three decades of this century saw a growing realization by many County Councils that a more positive approach was needed to preserve not only areas of countryside, but also important buildings. In Surrey, for example, 'preservation of the countryside was accompanied by attempts to preserve the built environment. Already, in the early years of this century, the County Council had appointed an Ancient Monument Committee, which had secured the preservation of a number of threatened sites and buildings, and the first edition of a 'list of Antiquities' had been published in 1934.'[6]

Whilst a few County Councils were prepared to purchase the occasional historic building for their own purposes if one became available, and thereby afford it some measure of protection, the loss of other fine old buildings and groups of buildings in the streets of our towns and villages during the inter-war years, appeared to cause only limited concern; buildings that, today, would unquestionably be considered as possessing 'listable' quality. This fact can best be illustrated by studying the many photographs of our street scenes, taken during the inter-war years, and noticing the loss of many fine buildings that has since taken place.

After the First World War, County Councils embarked upon a programme of establishing smallholdings, which were used as a way of encouraging people back to the land, whilst, at the same time, giving war veterans the opportunity to take up farming as tenant farmers. During the 20s and 30s, County Councils were able to acquire extensive land holdings, taking advantage at that time of the recession in agricultural land prices. These smallholdings provided a ladder by which experienced agricultural workers could have a chance to become farmers on their own account. As was

(a)

(b)

Rural cottages at Enham, Andover, before (a) and after (b) reconditioning in 1935. This is a particularly sensitive restoration, retaining much of the original quality of the building, but, unfortunately there were many other examples where this was not the case. (From

100 years of Progress – Hampshire County Council 1889–1989 (1989) by Gillian Ruston, published by Hampshire County Council and reproduced with their kind permission.)

to be expected some of these buildings contained farmhouses and buildings of varying historic interest, but for the most part the houses for the farmworkers were generally in poor condition. This was in contrast the large private estates where estate managers kept their buildings in good repair. Although rural District Councils at that time had the responsibility for providing adequate rural housing accommodation for agricultural workers, County Councils assumed a responsibility as well.

A lack of suitable dwellings for agricultural workers meant that County Councils needed to modernize those buildings on their estates which were damp, dark, ill-ventilated and without water and sanitation. With the aid of central government grants, under the Housing (Rural Workers) Acts 1926 and 1931, Councils were able to undertake the reconditioning of some of the worst cottages. Unfortunately, any intrinsic vernacular quality that these buildings might have possessed was very often lost in the process of 'modernization'. It is easy, with hindsight, to be critical of these improvements but public attitudes at the time had little regard for any historical qualities that some of these rural dwellings may have had, and the concept of a listed building was still some years away. The need to keep agricultural workers on the land, at a time of rural depopulation was an incentive to bring as many of these cottages up to habitable standards, however much 'authentic character' was lost in the process.

Again, after the First World War County Councils foresaw that the growth in motor traffic

would demand completely new highways and bypasses for our towns. The rapidly expanding suburbs of London were some of the earliest locations for bypasses, or 'loop-roads' as they were then called. Bypasses for Sidcup and Chiselhurst, in Kent, and for Kingston-upon-Thames, Leatherhead and Guildford, in Surrey commenced during the 1920s and early 1930s. Although these were essentially traffic measures, they did bring, for a short while, a degree of environmental improvement to the towns themselves.

Elsewhere in the country, existing roads were becoming inadequate to cope with the growing volume of traffic and hence the all too familiar programme of local road improvement schemes got under way to widen, straighten, grade and ease bends in an effort to make them safer and more suitable for motor traffic. In some cases this was often carried out at the expense of the character of the local scene, and this was particularly so where settlement lay astride a main road.

THE POST-WAR YEARS

The Town and Country Planning Act, 1947 provided for a listing procedure of buildings considered to possess architectural or historical significance, and the Historic Buildings and Ancient Monuments Act, 1953 enabled grants to be made by central government for historic buildings and Ancient Monuments. A distinction was drawn between Ancient Monuments which

(a)

(b)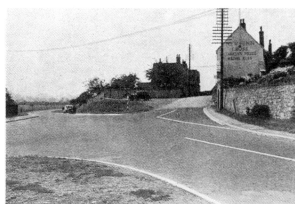

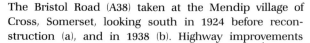

The Bristol Road (A38) taken at the Mendip village of Cross, Somerset, looking south in 1924 before reconstruction (a), and in 1938 (b). Highway improvements have resulted in the loss of village character as is shown in the later photograph. (Reproduced with kind permission of Somerset County Council.)

were generally unoccupied and listed buildings, although there are instances where a structure may enjoy both designations.

Today, our archaelogical sites and historic buildings are a valuable asset worthy of our protection, not just for their architectural or historic value, but also because they are tangible and visible examples of our own social history and have great educational value. There can be very few people who do not get pleasure and delight from visiting our historic buildings and learning of their history and the lifestyles of their inhabitants. The National Trust movement can bear witness to this.

It was recognized during the 1960s that the statutory identification alone of individual buildings possessing architectural or historical interest did not necessarily guarantee the protection of the character of historic areas, which was so often provided by groups of buildings, and, indeed, whole streets. It was therefore accepted that buildings could be listed for 'group value'. In 1967, as a further and logical development of this approach, the Civic Amenities Act was passed, introducing the concept of Conservation Areas. This was a Private Member's measure, with all-party support introduced into Parliament by the Rt Hon. Duncan Sandys MP, President of the Civic Trust, the national environmental charity founded in 1957.

The conservation of historic towns was now assuming greater importance as part of the planning function. As early as 1967, the then Minister of Housing and Local Government,

Anthony Greenwood, had stated that conservation of our historic towns was 'an aspect of town planning that is now receiving more and more attention: the kind of planning which is needed in order to preserve, in a positive way, the good things our towns already possess'.[7] Later, his successor was to commission detailed conservation studies of four cities, York, Bath, Chester and Chichester, in order to ascertain exactly the kind of problems and possibilities there were in formulating positive conservation policies, that could be generally applied.

The conservation movement had gained considerable momentum, and indeed recognition in the late 1960s and early 1970s. Under the auspices of the Council of Europe, European Architectural Heritage Year was designated for 1975. In the United Kingdom, the Civic Trust provided the Secretariat and co-ordinated the national effort for the year. This event, perhaps more than any other, can be seen as a landmark in the growth of the conservation movement. Quite apart from the efforts that were made throughout this country and on the continent, in promoting conservation schemes, other results were to be far reaching. The inclusion on school and college curricula of an appreciation and understanding of our environment was an important step, as was also the setting up of a fund, to be called the Architectural Heritage Fund, which would provide a source of financial aid to organizations with charitable status to enable them to undertake restoration schemes. Over £8 million has been loaned to projects since the Fund's inception, and many of the schemes in this book have been greatly assisted by the financial loans provided by this fund.

THE CONSERVATION SCENE SINCE 1974

The reorganization of Local Government in 1974 divided the planning responsibilities between the County Councils and the newly formed District Councils. A major role for the County Councils was the preparation of their County Structure Plans, where policies for the protection and enhancement of the built heritage would stand alongside other development policies, whilst the District Councils would be able to include detailed conservation proposals in their Local Plans, often accompanied by specific design guidance. Martin Shaw, Director of Planning and Property at Norfolk County Council has emphasized that 'any appraisal of the present state of county planning must give prominence to the positive economic, industrial, tourism and environmental programmes being implemented by County Councils'.[8]

Vicars Close, Wells. (Reproduced with kind permission of Somerset County Council.)

County policies emphasized that new development proposals would be judged against many factors including heritage and conservation issues, issues that would assume greater importance than had been the case hitherto. The continuing work of designating Conservation Areas has now been chiefly carried out by District Councils, thus ensuring that the major historic areas in each County are identified and policies drawn up for their protection and enhancement. Similarly, this identification serves as a basis for future planned expenditure by both County and District Councils on enhancement and Town Schemes.

Before 1974, most County Councils had built up specialist teams to handle their conservation work, including architects, town planners, surveyors, archaeologists, historians and archivists, each with a particular area of expertise. This included work on the preparation of the archaeological Sites and Monuments Record, conservation area designation, enhancement schemes, historic building advice, as well as considering grant applications and development proposals affecting listed buildings. With the District Councils now undertaking much of this work, they, too, sought their own specialist staff, although some requested County teams to resume this work on their behalf, especially in the early years. Indeed it has been an encouraging feature that over the seventeen years that have passed since local government reorganization, there has been an eagerness for both County and District teams to work closely together in their conservation work, with many projects being jointly funded and implemented. This is very apparent in the funding details that are shown for many of the projects in this book.

At this time the Department of the Environment was advised by the Historic Buildings Council for England on matters relating to historic buildings, listing, conservation, grants, etc., and by the Ancient Monuments Board on archaeological issues. With the development of combined records of both historic buildings and archaeological sites by County Councils in their Sites and Monuments Records, and the growth generally in concern for a single approach to all issues relating to 'heritage conservation', it was seen to be essential that these two groups should be effectively amalgamated as a separate executive agency advising the Department of the Environment. These ideas arose as proposals in *The Way Forward* published in 1982, and were later established in legislation in the

National Heritage Act, 1983, which set up the Historic Buildings and Monuments Commission, better known to us today by its shorter title, English Heritage. 'No decision-making powers were delegated to the Commission except in relation to grants, but the National Heritage Act, 1983, made the Commission the Secretary of States statutory advisors on a range of historic buildings and ancient monument matters. The Historic Buildings Council for England and the Ancient Monuments Board were wound up, but the Commission adopted its own committee structure to ensure it still had access to expert outside advice in presenting its views to the Secretary of State'*. Welsh Historic Monuments, also better known by their title, Cadw, was set up towards the end of 1984 to undertake a wide variety of ancient monument and historic building statutory and marketing functions on behalf of the Secretary of State for Wales. Cadw undertakes in Wales the duties and functions which are carried out by English Heritage and the DoE in England. Cadw is also an Executive Agency within the Welsh Office, and its staff have responsibility for ensuring the statutory duties set out in the various planning and ancient monuments Acts are administered. The Secretary of State is empowered, under the Historic Buildings and Ancient Monuments Act, 1953, to make grants available towards the repair of buildings considered by the Historic Buildings Council for Wales, the Department's independent advisory body, to be of outstanding architectural or historic interest. The Historic Buildings Council and the Ancient Monuments Board advise Cadw on related historical and monument matters.

In 1983, an accelerated programme for the resurvey of Listed Buildings was undertaken for the whole of England and Wales, by the Department of the Environment (DoE) and the Secretary of State for Wales. This would provide an up to date source of information for both central government and local authorities in carrying out their conservation and listed building work as well as providing a comprehensive catalogue of the architectural heritage of a country. The re-survey was carried out on a county-by-county basis, and besides looking again at the older urban lists – many of which were nearly a quarter of a century old – they were now to include a greater proportion of Victorian and Edwardian buildings, as well as other examples of local traditional architecture, such as farm

buildings and road-side features, including toll houses, signs and milestones. In some instances in England, and with the agreement of the Department of the Environment, the initial surveys were undertaken by staff in 22 County Planning Departments, where there were appropriately trained staff. The exercise was largely completed in England in 1987, although attention is now being given to some of the remaining urban lists that were excluded from the earlier survey. In Wales, where Cadw are undertaking the work, the listed building survey has recently been speeded up, but is yet to be completed.

As for archaeological sites, English Heritage, on behalf of the Department of the Environment, is undertaking a review of the present national lists of Scheduled Monuments, and identifying others which should be scheduled. There is little doubt that this survey, called the Monument Protection Programme, will significantly increase the number of Scheduled Monuments and thereby give a greater degree of protection for the sites. Much of this work is being carried out in conjunction with professional archaeological staff in County Councils, and extensive use is being made of County Councils' computerized Sites and Monuments Records.

County Education Authorities have adopted major initiatives in bringing heritage issues, in their widest context, into the classroom, whilst

Elvet Bridge, Durham. Part of the pedestrianization scheme, carried out jointly by Durham County Council and Durham City Council to mark European Architectural Heritage Year, 1975. (Reproduced with kind permission of Durham County Council.)

local authorities, together with English Heritage and Cadw, have promoted extensively their wealth of publicity material on the subject. Alongside this there has been a steadily growing awareness by the public of 'heritage' issues, no doubt due to the work carried out by the Civic Trust and the numerous local preservation societies, Historic Building Preservation Trusts and others.

The recent Government White Paper on the environment, 'This Common Inheritance', emphasizes that heritage issues are now enshrined in that all-embracing term 'environment'. The government is committed to preserving our heritage of historic buildings together with historic sites and landscapes. A five-point programme is projected that will provide for (i) strong legislation to protect buildings and sites from danger; (ii) an up-to-date record of our historic sites; (iii) financial support where it is needed; (iv) looking after properties in its care; (v) encouraging greater understanding of the heritage.

The continued use, and indeed respect for our old buildings and historical sites must be seen in the context of a much wider responsibility for our land and its economic survival. The term 'heritage' in this book should not be taken to imply a 'museum-piece' approach to conservation, but rather to indicate a positive and constructive attitude to this country's historic sites and buildings so that they can play an increasingly significant and meaningful role in our lives. By caring for, and investing in, the buildings of our past, we are showing not only good husbandry but a confidence in the future that we can hand on. The County Councils along with many others have clearly shown their commitment to this work and the trust put in them has been well repaid as the many examples in this book demonstrate.

Our built heritage is surely better protected and cared for today than at any time in the past, but like freedom, its price is eternal vigilance. It has taken nearly one hundred years to achieve this position, during which time, unfortunately, many worthy buildings have been lost. In 1975, Lord Holford, a President of both the Royal Institute of British Architects and the Royal Town Planning Institute, said:

> The English heritage is rich and varied. It is also contained in a small, densely populated and enchanting island. The important thing is that it is still so largely here – visible and visitable, appreciated and valued, talked about and written about as it never was before. As tastes change, and every generation evokes a fresh response from different periods of history, it is obvious that the inheritance should be kept as intact as possible and not reduced on purely moral or aesthetic grounds. A characteristic of the English 'heritage' is that it has, to a marked degree, the appearance of being lived in. Hundreds of historic buildings, from barns to palaces, exhibit a continuity of use which is still visible, despite the adaptations and additions of the past.[11]

REFERENCES:

1. Wilkins-Jones, Clive (Ed) (1989) *A Hundred Years of County Government in Norfolk.* Norfolk County Council, Library and Information Service.
2. 'Jubilee of County Councils, 1889–1939' (1939) County Councils Association
3. The Housing, Town Planning, etc., Act 1909.
4. Alexander, M.J. (1978) *Guildford As It Was,* Hendon Publishing Co. Ltd.
5. *Britain's Historic Buildings – A policy for their future use* (1982) British Tourist Authority, Working Party on Alternative Uses for Historic Buildings (ISBN 0 7095 0670 8).
6. Robinson, David (1989) *Surrey Throughout the Century 1889–1989,* Surrey County Council.
7. Anthony Greenwood, Minister of Housing and Local Government, (1967) *Historic Towns,* HMSO.
8. Shaw, Martin (1989) in *New Directions for County Government* (Ed Ken Young), Association of County Councils and the Institute of Local Government Studies.
9. Ross, M. (1991) *Planning and Heritage – Policy and procedures,* Chapman & Hall, London.
10. Summary of the Government White Paper (1990) *This Common Inheritance,* HMSO.
11. Lord Holford (1975) *Our Heritage of Landscape and Building,* The George Johnson Lecture, South Western Electricity Board.

MAP 1

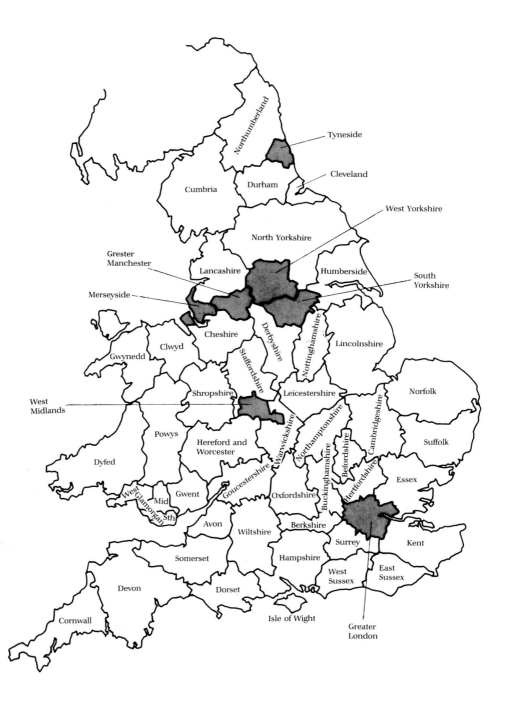

County boundaries in England and Wales.

MAP 2

The National Parks of England and Wales.* The Broads is not a National Park, but has equal status. (Reproduced with permission of the Countryside Commission.)

1

ARCHAEOLOGY

PROJECTS

Drawing overleaf shows Comeston Medieval Village, South Glamorgan.

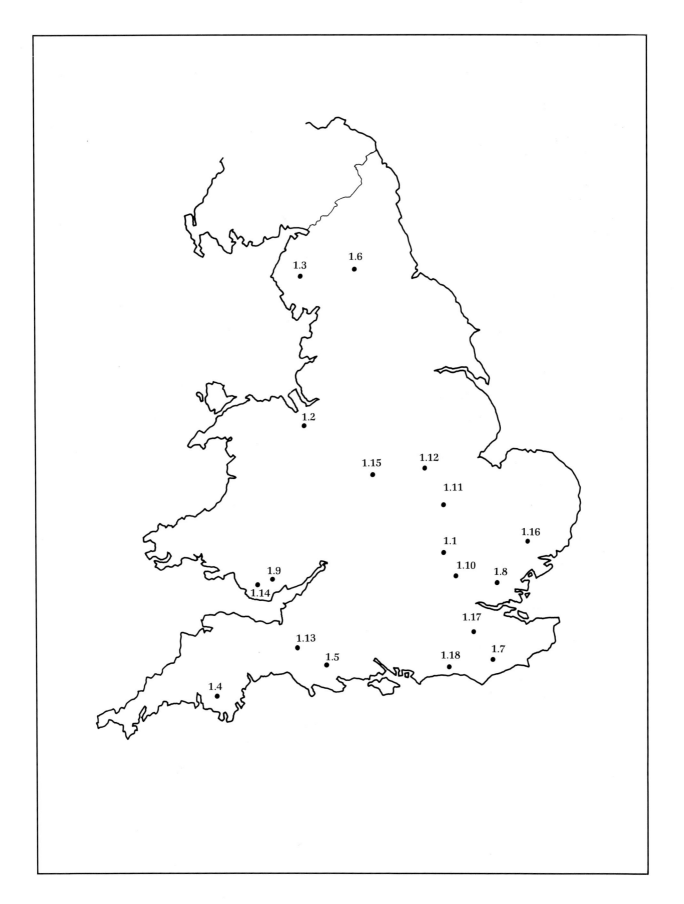

INTRODUCTION

Interest in sites of antiquity can be traced back at least 450 years, for it is recorded that John Leland was appointed Antiquary to Henry VIII in 1533 with a commission to search the length and breadth of England and Wales for surviving antiquities and monuments of all types.[1] However, just over 100 years ago, in 1882, archaeology became the first of what we would now call the 'environmental' disciplines to have the backing of Government legislation, with the Ancient Monuments Protection Act. The scholarly amateurs and writers of the time, following their interest of recording prehistoric monuments, laid down the foundations of what was to become in later years a thorough approach of research, recording and conservation.

For many years County Councils often supported archaeological research and data collection through their Museum service (or Local History work). Many Counties had active County Societies or Local Archaeological Trusts and Natural History groups who undertook archaeological research and excavation. Today, the scholarly amateur has been largely replaced by professional archaeologists, often working within County Planning Departments or in the Museum service. They take their place alongside their planning colleagues in proposing policies, promoting archaeological work, guiding research into sites, as well as adding to the County Sites and Monuments Record – a range of work that has expanded considerably over the last 25 years.

It is important, however, to emphasize the large amount of work undertaken by those local archaeological societies in surveying and recording sites and monuments. The Surrey Archaeological Society was formed in 1852, as were many others during the second half of the nineteenth century, 'in response to a growing interest in local antiquity'.[2] The present Archivist to the Surrey County Council relates that: 'From an early period the Society pressed for the preservation of antiquities and may have been partly responsible for the County forming, in 1911, the Ancient Monuments (Special) Committee. The Council then prepared a schedule of all Surrey Antiquities of importance. This later became the List of Antiquities of Surrey which was published by Surrey County Council in a number of editions, the last being produced in 1976.'

The landscape we see today is the result of human occupation and management over many thousands of years. It has been exploited, shaped, cleared and farmed to provide shelter, defence and a livelihood. From archaeological sites we can glean knowledge of our predecessors' lifestyles, their struggle for survival, their diet, and their methods of farming and husbandry. We are often dealing with very delicate and fragmentary remains which, once destroyed, are gone forever. The stone circles, the barrows, hill-forts and other earthworks, the remains of dwellings and farmsteads, together with fragments of pottery and other artifacts, are the pieces of a jigsaw which, when assembled, provide us with the only authentic picture we can get of our past. Sir Winston Churchill's oft quoted remark is apt: 'The past must be studied if the future is to be successfully encountered'.[3] The Department of the Environment has recently stated that archaeological remains are a finite and non-renewable resource which should be preserved in situ wherever possible.[4]

THE DEVELOPMENT OF THE COUNTY SITES AND MONUMENTS RECORD (SMR)

At the time of the Second World War, when large areas of the land were being prepared for military and defence purposes, many archaeological sites were revealed and needed to be recorded quickly. Unfortunately, some sites were lost, chiefly due to the understandable haste in constructing airfields and military camps in often 'virgin' areas of our countryside. However, the 'scientific' excavation of others before removal was one of the war-time tasks of the then Ministry of Works who also got involved in carrying out emergency works to bomb-damaged historic buildings. In the two decades following the War, and the establishment of Town Planning units in many County Councils, the appreciation of our archaeological heritage was developed and, at a time when much town and city redevelopment was underway, was recognized as an essential aspect of both future planning and control.

In 1969, the Walsh Committee (set up in 1966 under Sir David Walsh) recommended local authorities be urged to compile consolidated records of all known ancient monuments if they were not already doing so, and, at the same time, consider whether adequate professional archaeological assistance was available to them. Over the past twenty years, many County Councils have started to compile their Sites and Monuments Records (SMRs) as an ongoing review and record of archaeological sites. It is an index to known archaeological sites and historic landscape features in a particular county, with their location being recorded on Ordnance Survey maps, and a computerized data-base containing summary information. The County SMRs have been recognized by the Department of the Environment as central to the work of local planning authorities. They are used to provide archaeological information which is considered when formulating planning strategies, carrying out development control and the protection and management of important sites. In addition, archaeological sites are being increasingly recognized by local authorities as having an important role to play in the educational, tourism and recreational work of County Councils activities.

All Counties have now established an SMR and staff to administer it, constituting in itself a considerable source of archaeological information throughout the country. As computer technology becomes established, almost all previously manually-based records are being transferred to them for the additional flexibility, compact storage, and speedier input and retrieval they provide. In Cheshire, for example, the SMR was commenced in 1974, and from the beginning was stored on the County mainframe computer, later to be transferred to personal computers in an enhanced form with a map base and indexed paper record. It contains over 4500 archaeological sites, ranging from the Palaeolithic period to the Industrial Revolution. Again, at Nottingham County Council, the SMR covers over 6000 known archaeological sites and historic features, whilst the 14000 sites held on the Somerset County Council's SMR include sites ranging from their small prehistoric barrows to large areas of countryside where

remains of extensive Roman and post-medieval mining are to be found. Indeed, the protection and identification of extensive areas of landscape, for example in Cornwall and Cumbria, has also influenced the designation and boundaries of Environmentally Sensitive Areas, and 'historic landscapes'.

A review of the present lists of monuments scheduled under the Ancient Monuments Acts, is currently being carried out by English Heritage and Cadw in order 'to identify, or redefine, those which should be scheduled as being of national importance. A report had been prepared in 1984, which estimated that there were then, in England, over 300000 recorded sites and finds, and that the eventual number could be over 600000. In order to protect a reasonable sample of England's archaeological resource, it was assessed that some 60000 rather than the present 13000 monuments might need to be identified for rescheduling'.[5] Where requested, County Councils are assisting English Heritage and Cadw in this work, and when this programme is completed it will put the record of the archaeological resource of both England and Wales on a similar footing to that of the revised lists of listed buildings.

RECENT LEGISLATION AND GUIDANCE

The Ancient Monuments and Archaeological Areas Act 1979, at the time, was a considerable milestone for archaeology, and gave additional powers to both the Secretary of State and local authorities over the protection, recording and management of archaeological sites, as well as introducing the concept of Scheduled Monument Consent, replacing the earlier method of simply giving notification to the Secretary of State of an intention to carry out works to a Scheduled Monument.

The 1979 Act also recognized the problems confronting local authorities when developments took place on known archaeologically sensitive sites, and introduced a requirement, in certain defined areas, for developers to allow access for excavation and recording, prior to their ground works commencing. However, the matter of payment for this work was not defined, and many local authorities and local archaeological groups were often unable to meet the cost of anything other than a very limited 'watching brief'.

Towards the end of 1990, the Department of the Environment produced further archaeological advice in the form of the Planning Policy Guidance Note No. 16, *Archaeology and Planning*, aware of the growing public interest in archaeology after issues such as the Rose Theatre discovery in London, and the development of the Sites and Monuments Records by the County Councils. Its proposals can be seen as a major step forward, and places archaeology firmly centre stage with the planning process. The Government has now unambiguously identified archaeology as a material consideration in the determination of planning applications. It requires that Development Plans prepared by local authorities should indicate policies for the protection, enhancement and preservation of sites of archaeological interest, together with their setting. This Guidance Note provides a firm foundation for archaeology and with the provisions of the 1979 Act, gives a wide measure of protection for archaeological sites well into the 1990s.

RESCUE ARCHAEOLOGY

During the past 25 years, most urban centres in this country have witnessed tremendous redevelopment pressures. Undiscovered archaeological sites can often be the innocent victims of such urban redevelopment schemes, unless knowledge of the archaeological importance of a site is known beforehand. However thorough and detailed a SMR is, it is only a record of what is known already. Much is suspected and is frequently identified as having 'a high potential' or as being an 'area of archaeological importance' but hard factual information may not be currently available.

As is to be expected redevelopment within the centres of historic settlements frequently brings to light new archaeological information. There have been several recent cases, for example in York and London, where extensive and well preserved archaeological remains have been revealed during the archaeological excavation of a site prior to its redevelopment. It is often difficult to assess the importance of archaeological remains on the evidence contained within the SMR. In order to enable local planning authorities to make informed decisions, many County Councils now have policies within their Structure Plans which require applicants to provide the planning authority with

further archaeological information. Where archaeological assessments and evaluations are made, they are frequently carried out to detailed specifications set by the County Archaeological Officer. The assessment work is often carried out by professional consultants or by the local archaeology unit which in some instances is part of the County Council as at Essex, Norfolk, Suffolk, Bedfordshire and Humberside.

Once the importance of a site has been demonstrated by an evaluation, the local authority can then determine what measures are appropriate to ensure the preservation of the archaeological remains. In many instances this has resulted in legal agreements between local authorities and developers where the applicant is required to make provision for site recording, rescue archaeology and the publication of the evidence. Since the mid 1980s, County Councils in conjunction with District Councils in England and Wales have often secured many millions of pounds of private funding to be spent on Rescue Archaeology. The examples described in greater detail in this chapter of the rescue excavations at the Butter Market site in the centre of Ipswich, undertaken by the Suffolk County Council's Archaeological Unit and at Drayton Basset in Staffordshire, show how archaeological information needs to be recorded prior to site redevelopment, if its destruction is unavoidable.

Redevelopment pressures, particularly in historic urban areas, place an increasing demand upon the sources of funding for archaeological recording. Similarly, the construction of new road schemes by both the Department of Transport and County Highway Authorities has affected many archaeological sites, a number of which have only been recorded during roadwork construction. During the widening of the A66 in County Durham, however, the opportunity was taken, when a joint team of archaeologists from both Durham and Cleveland County Councils worked with English Heritage and the Department of Transport to record the many archaeological sites revealed during the work. This scheme is described in greater detail in this chapter (Project 6).

Where historical structures need to be accurately recorded, whether they are Ancient Monuments, industrial archaeological structures or historic buildings, it is possible for local authorities to request a photographic recording by the Royal Commission on the Historical Monuments of England, (RCHME). This process is known as photogrammetry, and can be particularly useful where large buildings are concerned, or where details, or, indeed, elevations are inaccessible unless expensive scaffolding is erected to enable the more familiar measured surveys to be done. Photogrammetry can also be used to great advantage in recording continuous street facades of historic buildings, where individual access for conventional measurement would be difficult.

Surveying and protecting off-shore sites and shipwrecks is another aspect of Rescue Archaeology that is being undertaken by some coastal County Councils, such as East Sussex and the Isle of Wight. This work has also been supported by English Heritage and the Royal Commission on the Historical Monuments of England.

0   1   metres   2   3

A 'stone-by-stone' drawing of the south-eastern porch of Glastonbury Abbey Barn, Somerset. The porch was recorded in detail by drawing and photogrammetry prior to its repair. The barn is a scheduled Ancient Monument. (Reproduced with the kind permission of Somerset County Council.)

SITE MANAGEMENT AGREEMENTS

Archaeological remains occur in a wide variety of landscapes and environments; it is often the responsibility of the County Council working with English Heritage, and Cadw, to ensure that appropriate measures are taken to preserve significant remains in the best way possible. Often of great concern to local authorities is the proper management of archaeological sites in private ownership. This is particularly so where there is likely to be damage caused, for example, by vehicular or pedestrian access, ploughing activities, inappropriate cattle grazing and stocking levels and uncontrolled tree and scrub growth. In these situations a management agreement is helpful to both parties. Devon County Council has, for instance, introduced an Environmental Land Management Scheme, and has used this to form the basis of an Agreement with the owner – a local charity – for the management of an Iron Age hillfort at Loddiswell providing for environmental and recreational benefits. A description of the project is given in this chapter (Project 4).

GRANTS

Much of the archaeological work carried out by County Councils is jointly funded with assistance from English Heritage and, in Wales, Cadw. Some of the work shown in the following examples would certainly not have been possible without this support. In other instances, District and City Councils and private organizations and individuals have made valuable contributions. English Heritage and Cadw are empowered to help local authorities purchase a monument when it is considered to be of exceptional importance, or when it is opportune to do so to ensure its longterm preservation, and the project from Somerset (Project 13) shows how three important sites were recently purchased by the County Council for this very reason. English Heritage and Cadw, together with local authorities, can offer Site Management agreements to occupiers of monuments in farmland, usually in the form of grants, and in some cases, capital costs can also be made.

The recent Planning Policy Guidance, Note 16 on Archaelogy and Planning, the possibilities for Site Management agreements, coupled with an increased importance and use of the SMRs, has strengthened the role of archaeologists and town planners. All counties in England now have a full-time Archaeological Officer and an expanding SMR. In Wales, Clwyd County Council, for example, has appointed a 'green archaeologist', demonstrating that archaeological sites form an important part of our countryside and that an integrated approach to countryside management is essential.[6] The protection, conservation, management and enhancement of the archaeological resource which survives in this country is becoming an increasingly important consideration in planning issues, reflecting the growing concern over the recent years for all matters affecting the environment.

The archaeological projects in this chapter indicate different facets of the archaeologist's work. While the growing emphasis on *in situ* preservation is likely to reduce the need for expensive one-off excavations, the demands for archaeological research on historically, important sites do not diminish.

The schemes illustrated in this chapter include excavations at Prehistoric and Roman sites, as in Gwent, Bedfordshire, Essex and West Sussex to the study and recording of medieval settlements and buildings in Northamptonshire, Nottingham-shire, Staffordshire, Surrey and South Glamorgan. The protection, and often the acquisition, of archaeological sites and landscapes, for example in Cumbria and Dorset, enables increased public awareness, whilst promoting archaeology into educational and community programmes, is illustrated in the schemes from East Sussex, and County Durham.

REFERENCES

1. Darvill, T.C. (1987) *Ancient Monuments in the Countryside – an archaeological management review*, HBMC.
2. Alexander, M.J. (1978) *Guildford As It Was*, Hendon Publishing Co. Ltd.
3. Ministry of Works (1949) *War and Archaeology*, HMSO.
4. Planning Policy Guidance Note No. 16. *Archaeology and Planning* 1990, Department of the Environment.
5. English Heritage (1988) *Conservation Bulletin* No. 6 (October).
6. *Clwyd Archaeology News* (1990) (Spring).

BEDFORDSHIRE

PROJECT 1.1, The discovery of Roman Sandy

The unexpected discovery of a Roman skull in the newly opened part of Sandy Municipal Cemetery posed a problem and provided an opportunity. Disruption of future burials was inevitable unless the ancient remains could be cleared. Grave digging would systematically destroy part of Sandy's rich but elusive history, for the cemetery was placed over part of the Roman town. This was the first opportunity to reveal a substantial part of Sandy's heritage, known only from stray finds for the last 400 years.

The first stage in solving the problem was to check whether the skull was a stray and isolated find or whether there were likely to be more. This was solved by the County Planning Department's Archaeology Service undertaking a trial excavation under Home Office Licence; exhumation of any human remains requires a licence from the Home Office regardless of their age. The excavation took place over the Christmas period 1987/88 and proved beyond doubt that the area was a Roman burial ground containing both adults and children.

The next stage was to raise the funds for a major excavation; the costs were estimated to be in the region of £60 000 for the first season's work. Fund raising started in earnest with a 'Save Sandy's Roman Past Appeal', launched at the Royal Society for the Protection of Bird's (RSPB) head-quarters at Sandy and under the patronage of a local dignitary, Lord Pym. The project had the personal support of the then Chairman of English Heritage, Lord Montagu of Beaulieu, as well as that of the Mayor of Sandy and the Chairman of the Bedfordshire County Council.

Support came in many forms. The initial grants were: County Council, £10 000; Sandy Town Council, £10 000; English Heritage, £10 000 and Mid Bedfordshire District Council, £500. This was closely followed by £10 000 from the County Council who adopted the project as a Centenary project; £10 000 from English Heritage, as a recognition of the importance of the archaeology and £1500 in cash donations.

Many thousands of pounds were given 'in kind' – fencing, accommodation, heavy plant, tools and equipment, volunteer labour. Expensive scientific analysis was given by English Heritage's Ancient Monuments Laboratory. English Heritage has also agreed to underwrite the post-excavation phase of the project.

The first major technical problem was the unusual sensitivity of the site. Excavating within a cemetery in use needed special tact and care, and one of the first actions when the trenches were opened was to place discreet screening around the excavation. This was also a condition of the Home Office Licence which required the exhumation to be undertaken with decency. Negotiations had to take place with people who had already purchased plots in order to achieve the necessary clearance of ancient burials.

The public were fascinated and maximum use was made of the excavation as a source of heritage education. Over 2000 people came to Open Days with guided tours and displays. More than 2500 children had talks, tours and their first 'hands on' experience of living history. The excavation was made accessible to the public on all levels and each child was given a certificate to prove that he or she had visited Sandy's Roman Past.

Thirteen burials have been found so far, together with the layout of part of the Roman town with its

Excavation in the early stages at Sandy: buildings are just beginning to appear as is the course of a Roman road. (Reproduced with kind permission of Bedfordshire County Council.)

Part of a large Romano-Celtic dedicatory sculpture found at Sandy. (Reproduced with kind permission of Bedfordshire County Council.)

1.2

roads and buildings, revealing something of its everyday life and industry. A number of major finds will enhance local museum collections. They include nearly 700 coins, fine jewellery, carved ivory, toilet implements and a rare sandstone sculpture depicting local gods. These, together with pottery, animal bones, seeds and building materials will help to reconstruct the jigsaw of life in Sandy between the first and fifth centuries. The skeletons when studied will reveal much about the health of the local population. A permanent and growing picture of Roman Sandy is emerging for present and future Sandy residents to enjoy.

Sandy is not so called for nothing! The excavation was timed to try to avoid the worst that hot sun can do to delicate sand-cut features.

Sprinklers were donated by local businessmen to damp down the sandy soils. Finds were so abundant that they outstripped the available storage space – more was provided in a secure store by another local businessman. A local land-owner solved the archaeologists' accommodation problem by providing a camping field close by.

Finally the ground needed to be reinstated to a condition where it would take grave digging without problems. Extra soil and sand were brought in and compacted with the excavated material in order to give a good solid base. With the top levelled and re-seeded no-one would know that the archaeological excavation took place there.

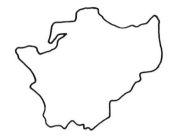

CHESHIRE

PROJECT 1.2, The Cheshire County Council Sites and Monuments Record

A fully maintained and exhaustive record of a county's archaeology underpins all archaeological work in a county. The Cheshire County Sites and Monuments Record (SMR) was first computerized in 1974 on the County's IBM mainframe computer. However, there were several limitations to this system and in 1986 a complete overhaul and enhancement of the old record began with the establishment of the temporary post of Sites and Monuments Computerization Officer. The post was funded by English Heritage for two and a half years as part of a nationwide enhancement programme of county SMRs. The new system is personal computer (PC)-based and uses the Superfile program, which is supported by English Heritage.

So that the initial computerization and enhancement could be completed within two to three years, limits were set on the type of information that would be included. All sites and finds ranging in date from the prehistoric period to 1700 AD are included in whatever form, i.e. standing sites (this includes all pre-1700 listed buildings), finds, 'sites of' (i.e. where there is no surface trace) and place names. Certain categories of information, such as all post-1700 sites and industrial sites were omitted. The temporary post created to computerize the SMR has now been converted into the permanent post of Archaeological Officer. Part of the duties of the Archaeological Officer includes the maintenance and

```
-------------------------------------------------------------------------
CHESHIRE COUNTY COUNCIL
SITES AND MONUMENTS RECORD                    Record number: 2293 /   /
Site name:
Parish   : Henhull                :                          Map: SJ65SW
District : Crewe & Nantwich             Ngr type: 8fig Ngr: SJ  6483  5345
-------------------------------------------------------------------------
Form    : Finds only           :    Form      :                  :
Period  : Prehistoric          :    Period    : Bronze Age       :

Feature : Axe-metal            :    Feature   :                  :
                               :              :                  :
Function :                     :    Function  :                  :
                               :              :                  :
Element :                      :    Element   :                  :
Site type:                                                       ;
Related Rn:      /    /             Treasure ref:
Event: Metal detecting      Worker: Anderson R    Year: 0    1990 -    0
                                       :              :          :    -
Condition:            Survival:          Area:
Site status:            :             Area status:        :
Owner type :
Owner      :

Occupier   :

Comments: Bronze Age palstave found in 1990 by Mr Ross Anderson with a metal
   detector (1). Palstave has shield pattern and is c.26cms long x c.6.5cms wide
   across the splayed blade. In very good condition, apart from damage to the
   haft end. Drawing and photograph (2). Group I shield pattern palstave.
   Northwards there is only 1 good parallel from Cartmell, Lancs. The examples
   from Manchester (Davey 36) and Delamere (Davey 39) are similar, but one has
   to go to the Marches and Shropshire for good parallels to the shape -
   Asterton Pralley Moor and Knockin Castle; Wem, Shropshire; Pentrevoelas/
   Ereiviat Road, Denbs and Llanidloes, Montgom. The shape is that of the
   Llandrinio palstaves of Shropshire-Montgomeryshire, though these tend only to
   have a crude hollow or a rib below the stop. All in the later Acton Park
   development phase (3).

---References---
   1 : Oral report to SMR                                         : SMR
Anderson R                          : 1990 : 0          : Note    : Yes
   2 : Drawing and photograph                                     : SMR
Grosvenor Museum and CMSU           : 1990 : 0          : Illus   : Yes
   3 : Written report to SMR                                      : SMR
Coombes D & Burgess C               : 1991 : 0          : Note    : Yes
   :                                :      :            :         :   :

                                    :      :            :         :   :

---Finds---
   1 : Bronze Age          : Bronze          : Palstave         : 1
Decorated              :                 : Private   :
   :                      :                 :          :         :

   :                      :                 :          :         :

   :                      :                 :          :         :

Compiler/amender: JC     Date(YY/MM/DD): 91/04/23   Continuation record: No
```

Cheshire County Sites and Monuments Record. A typical example of a primary computer record. (Reproduced with kind permission of Cheshire County Council.)

updating of the record to ensure that it is a reliable record of the county's archaeology.

With the creation of an up-to-date and accessible archaeological record, it is now possible for archaeology to play a full part in the planning process. Each District has an abridged extract of the SMR for development-control purposes and they are being encouraged to add the information to their development-control maps. All District planning lists are also checked by the Archaeological Officer to ensure that archaeological constraints are identified. Archaeology also plays a part in local plans and 'areas of archaeological potential' have been identified in several towns, using the information in the SMR. The SMR is also used not only to answer enquiries from consultants and prospective developers and offer advice on the appropriate archaeological response to be given, but it is also consulted by private researchers and students. Ways are now being explored of making the record accessible to schools.

Future developments of the SMR include the creation of an hierarchical arrangement of sites to give District planners more guidance when dealing with archaeological sites; the identification of areas of archaeological constraints on maps and the use of the County's digital mapping facilities.

Cheshire County Sites and Monuments Record. Backup files may contain fieldwork reports, photographs, press cuttings and other material. (Reproduced with kind permission of Cheshire County Council.)

CUMBRIA

PROJECT 1.3, Protecting the County's 'historic landscapes'

While Cumbria contains many important ancient monuments such as Castlerigg stone circle, it also contains areas of unenclosed common or upland where ancient remains cover many hectares. The cairnfields, such as Thwaites Fell found predominantly on the western and south western fells of the Lake District National Park, are a good example of one such 'historic landscape'. Another is provided by the limestone escarpment of the Upper Eden Valley, where a wealth of individually important sites, such as burial mounds and Romano-British farms, are juxtaposed in a palimpsest with later field systems and limestone pavements, as at Great Asby.

In 1979 the County Council recognized the importance of these 'landscapes', as opposed to individual monuments, and sought to protect the most important or most extensive of them by a clause in the Cumbria Bill then going through Parliament. The purpose of the Bill was formally confirm the powers of the County Council; perhaps not surprisingly, byelaws to protect historic landscapes met with some opposition and raised questions of how they might be 'policed'. When the Ancient Monument Division of the Department of the Environment (now English Heritage) agreed to undertake a re-evaluation of the sched-

uling in these areas the relevant clause was omitted from the Bill.

Since then the survey has been undertaken by Lancaster University Archaeology Unit (but only in the Lake District National Park). It is, however, likely that only parts of the landscape will be scheduled by English Heritage and then as specific types of monument, e.g. 'cairnfield', 'rectilinear field system', and not solely as 'landscapes', where their importance derives from their being palimpsests of different periods and 'monument' types. At the same time the protection afforded to certain areas by Limestone Pavement Orders was weakened when the legislation was changed to allow landowners to remove stone from 'man-made features'.

The protection afforded to 'historic landscapes' is thus limited. In the Lake District National Park it depends on management policies by the National Trust and Park Authority, and throughout the County on those Structure Plan policies which refer to historic landscapes. But clearly many activities which might damage or alter the character of historic landscapes are outside the control of the planning authorities and the need remains for Management Agreements or the modification of the concept of 'Areas of Archae-

Cairnfields at Thwaites Fell. (Reproduced with kind permission of Cumbria County Council.)

Field systems and limestone pavements at Great Asby. (Reproduced with kind permission of Cumbria County Council.)

ological Importance' in the 1979 Ancient Monuments and Archaeological Areas Act to include rural areas.

Another method of protecting such landscapes is that of appropriate farming – whether by commercial organizations or amenity bodies. Here attention might be drawn to the coppice woodlands which are a major element in the landscape of South Lakeland. They were originally established to fuel blast furnaces but also supported gunpowder works, bobbin mills, bark peeling (for tanning), besom and swill basket-making and while some of the blast furnaces are now protected by scheduling, the associated woodland is often derelict and becoming 'high strand' forest. The implementation of a 'Broad-leaved Woodland Strategy' by concerned bodies, including landowners, the Forestry Commission and the Local Planning Authorities, is seen as a means of pursuing appropriate management techniques. At the same time the encouragement of 'coppice trails' and special weekends or events featuring traditional crafts such as charcoal burning and chair bodging is seen as a means of focusing attention and interpreting this particular historic landscape.

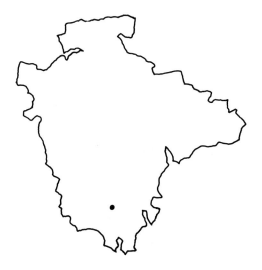

DEVON

PROJECT 1.4, Environmental Land Management Scheme

One of the first projects tackled through Devon County Council's innovative Environmental Land Management Scheme (ELMS), is the site of an iron age hill-fort near Loddiswell in South Devon. Blackdown Rings is an impressive ancient monument which, because it is superbly located on high ground, commands extensive all-round panoramic views. Field evidence suggests that it was originally an Iron Age hill-fort defended by a bank and ditch, with a counterscarp bank on the outside. Subsequently, at the time of the Norman Conquest, a castle was constructed within the enclosure, making use of the hill-fort defences. Today only the mound, banks and ditches remain; a series of low terraces and platforms outside the hill-fort site perhaps indicate traces of some settlement beyond the defended enclosure.

The whole 13-acre site was recently donated to the Arundell Charity, a small local charity which did not have the resources to manage it properly. It has been let for summer grazing by sheep and occasionally cattle. The animals have caused some erosion of the features and most of the more inaccessible areas had been invaded by scrub. Similarly, because of its situation, the site was visited by a significant number of people who also unwittingly tended to contribute to the erosion of some of the more sensitive archaeological features.

The site was desperately in need of being cared for, otherwise this part of our built heritage would only have deteriorated further and perhaps be damaged irreversibly. On the other hand, the site offered tremendous potential as a landscape, wildlife, recreational and educational resource. This is

Blackdown Rings, Loddiswell. Aerial view. (Reproduced with kind permission of Devon County Council.)

BLACKDOWN RINGS

Blackdown Rings is a large Iron Age hillfort with a small medieval castle inserted into its north-west corner.

The castle was of motte and bailey form. It may have included a timber tower rising from within a large mound of earth and rock surrounded by a ditch.

The tower was approached from the bailey (attached courtyard) by a bridge over the ditch which led to a defended entrance.

The bank and ditch which defended the bailey were crossed by a timber bridge leading from the Iron Age enclosure, now used as a large second bailey.

During the Norman Conquest of the South West early in 1068, a large army led by William I may have occupied the outer enclosure.

A Norman or Breton Lord may later have built the motte tower as a residence, his immediate followers living in the outer bailey.

This notice was prepared by the Devon Archaeological Society and funded by Devon County Council and English Heritage.

Artist's impression of the motte from the bailey entrance. Drawn by Piran Bishop

Blackdown Rings, Loddiswell. Artist's impression. (Reproduced with kind permission of Devon County Council.)

where the ELMS scheme became important and provided an ideal opportunity.

ELMS is based on establishing partnership agreements with land owners/managers whereby environmental and recreational benefits are secured for the public in return for grant aid and other support. More than 40 projects have been agreed overall up to the end of 1991/92. In respect of Blackdown Rings, the Arundell Charity was keen to enter into such a partnership agreement with the County Council. Plans were drawn up for the management of public access, the provision of recreation facilities, the enhancement of the site as a landscape feature, the promotion of wildlife and for the interpretation of this important and rich heritage site. Being a Scheduled Ancient Monument, these proposals had to be discussed with, and approved by, English Heritage. Other organizations were also involved, and in particular South Hams District Council as the site fits in well

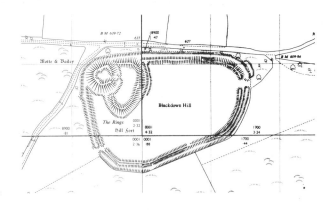

with the District's emerging recreation strategy. The site is now officially open to the public.

The ultimate package which has been developed is providing benefits to the landowner as well as to the public and various agencies involved. Perhaps more important though, a means has been found to care for yet another part of our heritage.

DORSET

PROJECT 1.5, Restoration of the Giant and viewing lay-by on the A352, Cerne Abbas

The Cerne Giant is one of the County's most outstanding features and forms an important tourist attraction. Facing west on the hill above the site of the medieval monastery, it is within the Cerne Abbas Conservation Area and is a Scheduled Ancient Monument. The figure is outlined by narrow chalk-filled trenches no more than 0.6 m (2 ft) wide. In the past its condition has been maintained by periodic scouring by local people, an activity which, according to tradition, used to occur every seven years. The date of the Giant has been much discussed, but his general resemblance to Hercules suggests a Romano-British date, perhaps of the second century AD. The figure was given to the National Trust in 1920 and has been maintained by the Trust since then. Recent measures to stop erosion and improve the setting have included the erection of a new and longer perimeter fence which now includes the Trendle, an earthwork above the Giant.

Cerne Abbas Giant. Dorset County Council contributed towards the cost of its resoration and provision of a viewing lay-by. (Reproduced with kind permission of Dorset County Council.)

RESTORATION OF THE GIANT

In 1979 the National Trust was faced with the major problem of renovating the Giant. This was a skilled operation which was last done during the 1950s. Basically it involved recutting the outline trenches and filling them with compacted new chalk.

VIEWING POINT LAY-BY

The most popular spot for viewing the Giant is the wide grass verge on the east side of the Dorchester–Sherborne Road (A352). Unfortunately, by 1970, as a result of vehicles parking and manoeuvring, the verge was seriously eroded and presented an untidy feature at the entrance to Cerne Abbas. The best solution was to construct a permanent viewing point in the form of a lay-by.

The County Planning Department, principally through the County Archaeologist, had been involved in detailed discussions and planning for this work with the National Trust, the Nature Conservancy Council (now English Nature), the Dorset Naturalist Trusts, the Department of the Environment and the adjoining landowner. The County Surveyor was involved in the design and construction of the viewing lay-by. The information panel put up near the lay-by was a joint National Trust and County Council project with two bodies carrying out a new survey of the Giant and the Trendle.

In financial terms, the County Council's contributions of £2000 towards the final bill of approximately £23 000 for the restoration of the Giant was relatively modest but greatly appreciated, as was the £500 (50% of the costs) towards the construction of the viewing lay-by. The main feature is the involvement of the County Council in a co-operative and comprehensive approach by various organizations and the landowner in the restoration of this renowned hillside figure.

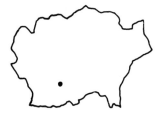

DURHAM

PROJECT 1.6, Survey and excavation alongside A66 widening, Bowes to Brough

To the west of Bowes, Co. Durham, the A66 Trunk Road runs over the Stainmore Pass. This is one of the most important routes across the North Pennines and has been used for thousands of years. The Pass has seen prehistoric traders, Roman legions, Viking adventurers, Scottish invaders and Victorian mail-coach travellers. This area, not surprisingly, is rich in archaeological remains. A 9.6 km (6-mile) stretch of the road is being made into a dual carriageway between 1990 and 1992 and the A66 Archaeological Project was set up to investigate and record the archaeological sites most at risk from the improvement scheme. The Project was fully funded by English Heritage and administered by Durham County Council (Education Department: The Bowes Museum) in conjunction with Cleveland County Council's archaeological service. This exercise in corporate management between adjacent counties was designed to make maximum use of local authority archaeological provisions and has proved immensely successful.

The A66 Project has attempted to carry out a full landscape survey of the road and surrounding countryside. Rather than examine individual sites in isolation it has tried to place them in a broader environmental and archaeological context and thereby explore the way that the land has been used and modified over some six thousand years of human history.

Fieldwalking and aerial photography allowed a full survey to be made of the archaeological monuments and led to the discovery of sites ranging in date and type from Middle Stone Age hunters' camps to nineteenth-century quarry tramways. This survey also enabled the Project to itemize those sites in need of full recording. As a result of this nine sites have been excavated on

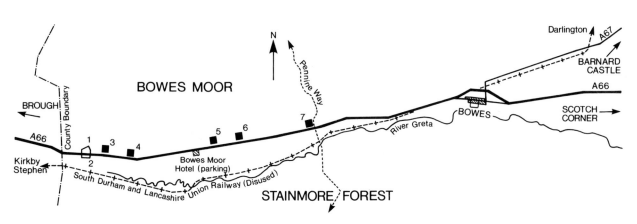

The Roman Marching Camp at Rey Cross. The new dual carriageway will cut through the camp south (right) of the existing road. This was the area excavated as part of the project. (Reproduced with kind permission of Cleveland County Council Archeological Unit and Durham County Council.)

the line of the dual carriageway including an important Roman signal station and part of the Roman marching camp at Rey Cross. Work at this last site proved to be extremely interesting, and preliminary dating from the pottery suggests that the camp, although built in the first century AD, was reused in the third century AD. The recording programme also covered the survey and photography of threatened buildings. These included eighteenth-century field barns and farms and a Victorian chapel.

Another important element of the Project was the programme of environmental research and sampling undertaken through Durham and Newcastle Universities. A large core of peat was cut

Removing a peat sample for pollen analysis. (Reproduced with kind permission of Cleveland County Council Archeological Unit and Durham County Council.)

from the moor and scientifically examined. A study of preserved pollen in the peat (combined with selective radio-carbon dates) has built up a picture of how the vegetation and use of the moorland has changed over the millennia. When this information is compared with smaller soil and pollen samples from individual excavations it will allow the environment of those sites to be recreated and can also aid in site dating. The environment work, when combined with the archaeological information from survey and excavation, will provide valuable evidence on the evolution and use of the Stainmore landscape.

A final and essential element of the Project was publicity. Free leaflets were provided on all aspects of the work and interpretation signs erected at the main sites. A possible association between one of the sites and the grave of Erik Bloodaxe, last Viking king of York, ensured continuous media coverage. It was realized however, that not all the sites could be made accessible to the public and so a programme of temporary displays at the nearby Bowes Museum, Barnard Castle, presented background information on the work. The survey and excavation part of the Project ran from 1989 to 1990. Post-excavation will continue until 1992 when a full archaeological report will be produced.

EAST SUSSEX

PROJECT 1.7, Michelham Iron Age round-house

East Sussex has a particularly rich archaeological heritage which can be shared by residents and visitors alike. The presentation and preservation of this resource is an increasingly important task faced by East Sussex County Council. Whilst the statutory protection of certain sites, combined with sensitive management policies, is one way of tackling this problem, encouraging an interest in the past is perhaps the surest way of conserving our heritage for the future. In pursuing this policy, archaeologists from East Sussex County Council's Planning Department have, over several years, instigated and sponsored the East Sussex Archaeology Project, an educational and interpretive venture. Originally formed in 1984, under the Community Programme Scheme, the project now works within the Employment Training Programme. Its first undertaking was the 'Schools Archaeological Roadshow', which aimed to make children in Primary and the lower levels of Secondary education aware of the importance of their archaeological heritage. The roadshow sessions involved pupil-centred activities, based on primary sources. An instant success, the roadshow rapidly became an established requirement for many schools.

By 1989 it had become clear that there was significant potential for a permanent open-air centre dedicated to a higher level of 'hands-on' activities involving projects that could not be attempted within a classroom environment. Several schools had already created temporary wattle-and-daub structures within school grounds and it seemed that a full-sized replica of an 'Iron Age round-house' would form the ideal focal point for such a centre.

The ancient technology activity centre and exhibition was officially opened during Environment Week 1990, and a May Day festival promoting the centre attracted over 1300 visitors. The latest addition to the centre is a full-sized replica of a Romano-British pottery kiln for firing pottery made by the children. Other activities provided for schools include building, weaving, cultivation and food production.

The response from teachers, pupils and members of the public has been extremely positive and encouraging. Most of the activities are designed to work within the guidelines recommended by the National Curriculum, Technology and History Working Group reports. Teachers are finding that this, together with the natural cross-curricular

Reproduction Iron Age round-house under construction. The framework is ready to receive daub (plaster) on the wattle (basket-like infilling). (Reproduced with kind permission of East Sussex County Council.)

nature of the project, is of particular value. The project now has a full schedule and caters for several school parties each week.

A number of possible locations, including school grounds, were investigated but all proved impracticable. Then the Director of Michelham Priory, a property of the Sussex Archaeological Society, showed interest in the proposal and a suitable area was found within the Priory grounds where the project could be located. The 5 m (16.5 ft) diameter round-house, constructed with wattle-and-daub walls, was erected by project members helped by local school children and traditional craftsmen. The construction cost

Reproduction Iron Age round-house at end of construction. (Reproduced with kind permission of East Sussex County Council.)

around £1000 and local firms made generous donations of materials. Ongoing expenditure is required for activity materials (e.g. potting clay, weaving yarns, corn for grinding etc.), whilst technical items (such as a thermocouple for recording kiln temperatures) have also been purchased. An accompanying exhibition was produced in-house, at comparatively low cost, using desk-top publishing software.

ESSEX

PROJECT 1.8, Butt Road Roman Church, Colchester

When Essex County Council announced plans to build a new police station in Colchester in the 1970s, it was already known that the site contained all that remained of one of the cemeteries which lay beyond the walls of the Roman settlement. It was also known that the remains of a building were to be found on the site, as the result of observations in a sand-pit by an amateur archaeologist in the 1840s, the date when most of the cemetery was destroyed by gravel extraction. Later, in 1935, a small part of the building was exposed, and as a result, it was thought to have been a shrine or temple built about AD 150–200.

In view of this important archaeological evidence, the Essex County Council allowed, and, indeed, along with English Heritage and the Colchester Borough Council, grant-aided the Colchester Archaeological Trust to excavate the site and to record as much as possible of what remained. The excavation also aimed to locate precisely the Roman building, so that the new police station building could be positioned to avoid it, thus enabling the remains of the building to be preserved in their entirety for display at a later date.

The excavations took place between 1976 and 1979, and revealed that, in fact, there were two different cemeteries at Butt Road. Lying at a lower level, pagan burials were indicated by 59 graves which were aligned north–south and were accompanied by objects and personal ornaments. Many of these graves were much damaged by the later grave digging of the upper level cemetery during the fourth century, for what appeared to be

Christian graves. Here were over 600 graves, in an east–west alignment, in tightly packed rows, and containing items such as footwear, armlets, necklaces and hair-pins.

As well as uncovering the graves, the building was also located, and identified as a church,

Remains of pagan burials at Butt Road site, Colchester. (Reproduced with kind permission of Colchester Archeological Trust.)

26

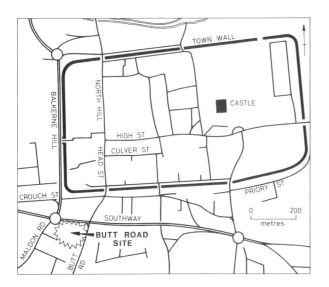

Artist's reconstruction of the Butt Road Roman Church in c.AD 320 (drawn by Peter Froste). (Reproduced with kind permission of Colchester Archeological Trust.)

Remains of the Butt Road Roman Church after completion of the project. (Photograph by Totem, Van Cols Ltd of Colchester.) (Reproduced with kind permission of Colchester Archeological Trust.)

probably built around AD 320. This was immediately recognized as being one of the most important early examples of a Roman church anywhere in Britain. Because building work on the police station did not start until 1988, the opportunity was taken to complete the excavation of the church, and consolidate the remaining walls as part of a permanent public display. The external walls of the Roman church were clearly discernible immediately below ground level and were of stone and brick. Roof tiles were found indicating a tiled roof and the floor was probably earth or sand. At the eastern end was a curved wall in the shape of an apse whilst inside, wooden posts formed short northern and southern aisles and a transverse screen, indicating a form of church layout that was to be adopted by Christian churches for many centuries to come. Of particular interest to those speculating as to the appeerence of the building, was the discovery of five complete examples of oil lamps, indicating that the interior would have been quite dark, with small windows.

The cost of the consolidation works to the church and its display was borne by Essex County Council and amounted to around £6500. The work was carried out by the Colchester Archaeological Trust and an additional £2300 was provided by the Colchester Borough Council. Additionally there has been considerable archaeological support from the County Archaeological Section of the County Planning Department.

The project resulted in a new heritage attraction for visitors to Colchester. A 'popular' booklet about the site was written by the Colchester Archaeological Trust and published in time for the official opening of the church in 1989, the costs of £2500 being met by the Essex County Council.

As a result of the extensive site discoveries, the siting of the new police station was slightly changed to allow the remains of the church to be displayed in a better setting.

GWENT

PROJECT 1.9, Caldicot Bronze Age excavation

A major dilemma faced Gwent County Council and Monmouth Borough Council acting jointly to provide an amenity lake at Caldicot Castle Country Park when highly important Bronze Age remains were discovered at the site in 1988. Work on lake construction was suspended until the Glamorgan–Gwent Archaeological Trust undertook a limited excavation during the summer of 1989. Discoveries to date include much well-preserved ancient timber, some deliberately shaped into large planks, which had been part of a timber structure incorporating massive posts driven into the bottom of a former channel of the Nedern Brook. A large number of interesting finds have been found associated with the timber, including a bronze chape (part of the sword scabbard of a warrior) and a sizeable fragment of a sewn plank boat, the first discovery of this type of prehistoric vessel from western Britain, which has created considerable public interest.

The waterlogged nature of the deposits in the valley bottom has ensured that evidence has survived which should enable archaeological scientists to work out many details concerning the environment of the area at the time when the prehistoric structures were in use. These finds already rank the Caldicot site as one of the most important in north-west Europe, let alone Wales. Within Britain its closest parallel is at Flag Fen near Peterborough.

While the local authorities had at first been determined to resume work on the lake following the initial archaeological dig, there was considerable media and public demand for the site to be subject to a much larger excavation. The Glamorgan–Gwent Trust was called upon to provide detailed estimates for a full excavation. These estimates involve a total cost of £376 000 of which Cadw, the Welsh Historic Monuments body, will find £303 000, for a five-year funding programme of measures for the archaeological excavation of the whole lake-bed area and conservation of the finds; the local authorities will find £73 000. The excavation, the largest of its type ever attempted in Wales, is being conducted by the Glamorgan–Gwent Archaeological Trust. A public appeal is being mounted to raise funds for display of the finds and visitor interpretation of the site and the Caldicot Trust has been particularly supportive in this respect.

The finding of part of a boat attracted considerable media attention. It was resting on the bed of the old river channel, and turned out to be the lowest strake of a vessel constructed of planks which were 'sewn' together with roots, probably of yew. A few similar vessels have been recorded almost entirely from the Humber, and they date to the second millennium BC, although there is a

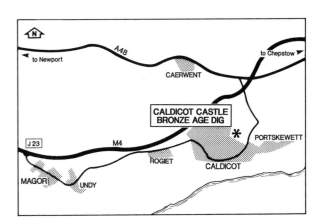

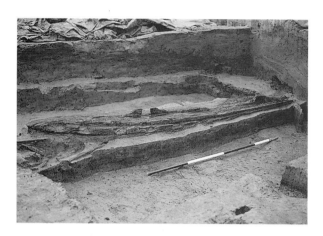

The Caldecot boat-strake, during the course of excavation (2-m scale). (Reproduced with kind permission of Glamorgan–Gwent Archeological Trust.)

One of the larger structures excavated at Caldicot, possibly a fishing trap. (Reproduced with kind permission of Glamorgan–Gwent Archeological Trust.)

similar but later Danish example, and indeed similarly constructed vessels are still in use in the Indian ocean. The Caldicot find however is of particular importance because of its discovery in an archaeological context (largely lacking for the Humber boats) and because of the considerable advances made in conservation techniques since the discovery of the Humber vessels. The Caldicot vessel would have been originally about 15 m (50 ft) long and paddled rather than sailed or rowed. It would have been capable of carrying cargo across the Severn, and indeed the pottery from the site points to contacts with south-west Britain and with Wessex. The weak point in the design of such a boat would have been the roots threaded through the sewing holes, and it is possible that the vessels would have been dismantled for storage (perhaps underwater) each winter and reconstructed in the spring.

Lifting the boat from the clay and silts in which it lay and removal for conservation provided the excavation team with difficulties, for few, if any, pieces of wood this size had been successfully recovered before. However, specialist advice was sought from a number of sources, and for several weeks during which the remains were carefully excavated and recorded *in situ* the various options were considered. The technique eventually adopted involved sliding a heavy-duty plastic sheet under the vessel which would cut through the clay in which the wood was embedded, lifting the boat on its plastic sheet on to a specially constructed pallet, and then manhandling pallet and boat off the site to a storage tank, where after further investigation the lengthy processes of

Caldicot Bronze Age excavation. Staff operating from scaffolding rig. (Reproduced with kind permission of Glamorgan–Gwent Archeological Trust.)

conservation will commence.

The programme of 'preservation by record' (a euphemism for very strictly controlled destruction) ensures that the public should be able to benefit from this important resource and to observe the work in progress. The location of the site within a Country Park was clearly of benefit. Walkways and viewing platforms have been provided together with an on-site exhibition, setting the site in its prehistoric and geographical context, which is staffed by the Caldicot Trust, a local amenity society. Promotion of the site is also actively being undertaken. Although it is not possible to expose more than a small proportion of the site to the public gaze, the fact that it is primarily organic artefacts that the visitors are invited to look at is usually a welcome novelty. These are not the familiar pottery beakers and stone axes, but items which speak a little more directly about the immediacies of human activity, such as the toolmarks left on a wooden plank three thousand years old, which appear as fresh as if they had been fashioned the previous week.

Waterlogged sites present a number of technical problems. The processes of excavation upset the physical and chemical equilibrium in which the finds have remained for centuries, and deterioration can set in rapidly. One of the major problems is desiccation, so much of the site is carefully covered in plastic to keep the timbers moist and shaded from sunlight. Exposed areas are constantly sprayed with water. Each piece of wood (and the site contains many hundreds) has to be painstakingly recorded and examined for such features as carpentry methods, the impressions left by Bronze Age axes, tree-rings (which in turn can enable the calculation of the precise date in calendar years when the tree was felled), evidence of prehistoric woodland management methods such as coppicing, and the holes bored by prehistoric insects. During these various analyses the wood has to be kept in tanks filled with water. A certain proportion of the wood will be selected for conservation and eventual display, and this part of the process is being carried out by Monmouth Borough Council Museums Service, who are working closely with the archaeological team.

Another difficulty is the extremely fragile nature of the archaeological deposits; the excavation team cannot work directly on the ground, but has to operate from a scaffolding rig raised above the surface of the site. Movement of personnel, spoil, finds and samples therefore presents a set of logistical problems not encountered on more conventional 'dry' sites. The technical problems of investigating such a site are however more than compensated for by the quality of data which survives. The Late Bronze Age is a period about which comparatively little is known, and this factor would make Caldicot important in any case. Its particular importance lies in the range of evidence preserved and the apparently special nature of the remains.

A major component of the programme will be the examination of plant remains, pollen, molluscs, animal bones and various microorganisms which are preserved within the sediments. Conventional sites which have not been waterlogged yield artefacts which are the most part inorganic, such as pottery and stone. Yet it is organic artefacts of wood, leather, basketry, textiles and many other materials which actually make up the everyday fabric of human life throughout prehistory and even in our own age.

Given the importance of the Caldicot site, the most desirable outcome would ideally have involved preservation so as to conserve a valuable and non-renewable archaeological resource. Despite considerable efforts on behalf of the local authorities, Cadw and the Glamorgan–Gwent Archaeological Trust to achieve this aim, no certain method could be found of arresting the processes of deterioration which had been set in train by the disruption of the environmental characteristics of the site. One further difficulty is that the total extent of the site beyond the limits of the lake excavation is unknown at present. Post-excavation analyses of the data will lead towards a published account of the discoveries and their significance, whilst the artefacts, following conservation, will be available for public display.

FURTHER READING

1. Pyor, Francis (1991) *Flag Fen – Prehistoric Fenland Centre*, English Heritage.

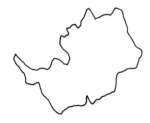

HERTFORDSHIRE

PROJECT 1.10, Hertfordshire Archaeological Trust

Hertfordshire is a county with a rich archaeological heritage that includes remains of every period from early prehistoric times to the present day. The County Archaeological Record, which is maintained and held by the County Planning and Environment Department, lists over 6000 known sites and findspots, and over 500 areas of particular importance and potential have been identified throughout the county. Many of these sites are of national importance.

Hertfordshire is also under intense development pressure. Its pretty countryside and fertile soils, its proximity to London, and the creation of a clutch of 'new towns' in this century has created a wealthy but crowded county. The result is a constant demand for land for housing, farming, roads, business, leisure and recreation. In its turn this demand has put enormous pressure on both the man-made and the natural heritage.

Archaeological remains form a part of that man-made heritage, consisting not only of completely buried remains, but also upstanding earthwork sites and standing structures. By its very nature, this archaeological heritage also contains a hidden element. The management of this archaeological heritage in the context of the county's development pressures, and maintaining a reasonable balance between development and conservation is a demanding process. In a few cases the argument for the latter will be so overwhelming as to warrant rejection of development proposals; in a few others it may prove possible to marry the two, but in most cases development can only proceed by the destruction of archaeological remains. This need not mean total loss, however; in such cases,

Recording a third-century AD corn-dryer during excavations in advance of housing development at Chells Manor Village, Stevenage. (Reproduced with kind permission of Hertfordshire Archeological Trust.)

it is now standard practice to ensure, usually through the normal planning process, that the sites of such developments are fully investigated before construction begins.

Such provision begs the question of resources, and also of an available and appropriately qualified organization to carry out such 'rescue' archaeology. This was indeed a problem in Hertfordshire until 1986. Until then the county was covered by three professional archaeological organizations, two of which were run by the District Councils of St Albans and North Hertfordshire, with the third being an independent unit. It was very difficult for the two District Council units to operate outside their District areas, and the independent unit was then experiencing severe financial problems. The situation was rightly described in a report to the County Council in October 1985 as 'patchy'. The County Council decided to grasp this nettle firmly. The ailing independent unit was restructured, revitalized, and most importantly, refinanced, as the 'Hertfordshire Archaeological Trust', which was formally established on the 7 July 1986.

The County Council saw its primary responsibility as the provision of a secure base for the new organization, and to this end has contributed an annual sum as 'core funding' from the outset. The original figure of £20 000 in 1986 has now risen to £52 000 in the current (1991/92) financial year. The County Council was also extremely keen to involve the District Councils as 'core supporters', and in the 1990/91 financial year, six District Councils in Hertfordshire contributed £22 650. This core support was never intended to do otherwise than provide a base on which the Trust could build, and the bulk of its income (£286 000 in 1990/91) now comes from the private sector through 'developer funding' or from English Heritage. This mix of private and public support has proved highly successful, and has enabled the Trust to ably fulfil the County Council's original aim which was to provide a genuinely county-wide archaeological service. Its development has transformed the provision for rescue archaeology in Hertfordshire. It perfectly complements the database maintenance, monitoring and conservation work of the County Council's own archaeology service, which has no effective field capacity; it enables the Local Planning Authorities to give reality and credibility to their policies for the archaeological heritage, (a provision that has become even more crucial since the publication of the DoE Planning Policy Guidance Note No. 16 on Archaeology and Planning), and it allows commercial developers to deal with a well-founded professional archaeological organization that is, like themselves, within the private sector. The Hertfordshire Archaeological Trust is a success story chiefly because of the initiative and support of the County Council.

NORTHAMPTONSHIRE

PROJECT 1.11, Village origins, Raunds and West Cotton

Northamptonshire County Council created an Archaeology Unit in the 1970s to provide a professional response to the threats to the County's archaeological remains. The first step taken was the rapid compilation of a Sites and Monuments Record which demonstrated that there were extensive areas of the County where the archaeological evidence had been destroyed, in particular by recent development. However, there was still a remarkable survival of remains over many areas of the County. The awareness of the quality of archaeological remains was highlighted by the fact that there were major land use changes about to take place – plans for mineral extraction, roads, and urban and village expansion.

In line with a strategy which acknowledged the disciplines of geography as much as of archaeology (Archaelogical Priorities; Proposals for Northamptonshire), the Archaeology Unit adopted, in 1978, a policy of according a higher priority to certain areas of the County for further archaeological study, chosen because of their comparatively good archaeological survival and because of their significance as centres of human settlement over long periods of time. This has shaped the Council's response to the choices necessary in rescue archaeology during the 1980s.

Archaeological rescue excavations had already started, with English Heritage support, at the well preserved Saxon and medieval site at the village of Raunds, in East Northamptonshire. As this excavation proceeded, it was recognized that the village, and its surroundings, provided a sample area of Midland landscape where archaeological evidence could be recovered to assist in the understanding of the origins of the English village, from late prehistoric to post-medieval times. In 1984, English Heritage accepted the project in principle as a 'priority area', and agreed to support a programme of rescue excavation through long-term funding.

A thorough search of the ground surface was made to collect scatters of pottery, building fragments and other artifacts from every available field in the 40 km^2 (15.5 square miles) area chosen, combined with large-scale excavation of threatened remains of settlements and cemeteries in the Raunds area. The whole region has been subject to major development in recent years, and sites have been excavated ahead of quarrying activities, housing development and road construction schemes. The budget of the project has been between £2.5 and £3.0 million, and has involved co-operation between the Northamptonshire County Council, the East Northamptonshire District Council, English Heritage and the Manpower Services Commission, as well as developers and land-owners, to ensure preservation of some sites and the excavation of others in advance of development.

Aerial photography, geophysical prospecting, and detailed field scanning have been used to discover the presence of ancient settlements across the mainly arable fields of the area. Within the

Excavations in progress at West Cotton, a key site of the Raunds Area Project. (Reproduced with kind permission of Northamptonshire County Council.)

towns and villages, development land has been trial-trenched to provide similar information, and a detailed picture of the archaeology of the selected area has been established. This can be used to select sites for preservation or further investigation.

INITIAL RESULTS AND DISCOVERIES

The arrival of the first farmers, before 4000 BC, was marked by widespread tree clearance and their large earthen burial monuments have been found under later flood deposits on the valley floor. The Neolithic long barrow at South Stanwick is probably the earliest burial mound in the area. At West Cotton, seven monuments formed a ritual focus for 2000 years; they were built, refurbished and re-used from about 4000 BC to about 1500 BC and included a huge 'long mound' approximately

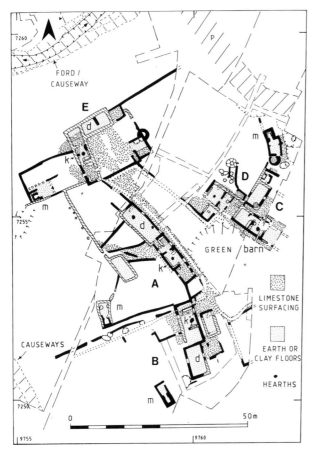

a large house with fine mosaic floors and integral bath-suites. Beside the villa lies the 'home farm' of barns and granaries while nearby must lie the, as yet, undiscovered remains of a Roman temple or mausoleum, because fragments of sculptures of gods and captives have been found re-used in the villa walls. The most remarkable discovery is the foundations of an estate of small stone cottages of the farm workers which spread over some 30 hectares (74 acres) around the villa. For the first time this excavation has revealed the complete agricultural settlement which supported the wealthy villa owner. Only 1.5 km (1 mile) to the south of this site another villa has been excavated. Here was the earliest known 'barn conversion' from a mill and barn to a substantial residence in the fourth century AD. The wealth of these sites shows the remarkable agricultural productivity achieved in Northamptonshire during Roman times.

In the fifth century AD there began what is known as the 'Dark Ages'. The only evidence that has been found of any occupation in the valley has been the discovery of the remains of two huts at West Cotton. On higher land, at Raunds itself, timber halls and sunken floored huts represent the farming communities typical of the period.

It now seems that the medieval villages of the area had their origins in the late Saxon period, perhaps the ninth century. At the small hamlet of West Cotton, a new settlement was created within regular planned plots, as a 'green field' development. Large timber buildings were set within a defined enclosure, adjacent to a water mill, forming a manor. A similar development occurred in North Raunds, where the timber buildings of Furnells Manor included a large hall and service wing and, by the tenth century, a small stone church had been added. By the twelfth century, the buildings were replaced in stone and Furnells Manor continued in use until the fifteenth century. At West Cotton, the Manor was replaced in the thirteenth century by a group of cottages, each representing a small farm. To date, about half of the hamlet has been excavated, indicating a site where the buildings themselves are unusually well preserved, with, in some instances, walls still standing up to 1 m (3 ft) in height. During the fifteenth century, economic changes following the 'Black Death', together with continual problems of severe flooding in the area, made the dwellings on the valley floor uninhabitable, and so West Cotton was deserted. The villages on higher ground, such

135 m (148 yards) long, 15 m (16.5 yards) wide and over 1 m (1 yard) high. Alongside, other enclosures and a timber platform descending into the river were probably used in the funerary rites. The monuments were apparently planned to form alignments, perhaps related to lunar and solar positions.

Later, around 2000 BC, round barrows were added to the group, each with a circular mound over a primary burial of a single individual, often accompanied by flint tools and pottery vessels. From around 1500 BC, the monuments were abandoned.

The next finds excavated are from the Iron Age (500 BC to 43 AD). Aerial photography above Irthlingborough has revealed a hill-fort, the residence of the local Celtic chieftain, and under Stanwick villa an extensive settlement of timber round-houses and granaries has been excavated.

In the Roman period (43 AD to 410 AD) there was a considerable increase in population density and many settlements are known already. The excavation of a Roman villa and settlement at Stanwick, in advance of gravel extraction, is one of the largest undertaken in Britain. This villa was as at Raunds and Stanwick, continued to flourish, presenting the village pattern that is evident today.

INTERPRETATION AND PRESENTATION

The emphasis now being given to the project is to complete the fieldwork and to set down and publish the results of all the thorough research and excavation work that has been completed so far. The project has attracted a high level of public interest and this has been catered for by lectures, guided site visits, and the presence of small displays on site. The County Council has made considerable use of the project as an educational resource. Although the excavated remains will be removed by development, some sites have been selected for preservation and it is hoped that a major exhibition of the evolution of the landscape based on the Raunds project can be established for the future.

This project has absorbed a lot of time, energy and finance, but it is hoped that these efforts have provided a valuable survey into the making of the English landscape. This project could not have proceeded without the help of English Heritage and the Manpower Services Commission who provided much of the labour element so necessary for these schemes. The co-operation of the local authorities, industry and private individuals has, clearly, been a key factor in the success of the project.

NOTTINGHAMSHIRE

PROJECT 1.12, Wansley Hall near Selston

Whilst considerably altered over the centuries, the building at Wansley Hall represents an all too rare example of a Norman-type first-floor hall house probably built as early as 1200 AD. Last inhabited in 1960, and fast falling into dereliction, the Nottinghamshire County Council resolved in 1981 to undertake an ambitious research and recording of the building to determine its historical interest, and to conserve what remained of the structure.

From its origins in the early Middle Ages, the house has been altered and added to over the centuries as the need of its various owners changed. Some fifty examples of Norman domestic architecture are known in the British Isles, though many are fragmentary. Most of these date from the latter half of the twelfth century. Such buildings would have been modest in size, and, as at Wansley, have contained a ground level undercroft, with a first-floor hall over, reached by outside steps. A building of this layout usually indicates that it was the home of a person of considerable status. Although much dereliction has set in, there is no doubt that the remains are of considerable archaeological importance; conserved as a consolidated ruin, they are a rare survival of early domestic architecture in the County.

Wansley stands on a elevated site near to the hilltop village of Selston. It is the site of the Medieval manor of the de Wandeslie family. The manorial estates of Wansley are mentioned in the Doomsday Book and took up a sizeable portion of the land in Selston parish. Research has shown that there was probably an estate, within which some 24 hectares (60 acres) belonged to the home farm, together with over 40 hectares (100 acres) of open woodland, although this would be nowhere near the extent of the total land at Wansley, under cultivation in 1086. By around 1300, the estate appears to have covered some 1215 hectares (3000 acres), and shortly before this date, there is documentary information of the ownership of the Hall by Ralph de Wandesley.

From 1302, again from documentary evidence, the fortunes of the Hall changed as the estates passed through a series of different owners and tenants. The property and its lands lost considerable influence in the region, chiefly due to the sale and splitting up of the estate, until by the end of the sixteenth century, the Hall estate had reduced to but one of a number of farms. It was as a small farm holding that the Hall was last used, when, following a serious fall of masonry and roofing, the building was vacated in 1960.

The original form of the Manor House probably consisted of a basement or undercroft, of one or two chambers, possibly used for safe storage. Above was the main room, the Hall, and possibly a smaller chamber, called a solar, at the east end with a garderobe, or latrine. The surviving building does not tell all the story. Such medieval houses normally had a range of other buildings, each under its own roof, often timber framed and thatched, providing cover for the pantry, bakehouse and brewhouse, as well as for stables. The

Wansley Hall. A short length of oak close stud screen, which is probably of sixteenth-century date. (Reproduced with kind permission of Nottinghamshire County Council.)

Wansley Hall. Remains of a Tudor period sixteenth-century fireback of narrow bricks arranged in a herringbone pattern. (Reproduced with kind permission of Nottinghamshire County Council.)

Wansley Hall. Eighteenth-century oven. (Reproduced with kind permission of Nottinghamshire County Council.)

Hall would have been the administrative centre for the farming estate, with many agricultural barns nearby. From documents it is known that a private chapel existed on, or adjacent to the site. A well shaft has already been located a few feet from the Hall, as would be expected for a site that is above a convenient stream for its water supply. There has been no archaeological excavation at Wansley to date, but a geophysical survey over part of the environs suggests further traces of buildings below ground.

The northern section of the ruin, arranged on an east-west axis, is the remains of the original Hall, the south wing being a much later addition. The Hall is approximately 7.6 m (25 ft) wide and 12.8 m (48 ft) long overall, which compares quite interestingly with the dimensions of another well known Norman hall house, Boothby Pagnall Manor House in Lincolnshire, which measures 7.6 m (25 ft) wide by 17.0 m (55 ft).

Nothing of the original interior survives although a short length of oak close stud screen still exists which probably dates from the sixteenth-century. There has been, as is to be expected, a considerable amount of damaging alterations carried out each century, and it is unlikely that much will be recovered from the early days of the Hall. There are remains of a Tudor period fireback of narrow bricks arranged in herring-bone pattern, and of an eighteenth-century oven. There are no surviving main windows, although fragmants of three original small windows survive, two on the west end of the Hall and one low down at the west end. The Hall is built in a local sandstone, called Coal Measures sand-stone, in coursed rubble stones. There survives an original plinth along much of the north and west end walls, although little exists of the original doorways.

Following abandonment of the building, decay rapidly set in and the building deteriorated to an

Wansley Hall. Interior view before restoration, with timbers removed. (Reproduced with kind permission of Nottinghamshire County Council.)

Plan of Development and Extension

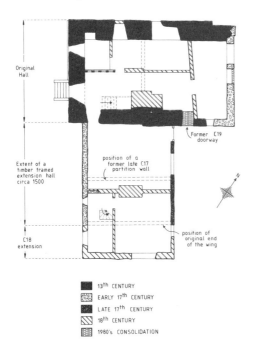

Original
Hall

Former C19
doorway

Extent of a
timber framed
extension hall
circa 1500

position of a
former late C17
partition wall

C18
extension

position of
original end
of the wing

N

■ 13th CENTURY
▨ EARLY 17th CENTURY
▨ LATE 17th CENTURY
▨ 18th CENTURY
▨ 1980's CONSOLIDATION

alarming degree. Roofs collapsed and chimney stacks fell, window frames fell out and trees grew close all round. The County Council's initiative to conserve the historic remains as a conserved ruin were directed by the Heritage section of the Planning and Transportation Department. Site labour in carrying out the work of clearance and consolidation was provided by the, then, Community Programme Agency. The costs of the works were £6200, which was met equally by the Nottinghamshire County Council and the Ashfield District Council, with a small contribution being made by the Selsdon Parish Council. The costs do not include labour nor the 'hidden' costs to the County Council of providing considerable archaeological advice throughout the scheme. The work consisted of the removal of all the decaying material which had fallen within the house walls, together with young saplings and bushes which had grown within the walls. Decayed timber lintels over openings had to be carefully taken out and replaced with concrete ones where this was essential for stability. Some parts of the stonework on the south-wing gable had to be carefully taken down because it was unsafe and rebuilt from photographic evidence. All the existing stonework and brickwork needed extensive repointing.

The repairs to the ruin were carried out by largely unskilled labour, who were trained as the work progressed. They were supervised by the staff of the Heritage section of the County Council, to ensure archaeological evidence and historical accuracy was retained. Their completed work is very creditable and has ensured the survival of a most important medieval manor house. Work on consolidating the building was completed by the end of 1988. The building is still privately owned and permission is needed for access.

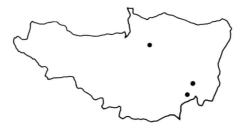

SOMERSET

PROJECT 1.13, Preservation and management of archaeological sites

Within the County of Somerset there is a range of archaeological sites and monuments, the majority being in private ownership. The long-term protection and management of such sites is often related to the care and attention given by their owners and custodians. The County Council owns a number of estates in Somerset, containing a variety of archaeological interest. While most of these sites had been acquired for agricultural or land management reasons, the County Council has recently pursued a policy of purchasing important archaeological sites to ensure that a representative sample of type sites from all historical periods is brought into public ownership and the sites are protected from development which might otherwise damage them. There are several hundred archaeological sites, findspots and historic landscape features identified on County Council-owned land. These range from Bronze Age barrows on the Mendip Hills through to extensive post-Medieval mining remains at Charterhouse (Mendip) and a nineteenth-century brick kiln at Bridgwater. The important archaeological sites in the county are scheduled as ancient monuments, and the County Council has

a responsibility to maintain and interpret sites in its guardianship.

An essential element for the long-term protection of any archaeological site is the production of a management plan to demonstrate how the landscape can be preserved and managed economically without detriment to the site. An awareness of appropriate grazing and stocking levels and the use of sheep and/or cattle may be crucial to ensure earthwork sites under pasture are protected from over-grazing and cattle poaching. A variety of land-management issues, likely visitor pressure, space for occasional car parking, site interpretation facilities and the production of trail guides and leaflets is used to enable visitors and residents to gain a better appreciation of their historic environment.

The County Council has acquired several major sites during the past five years, each one being an important example of a medieval settlement, with substantial financial support offered by English Heritage to meet the purchase costs. The decision was taken to purchase three sites, all Scheduled Monuments which were for sale and considered to be under threat.

Aerial view of Nether Adber deserted medieval village. The remains of the village houses, banks, ponds and ditches are clearly visible surrounded by medieval ridge and furrow fields. (Reproduced with kind permission of Cambridge University Collection of Air Photographs.)

DEER LEAP (RAMSPITS), NEAR CHEDDAR

There is an increasing awareness between archaeologists and ecologists that many sites of archaeological interest are often of nature conservation interest as well. At Deer Leap, on the south-facing slope of the Mendip Hills, an area of nearly 20 hectares (49.5 acres) was purchased containing settlement evidence of medieval date. The earthworks include house platforms, field boundaries, trackways and an impressive series of medieval lynchet fields, marking the attempts

of the medieval farmers to cultivate the land. A nineteenth-century former cattle barn at one of the farm sites has been repaired by the County Council to house a series of interpretation panels, outlining the landscape history of the Mendip Hills and providing information for visitors. This site was purchased in 1989 by the County Council, for £27 500 with the assistance of a grant from English Heritage, of £6875.

NETHER ADBER, A DESERTED MEDIEVAL VILLAGE

At Nether Adber, 5 km (3 miles) north of Yeovil, the earthwork remains of a deserted medieval village covering 9 hectares (22 acres) was purchased by the County Council in 1989 for £50 000 with a £45 000 grant from English Heritage. The site contains some of the best preserved house platforms in the eastern part of the county, as well as streets, ditches and closes that are still clearly visible. A recent survey by the Royal Commission on the Historical Monuments of England, has recorded all the earthwork remains in these fields.

Nether Adber is first recorded in the Domesday Book of 1086 and other documents record that in the fifteenth and sixteenth centuries the population declined. Aerial photographs taken in the 1960s clearly show that the site was at one time more extensive than it is today. Parts of the earthworks were destroyed by tipping and levelling in the 1970s; the moated site and adjacent fish ponds in the northern field have been partly levelled but can still be traced on the ground.

The main aim of the management plan is to ensure that the earthworks are not affected by cattle poaching or over-stocking, and grazing is monitored on a regular basis. Fence repairs, hedge laying and some tree planting to re-establish hedges has already started on part of the site. Due to the local interest in the site, consideration is being given to the display of visitor information nearby, together with a small car park.

MARSTON MAGNA MOATED SITE

The Medieval earthworks at Marston Magna, covering an area of 2.25 hectares (5.5 acres),

represent one of the best preserved examples of a Medieval moated site in Somerset. When viewed from the air the rectangular shape of the platform is clearly visible. It is likely that there was a building on the platform, although its exact position has not been determined. In contrast with Nether Adber, the earthworks at Marston Magna are likely to represent the remains of a manorial centre rather than typical village earthworks.

The main feature is the platform which is surrounded by a ditch approximately 2–3 m (6.5–9.8 ft) deep and 10 m (33 ft) across. The moat is wet for part of the year and is joined at its eastern end by a medieval fishpond, now dry, but it contains some water during periods of heavy rainfall. Surrounded by its common fields the association between the moat, church and churchyard and the existing road pattern is clearly visible.

A management plan for this site has been drawn up which recommends that the site should ideally be grazed by sheep to keep the grass short and to prevent erosion of the steep banks by cattle. Situated at the edge of the village the site is frequently used for walking by local residents and an interpretation panel has been erected on the site. The County Council purchased the land in 1986, for £23 000 and were assisted by a contribution of £2000 from the Marston Magna Parish Council, and a grant of £8500 from English Heritage.

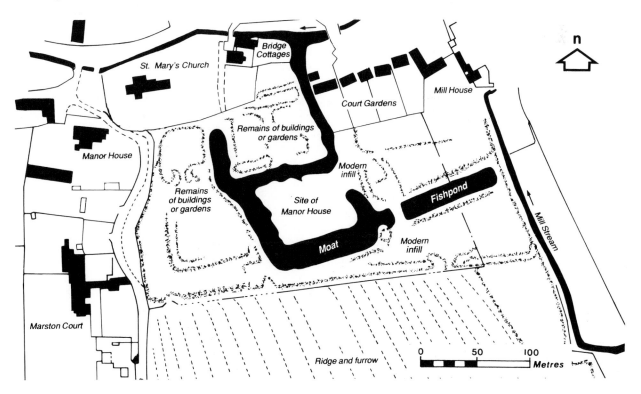

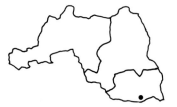

SOUTH GLAMORGAN

PROJECT 1.14, The restoration of Cosmeston Medieval Village

Cosmeston Medieval Village is a heritage project unique in Britain, involving the excavation and full-scale reconstruction of a medieval community on its original site. It is situated in the picturesque surroundings of Cosmeston Lakes Country Park in the County of South Glamorgan, and is only 15 minutes drive from the centre of Cardiff.

The archaeological importance of the Cosmeston project lies principally in its size. Other medieval settlements have been excavated throughout the country, although far fewer in Wales than in England, but the scope of these excavations has usually been limited both in size and in duration, such limited excavation can sometimes lead to a distorted interpretation. At Cosmeston, however, the archaeologist has the opportunity to excavate a large portion of the settlement over a long period of time and to use the results to shed light on similar sites where the excavators have not been so fortunate.

Perhaps the most exciting facet of Cosmeston Medieval Village is the reconstruction programme. The ultimate goal of the project is nothing less than the presentation of a complete and working community of rural Wales in the early fourteenth century. A particularly important feature is that the excavations are being interpreted and presented to the visitor in a way which is not only educational, but entertaining.

Cosmeston probably came into existence sometime between 1100 AD and 1200 AD – a castle is first mentioned in 1166. Artifacts from the Stone Age and Roman periods have been found, but no evidence of an earlier settlement. The medieval community took its name from the Costentin family of Northern France who came to Britain with the Norman invaders in the eleventh century.

In the second decade of the fourteenth century the village had a new lord, William de Caversham. Why the land changed hands is not known, but this was a time of great hardship. Deterioration in the climate of Northern Europe brought forth colder and wetter weather. As harvests failed and

Aerial view of Comeston Medieval Village taken in 1984. (Reproduced with kind permission of South Glamorgan County Council.)

disease devastated livestock the fires of rebellion began to smoulder among the native Welsh. Llewelyn Bren, Lord of Senghenydd in the high-lands of Glamorgan, led his people in a war that was to end with his capture and execution, but not before much of Glamorgan lay devestated. Perhaps these troubles were the final straw for the Costentin family, who would have been finding the village less and less profitable as population and production declined.

The interpretation of Cosmeston's archaeology suggests that de Caversham made a concerted

Comeston Medieval Village. Reconstruction of the bakehouse taken in 1985. (Reproduced with kind permission of South Glamorgan County Council.)

Comeston Medieval Village: completed byre, taken in 1984. (Reproduced with kind permission of South Glamorgan County Council.)

effort to revive the community with the construction of a series of new buildings. A silver penny of Edward I, minted in 1297, was found in the wall of one of these structures, the degree of wear on the coin helps to date the construction of the buildings to the early part of the fourteenth century. The modern reconstruction of the village is based upon this period of renewal. de Caversham's attempt to inject new life into the community was short lived. The population continued to decline, with the plague years of the later fourteenth century completing Cosmeston's transition from community to a scatter of partially deserted hovels as the Black Death stalked the land.

Cosmeston was not to disappear totally, for up to 150 years ago records show that the village was now the site of three cottages and two farms.

The medieval village was discovered when excavations, carried out by the Glamorgan–Gwent Archaeological Trust, were undertaken in the vicinity of an earthwork known as Cosmeston Castle, in response to the threat of an adjacent development. The first excavation was limited, but further research, examining the surrounding landscape, and documentation suggested the existence of a manor, village and surrounding fields. Both the South Glamorgan County Council and the Vale of Glamorgan Borough Council appreciated that this could be an important site, and as it lay within the Country Park administered by the two authorities, they commissioned a second and much more extensive excavation programme which confirmed the existance of these features.

The excavation site, which covers approximately 6000 m² (6564 square yards) still leaves many more artifacts and buildings of the medieval community to be uncovered. Records and earthworks show the existence of a manor house, church, dovecote, mill, fishponds and orchards, as well as additional domestic and agricultural structures.

The interpretation of the structures was to present difficulties as no peasant buildings of the period of around 1300 AD had survived in the area. Guidance as to what these structures would have looked like was based upon the interpretation of the archaeology, vernacular building methods known to have been used by medieval stone masons and carpenters, and the necessities of medieval life.

Furthermore, and not surprisingly, there was the lack of a workforce skilled in medieval building techniques! These problems of reconstruction

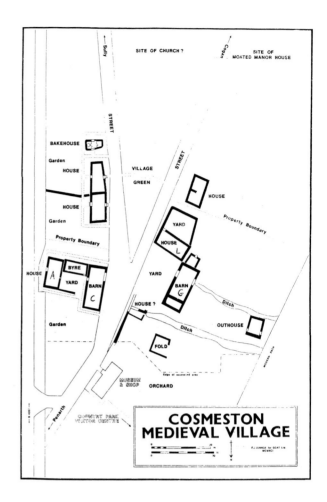

were overcome by the use of highly qualified archaeological staff backed by an extremely supportive and highly motivated workforce who learnt techniques and skills during the reconstruction. The experience gained by staff involved with the project and contact with other archaeologists and historians has ensured that the reconstruction of the buildings is as authentic as possible.

In the early years of the restoration programme, labour was available through the Manpower Services Commission (MSC). This enabled materials to be obtained locally and reconstruction work to be undertaken relatively cheaply, in much the same way as would have happened in medieval times. The workforce gradually improved their medieval building skills, but with the demise of the MSC scheme during autumn of 1988, continuation of the project was threatened.

Private sponsorship, donations and financial support from both South Glamorgan County Council and the Vale of Glamorgan Borough Council ensured the project's future. The two authorities initially funded the village restoration on a contractual basis, and then in 1991 they took over the direct management of the project. With the support and active encouragement of Cadw, and using a team of archaeologists and builders, work on the restoration programme continued. Provision was made on site for a small museum displaying various artifacts and features of the village, and as an additional attraction to the public, tours are given by guides in medieval costume.

Direct control of the project has enabled the two authorities to promote the medieval village in conjunction with the adjacent Cosmeston Lakes Country Park which attracts up to 350 000 visitors a year.

The cost for the project to date has been in the region of £437 000. With the demise of the MSC scheme, the two authorities have been the main financial contributors to the project. However financial assistance has also been given by the Prince of Wales' Committee, and a number of private companies.

Although the cost of the excavation programmes can be quantified, those for the reconstruction work have been difficult to assess, mainly because the work involves using building methods and techniques now long forgotten, and skills that had to be learned as work proceeded.

South Glamorgan County Council and the Vale of Glamorgan Borough Council have jointly funded a feasibility study by consultants to investigate the future marketing of the project with a view to making the medieval village even more attractive to the visitor. The fact that excavation and reconstruction works are still being undertaken means that the visitor is treated not only to an example of a working medieval village, but is also given an insight into the workings of archaeological excavation and interpretation.

STAFFORDSHIRE

PROJECT 1.15, Excavations at Drayton Bassett Manor House

In 1988 contractors uncovered evidence of one of Staffordshire's best archaeological sites during construction of a housing development at Drayton Bassett near Lichfield. Investigation soon showed this to be the remains of an impressive medieval aisled hall, the predecessor of Drayton Manor, home of Sir Robert Peel. The task of mounting a 'rescue' excavation, and of recording this remarkable discovery had to be faced at short notice.

Urgent site discussions led to a revision of construction schedules and the transfer of a Community Programme Agency team of archaeologists to the excavation site. Sometimes working alongside construction machinery and mechanical excavators, the archaeologists remained on site for six months, recovering artefacts and piecing together the story of the site. Technical supervision was provided during the course of the project by an archaeologist from the County Planning and Economic Development Department's staff.

A medieval moat and bridge were amongst the first discoveries, soon to be followed by the excavation of a well and corn-drier, and then the foundations of a large aisled barn. The bones of deer from the hunt and fragments of continental glass and pottery pointed to the high social status of the site, but the final triumph came in the closing weeks of excavation. The Norman manorial aisled hall of the Bassetts of Drayton, with an arcaded undercroft in the crosswing, provide

a spectacular culmination of a remarkable collaborative rescue excavation. The finds from the excavation were subsequently presented to the nearby Tamworth Castle Museum by the developer, who also produced a short publicity brochure for the site.

Funding for the project was largely derived from the Manpower Services Commission (£18 500). Costs of materials and fees for specialist reports on the archaeological material were met by the County Council, including the appointment of a temporary assistant within its Archaeology and Conservation Section to prepare a report for publication. Total County Council input amounted to £4300.

(See Plate 1.)

(*Reproduced with kind permission by Lovell homes.)

The front and back faces of 'Jetton', used as unofficial currency for bartering.*

50

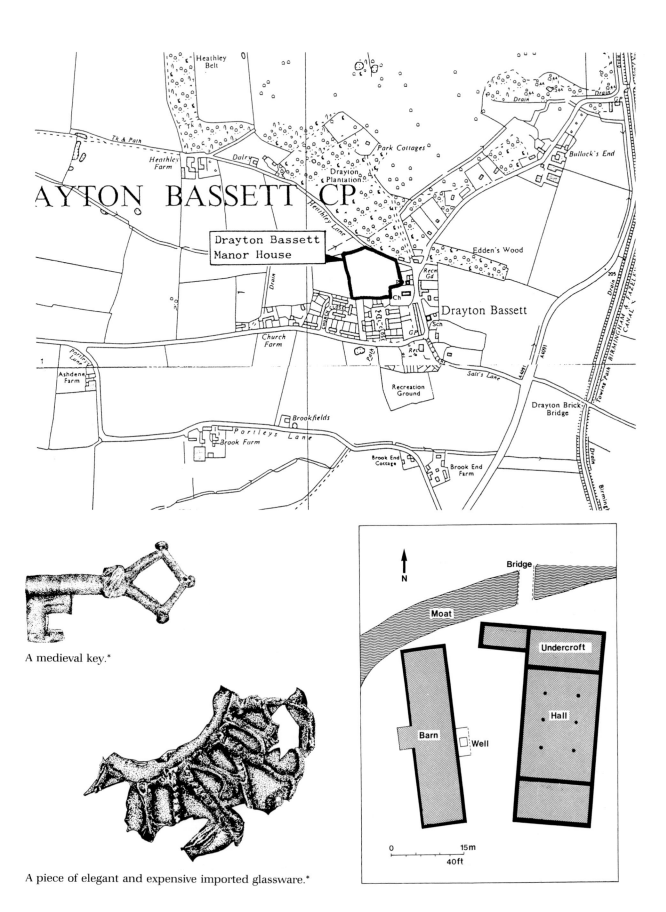

A medieval key.*

A piece of elegant and expensive imported glassware.*

51

SUFFOLK

PROJECT 1.16, Excavations at Butter Market in Ipswich

Rescue excavation in Ipswich since 1974 has shown that it is one of England's first towns, founded in the early seventh century, probably by the East Anglian Royal House, whose burial ground lies at nearby Sutton Hoo. By the ninth century the town covered about 50 hectares (124 acres) coinciding with the modern town centre. The recent development boom in the town has brought an unprecedented threat to archaeology both above and below ground, but it has also provided a unique opportunity to examine the origins of the town, and by analogy, English towns in general.

In 1988 one of the largest and most important urban rescue excavations in this country was undertaken by Suffolk County Council's Archaeological Unit, south of the Butter Market, Ipswich, prior to the construction of a massive new shopping centre. The Butter Market site was of major importance archaeologically for a number of reasons. Firstly, it lay in the centre of the Anglo-Saxon town (and modern town) which had never been sampled by excavation. Secondly, it provided the opportunity for the large-scale excavation which is necessary to reveal changing urban landscapes, i.e. the density of buildings and their relationship to streets, tenement sizes, nature of boundaries etc., all of which is crucial to the understanding of urbanization as a process. Thirdly, the development area coincided with the precinct of the town's Medieval Carmelite Friary about which very little was known apart from a bare historical outline.

Despite the extent of the redevelopment, and its proximity to the centre of the town, there were few standing buildings of merit on the site and only one isolated Listed Building, proposed for demolition. These were recorded before demolition at a cost met by the site developer. Of the surviving archaeological deposits, about 4500 m^2 (5382 square yards) were threatened with certain destruction by the inclusion of two levels of basement car parking in the development scheme. With the advice of the County Archaeologist, outline planning permission was granted

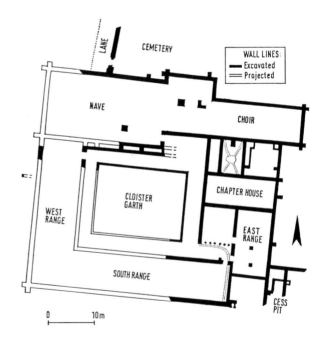

Cellar of a typical tenth – eleventh century Ipswich town house. Holes for the wall posts can be seen bordering the clay floor. (Reproduced with kind permission of Suffolk County Council.)

by Ipswich Borough Council subject to agreement being reached to ensure that an adequate record was made of deposits prior to development. The developers built a 12-month excavation period into their programme (later extended to 14 months) and agreed to provide funding of up to £280 000 to cover excavation and post-excavation costs. As it turned out the site was more productive than predicted, and additional funding for the project was provided by English Heritage.

The sequence of occupation uncovered on the site started, unexpectedly, with a cemetery, dating from the seventh and eighth century. This was undoubtedly the burial ground for the town at this period which lay immediately to the south of the Butter Market site. Despite extensive disturbance by later features some eighty graves were excavated which will provide a unique insight into the town's first urban residents.

In the early ninth century, burial ceased on the site, and the town expanded rapidly northwards over the cemetery. Two gravel-surfaced streets were laid out and their frontages were soon developed with timber buildings. This ninth-century occupation is association with intensive craft activity including potting, bone and antler working, and bronze smithing, reflecting the heavy emphasis of the town's economy as a whole on craft production.

Occupation in the tenth and eleventh century was less intensive, with buildings set well back from the streets and more widely spaced than in the ninth century. The building types also change with the introduction of what appears to be a specifically urban house-type – the cellared building. These buildings, with weatherboard cladding on a stout oak frame, are two storied with the lower storey either a full basement or semi-basement. This occupation ends abruptly in the late eleventh century with the burning of these buildings presumably either to clear the site of run-down property or as a deliberate aggressive act by the newly arrived Norman overlords. Domesday Book records a reduction of the town's population from about 2700 to 1000 between 1066 and 1086 and there can be no doubt that economic disaster had struck.

The Butter Market site appears to have been waste ground throughout the twelfth and thirteenth centuries until it was acquired by the Carmelite Order in 1278 in order to build a Friary. By the end of the fourteenth century they owned almost exactly the same parcel of land that is currently under redevelopment. Excavation uncovered virtually the entire ground plan of the Friary, with its church, nearly 60 m (66 yards) long, and great cloister to its south. Finds include large quantities of stained glass, floor tiles and architectural fragments crucial in any attempt at reconstructing its three-dimensional form. The Friary was largely demolished at the Dissolution in 1538, but part of the claustral range survived, for use as a County Gaol, until the later eighteenth century, when it was cleared to make way for a provisions market in 1809.

Throughout the excavation there was a high level of public interest and media coverage. Unfortunately, public access to the site had to be strictly limited as demolition contractors were working alongside the excavation. Some school visits were possible and conducted tours were arranged outside working hours. To cater for public interest, an exhibition, updated throughout the excavation, was mounted in a Portakabin with easy access from the highway and with a good view out over the excavations.

SURREY

PROJECT 1.17, Excavations at Hextalls, North Park Farm, Bletchingley

A large area at North Park Farm, Bletchingley, was proposed for sand extraction several years ago. It included a small sub-rectangular earthwork known as Little Pickle, marked out by ditches and banks, but there was no other indication of archaeological potential. Preservation of the earthwork was not thought to be an option, mainly as it would have meant the sterilization of a major part of the proposed sandpit (because of the batter required for the sides of the pit in a very deep working), and also because it is difficult now to locate acceptable sites for the extraction of sand of this quality in Surrey.

A programme of archaeological work was therefore agreed with the mineral company operating the site. The work was funded by the company and small-scale excavations and survey over two or three years led to the discovery of a major occupation site buried in the field adjacent to the earthwork. Testing of this site indicated that it was very extensive and discussions were held with the company and English Heritage to find ways to set up the major excavation that was clearly required. Funding was provided by both these organizations and Surrey County Council and the whole area was excavated in 1988–89. The overall cost of the project will eventually be in the region of £60 000, split fairly equally between the mineral company and English Heritage, with a small contribution from the County Council.

It should be noted that English Heritage were only prepared to assist with the funding of this excavation because there was already a planning permission for the site. They made it clear that their current policy is that developers of every kind should fund *all* the archaeological work required as a result of their developments. However, there will always be circumstances where it is not possible for this policy to be applied, and it is essential that English Heritage continues to be in a position where it can grant aid rescue excavations when they cannot be funded in

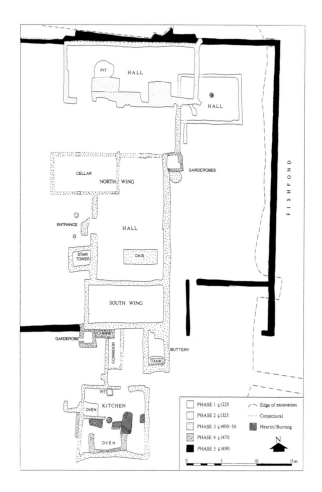

Hextalls Manor House. View looking north of work in progress in the area of the fifteenth-century kitchen. (Reproduced with kind permission of Surrey County Council.)

any other way, or where funds from other sources are insufficient.

The archaeological work was carefully phased in with the working of the sandpit and the agricultural use of the land. It was carried out by the archaeological team based in the County Planning Department, assisted by local archaeologists and historians. A large area was stripped of its topsoil and then the archaeological deposits were examined. Prehistoric, Roman and Saxon artefacts were found on the site, but the earliest building located was a hall house of early thirteenth century, with a circular tile-on-edge hearth and associated buildings. The hall had been demolished and a more elaborate hall then constructed in the fourteenth century. This building remained standing but its function as the main hall was usurped by a later stone-built hall between two wings, one having a cellar, with associated service rooms and a detached kitchen to the south. In the late fifteenth or early sixteenth century, the whole complex was brought together by making walled courtyards to front and rear. The courtyard at the front had a gatehouse with attached cellars. The final complex had thus developed into an early Tudor country house, with outer and privy courts, a piped water supply and a water tower, a large

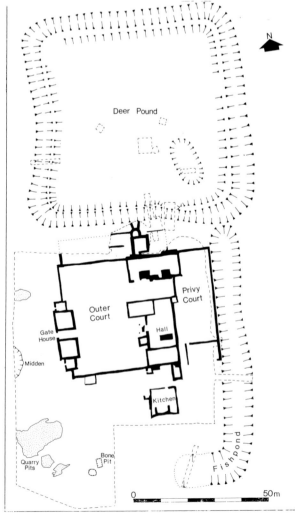

Deer Pound

Privy Court

Outer Court

Gate House

Midden

Hall

Kitchen

Fish Pond

Quarry Pits

Bone Pit

N

0   50m

fish pond and an attached deer pound (the earthwork already mentioned). It was eventually demolished in the period 1550–59.

It has now been possible to link evidence from documentary research with that from the archaeological site. It seems clear that it must have been originally the house belonging to a family whose name was rendered in Latin as Venator (the huntsman), a clear link with the deer park known to have been in existence from at least 1223. It was eventually known as Hextalls after Henry Hextall who owned the estate from about 1460 to 1493. He was probably responsible for the development of the courtyard complex. In the early sixteenth century, the estate was bought by the Duke of Buckingham who also held the adjoining estate, on which he built a Tudor great house, the remnants of which are now known as Place (Palace) Farm. After his execution for treason it was given in due course to Anne of Cleves as part of her pension arrangements. Clearly Hextalls was eventually demolished as only one large house will have been needed for the estate. It was only the discovery of the archaeological site which has made it possible to understand these various documentary references.

This work illustrates once again that totally unexpected archaeological finds can be made at any time. The presence of a Tudor courtyard complex so close to a known site of the same kind was completely unexpected. In this case the cellars of the Tudor gate house survived to almost their full height completely invisible below the field. The work also illustrated how well the mineral operator, English Heritage, the County Council and local amateur archaeologists could work together; this close co-operation relied greatly on the professional archaeological team being locally based, in the County Planning Department.

WEST SUSSEX

PROJECT 1.18, Excavations at Chanctonbury Ring, Hill-fort

Before the October 1987 storm, Chanctonbury Ring was readily recognizable in the West Sussex landscape as a prominent hilltop tree clump from a wide area of the surrounding South Downs. The landowner, Harry Goring, great-great-grandson of Charles Goring who first planted the Ring at the end of the eighteenth century, felt that the replanting of Chantonbury Ring was not just a matter of family duty, but an issue on which there was widespread public support.

However, set against the historical perspective of human activity on the Sussex Downs which stretches back thousands of years, the evocative image of Chanctonbury Ring as a hilltop tree clump is a comparatively recent phenomenon. Less well known is the fact that the site is an Iron Age hill-fort, scheduled as an Ancient Monument, under the Ancient Monuments and Archaeological Areas Act (1979). The hill, where Charles Goring played as a boy and determined to plant his trees, is crowned by the bank and ditch of the hill-fort which later became the focus for a Romano-Celtic temple. Substantial foundations of this temple site survive[1] but previous excavations have shown that the roots of the beech trees which spread widely through the shallow topsoil covering the chalk were causing damage to these buried structures.

How could a replanting scheme be achieved which balanced a strong desire to recreate a potent symbol of the South Downs landscape with the need to preserve a statutorily protected ancient monument? One solution would be to provide for a 'glade' which respected the buried foundations of the Romano-Celtic temple, but still produced the desired hilltop clump effect when viewed from outside. Apart from the central temple site, the

planting scheme left a second 'glade' in an area to the south-west where excavators in the early years of this century discovered foundations of a second structure, allegedly of a curious kite-shaped plan.

(a)

(b)

Chanctonbury Ring. (a) Irregular polygon of the second temple building under excavation (view from east, looking west); (b) south-west corner of the second temple (view from south). (Reproduced with kind permission of West Sussex County Council.)

CHANCTONBURY RING

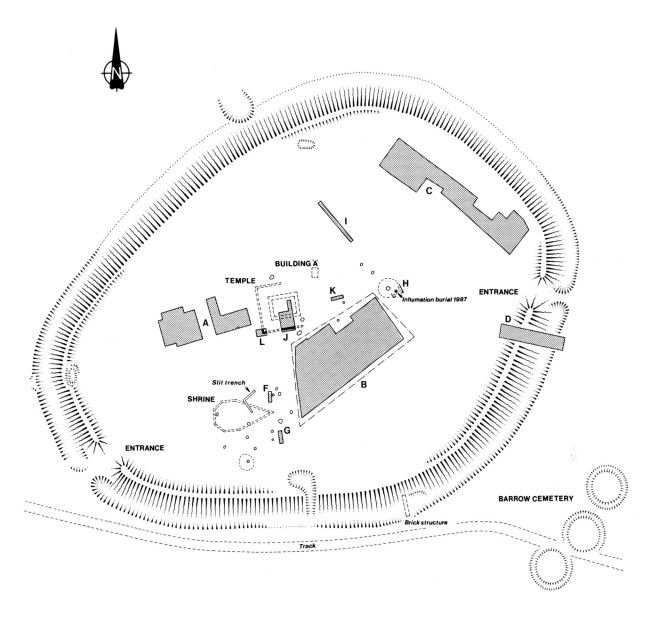

BUILDING A

TEMPLE

ENTRANCE

A

K

H

Inhumation burial 1987

D

L

J

B

Slit trench

F

SHRINE

G

ENTRANCE

C

I

ENTRANCE

BARROW CEMETERY

Brick structure

Track

0   50 Metres

It was important to assess the full extent of buried structures within the embankment of the hill-fort to ensure that remains vulnerable to tree roots would not be damaged. At the same time, a planting scheme which left too many 'glades' within the Ring would diminish the impression of a canopy of leaves and could lead to trees being lost in future gales through wind turbulence.

Following the events of October 1987, the Countryside Section of West Sussex County Planning Department liaised with the landowner to established a plan of action. English Heritage were contacted to set in motion an application for Scheduled Monument Consent required under the 1979 Act. Before determining which areas would be safe to replant, English Heritage commissioned an archaeological assessment involving trial trenching to confirm whether the areas considered for replanting held sensitive structures and would therefore be at risk from future root action. A series of trenches a metre wide were excavated radiating inwards from the ditch and bank towards the temple in the centre. The work was carried out by the Field Archaeological Unit of the Institute of Archaeology, London, in December 1989. The results indicated that apart from the areas of known sensitivity, there were no further structures which would be at risk from replanting.

As the 'kite-shaped' building, partially revealed in 1909, was still very much an archaeological puzzle, West Sussex County Council with consent from English Heritage, funded its own assessment to investigate in March 1990. Besides resolving the question of the 'kite-shaped' plan, which was virtually unknown to archaeology, further excavation would serve other objectives. Firstly, a detailed analysis of the impact of tree roots on buried structures would provide English Heritage with a case study to set down guidelines in the management of other scheduled monuments affected by root action. Secondly, if followed by a more extensive area excavation to locate and plan sensitive archaeological features, the assessment would indicate where extra planting could thicken up an area otherwise vulnerable to the prevailing south-westerly winds. A more radical alternative would be total excavation. Although this would theoretically 'preserve by recording', in practice it is a destructive process in which *in situ* structures may be removed to record earlier features or phases of activity beneath. By creating an archaeologically sterile area, the conflict between tree roots and sensitive deposits is removed, but it would be contrary to government guidelines on preservation and the spirit of the 1979 Act.

The archaeological assessment in March 1990 successfully located foundations of a building and traces of a second, but far from being kite-shaped they proved to be of conventional rectangular plan. As the surviving wall footings are only one flint deep, interpretation of the true wall alignment among the general scatter of flints is not an easy task. The plan produced after the partial excavation of 1909 must therefore be pardoned as an imaginative reconstruction. The most significant discovery in the March assessment was a portion of *in situ* tesselated floor consisting of

small sandstone blocks roughly an inch square. By chance, this floor had survived in the south-west corner of this building, protected where the two walls met. Elsewhere in the vicinity, isolated tesserae were appearing suggesting that tree roots had disturbed most of the remaining areas of floor. One large beech straddled the outer corner of the building close to the area where the floor was intact. Had this tree been one of the thirty or so large specimens which came down in the gales of January 1990, such valuable archaeological information could well have been lost. Each tree as it topples may tear up a root pan of considerable diameter and take with it any archaeological features which the roots have penetrated.

The archaeological assessment of December 1989 funded by English Heritage as a precondition of scheduled monument consent for replanting and the March 1990 assessment funded by West Sussex County Council each cost £2500. This investment is really just the beginning. Now that it has been demonstrated that there is a building (or buildings) associated with the temple further recording to recover a full groundplan is the next logical step. Hopefully this will lead to a better understanding of ritual centres in Romano-British culture where the classical gods of the Graeco-Roman world were absorbed into native British cults. In the future, once the trees have matured, there will be ample scope for an interpretation centre at Chanctonbury Ring to incorporate the findings of forthcoming and preceding excavations. The planting scheme has even allowed for an avenue of trees leading to the central temple site in accordance with evidence found at other temples that suggests they were approached along a ceremonial marked path.

REFERENCES

1. Mitchell, G.S. (1910). *Sussex Archaeological Collections*, **53**, pp. 131–7.

FURTHER READING

1. Bedwin, O. (1980). Excavations at Chanctonbury Ring, West Sussex. *Britannia*, pp. 173–222.

2

INDUSTRIAL ARCHAEOLOGY

PROJECTS

Drawing overleaf shows Porthgain Harbour, Pembrokeshire Coast National Park.

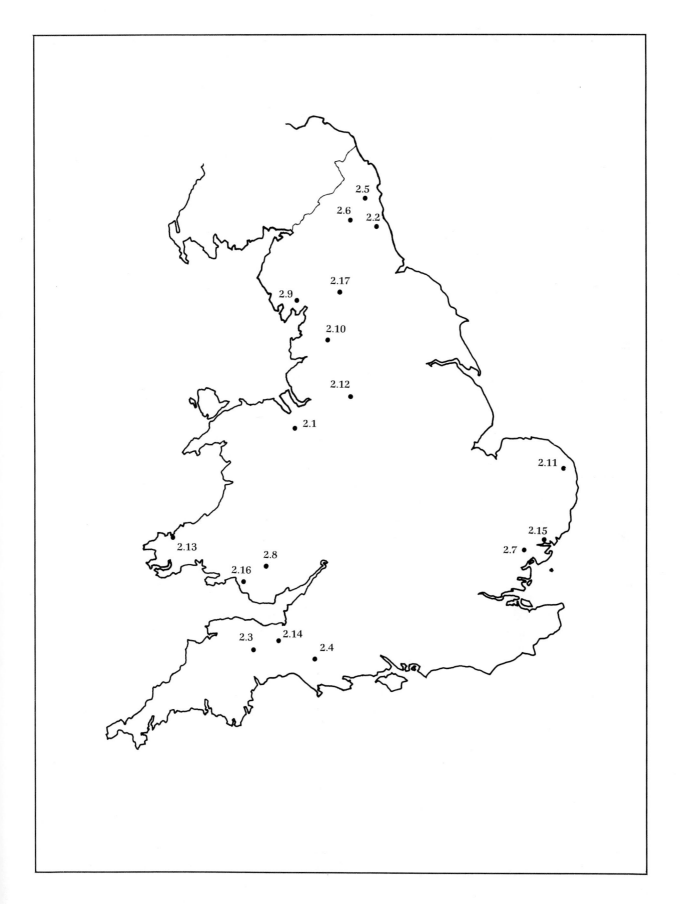

Until recent years Industrial Archaeology tended to be the specialist interest of small groups of enthusiasts. Today there has been a dramatic increase in the appreciation of the subject and this is, no doubt, because it is possible to identify more closely with this country's pioneering industrial achievements and the way of life of people who worked in a period often not more than a few generations ago.

Few aspects of our heritage draw more public interest than the monuments and machines of our industrial past. Not only to the archaeologist are these features of immense interest, they are quickly being recognized as an essential element in the understanding of the development of our present-day industrial scene – an aspect of social history that features in many educational initiatives.

This chapter looks at the work that County Councils are undertaking, often in collaboration with District Councils and others, in rescuing and restoring some of the best examples of our industrial heritage. Some structures like mine workings have been derelict for many years and are now no more than historic ruins; others, such as warehouses and textile mills still stand, but are no longer used for their original purpose. Indeed, these mills count for a great number of the larger industrial buildings now vacant. Ten years ago, for instance, in the Lancashire/Yorkshire textile area, local authorities faced a monumental task in finding new uses for the mills and warehouses where floor areas were approaching a million square feet per building at times![1] Some have been successfully converted to other uses, such as housing or offices, or adapted by subdividing the spaces to form small industrial or business units. These conversions, if carried out in a way that still retains the essential integrity of the building, can provide a cost-effective way of utilizing an existing structure, whilst at the same time provide essential employment. The example from Lancashire, of Helmshore and Whitakers Mill (Project 10) shows how a derelict textile mill has been restored to form a County Textile Museum.

Other buildings, which have lain empty and disused for many years, are often able to be restored sympathetically and returned to their original uses, although this will usually be in the form of working exhibits, rather than genuine industrial production. This is a particular area where local authorities are well suited to promote such initiatives as part of their educational and museum responsibilities.

It is interesting to note the work of County Councils in restoring buildings associated with the agricultural activities of their area. Norfolk has been involved with a Trust in restoring the water-pumps, watermills and windmills so reminiscent of the East Anglian countryside (Project 11), whilst Suffolk illustrates the restoration of Buttrams Mill, a tower mill, at Woodbridge (Project 15), work that is still proceeding. The corn mill at Sturminster Newton in Dorset (Project 4) has been restored by the County Council, again working through the activities of a Trust. Other watermills at Essex (Project 7) and Cheshire (Project 1), have also been restored to working order, work that has been achieved with the co-operation of many organizations and individuals.

Five schemes illustrated in this chapter relate to lead mining and iron workings, whilst one involves the development of a colliery museum. They all show a variety of restoration schemes where public display is an important element in the public appreciation of our industrial heritage. There is little doubt that these structures can, when properly conserved and imaginatively promoted, achieve a high level of interest and a source of pleasurable learning.

The conservation of such relics is not without its particular problems. In the case of masonry structures that have fallen into decay and have been exposed to the weather for many years, the soundness and stability of the stone or brickwork itself will need careful repair, often with materials that need to match the original as closely as possible. Where public accessibility is to be considered, a balance will need to be struck between limited restoration and stabilization of the existing fabric. Many engineering structures are built with cast-iron components, where repair or replacement can be both difficult and costly.

Where structures need to be adapted to suit new uses, then the Building Regulations may pose further difficulties. In mills and warehouses, for example, low ceilings, the pattern of structural support and low ratio of window to wall may not comply with modern requirements. Again, modern fire regulations often create more difficulties for older industrial buildings, because the cast iron so often used in construction has been considered to have a low fire rating. Fire doors, modern floor-loading requirements, compartmenting and additional means of escape are further examples of the problems that await the enthusiast who wishes to undertake the rehabilitation of

Artist's impression of a plateway in operation transporting raw material to the Monmouthshire and Brecon Canal wharves. (Reproduced with kind permission of Mike Blackmore.)

some of this nation's industrial buildings. Where working machinery is involved, for instance in working watermills and pumping stations, wire guards are required to protect people from machinery and other measures which often detract from the visual integrity of the building.[1]

Railways, industrial tramways and canals each have their own aura and character as well as enthusiasts! The first two are generally beyond the scope of this book and are more than adequately dealt with in other publications. However, the progressive restoration of abandoned and derelict canals is an important area of conservation work in which many local authorities are involved, either as owners of canals or, more often, in conjunction with British Waterways. Two canal restorations feature in this chapter, both from the south-west of England, a region possessing few canals, but popular with tourists. In terms of industrial archaeology, each of these has clearly been a success, enabling a historic waterway to be

re-opened once more to navigation, whilst providing an additional recreational facility for the public to enjoy.

Today industrial archaeology is a most popular and valuable area of the work of the conservation officer and archaeologist, and one where often restricted financial resources have an important 'pay off'. It is to be hoped that the illustrated examples in this chapter will encourage all those with a responsibility for our industrial heritage to continue with the enthusiasm that has already been shown. The long-term conservation of this heritage requires the co-operation of a wide range of national bodies and local authorities working in conjunction with industry and the private sector. It also needs flair and initiative coupled with professional expertise to ensure that important industrial remains are protected and restored in an appropriate and imaginative way.

REFERENCE

1. British Tourist Authority (1982) *Britain's Historic Buildings – a policy for their future use.*

FURTHER READING

1. Binney, M., Machin, F. and Powell, K. (1990) *Bright Future – the re-use of industrial buildings*, SAVE Britain's Heritage.
2. Cossons, N. (1987) *The BP Book of Industrial Archaeology*, 2nd edn, David and Charles.
3. Falconer, Keith (Series Editor) (1977) *The Batsford Guide to the Industrial Archaeology of the British Isles.*
4. Hudson, K. (1989) *Industrial Archaeological Sites from the Air* – Cambridge University Collection, Cambridge University Press.

CHESHIRE

PROJECT 2.1, Restoration of Stretton Mill – a working cornmill

The cornmill was the hub of a medieval village's economy; since all the tenants' grain had to be ground there, it was their only source of flour for bread, and for the lord of the manor it was a sure source of revenue. There are references to some 700 sites in Cheshire where a watermill or windmill has stood at some time since the eleventh century. In 1974, only two watermills were in working order. Now three further watermills, including Stretton Mill, have been restored. There is no working windmill, but one may be restorable.

Stretton Mill is one of the most interesting watermills in Cheshire. On a medieval site, the present building dates from the sixteenth to nineteenth centuries. It has one overshot wheel and

Stretton Mill. Sluice repaired, pool dredged and building restored. (Reproduced with kind permission of Cheshire County Council.)

one breast wheel driving separate trains of machinery, one largely of timber dating from the eighteenth century and the other substantially of cast iron from the nineteenth century.

Up to 1974, cornmills were regarded as industrial buildings which the Department of the Environment was seldom willing to list. Stretton Mill was semi-derelict, unused since the 1950s and, with no available tenant, a burden to its owner. The County Council's Conservation Officer appreciated the interest of the building and its machinery, but it was not listed until 1972. The intention was to acquire the mill and restore it as a working mill museum in the face of financial retrenchment then facing many councils. The only practical course was to secure the partnership of as many individuals and organizations as possible, so that the expenditure to be faced by each would be manageable.

The County Council's Museum Service agreed to take on the mill as a working museum, provided that the County Planning Department could secure its purchase and full restoration, with the necessary facilities for visitors. The owner conveyed the mill to the Council for a peppercorn; the Manpower Services Commission financed Job Creation Scheme labour to carry out essential building repairs; the Water Authority dredged the mill pool and repaired the sluice; the Science Museum gave £2066 towards machinery repairs; two structural engineers (father and son), expert in the restoration of cornmills rebuilt the two waterwheels and the machinery, charging only for their expenses and the cost of materials; the Countryside Commission paid half of the car park and landscaping and the County Council bore £19 000 of the £50 000 cost of the works. The public gained a mill museum in west Cheshire comparable in interest with the National Trust's Nether

Stretton Mill. Overshot wheel rebuilt by Dr Cyril Boucher. (Reproduced with kind permission of Cheshire County Council.)

Alderley Mill in the east of the county. The County Council's Historic Buildings Officer specified and supervised the building restoration and their Chief Environmental Engineer managed the civil engineering and external works.

CLEVELAND

PROJECT 2.2, Lazenby Bank, Teesside

As part of the Cleveland Urban Fringe Scheme, the project at Lazenby Bank involves aspects of archaeology, industrial archaeology and the conversion and reuse of listed buildings, together with the necessary site interpretation. The project is a partnership with industry. Over 100 hectares (247 acres) of predominantly woodland hillside is leased for a peppercorn, from I.C.I., the company which owns the land. It includes a grade II listed building of industrial archaeological importance and a Victorian school, also listed grade II. There are other structures of industrial archaeological importance relating to the ironstone mining for which these buildings were constructed, and the site includes part of a scheduled ancient monument, Eston Nab Iron Age hill-fort, which, at 242 m (793 ft) above sea level, overlooks the Tees valley from its elevated position.

THE INDUSTRIAL BUILDINGS

The industrial archaeological interest of this site centres around the range of buildings erected in connection with the extensive ironstone mining at Lazenby Bank. The Guibal Fan House Building was constructed to ventilate the mine and is listed Grade II, being built around 1870. Various structural repairs have been required, and as part of the structure is underground, various restrictions to access apply. The building itself is a very early example of *in situ* cast concrete, using blast furnace slag as the aggregate. Although not unique, the building is thought to be the only example in Britain which is accessible to the public. Steel gratings over the entrance apertures prevent unsupervised access.

Guibal fan house (The *S.S. Castle*) at Lazenby Bank (*c.*1870). (Reproduced with kind permission of Cleveland County Council.)

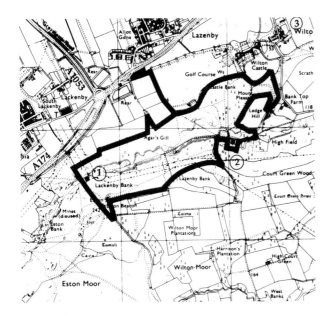

Wilton Old School (1854) now an interpretative/education centre. (Reproduced with kind permission of Cleveland County Council.)

'New Bank Top' is a complex of structures surrounding the open ventilation drift. The drift itself is a brick-lined tunnel which has required considerable rebuilding to ensure public safety, and it is open as far as 30 m (32 yards) into the hillside. There are also remains of a furnace and chimney for ventilation, foundations of an iron-cased Guibal-type ventilating fan, the engine bed and remains of the engine house for the fan. There are also the massive foundations of a steam-powered hauler (acting along a rope-hauled wagonway, now a footpath), the foundations of an electric motor house which superseded the boiler house for the hauler, two massive concrete piers formerly supporting a brake house, a 'centre kip', a sunken wagon siding with stone retaining walls and the remains of a stable building. The Keith fan was a small electric-powered ventilating fan of which the remains have now been consolidated along with the accompanying drift which it ventilated.

The Local Industrial Archaeological Society has surveyed and reported on the Guibal fan. The Keith fan has also been recorded and the remains of the mine complex at New Bank Top are well documented.

The mine closed in 1949, and it is only recently that concern has grown that this feature of our historic heritage should be conserved in such a way that visitors could come and appreciate the workings of a late Victorian mine. All the remains of the mine structures and buildings have been consolidated and made safe for public access. With the exception of the New Bank Drift, where public safety was a priority, the minimum amount of work has been done. Here the soil level has been lowered to its original height and approximately 5 m (5.5 yards) of the drift mouth has been rebuilt.

Wilton Old School, built in 1854, has been converted internally to provide an interpretive/education centre for school groups and visitors. The industrial archaeological sites are publicized and promoted at a wide variety of outlets. Educational use is being developed through a warden service and there is both on- and off-site interpretation in the form of pamphlets and panels on site. The five-year programme of work to the school has cost, during the first four years, over £13 000.

DEVON

PROJECT 2.3, Grand Western Canal, Tiverton

John Rennie was the engineer who supervised the design and construction of the Grand Western Canal, which, together with the Bridgwater and Taunton Canal (also mentioned in this chapter, Project 2.14), was an ambitious attempt to provide a waterway between Bristol and Topsham, the port of Exeter, and hence connect the Bristol and English Channels. Such a canal would have allowed goods to be shipped from the Midlands to the south of England, avoiding the hazardous south-west peninsula. Today only the 22.5 km (14 miles) of the Bridgwater and Taunton Canal and 17.7 km (11 miles) of the narrower Grand Western Canal remain as navigational waterways. The two canals do not link as they once used to, and the Grand Western is now limited to a stretch between Tiverton and Lowdwells, close to Westleigh on the Somerset border (Site plan: Project 2.3).

The last horse-drawn tub boats worked on the Grand Western Canal until the 1920s after which it fell into disuse until local people persuaded the County Council and the Mid Devon District Council to acquire it from the British Waterways Board (now British Waterways), which also endowed it with £38 750, in May 1971.

The building of the canal in 1813 had presented many problems for those early navigators. Works at Halberton, some five kilometres (three miles)

Grand Western Canal before restoration. Weed-chocked section at Burlescombe. The old railway bridge in the background connected the quarries with the main line. (Reproduced with kind permission of Devon County Council.)

east of Tiverton, proved in their day to 'be most difficult and expensive' with high cuttings through hard rock, and the occurrence of porous sand.

With the restoration works commencing in 1974, very similar problems were encountered in the same region. Leaks abounded, and the canal had to be lined with over 300 m (330 yards) of butyl

plastic sheet, which lasted until 1988, when further repairs were necessary due to increasing failures and water loss. The possible costs of relining this length of the canal caused great concern to the two Councils, and a suggestion at the time to drain off the leaking length and to abandon it was considered. There was, however, a strong feeling that the canal should be maintained as a navigable waterway – a feeling that was supported by this being the cheaper of the two options. By April 1990, tenders were invited for the necessary repairs, which required a high density polythene sheet to be laid over a length of 1200 m (1330 yards). This cost £440 000 and contained a guarantee that the works should avoid any further leaks for 40 years.

The Grand Western Canal contains no dramatic structures such as locks and viaducts and tunnels (over the restored length), nor are there any warehouses along its banks. An old wharf house has

Renovated Wharf House with wharf for unloading stone. (Reproduced with kind permission of Devon County Council.)

Horse-drawn boat on canal near Tiverton. (Reproduced with kind permission of Devon County Council.)

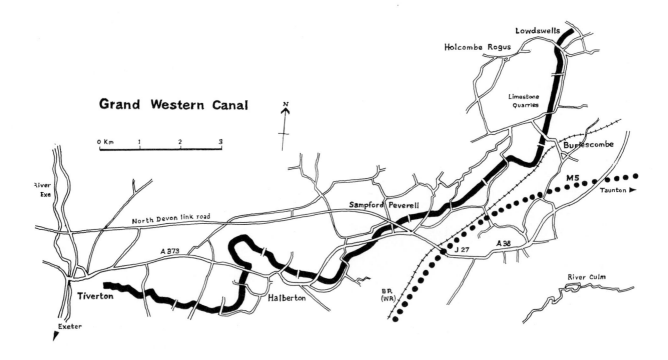

Grand Western Canal

0 Km   1   2   3

N

River Exe

Lowdswells

Holcombe Rogus

Limestone Quarries

Burlescombe

M5

Taunton ►

North Devon link road

Sampford Peverell

A 373

J 27   A 38

River Culm

Tiverton

Halberton

B R (WR)

Exeter

been renovated with a wharf for unloading stone. Its beauty today no doubt lies in the way in which it unobtrusively blends discreetly into the glorious Devon countryside. Many of the bridges are either built of locally quarried stone, or brick, made from Devon clay from nearby brickfields. In order to avoid costly earthworks and cuttings, the canal, near Halberton, takes a wide sweep of nearly 1.6 km (1 mile) in order to maintain a constant contour. A deep cutting at the eastern end of the canal was necessary in order to keep the summit level low and to reduce the problems of providing an adequate water supply. The excavation of this cutting accidentally solved the water supply problem as naturally occurring springs were revealed, which, to this day, provide the canal with its water.

The canal's value as a centre of water-based recreation and enjoyment cannot be overstressed, for in this part of the south-west there are few canals that are available for navigation. A privately owned horse-drawn boat, regularly using the canal during the summer months, has attracted visitors for many years now, and this year, it is confidently expected that the number of visitors coming to the canal will exceed 300 000. The 17.7 km (11 miles) of towpath provide easy walking through an ever-changing scenery, and there are good car parks at Tiverton and Sampford Peverell. There are picnic sites at Tiverton, Tiverton Road bridge, Halberton and Sampford Peverell.

The County Council has since designated the canal a Country Park, and in 1990, The Grand Western Canal Trust was formally constituted, and a member of this Trust represents its views on the Canal Advisory Committee.

DORSET

PROJECT 2.4, Restoration of Sturminster Newton Mill

Sturminster Newton is a small market town in north Dorset located at a bridging point across the River Stour. Sturminster, the main settlement, is located on the north bank and is linked by a fifteenth-century bridge to the small settlements of Newton and Bridge on the south bank. Between Newton and Bridge, overlooking the bridge, is the 'castle', a scheduled ancient monument, consisting of the ivy-clad remnant of a medieval manor house within the earthworks of an Iron Age Fort. The seventeenth-century mill and its weir, approximately 238 m (260 yards) upstream from the bridge, complete this attractive scene (Location plan b: Project 2.4).

The existence of mills at Sturminster is recorded in the Domesday Survey of 1086. It is likely that one of these mills was the predecessor of the present mill which dates partly from the seventeenth and partly from the eighteenth centuries (Fig. 2.8). A feature of the Mill is its water turbine which was installed in place of the traditional water wheel in 1904. This more efficient use of water power, which had been developed during the nineteenth century, is based upon the principle of a horizontal as opposed to a vertical wheel. Sturminster Newton Mill offers an opportunity to see how a mill works – from the delivery of grain to the final product, and to compare the age-old process of stone grinding with more recent milling machinery.

Concern for the future of the mill, one of the few still working in Dorset, began in the 1970s. At that time it was leased to a local farmer who used part of it to grind small quantities of animal feed in return for maintaining and operating the hatches. Both the owner, Mr Anthony Pitt-Rivers, and the County Council were keen to preserve the mill and in 1974 the decision was taken that, whilst there was no short-term problem, it would be sensible to start planning for the time when the tenant retired.

PHASE I

A prerequisite for a working watermill is an adequate supply and head of water. The levels and flow of water in this stretch of the River Stour are controlled by a series of rolling bays and hatches at Cutt Mill (disused) approximately 3 km (2 miles) upstream, at Sturminster Mill itself and at Fiddleford Mill (still operational and also leased to a local farmer) a similar distance downstream. The river is also important as an amenity feature and for fishing.

The Wessex Water Authority were most co-operative, and in 1976, following a detailed survey, produced a report on the conditions of the rolling bays, hatches and stability of the banks at the three mills, together with recommendations for repair and bank stabilization. In 1977 it was agreed to raise the estimated £27 500 for the necessary works at Sturminster and Fiddleford. Contributions were received from: The Rivers Estate (£5000); The Angling Club (£5000); Wessex Water (£8000); Sturminster Newton Parish Council (£2000); North Dorset District Council (£3500); Dorset County Council (£3500), a total of £27 000. The works were implemented in August of that year.

PHASE II

In September 1977 a meeting was held to discuss the preservation of Sturminster Mill. The formation of a Trust was agreed in principle, initially to be advised by officers from the County Council's Planning, Solicitors, Treasurers and Valuers Departments. During 1978 and 1979 the owner and representatives from the County, District and Parish Councils considered the options and problems involved in preserving the mill, i.e. whether it should be a commercial mill; a commercial mill, but with access for court visitors; mainly for visitors, with the mill gently operating or a museum piece.

A small working party was set up headed by the then Chairman of the County Council's Planning Sub-Committee whose family had long associations with milling in Dorset. Under his direction, the officers investigated all the possibilities and

Sturminster Newton Mill restored. (Reproduced with kind permission of Dorset County Council.)

associated problems – technical, insurance, safety, management etc. A great deal was learned by visiting several working mills and talking to the millers. Mr Ellis of Headley Mill gave advice and also came to Sturminster on two occasions to assist on technical aspects of restoration. The Sturminster Rotoract Club gave help in clearing out the Mill. This arduous and dirty task took three weeks during which time, with Mr Ellis' help, vital pieces of equipment, including the stones, were discovered beneath years of accumulated dirt and rubbish.

By October 1979 it was possible to update and finalize the schedule of repairs and necessary additional work, such as installation of electricity and construction of a car park. Fortunately, the

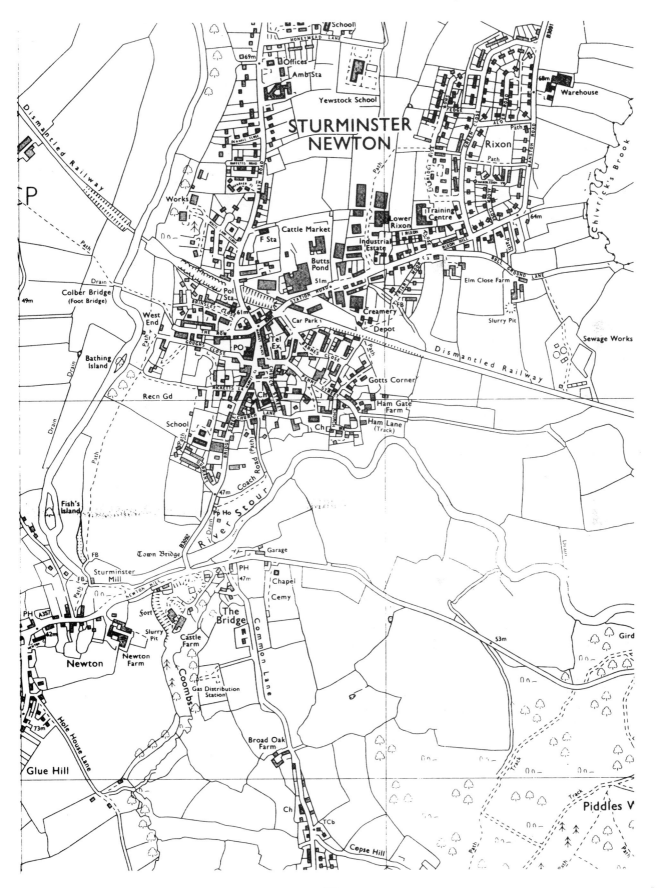

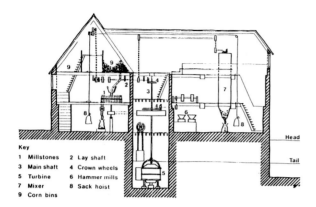

Key

1 Millstones   2 Lay shaft
3 Main shaft   4 Crown wheels
5 Turbine   6 Hammer mills
7 Mixer   8 Sack hoist
9 Corn bins

Sturminster Newton Mill. Preparing the stone for dressing. (Reproduced with kind permission of Dorset County Council.)

turbine, main drive and lay shafts were found to be in reasonably good working order; other old machinery was capable of repair, some missing parts could be 'borrowed' from other disused mills or new equipment installed at a reasonable cost. The estimated cost was £18 000. By February 1980, a total of £17 488 had been raised from Dorset County Council (£7180); North Dorset District Council (£7500); Sturminster Newton Parish Council (£1000); DoE (£1808). Subsequently the Sturminster Newton Carnival Committee donated £100 which gave a working fund of £17 588.

During 1980, details were finalized and preparations made in readiness to take over the Mill when the tenant retired and vacated the Mill at the end of the year. The first formal meeting of prospective trustees took place in December 1980, at which it was formally agreed (i) to form a Limited Trust Company with seven trustees, two from each of the Councils and the owner of the Mill; (ii) that sufficient funds were available to cover the cost of the repair work; (iii) that work on the more urgent structural repairs should be put in hand and (iv) prospective tenants would be interviewed.

In February 1981 work on restoring the Mill began and a tenant miller appointed. Restoration work continued from February to June. The tenant miller worked on the machinery and volunteers from Guy's Marsh Borstal worked at weekends clearing footpaths, verges and the river banks. In July 1981 Sturminster Mill, although not quite ready, was opened to the public because of the

great interest in the project. During that year, excluding school parties, approximately 4000 people visited it.

In 1982 restoration work continued, a car park and picnic area were constructed, and toilet facilities provided. There were improvements to the river-bank, trees and shrubs were planted, and fences, steps and gates erected. On 22 September 1982, the Sturminster Newton Trust Co. Ltd officially came into being. It is a private company with the seven trustees as the directors. The Mill is leased to the Trust at peppercorn rent, and the trust in turn, sub-leases it to the miller. The Trust's income is derived from the rent paid by the miller and 50% of the profits from visitors. All income is ploughed back into the continuing work of maintaining and improving the Mill.

DURHAM

PROJECT 2.5, Restoration of Causey Arch, near Stanley

The Causey Arch, also known as the Tanfield Arch, is claimed to be the oldest single span railway arch in the world. It is over 260 years old, is a Scheduled Monument and is listed Grade I in the Department of the Environment's List of Buildings of Architectural or Historic Interest. It has a clear span of 31 m (102 ft) at that time the largest span in England and the crown of the arch stands 25 m (82 ft) above Causey Burn. Time and weather had an effect on the Arch; trees, seeded from salves in the joints of the stonework, grew over the years to a considerable size with consequent damage to the surrounding structure. Water penetrated into the interior of the Arch and washed out the mortar joints and caused the surface of the Arch soffit to disintegrate. Although the Arch was in no danger of collapse, it did constitute a hazard to anyone underneath. Also the 9 m (29 ft) high rock face supporting the eastern abutment showed signs of severe weathering and deterioration which, if left unchecked, would eventually constitute a danger to the Arch.

Durham County Council purchased the Arch and surrounding land to create a Picnic Area and decided to restore Causey Arch. Responsibility for the scheme was undertaken by Durham County Council in close consultation with the Department of the Environment. Overall financial control and planning aspects were under the direction of the County Planning Officer, and the works were designed, carried out and supervised by the County Engineer. The Departments together now form the Environment Department.

Decaying stone in the arched soffit was identified and resin injected to prevent further deterioration. Trees located in accessible positions were dug out and other trees were cut back and killed by chemical treatment. Stonework affected by the trees was rebuilt. As mortar was missing from the stonework joints to a considerable depth a contract was let to 'pressure point' the walls so that maximum penetration of the new mortar could be achieved. Missing or weathered stones were replaced using stones found on site chiefly from the collapsed causeway; badly aligned areas of stonework were taken down and rebuilt. The final pointing was done by hand.

Early prints showed that no railings were provided on the original structure but present-day safety regulations demanded that appropriate railings be installed. These were placed about 2 m (6.6 ft) back from the face of the bridge to reduce their visual impact when viewed from below.

The sandstone face supporting the east abutment was fissured and of poor quality, the rock having weathered away in the weaker areas leaving overhanging blocks which tended to fracture at the back and fall away. A large number of rock bolts were installed to hold the various parts of the face in position. In addition, grout was pumped into fissures in the rock through the holes drilled for the rock bolt and over 100 tonnes of cement were used in this operation. The void beneath the overhang was filled with concrete and the surface was cast as individual rocks to match the natural rock above. The rhythm and scale of the original sandstone cliff was carefully matched. This skilful concrete repair work won the 1988 Construction Award of the Northern Counties Association of the Institute of Civil Engineers and a Commendation in the 1988 Civic Trust Award.

(See Plate 2.)

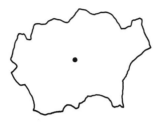

DURHAM

PROJECT 2.6, Killhope Lead Mining Centre and Park Level Mill, near Stanhope

Lead was mined in the North Pennines in the Middle Ages, and possibly earlier. Remnants of this once great industry are strewn across these northern hills: miles of man-made caverns (stopes) and tunnels (levels) created at altitudes of 550 m (1800 ft) on the Durham, Northumberland and Cumbrian borders.

Park Level Mill, built about 1877, was situated adjacent to a lead mine and was used to crush and dress the lead ore (galena) from the hills of Weardale. The adjacent mine had been driven, some twenty years earlier, to cut across a series of vertical veins of lead ore, and connect to Killhopehead Mine 3 km (2 miles) away. Motive power for the operations was provided by both human effort and water power, Park Level Mill having a massive, wrought-iron wheel, 10 m (34 ft) in diameter, which was driven by water flowing from a series of nearby reservoirs.

The extraction of lead declined during the second half of the nineteenth century, and by 1900 it had ceased totally in the region. Killhope closed at this time. During the 1930s it was scoured for reusable materials, and, although ignored during the 1939 war effort for scrap-iron as it was too remote, it was advertised for sale and demolition in the 1950s. During all these years, the buildings and workings became progressively derelict and dangerous.

However, the whole area in which these workings were situated was a popular spot for visitors and tourists, and a small picnic site was established nearby in the late 1960s. At the time of the Durham County Council's lease of the site in 1968, not only were the buildings extremely unsafe, but the whole site was often wet in summer and frozen in winter. The river, the Killhopeburn, frequently spilled into the workings in times of flood. In the late 1970s the County Council had fenced off the wheel and some of the buildings which were considered too dangerous. There was virtually no information available about the site and buildings. All these factors made it very difficult to consider even a strategy for repair and restoration. It was considered by many, however, that these remains of the lead mining industry were a significant heritage landmark in the North Pennines, and the Durham County Council agreed that efforts should be made to conserve the structures. Demolition was never a consideration, and, indeed, the main buildings and the large water wheel are Scheduled Ancient Monuments.

Discussions took place, both with 'experts' in the lead industry and English Heritage, and the County Council's archaeologist, to determine the importance of the site and what strategies should be adopted for its preservation and presentation. Discussions were also held over likely funding with English Heritage and the Countryside Commission. A strategy was drawn up by the County Council for saving the monument and was submitted to its Environment Committee. This included the provision of a tourist information point (after discussions with the Northumbria Tourist Board) and for the repair of the structures as an initial step.

Restoration of the buildings proved very difficult and there was little living or documentary

Killhope Lead Mining Centre. Base teams and dressing floor. (Reproduced with kind permission of Durham County Council.)

Killhope Lead Mining Centre. Brunton Buddle Water Wheel and dressing floor. (Reproduced with kind permission of Durham County Council.)

Killhope Lead Mining Centre. (Reproduced with kind permission of Durham County Council.)

accounts of the working methods of the Killhope site. In the meantime, substantial repairs were necessary to stone walls, lintels, roofs and their trusses, stone flagged floors and water channels. Apart from the crusher area, attention needed to be given to the two main buildings on the site, the Jigger House and the Buddle House. The former accommodated the main dressing plant, and was where the lead was separated from the rock and spar in the ore, by the force of water. The Buddle House contained four Cornish buddles, which were circular, inverted cones over which water, containing a mixture of lead and sandy mud was fed, separating out the finer particles of lead. Attention also had to be paid to the repair of both the water races and a short mineral trackway between the dressing floors, where the lead ore was dropped, the work being carried out after archaeological research and inspection. The main bridge over the Killhopeburn was rebuilt after having been washed away in floods in 1983, and three aquaducts were constructed, one to carry the tail race. The mine shop was to be fitted out as a visitor centre, and this required considerable stonework repairs and reroofing.

In 1980 it appeared that a repair and consolidation exercise would be sufficient to ensure at least the survival of the structures, but inevitably, as more was learnt of the intriguing processes that were carried out, and archaeological research work uncovered more of the layout of the structures that were erected for the purpose, it was clear that a more substantial programme of restoration would be needed.

Funds were made available by the County Council for a four-year programme of work, backed by English Heritage and the Manpower Services Commission. This work was confined to the Ancient Monument site, although, later, work to the forestry area was assisted financially by the Countryside Commission. Additionally some grand aid from the EEC European Regional Development Fund was awarded, and there were contributions from many commercial undertakings. A gift of two water wheels was made by the Friends of Killhope. Since 1980, Durham County Council has set aside a gross capital budget of £790 000 for the restoration of the Killhope Lead Mines complex. English Heritage has offered a grant of almost £25 000, the EEC Rural Development Fund £160 000, and the Countryside Commission £96 000.

The Manpower Services Commission undertook the considerable labour implications and met the costs of employment and transporting men up to 40 km (25 miles) to and from the site, and the hiring of plant. Enticing a young labour force on to a snowy, rainy site some 460 km (1500 ft) above sea level, remote from any sizable community was far from easy, especially in the early days of the scheme, and it speaks well of the enthusiasm that was engendered on the site, that the work of restoration was achieved.

The site officially opened in 1984 when it was estimated that some 25% of the visitors were tourists. Today that figure would probably be nearer 75%. During the winter months, and outside the peak visitor season, school parties are catered for. Killhope attracts around 40 000 visitors a year, and with the recently constructed visitor centre open in 1991, it is anticipated that this will increase to 60 000.

The work has been planned and carried out under the direction of the Durham County Council's Environment Department by their Design and Conservation team. The successful realization of this project has been the result of dogged determination and much frustration, but the County now has a fitting monument to a past industry – and to those who worked in it – in one of the most inhospitable sites in Britain, now giving pleasure to many.

(See Plate 3.)

ESSEX

PROJECT 2.7, Thorrington Tide Mill

At one time, most towns and villages in Essex possessed a windmill or watermill to provide flour for their daily bread. Watermills were normally sited on rivers, where the flow or fall of water would turn their wheels, but sometimes the ebb of the tide in an estuary was used for this purpose. Such a mill still survives at Thorrington, between Colchester and Brightlingsea, and is the only example of a tide mill in Essex to retain its water-wheel and machinery.

Essex County Council was possibly one of the first local authorities to recognize the technical and landscape importance of traditional mills, and as early as 1937 began a scheme of preserving selected examples, which has continued to the present day. The County Council allocates an annual budget for the upkeep of mills, and employs a full-time millwright in the Planning Department to look after the five mills in the County's care. In addition to the direct acquisition and preservation of mills the millwright is available to give technical advice to private owners of mills within the county. A part-time Mills Visit Supervisor is also employed to conduct parties of schoolchildren or interested adults over the restored mills, some of which may be seen working.

The County Council acquired Thorrington Mill in 1974, together with sufficient land to construct a car park for visitors. For the technically minded, the mill has a 4.9 m (16 ft) diameter by 1.8 m (6 ft) wide breast-shot water-wheel with 50 paddles geared to drive three pairs of 1.2 m (4 ft) diameter French burr millstones. The gear train consists of large toothed wheels, perhaps the most impressive

being the great spur wheel beneath the millstones. This is an all-wooden wheel, nearly 2.4 m (8 ft) in diameter with 108 teeth, each tooth being individually fitted into the rim and spaced to a hair's breadth. In addition to the millstones, the mill is equipped with a mechanical hoist for raising sacks of grain by water power, and also a 'reel' or rotary sieve, for removing bran from flour and hence making it a little whiter for domestic use.

There has been a mill on the Thorrington site since 1558, but the present mill dates from a reconstruction in 1831, this date being carved on the plinth brickwork and on a beam inside. The mill functioned by tidal power until 1926, assisted by a steam engine, but later became dilapidated until it was bought by a private owner during the Second World War. He carried out much needed repairs, and used the building successively as a seed store, piggery and a fowl house, eventually selling it to the County Council, who wished to preserve this last typical example of an Essex tide mill.

The restoration of a watermill is a major undertaking, and particularly so when the mill is subsequently required to function for demonstration purposes. The water-wheel channel had been deliberately sealed off long ago, and the lower half of the wheel itself was entirely buried in accumulated silt and rubbish. On cleaning the waterways it became apparent that the channel wall and the wall of the mill itself were undermined, and would need comprehensive repair even before the restoration of the working parts could begin.

Thorrington Tide Mill. (Reproduced with kind permission of Essex County Council.)

Thorrington Tide Mill. The restored water-wheel; repairs to the timber frame in progress. (Reproduced with kind permission of Essex County Council.)

The foundations of the mill were some 2.4 m (8 ft) below high tide level, so a coffer dam of steel sheet piling was needed to hold back the tide while the work of underpinning the building and constructing a new concrete apron proceeded. Fortunately the National Rivers Authority was very sympathetic towards the aim of restoring the mill and was able to carry out this specialist work under contract to the County Council. This phase was completed successfully despite the periodic 'spring tides' which would pour over the top of the piling and flood the work area, thus enforcing a break in the proceedings. Having placed the mill once more on sound foundations it was possible to reinstate the repaired water-wheel, together with its control sluice and associated mechanism. The water-wheel is mainly constructed of cast iron and many of its components were reusable, but where the iron had been submerged in salt-water mud, it had become quite soft, and the parts so affected had to be renewed. The wooden paddles and sole boards had disappeared, and had to be made anew. On May 10th 1990 the wheel turned by water power for the first time in over 60 years.

The next step was the repair of the timber-framed, weather-boarded mill building with its slated roof. Although apparently sound, the pine timbers had rotted in a number of areas, and more damage had been caused by rats gnawing cavities in the beams. This damage became evident upon stripping off the weather-board cladding, also overdue for replacement. New sections of pitch pine have now been scarfed into the timber frame where found necessary, and all the cladding has been replaced and painted. New cased sash windows to the original design have been incorporated. Work is going on to repair the floors and to reslate the roof, and when this has been done the mill will be ready for viewing, albeit not fully operational.

A future phase will involve the repair and recogging of the great spur wheel, and the renewal of worn parts in the final drive to the millstones. The millstones themselves will need attention in the form of 'dressing', i.e. levelling and regrooving the working faces so that they are once more able to grind wheat into wholemeal flour.

The cost of the whole project has been considerable; the work was broken down into annual phases calculated to be affordable from the funding available. The costs were estimated as follows: Stage 1, dismantling machinery, and repairs to waterwheel: £13 000; Stage 2, improving entrance and building car park: £39 000; Stage 3, repairs to foundations and watercourses: £60 000; Stage 4, reassembling water-wheel, repairs to machinery: £40 000; Stage 5, repairs to building: £55 000, making a total of £207 000.

The Planning Department's Budget for the Upkeep of Mills has met the cost of restoration over a five-year period, assisted by grant aid from English Heritage. The mill, which is listed Grade II* was declared to be 'outstanding' by English Heritage after due consideration, and a 25% grant was offered. This applied to work on the mill itself, but excluded the car park. The grant was conditional upon the mill being made available for public viewing – the original intention of the County Council.

When the current work has been completed, the mill will be opened to the public on a regular basis during the summer, and party visits will be available for those requiring a conducted tour, during which the working and history of the mill will be explained. Judging by the popularity of the County Council's preserved windmills, Thorrington Tide Mill in its delightful setting will become a 'must' for visitors.

GWENT

PROJECT 2.8, Govilon Wharf Warehouse restoration

The incidence of coal, iron and limestone in the valleys of South Wales led to its development as a major industrial area in Britain during the eighteenth century. In order to provide consistent supplies of the necessary raw materials as well as transporting the products, it was essential to establish a network of simple horse-drawn plateways linking with horse-drawn barges on the canals. Therefore, by the end of the eighteenth century, canals were being threaded through these hilly regions, able to connect to docks and wharves further downstream.

The Monmouthshire and Brecon Canal was one such route, and was opened for commercial traffic in 1799. Coal and iron were the basic commodities transported. Along the valley there were a number of collieries and ironworks, such as at Llanelly, and limestone quarries and collieries near Crickhowell. South-bound traffic consisted of agricultural produce, and later, a trade in flour between Kington and Merthyr was built up. It was normal practice for canals to have plateways, or tramways, using horse-power to connect to the industrial areas and the canal network became an essential part of the industrial success of the region.

The warehouse at Govilon on the north bank of the Monmouthshire and Brecon Canal 0.8 km (0.5 miles) from the village of Govilon was built in 1812 and used as a storage and 'transshipment' point for goods transferred between the barges and the adjacent Llanfihangel plateway, a 1.0 m (3 ft 6 in) gauge link to the local town of Abergavenny and beyond. Later, a further plateway from the Blaenavon Ironworks also used the building. It was originally built for storing pig-iron transported

by plateway from Crawshay Bailey's ironworks (see Project 3.10). The building was one of the few remaining warehouses dating from the early days of the canal, but had deteriorated badly. In 1973 it had been listed as a Grade II building. In 1979, with the approval of the owners, the British Waterways Board (now British Waterways), a submission was made to the Manpower Services Commission for a Project-based Work Experience Scheme which was to be sponsored by Gwent County Council. Approval for the scheme was given and an offer of grant-aid of £2300 was received from the Welsh Development Agency under its Environmental Improvement Programme. The Gwent County Council's Planning Department were to provide supervision and the British Waterways Board offered to provide comprehensive scaffolding for the warehouse.

The scheme was started in October 1979. The team consisted of six unemployed teenagers whose average age was 17 years, and a supervisor. The supervisor alone, who was only in his mid-20s

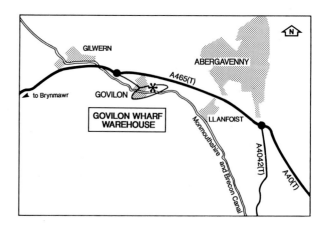

Govilon Wharf Warehouse.

Govilon Wharf Warehouse. Pen sketch.

himself, had any experience in building construction, but gradually the youngsters became quite adept at stonework, carpentry and concreting. The new windows, which are copies of the originals, were made by the teenagers themselves, using machinery at the Woodworking Department of the Pontypool College of Further Education.

Work carried out to the warehouse included the stripping of the roof, repairing decayed timbers, reslating the north elevation, fixing new ridge tiles, repointing stonework (internally and externally), rebuilding crumbling areas of stonework, making and inserting new windows and doors, laying a new concrete floor, rebuilding the external steps, constructing retaining walls and laying land drains around the warehouse. The scheme was finally completed in June 1980, at a cost of £4800, a figure which excludes labour costs.

By renovating the Govilon Wharf Warehouse, Gwent County Council and the British Waterways Board have ensured that it will contine to represent examples of early eighteenth century warehouses that were once to be found along the Monmouthshire and Brecon Canal. The completed scheme has attracted a revival of boating interests in the locality and has enhanced both the canal and its immediate surroundings. Since 1985, the British Waterways Board has taken over the building as its regional office, carrying out minor internal works to enable the building to be used for offices with meeting-room facilities, on the upper two floors, with canal maintenance accommodation on the ground floor.

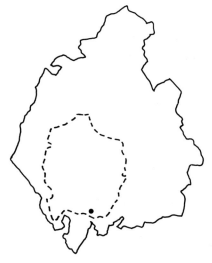

LAKE DISTRICT NATIONAL PARK

PROJECT 2.9, Duddon Iron Furnace

The Lake District has a wide range of archaeological and historic features, in particular the remains of once prosperous rural industries. In the eighteenth century the iron smelting industry relied on charcoal as a fuel, consequently the furnaces and forges were established in the well-wooded parts of the country such as Shropshire, Forest of Dean, South Yorkshire, the Weald and the Furness area of the Lake District.

Of the eight blast furnaces which were set up in the Furness area between 1711 and 1748, the one which survives in its most complete form is the Duddon Furnace, at the southern end of the Duddon Valley near Broughton-in-Furness. As with all the other furnaces, Duddon was carefully located within easy reach of iron-ore deposits, woodlands for fuel and water for powering the bellows. This blast furnace with its stores for charcoal and iron, together with workers' cottages was erected in 1736–37. The furnace ceased in 1867, by which time coke had become well established as the main fuel to smelt iron. The furnace buildings were abandoned and left to revert back to woodland, apart from the cottages which were inhabited until 1953.

In recognition of its national importance the furnace became a Scheduled Ancient Mounment in 1963. Through the interest of local industrial archaeologists the (then) Cumberland County Council managed to secure a 21-year lease on the furnace stack in order to carry out first-aid repair work in 1973, grant-aided by the Department of the Environment. This was very much a 'stitch-in-time' operation, but it did not solve the future management of the site.

During the negotiations in the 1970s, it was hoped that the Department of the Environment would agree to become guardians of the site, but a decision in late 1979 ruled this out because of Government economics. The National Park Authority (NPA) immediately took the initiative as the site lies just within the National Park. Following discussions with the new owner, who had just inherited the Duddon Estate, the NPA obtained a 50-year lease in 1981 on all the buildings apart from the now derelict workers' cottages. The owner intends to restore these in the future. The primary purpose of the lease was to take over the management of the site from the County Council (as the NPA now had full-time planning staff since 1974) and to carry out a programme of excavation and consolidation works. It was not the intention to improve public access at this stage, as a public bridleway passes close by the site. For safety reasons and to maintain control over the site, the NPA continued the County Council's

Duddon Iron Furnace. Photograph taken 30 years after closure of works (1867). Growth of trees in the top of the stack is already apparent. (Photograph first appeared in *North Lonsdale Magazine* in 1897).

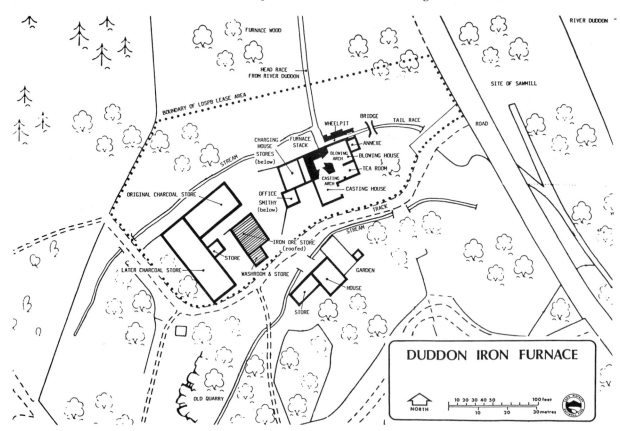

(a)

(b)

Duddon Iron Furnace in 1991 after 10 years of excavation and consolidation by the Park Authority. (a) Water-powered bellows blew air into the large opening in the foreground; (b) the large arched opening gave access to the hearth for casting the iron. (Reproduced with kind permission of the Lake District National Park.)

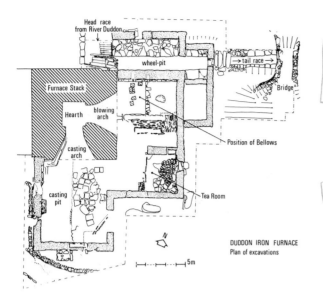

Head race from River Duddon

wheel-pit

→ tail race →

Bridge

Furnace Stack

Hearth

blowing arch

Position of Bellows

casting arch

Tea Room

casting pit

N

DUDDON IRON FURNACE
Plan of excavations

5m

practice of issuing permits to interested individuals or groups.

The first works carried out in 1980/81 were to fence the site and clear trees and undergrowth from within and adjoining the buildings and structure, with the NPA's own Park Management staff. It is ironic that the woodlands which originally attracted the iron industry to the area, could now, over time be responsible for destroying the remains. The Department of the Environment were unable to offer any direct labour help, but they provided a detailed schedule of works and an overall estimate of £35 000.

In autumn 1981, the NPA organized an 11-week archaeological excavation of the eastern section of this site to reveal the remains of the casting area, bellows room and wheelpit. This was the first excavation at any Lakeland furnace and it was grant-aided by the Department of the Environment.

Between 1982 and 1985 a programme of summer excavations was carried out, which included work to the floors of the standing buildings adjoining the furnace stack; completion of the wheelpit area; investigation of the hearth area of the furnace; clearance of the floors of the charcoal stores and preconsolidation and recording of the charcoal store walls. In 1982 the iron-ore store was reroofed by local contractors with Department of the

Environment grant aid. A major project to consolidate all the wall tops of the charcoal store was carried out successfully in 1986. The large charcoal store is a huge roofless building almost 30.5 m (100 ft) long and it was essential that the uneven wall-top profile was retained and not 'planed-off'.

In 1988 an NPA management plan was approved for Duddon Furnace. In essence it sets the context for future work on the site and in particular it recommends structural work on the two furnace stack arches. The main theme of future management is to retain the quiet character of the site and not to promote it actively as a tourist attraction. Visiting groups ranging from local historical societies to Council of Europe delegates have supported the NPA's philosophy. From past experience at other popular sites in the Lake District, once a site becomes busy and on the day tripper's itinerary, this brings with it serious problems of maintenance and site management. The NPA is not in a promotional role nor does it view such sites on a commercial basis. Its primary statutory duty is to preserve and enhance the landscape. Any further development could so easily destroy the special character of the furnace's setting.

In the near future when the consolidation work is completed and the site is made safe and free access is allowed, the intention is to erect an interpretive panel, alongside the public bridleway, which sets the geographical and historical context and explains the processes and functional nature of the buildings. Duddon Furnace is an impressive structure over 250 years old and any descriptive panels will require very sensitive treatment.

Since the NPA took over the management of the site in 1981 approximately £33 000 has been spent of which £9200 has been grant-aided by the Department of the Environment and English Heritage. The final phase of consolidation work is programmed for 1990/91 and further grant aid has been promised. By protecting and managing the most complete charcoal blast furnace in England, the NPA has ensured that a very important feature of the Lake District's industrial heritage has been saved for people to understand, appreciate and enjoy.

LANCASHIRE

PROJECT 2.10, Helmshore Textile Mills: Textile Industry Museum for Lancashire

Some schemes are carried out smoothly according to a preconceived plan; others are no less successful, but, as in the creation of the Museum of the Lancashire Textile Industry, have to change and grow in response to changing circumstances. The Museum is housed in two former textile mills at Helmshore, some 6.4 km (4 miles) south of Accrington. Although they stand no more than a few yards apart and up to 1852 were owned by the same man, their subsequent history, their prosperity and decline have been different, and this has affected the development of the Museum.

The older of the mills, Higher Mill, is perhaps the oldest textile mill in Lancashire; it was built in 1789 as a fulling mill and remained as such until it closed in 1967. It was powered by water; the reservoirs and the mid nineteenth-century water-wheel and fulling stocks (in which loosely woven woollen cloth was shrunk and thickened by soaking and pounding in a sort of detergent) survive in working order today.

The second mill, Whitaker's Mill, was built in the 1820s and rebuilt in 1860 after a disastrous fire. It started life spinning woollen yarn and weaving woollen cloth (which was then fulled next door) but, after several changes, it became a cotton spinning mill in the 1920s and remained as such for more than 50 years.

Long before Higher Hill closed, the importance of its antiquated machinery was recognized by

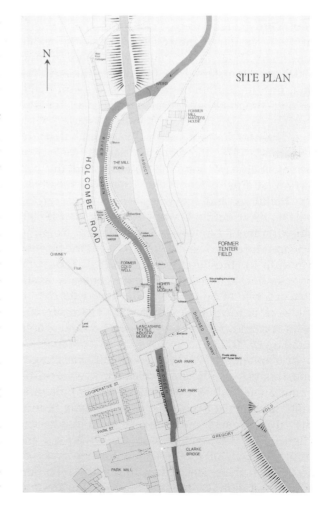

Helmshore Textile Mill (Higher Mill). (Reproduced with kind permission of Lancashire County Council.)

local enthusiasts who were keen to see it saved. As a result of their efforts the building and reservoirs were scheduled as an Ancient Monument and were bought by a Trust from the owners. In 1971 an important collection of early textile machinery, built up by Platt's of Oldham around 1900, was transferred to the upper floor of the mill, but the burden of guiding visitors and maintaining the building became too great for the Trust. Negotiations were therefore started with the County Council, with the result that, in November 1975, the Museum Service took over responsibility for both the building and the collection, at a peppercorn rent. The major repairs to the buildings and the water-wheel were carried out by the County Council at a cost of £45 000, although this figure was offset by a grant from the Science Museum of £8700. (Grants from the Science Museum for the Purchase or Repair of Industrial or Scientific Material (PRISM) are generally available at a rate of up to 50% of the approved cost of the work or the purchase involved.) The reservoirs were repaired, funded by DoE derelict land grants totalling £67 000.

At Christmas, 1978, Whitaker's Mill was closed, and this posed a major problem: if it were to be demolished and redeveloped as small industrial units, as seemed likely, this would greatly reduce the attractiveness and interest of the adjacent Higher Mill. Consequently, in 1979, with a grant from the DoE of £9300, and a further grant of £4000 from the Science Museum for the retention and restoration of the machinery, the County

Council bought both the Mill building and the machinery it contained for £71 340. Initial repairs to Whitaker's Mill amounted to approximately £65 000, of which nearly £20 000 was offset by grants from the DoE (Ancient Monuments) of £18 700, and over £1000 from the European Regional Development Fund.

The ground floor was the first area restored, and this was laid out to provide a shop, toilets and a cafe as well as a large display area illustrating the rise and fall of the Lancashire textile industry. Outside the Mill a landscaped area was laid out for car parking and picnics. The costs were considerable, even for this first phase, being in excess of £110 000. Of this, nearly £80 000, however, was awarded by way of grant aid. The English Tourist Board contributed £35 000; the Countryside Commission, for the outside works, £14 000; the European Regional Development Fund £27 000. The remainder was made up by contributions from local industralists. The North West Museums and Art Galleries also awarded a grant of £3500 towards the necessary safety systems for the display areas.

The remaining phases of restoration needed to include extensive work to the roof, and the remaining floors of the Mill, together with the replacement of heating boilers and energy conservation measures. These amounted to over £125 000, of which nearly £61 000 was received by way of grant from the European Regional Development Fund; the Historic Buildings and Monuments Commission (now English Heritage), £2000; and the English Tourist Board nearly £4000.

The original intention was that some of the machinery on the first floor of the old Mill workings should be removed to create more space for the display of other types of machine, but in the event no more than minor changes have been made. The spinning room therefore remains with its 87-year-old self-acting mules, which trundle back and forth across the floor to produce a soft cotton yarn on 714 spindles – an almost unique example of an early textile workplace just as it was when its machinery ran for profit rather than for educational purposes. For most people this is the highlight of the visit, since the machinery is demonstrated by men who used to work in the industry.

Development of the textile museum has now stopped, for a dozen miles away, on the outskirts of Burnley, there stands the last steam-powered cotton weaving shed to work in Britain, Queen

Helmshore Textile Mill. Water-wheel and fulling stocks. (Reproduced with kind permission of Lancashire County Council.)

Helmshore Textile Mill. Spinning on the mule floor. (Reproduced with kind permission of Lancashire County Council.)

Street Mill. After it closed in 1982, it was acquired by Burnley Borough Council and run by a Trust with the Council's assistance, but financial difficulties arose. Since the mill is too important to disappear and has obvious links with the spinning side of the industry this second working museum has been brought under the County's protection.

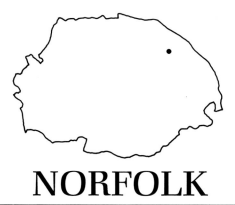

NORFOLK

PROJECT 2.11, Restoration of windmills, windpumps and watermills

Norfolk has a special heritage of windmills, windpumps and watermills. The extensive network of drainage channels throughout the vast marshland area of the Norfolk Broads relied on windpumps to raise the water into the higher river system. Over 70 of these windpumps have survived, at least in part, in contrast with the Fens where few remain. Norfolk also has some 123 cornmills and about 111 watermills. In the late 1940s, there was some concern amongst people living in the county over the fate of windmills throughout Norfolk. Pressure was brought to bear on the County Council to take the lead in their preservation.

Following a preliminary survey, the County Planning Officer drew up a list of 20 windmills and windpumps in 1957 and the Council accepted a short list of 18 for action. Funds were allocated and contributions attracted from industry and commerce. Initially, a separate deposit account was opened. It soon became apparent that a greater fund-raising drive was needed. It was decided, therefore, to establish a charitable trust to take advantage of covenanted donations and bequests, and the Norfolk Windmills Trust was founded on the 19 August, 1963. The Trust is run by five Trustees, nominated by the County Council.

From its modest start, the Trust's activities have expanded greatly. Direct action by the Trust, through freehold or leasehold ownership, has saved 18 mills. Grants from the County Council to private owners has helped to preserve a further

46 throughout the County. The County Council started by allocating £500 in 1960, whilst today, the Council's grant to the Trust is £32 000 per annum. Income from other grants, admissions,

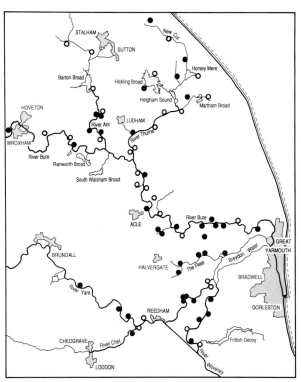

SURVIVING REMAINS OF WINDPUMPS IN NORFOLK

Windpumps { ○ Restored, converted or incapable of repair at start of Programme
● Being saved through the Windpump Protection Programme

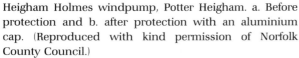

Heigham Holmes windpump, Potter Heigham. a. Before protection and b. after protection with an aluminium cap. (Reproduced with kind permission of Norfolk County Council.)

sales and fund raising, almost doubles this amount, enabling the Trust to sustain a programme of protection and restoration.

The repair of mills is a specialist subject requiring technical knowledge about their construction and operation. The Planning and Property Department of the County Council provides this technical advice to the Trust on a continuing basis. The mills repaired by the Trust are generally open to the public and there is great interest from local people, holidaymakers, schools and special groups. Looking to the future, there are now many protected mills which the coming generation will be able to restore and to enjoy. These would all have been lost if the County Council, and its Trust, had not decided to act.

Turf Fen windpump fully restored at Ludham. (Reproduced with kind permission of Norfolk County Council.)

PEAK NATIONAL PARK
PROJECT 2.12, Dirtlow Rake, Castleton

The carboniferous limestone area of Derbyshire has many sites where remains of the lead-mining industry can be studied. One of the best is Dirtlow Rake, 1 km (0.6 miles) south of Castleton. A 'rake' is a term used in Derbyshire for a mineral vein, and this one can be followed for 5 km (3 miles) from the edge of the limestone. Parts have been left undisturbed since the eighteenth and early nineteenth century when miners extracted lead ore by means of numerous shafts. Parts are now being worked for calcite, barytes and fluorspar.

The Peak Park Joint Planning Board (the National Park Authority) decided to initiate a re-clamation scheme on part of the rake which was left in an untidy state partly as a result of its chequered history. It contains a deep cut showing the pick marks of miners from mediaeval times (which was a favourite place for illegal tipping), shafts from later mining – some of which were in a highly dangerous condition – and the remains of lead miners' waste heaps which were removed earlier this century leaving an untidy surface.

The board approached the site owners (Blue Circle Industries) and proposed a scheme of land reclamation involving some safety works. The work included the removal of rubbish from the open cut, taking care not to damage the miners' pick marks and geological features. Open shafts were capped, mostly using grilles (which allow a view down, whilst allowing access for authorized explorers and egress for bats). Disturbed areas

were regraded and reseeded with a light sowing of fine grasses to allow the distinctive flora of lead-waste areas to recolonize. Trees and shrubs were planted to add to the diversity. A wall was built along the roadside to prevent unauthorized tipping or access, and a small car park was constructed for visitors in booked parties.

Derbyshire County Council designed and carried out the project, and shared with the Board the £16 000 cost of works that were not eligible for grant. The Department of the Environment paid 100% grant for most of the work, amounting to £116 000. The Board now manages the site.

A voluntary body, the Peak District Mines Historical Society, has brought to this site a crushing circle which had to be moved from a mineral site elsewhere. It consists of a circle of stone paving and the massive stone wheel which was rolled

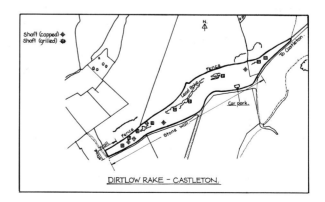

DIRTLOW RAKE – CASTLETON.

Dirtlow Rake. General view of the site. (Reproduced with kind permission of Peak District National Park.)

Dirtlow Rake. Crushing circle. (Reproduced with kind permission of Peak District National Park.)

round it by a horse or donkey to crush the mined material before sorting the lead ore from the unwanted rock.

Since completing the works, the site has been designated as a Site of Special Scientific Interest by the Nature Conservancy Council (now English Nature) for its geological interest. Due to safety considerations, only booked parties may visit the site. Bookings are made with the Quarry Manager, Hope Cement Works, Hope, via Sheffield. A leaflet will be available outlining the varying interests of the site and the recent history of co-operation to preserve them.

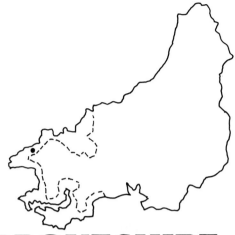

PEMBROKESHIRE COAST NATIONAL PARK

PROJECT 2.13, Porthgain Harbour

Situated amidst some of the finest coastal scenery in the region and a few miles west of Fishguard, is the tiny hamlet and harbour of Porthgain, once busy but now no longer used commercially. Its prosperity was sandwiched into 100 years between the 1830s and 1931, during which time its industry expanded, peaked, declined and died. Porthgain, in its heyday, exported around 40 000 tons of stone products a year, and boasted a local coastal fleet of nearly 100 vessels. It owed its short-lived prosperity to the abundance of slate found in the locality – together with fine deposits of granite and brickmaking material. Porthgain slates, granite and bricks, marked with the village name, were sent to England and Ireland during the period of Britain's industrial expansion. Later, competition from North Wales and the Midlands meant that trade eventually declined, exacerbated by the fact that Porthgain was not linked to any railway network.

However, the increased demand for crushed road stone that developed with the coming of the motorcar during the 1920s and 1930s meant that Porthgain experienced a renewal of fortunes, since coastal shipment was still a practicable means of transport. This trade lasted until 1931, when, virtually overnight, the harbour was closed,

leaving the workforce unemployed, the giant hoppers and crusher plant idle and the harbour and cottages empty. Throughout the Second World War and up to the late 1970s, the site remained derelict, and a gaunt reminder of the

101

Porthgain Harbour in 1910. Local fleet. (Copyright Roger Worsley; reproduced with kind permission of Pembrokeshire Coast National Park.)

Porthgain Harbour in 1910. Village industry. (Reproduced with kind permission of Pembrokeshire Coast National Park.)

once thriving industry that once stood here.

In 1979, a proposal was made by a Midlands-based firm, which has taken over the interests of the defunct Porthgain Village Industries Company, to sell the property. The 25 local residents, with local support, clubbed together to purchase their houses, with the knowledge that, if successful, the National Park Authority would buy the harbour, industrial buildings and the cliff-top area. Fortunately, the residents were successful in their bid to purchase, and, in 1980, the cottages, harbour and derelict industrial complexes were purchased by a consortium of tenants and the National Park Authority. The latter, as the result of further purchases, gained control of the coastal slopes on either side of the harbour.

Immediately after purchase, restoration of the six cottages, known as The Street, took place. Their original grouted roofs were replaced by beautiful Caernarvon slates, salvaged from the cargo of a vessel which had sunk off Ramsey Island, some 10 miles west of Porthgain some years earlier. The industrial buildings and the cottages are listed as being of Special Architectural or Historic Interest, and the whole village is regarded as a site of special industrial archaeological importance. Currently the National Park Authority is working on an improvement to the area and surrounding roads and has completed laying out a car park. Work is also complete on restoring the harbour walls, quays and the stone-crushing plant.

Apart from the work carried out to the cottages by the owners themselves, the majority of the acquisition and restoration costs were met by the National Park Authority. This has amounted to some £40 000 over the last 10 years. Cadw has been requested to assist with the consolidation and interpretation of the industrial archaeological remains. Further work is to be undertaken on a scheme to re-roof and restore 'Ty Mawr', a large building in the centre of the village for communtiy and public uses.

The National Park Authority has published a site card for Porthgain which gives a brief account of its early industrial history as well as explaining the facilities now available to the public. The site card – one of a series on Pembrokeshire's Sea Trading – is fully weatherproofed, making them ideal for field visits.

Porthgain Harbour. The derelict industrial buildings are now in the ownership of the National Park Authority. (Reproduced with kind permission of Pembrokeshire Coast National Park.)

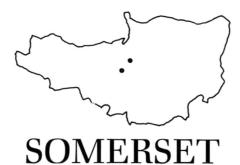

SOMERSET

PROJECT 2.14, Bridgwater Dock and the Bridgwater and Taunton Canal Restoration

BRIDGWATER DOCK

Bridgwater Dock was built in 1841 to provide safe harbourage for the increasing amount of shipping that was trading up the River Parrett to Bridgwater. It was built as a 'floating harbour', capturing the high tides of the Parrett behind massive timber lock gates and retaining high water in the Dock so that vessels could load and unload on an even keel; an operation that was difficult to accomplish when moored in a tidal river. The trade was mainly bricks, tiles and timber, fuel and foodstuffs. The Dock itself was the centre of considerable industrial activity right up until World War II, after which time trade declined, and the then owners, British Railways, closed the Dock and offered the 7-hectare (17-acre) site for sale.

Somerset County Council, anxious to conserve a unique, manually operated Dock that had remained much as it was when built, purchased it in 1974. As owners, they would then be in a strong position to influence the subsequent development of the adjacent semi-industrial land that was included in the purchase. A 10-year programme to develop the dockside and to enhance its historic features was adopted by the County Council in 1976, and in order to fund the restoration costs involved, the Council agreed that the proceeds from the sale of the remaining land could be ploughed back into the restoration work.

In 1973 the Dock complex, which included a grain warehouse, three sets of lock gates, a double bascule bridge carrying a public highway over the

Dock between the main basin and the tidal basin, together with footbridges, sluices and cranes had all been listed Grade II. In 1975 the entire area was included within the Bridgwater Town Conservation Area.

Immediate repairs were undertaken to the lock gates and chambers at a cost of around £150 000, and in 1983, work to stabilize the fractured south wall to the dock was undertaken. This required the insertion of 37 17-m (56-ft) long rock anchors into the ground below water level, at a cost of over £150 000. Another interesting restoration project was the repair of the double bascule bridge, which needed to be removed and rebuilt off site, while a temporary bridge was provided. The cost of this work was approximately £200 000. Together with other environmental works to railings, paving sluices and dock-side lighting, the total cost to the County Council amounted to just over £520 000, but this was offset by grants from English Heritage, Sedgemoor District Council and the Water Authority (now the National Rivers Authority) amounting to nearly £75 000.

Nearly 4 hectares (10 acres) of derelict land was available for housing development, and before the land was offered for sale to developers, the County Planning Department prepared a detailed design-guide to ensure the dockside development was sympathetic to the existing dock character. It was envisaged that both the Dock itself and the warehouse, a four-storey brick structure that contained over 4000 m² (4784 square yards) of floor-space, would be leased separately to a Marina

Bridgwater and Taunton Canal. Restored swingbridge. (Reproduced with kind permission of Somerset County Council.)

company, independent of the housing development. The warehouse and the Dock were leased by the County Council in 1983, the warehouse being converted into residential flats, dockside pub/restaurant, and laundry facilities for boatsmen. The water area has been transformed into a Marina, containing sea-going and canal boats.

The dockside housing, consisting of just under 150 dwellings, the conversion of the warehouse, and the establishment of the Marina were all carried out using private finance. This co-operation of private and public finance has resulted in the original concept for the Dock, drawn up 10 years earlier, being realized. From a conservation point of view the exercise has been successful and is a popular visitor attraction. From the financial angle, although conservation on this scale is bound to be expensive, the outlay by the County Council, including the initial purchase, has been covered by sales income.

BRIDGWATER AND TAUNTON CANAL

The Bridgwater and Taunton Canal was completed in 1827, connecting the River Tone at Taunton to the River Parrett, just south of Bridgwater. With the construction of Bridgwater Dock, to the north of the town the route of the canal was changed to enter the Dock, and thus provide direct access for barges whilst also giving a source of water to replenish the Dock.

For over fifty years, the canal barges carried considerable cargoes to and from Taunton, but this slowly declined with the competition of the railways, and, by 1906, all commercial traffic ceased. From that time, until World War II, the canal was kept in fair condition with the water channel full – acting as an essential land drainage channel – although the six locks fell into disrepair.

Bridgwater and Taunton Canal. Pen sketch of Lower Maunsel Lock.

In 1962, ownership passed to the British Waterways Board (now British Waterways), and in 1968, it was classified as a 'remainder waterway', the Board being relieved of navigational responsibilities the following year. With Somerset being a popular holiday county, it was inevitable, perhaps, that proposals to restore the canal to navigation, particularly for popular boating, were advanced.

In 1981, the County Council requested that the County Planning Officer carry out surveys to establish the feasibility of the canal restoration, and two years later, when a fully costed assessment had been made, the Council resolved, in association with the owners and the two District Councils through whose area the canal flowed – Sedgemoor District and the Borough of Taunton Deane – that a 10-year programme of restoration to full navigation be put in hand.

The 1983 study had estimated that the total costs to ensure navigation over the 22.5 km (14 miles) of canal would be £650 000, which included an annual sum for maintenance. These costs were to be shared equally by the various contributors. It was to be another two years before a practical start could be made. At the end of 1991 about 16 km (10 miles), from Bridgwater Dock, had been opened to public navigation, with a regular boat-trip service operating in the summer months.

A major aspect of the restoration works has been the replacement of the 'fixed' swingbridges over the Canal by new bridges capable of swinging open for boating, whilst being operated by one person. Designs resembling the Victorian originals were adopted, although as each bridge would now have to carry far heavier loads due to the increased weight of much agricultural machinery, steel would need to be incorporated into the bridge

The six locks needed repairs to both the chambers and the gates, and, as the public would now be using the canal, each lock had to have safety chains and ladders. Four small car parks and picnic sites adjacent to the canal have also been provided, the land purchase costs for these being grant-aided by the Countryside Commission.

Early on, at the start of restoration, a Canal Committee was set up, comprising representatives of the three Councils, also attended by British Waterways, in order to oversee progress and budgeting allocations. Latterly, this was supplemented with a Users Forum, at which many organizations and interest groups involved in the canal restoration could offer points of view as and when the work proceeded.

Once restoration has been achieved throughout the total length, it is the intention of the three local authorities to press for the present designation of 'remainder waterway' to be upgraded to 'cruiserway', and hence ensure the canal's continued protection, whilst possibly attracting additional 'amenity' funding from British Waterways. To this end, a 21-year maintenance agreement has already been entered into jointly by the three Councils with the Board, which ensures additional maintenance funds, incurred by the Board due to public navigation, are available.

In the early years of the restoration, considerable assistance was given by the MSC schemes, principally the Community Project teams, when over 30 staff were employed. At the demise of the Community Project, and with the work still unfinished, the County Council funded the retention of some of the site staff. This has enabled the project to proceed to the point where, within the next two years, it is hoped to complete the restoration of this canal.

(See Plates 4 and 5.)

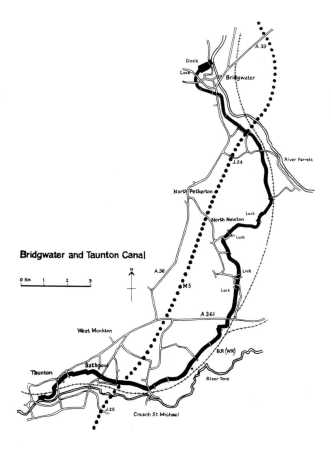

Bridgwater and Taunton Canal

structure. Each bridge, including strengthening the abutments, cost around £30 000 in 1988. Where other low bridges were encountered, mainly lightly used agricultural crossings, these were raised to achieve the necessary headroom of just under 2.5 m (8 ft), but only if there was sufficient space on the canal sides for the extended approaches. The cost of raising a bridge was appreciably cheaper, at about £5000 each.

SUFFOLK

PROJECT 2.15, Buttrum's Mill Restoration, Woodbridge

Buttrum's Mill is a particularly fine example of a tower mill, built in 1835–36 and last worked in 1928; it is listed Grade II*. The former East Suffolk County Council assumed responsibility for maintenance and public opening of the mill under a lease taken out in 1950. For about 30 years the mill was preserved in a 'static' condition; as well as being rather lifeless and unattractive to visitors, this led to the deterioration of the cap and sails which are designed always to face into the wind. By 1980 major repairs were needed which involved lifting off the cap and sails. It was recommended that the mill cap was put back so that it was able to turn, in order to reduce water penetration, and that the opportunity would be taken to fit shutters to the sails enabling them to turn.

A phased restoration was planned using millwrights under the supervision of a consultant architect. This was achieved from 1981–86, the new cap being lifted onto the tower in July 1982, and the final pair of sails in November 1984. The interior machinery was not returned to full working order, but to a condition which would enable the visitor to understand readily how everything functioned. This involved the replacement of various missing belt drives.

The cost of the repairs was in excess of £90 000, to which the Department of the Environment contributed grant aid of £38 800. The costs borne by the County Council were met from the Building Maintenance budget supervised by the County Architect.

The location of the mill, in a residential area close to a road junction and two schools, meant

Buttrum's Mill, Woodbridge.

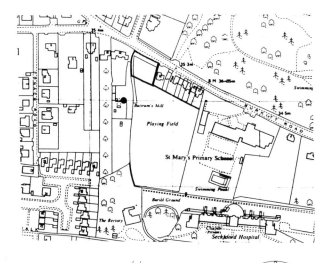

that visitor parking was a problem. The County's lease of the mill made provision for access but did not include any other land by it which could be used for parking. However, the County Council did own the adjoining land which was used as a school playing field. Following discussions with the County Education Officer and the school governors, agreement was reached for the construction of a small car park for mill visitors which would also cater for parents dropping off or collecting school children. The design and landscaping of the car park was dealt with in-house by Planning Department staff, and it was constructed in 1988. The surface is of rolled pea shingle. The cost was approximately £7200, which was met from the Positive Planning budget administered by the County Planning Officer.

In 1989–90 a six-board display was prepared for the ground floor of the mill. This covers the mill's history, restorations, an explanation of the internal machinery, the millwright, history of milling and

Buttrum's Mill. View inside the cap, showing brake wheel and striking gear for opening and and closing sail shutters. (Reproduced with kind permission of Suffolk County Council.)

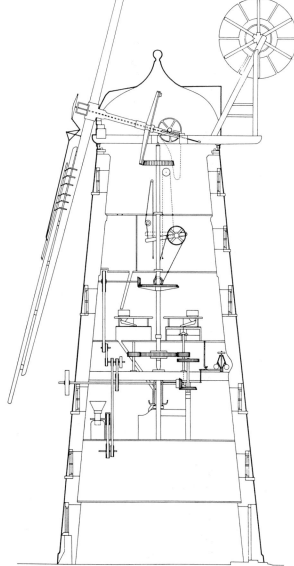

Buttrum's Mill. Section.

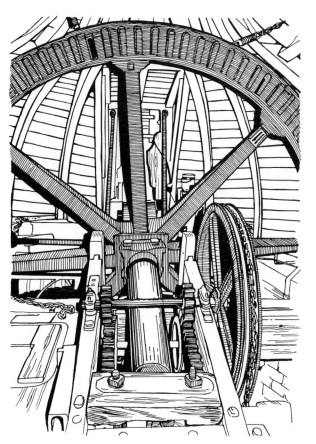

other mills in the town. A permanent electricity supply was connected to the mill, enabling the boards to be lit by individual spot lights. Local enthusiasts have set up a number of small exhibits on the ground floor to complement the display boards.

A warden was appointed for part of the 1989 season to enable the mill to be regularly opened at weekends, and to conduct organized visits by school children etc., on weekdays.

Since the restoration has been completed, the mill's owner has had the sails turning on many weekends. This has naturally attracted many extra visitors, who have found their visit much more rewarding than in the past. With improved sign-posting and publicity the mill should now be ready and prepared for the number of visitors it deserves.

WEST GLAMORGAN

PROJECT 2.16, Cefn Coed Colliery Museum

Cefn Coed Colliery, near Crynant, was a major anthracite coal mine in the Dulais Valley in West Glamorgan, employing over 1000 men during its heyday in the 1950s. Cefn Coed closed in 1968, and although the National Coal Board continued to use the site for the operation of the adjacent Blaenant drift mine a number of buildings of historical significance were threatened with demolition. After several years of neglect and several more of negotiation the task for preservation ultimately fell to West Glamorgan County Council.

The site was a difficult one to turn into a public area, squeezed as it was between the still working Blaenant Colliery and a busy main road. The key buildings were also at different elevations and access to many areas, although acceptable for an industrial site, were entirely unsuitable for public use. However, a restoration scheme was planned and implemented which would allow safe public access to the site for all visitors. Physical works were undertaken using a series of Community Programme schemes and under the supervision of the Planning Department staff an area of 0.6 hectares (1.5 acres) was leased from the National Coal Board under a 99-year lease. Work commenced in 1978, the first priority being the fencing off of the preservation site from the still operational Blaenant colliery. A programme of restoration of the major elements of machinery was then undertaken. The Engine House with its rare Worsley Mesnes steam winding engine was refurbished. In the Power House a huge air compressor was refurbished and the space from which a second compressor was removed for use elsewhere was

developed as an area for temporary exhibitions. A second exhibition outlining the history of the colliery itself was also created in a small annex of the Engine House. The creation of exhibitions to fill these spaces was achieved through a further Community Programme scheme employing a temporary Exhibitions Officer.

Cefn Coed Colliery Museum. Visitors on a guided tour of the Museum are shown the steam winding engine. (Reproduced with kind permission of West Glamorgan County Council.)

(a)

(b)

Cefn Coed Colliery Museum. Two of a number of draw-ings produced by West Glamorgan County Council as part of its interpretative display. (a) The compressor, winding engine, electrical and boiler houses and colliery chimney. All these structures were described in 1991 as 'an exceptionally complete colliery complex'; (b) juxtaposition of the museum (buildings to the left of the headframes) with the then working Blaenant Colliery. (Reproduced with kind permission of West Glamorgan County Council.)

The original Boiler House with its rank of six 'Lancashire' type steam boilers, was substantially refurbished internally and a public viewing plat-form built. Externally, substantial work was done to improve public access. Ramps were built in order to link buildings on different elevations. The constraints of the site meant that car-parking space could only be found some 200 m (220 yards) from the entrance to the site: space for 50 cars was created and an access road for pedestrians and service vehicles was built. Last but not least, a demountable toilet block and a temporary wooden ticket office were installed at the site entrance.

A further Community Programme Scheme pro-vided a small team of guides, and the site was opened to the public in time for the summer season of 1980, attracting 5000 visitors during its first year of operation. Originally named the Cefn Coed Coal and Steam Centre it has since been renamed the Cefn Coed Colliery Museum in order to achieve more effective marketing. The Museum has recently celebrated its 10th anniversary, and some 150 000 visitors have been received in total, with visitor numbers peaking at 17–20 000 per annum. During this time the site has undergone significant further development: new permanent toilets, office and shop/reception facilities have been built and a classroom has been added which is converted into a cafeteria during the peak summer season. A simulated mining gallery has also been built in a tunnel 2 m (2 yards) below the surface of the site. This is accessible to all visitors (including wheelchair users) and provides as far as possible the authentic 'feel' of life and work underground. All of this further develop-ment was undertaken through further Community Programme schemes. The huge steam winding engine in the Engine House has also been motor-ized, using specialist contractors.

It is clear from the above outline that the Cefn Coed project would not have materialized without the availability of Community Programme funding. During the years 1978–87 the MSC contribution to the project, including wages, was in the region of £360 000. The County Council's capital expendi-ture to 1990 (exclusive of in-house costs) was some £100 000. These limited resources were used care-fully and were augmented by aid in kind, including generous help from the NCB both on the site itself and in allowing and aiding salvage of exhibits and materials from other sites. The Welsh Development Agency has also provided grants of £20 000 for medium-sized projects involving refurbishment of roofs and of the brick chimney stack.

Since 1982 the Museum has been funded directly by the County Council. It currently has a staff of six permanent and seasonal staff and a gross revenue budget of £70 000 per annum, of which approximately £22 000 is recovered in income from fees and sales. Several major operational problems remain: the difficulty of access to high buildings, the fragility of their slate roofs and the difficulties of environmental control in these large spaces. Most difficult of all to solve is the awkward physical configuration of the site which is currently the greatest limitation to further development. The recent closure of Blaenant Colliery may provide an opportunity to solve many of these problems through expansion on to the Blaenant site with a consequent doubling of the area of the Museum. Despite these problems the Cefn Coed Colliery Museum has become a successful small-scale museum providing both a local service (some 2500 school children visit the Museum annually) and a contribution to local tourist provision (over 60% of casual visitors to the Museum are from outside Wales, including visitors from 41 countries during 1989). Visitor surveys over a number of years suggest that the Museum is successful in providing an educational experience, in the broadest sense of the term to its varied clientele.

(See Plate 6.)

YORKSHIRE DALES
NATIONAL PARK

PROJECT 2.17, Three lead smelting mills

The Yorkshire Dales area was once one of the main lead-mining areas in Britain. For centuries, perhaps even as far back as the Roman period, lead extraction played a major role in the economy of the area and the industry has had a major effect on the landscape. The most dramatic remains are directly associated with the mining, dressing and smelting of lead ore but the industry also had a marked effect on the development of the road and footpath network, on villages and hamlets and even on the fields and woodland.

Faced with dwindling reserves and increased competition from rich, easily worked lead ore deposits overseas, the industry declined rapidly in the late nineteenth century. The decline is mirrored in the population figures. In 1851, for example, 6820 people lived in the mining areas of Swaledale and Arkengarthdale; by 1891 the number had fallen to 3464 and by 1931 to 2543. The buildings and other structures associated with the industry were allowed to collapse or were used as sources of building stone. As memories of the industry faded its historical importance gradually became appreciated. Some of the buildings were listed as of 'Special Architectural or Historic Interest', while others have been scheduled as Ancient Monuments. Such formal protection however does not

prevent damage from natural decay, weathering or vandalism. In 1983, the Yorkshire Dales National Park Authority began to negotiate agreements with the owners of some of the more impressive and important sites and to initiate a programme of consolidation and interpretation. Three lead smelting mill complexes, Grinton, Old Gang and Surrender, in Swaledale are now the subject of management agreements and consolidation works are in progress.

Grinton Lead Smelting Mill and Peat Store, unlike those at Old Gang and Surrender, still retain their stone-slated roofs, probably because the buildings were until recently used for agricultural purposes. Some emergency repairs were carried out to the Grinton buildings in the late 1970s, and in 1987 the National Park Authority initiated a comprehensive scheme for total reslating, timber and metal treatment, partial repointing and rebuilding of recently collapsed stonework. This was grant-aided by English Heritage and carried out by a local building firm at a cost of £10 475. Although some purlins needed to be replaced, the main roof trusses, an impressive king post construction with a 16 m (53 ft) span, were found to be sound. Further emergency repairs were carried out to the buttresses of the Peat Store and a scheme

for consolidating this building has now received Scheduled Monument Consent.

By comparison the mills at Old Gang and Surrender were very ruinous. These mills share the same water supply, Old Gang Beck, are less than 1.2 km (¾ mile) apart, and of roughly similar dates, but are very different in character. Surrender is a relatively simple mill with 4 hearths, 2 on either side of a central water wheel pit, with double-decker flues merging into one ground-level flue towards the rear of the building. The mill ceased smelting in the 1880s and a century of natural decay and stone robbing had resulted in the interior of the building being little more than a pile of rubble. Most of this has now been removed and the building 'consolidated as found'. This involved carefully removing perished mortar and repointing and stabilizing the broken wall edges and tops. The mill is close to a popular picnic area and the Coast to Coast walk passes within 46 m (50 yards). Once consolidation work is finished on-site and off-site interpretation will be developed.

Old Gang is a much larger and in many ways the more impressive site. It is also more complex; the remains of at least two smelting mills have

Old Gang lead smeltering mill. The Yorkshire Dales contain many remains of industrial activity such as this mill near Reeth in Swaledale, which is being consolidated by the Park Authority. (Reproduced with kind permission of Yorkshire Dales National Park.)

been identified and, in the 1940s and 1950s, the newer mill building was utilized by a company extracting barytes from old mine tips.

In addition to the smelting mill remains, there are extensive mining remains – large hushes or open rake workings, shallow shafts, level entrances and huge spoil heaps – and a large dressing floor where the lead ore was cleaned and separated from other minerals prior to being smelted. The principal consolidation works at Old Gang, which include a significant archaeological excavation and recording component, are also being carried out by local contractors at an estimated total cost of £50 000. Once consolidation is complete low-key interpretation will also be provided at these sites, possibly as part of a lead-mining trail linking various monuments and remains connected with the industry.

3

HISTORIC BUILDINGS

PROJECTS

Drawing overleaf shows Belford Hall, Northumberland.

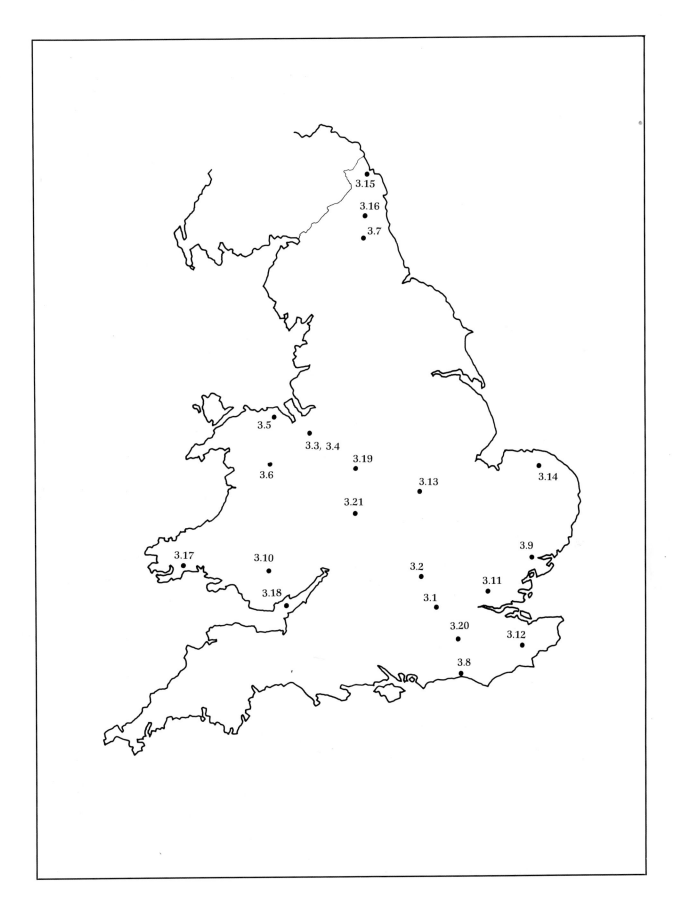

INTRODUCTION

It would be hard to imagine our towns and cities, and indeed our countryside, without old buildings; so much are they a part of the everyday scene that we tend to take them for granted, and overlook their importance. Each one is an example, in however small a way, of a combination of design and construction skills that provide us with a very visible history of building through the past 500 years. Past generations have lived and worked in them, with each period leaving its own imprint as the political and social history of this land unfolded. From the modest cottage to the mansion, our historic buildings are the very essence of what is termed our built heritage. Hopefully today, with extensive conservation legislation and a supportive public, their future is better assured than at any time in the past, although some will still be very vulnerable. This chapter looks at some remarkable examples of building restoration and renewal, without which many would have succumbed to either further neglect or the bulldozer.

The breadth of restoration work that County Councils, closely working with others, are undertaking is impressive, particularly at a time when local authorities are restricted in the amount of finance that is available for this kind of work. The buildings range from medieval structures, such as the massive Cressing Temple complex in Essex to the fifteenth century timber-framed town house at Wokingham, Berkshire, the magnificent restoration, after fire damage, of Missenden Abbey, Buckinghamshire, and the delicate reconstruction of the dovecote at Queniborough, in Leicestershire. They involve buildings from almost every architectural period and style; from Medieval and Jacobean houses in Staffordshire and Durham, a classical mansion in Norfolk, nineteenth century stone defensive houses at Nantyglo, in Gwent, and the flamboyant Victorian castellated castle at Bodelwyddan, Clwyd.

There is no doubt, however, that most of the workload of county conservation officers will be mainly with the problems and repairs associated with what Walpole termed the 'middling houses' after his Grand Tour in 1741, when he noted that such houses 'were only to be found in these islands'. [Olive Cook and Edwin Smith (1968) *The English House Through Seven Centuries*, Nelson.]

In some instances the County Councils' involvement has been one of initiating survey and research. Cheshire County Council's involvement in a research project for the famous Chester Rows is described in detail in this chapter. There is also the role that the professional staff in County Planning departments play in working with their District Council colleagues on joint restoration schemes, and advising owners and developers over the correct or preferred methods of repair.

The repair of redundant historic buildings often raises another important issue, that of new uses which must both be compatible with the building and economically viable. Unlike other objects of everyday life, which, when no longer suitable for their original use can either be discarded or stored, buildings can, and often do, outlive their original use. If the integrity of the architecture of the building is not diminished, and its character and setting safeguarded, then, with the skills of a conservation architect, new uses can often be accommodated satisfactorily. All around us we see examples: an empty warehouse now used as offices, or a country house as a company training and conference centre, residential home or hotel. The example at Belford Hall in Northumberland, where a large but derelict country mansion has been skilfully converted into a number of private apartments, shows how such an exercise can ensure a building's continued survival. In the same county, and providing a total contrast in scale, is the delicate restoration and thatching of a small stone cruck barn, possibly the last remaining example in Northumberland.

STATUTORY LISTS OF BUILDINGS OF SPECIAL ARCHITECTURAL OR HISTORIC INTEREST

This is an inventory, commenced after the Town and Country Planning Act, 1947, of those buildings and structures of architectural or historic interest from the earliest examples up to the very recent past. (In exceptional circumstances buildings erected even up to thirty years ago could be considered for listing.) By being included in the inventory, they are termed 'listed', and whilst in the early years of the legislation there were three Grades of listing, together with 'provisional lists' today we enjoy a simpler grading system of Grade 1, 2* and 2. The lists are drawn up and published by the Secretary of State for the Environment, and can be amended by both additions, and rarely, deletions as and when new information about a building is received.

These lists, which have recently been revised, provide a valuable record of our older building stock, county by county, with a brief description of each. The record will form the factual background to our heritage of historic buildings and forms the basis of local authority action, whether this be in individual historic building repair, enhancement work or Town Schemes in conjunction with English Heritage, and, in Wales, Cadw. In England there are over 500 000 listed buildings, but this represents only a small proportion, perhaps 2%, of the total building stock. Most listed buildings are privately owned and well cared for, bearing in mind the often disproportionate costs of repair and maintenance. The onus of keeping a listed building in good repair must rest, in the first place (as with all property), with the owner, but there will be instances where an owner is not able to, or declines to attend to repairs to his listed property with the consequence that the building's condition, and hence, its listable qualities are 'at risk' of being lost forever.

BUILDINGS AT RISK

Regrettably it is inevitable that there will always be a small number of listed buildings, whether they be domestic dwellings, agricultural buildings, industrial structures, such as warehouses, viaducts and windmills, and even some religious buildings that, usually because they are no longer used, fall into disrepair and which, if allowed to continue, could quickly result in the loss of the building.

Although the Repairs Notice procedure is available to local authorities, with default powers to acquire the building, or even to carry out specified works to protect the building, if these are not done by the owner the fact remains that some, unfortunately, continue to become derelict and neglected. English Heritage have been concerned about this for some while, and have recently been looking into the whole issue of buildings 'at risk'. In 1990–91 they carried out a sample survey to determine the extent of the problem. With assistance from survey teams from both County Councils and District Councils, English Heritage surveyed some 43 000 of England's 500 000 listed buildings and concluded that, whilst most were in reasonable condition, some 36 700 (7.3%) were at risk from neglect; this number could be doubled if buildings found to be vunerable and in need of repair were to be included. Not surprisingly, the survey found that, whilst over half of all listed buildings are in conservation areas designated to preserve or enhance their character, almost two thirds of those buildings catagorized as 'at risk' were not in conservation areas. Location is clearly an issue in determining the chances of a building's survival.[1] The aim is to encourage all local authorities to undertake their own survey of listed buildings in their area and compile a register of buildings at risk, so that, by 1995, the whole of England and Wales will have been covered.[2]

Derbyshire County Council, for example, have kept records of buildings 'at risk' for nearly twenty years now, and other county's can make similar claims. The example at Whitwell, illustrated in the chapter on Building Preservation Trusts, shows how a group of buildings, fast falling into decay, but nevertheless important as a group in the streetscape, were rescued by the County Council. They organized their restoration through their historic building repair scheme, an in-house revolving fund, which has addressed the increasingly worrying problem of unsympathetic alterations to modest houses in Conservation Areas.

Norfolk County Council have also published a survey of historic buildings at risk in their County. It emphasizes that there are over 100 derelict churches, a legacy of centuries of rural depopulation, as well as over 200 historic buildings that are suffering from neglect and decay.

10 Bentley Road, Forncett, Norfolk. A seventeenth century timber-framed cottage, showing emergency repairs to the thatch, while the owners decide what to do with the building.

THE CONVERSION OF HISTORIC FARM BUILDINGS

In recent years, the question of conversion and re-use of redundant farm buildings has been causing local authorities many problems. With the dramatic changes in farming practices in recent years, and the increased size of agricultural machinery, many traditional and historically interesting farm structures are no longer suitable for their original uses. That the countryside would be the poorer without these buildings is not questioned, but what to do with them and how to encourage new and appropriate uses which do not conflict with planning policies poses problems for local authorities.

Residential conversion, the usual suggestion, unless carried out with sensitivity, very often only succeeds in destroying the traditional features that the building originally displayed; other uses, such as workshops and small offices might in some cases be equally inappropriate. English Heritage and Cadw, whilst accepting that new uses can be the best way to ensure the continued life of a building, are however concerned that residential conversion is 'too destructive' and are prepared to offer advice on the problems associated with the retention of historic farm buildings.

In this chapter there is an interesting example of the re-use of disused barns at Seven Sisters in East Sussex, where an opportunity presented itself to convert these to a visitor centre for the area. Again, Kent County Council, supported by, amongst others, the Ministry of Agriculture, Fisheries and Food (MAFF), the Rural Development Commission and English Heritage, commissioned a Kent Farmstead survey in April 1990 to obtain a record of the pattern of farmsteads and traditional farm buildings, and devise appropriate policies for those involved in planning and rural agricultural interests.

In Hampshire, as in many counties, there is concern at the future of historic farm buildings. Survey work by the Planning Department of the Hampshire County Council 'has revealed that, of the seven hundred or so listed agricultural buildings, almost a quarter have been converted to other uses – in most cases residential. Of the eighteen Grade I and II* listed barns, only half remain in agricultural use. Generally the standard of design in the residential conversions has been poor, sometimes resulting in the building no longer being of "listable" quality. Standards of design are improving but there is much to be done by local planning departments to tighten control on the implementation of approved schemes'.[3] A working party has been set up by the Hampshire County Council and the District Councils together with the Isle of Wight to consider a policy 'package' to help tackle the problem of redundant farm buildings. In the chapter on Enhancement Schemes and Town Schemes, an interesting project in the Yorkshire Dales National Park is described, retaining the traditional field barns and walls that are such a feature of this valley landscape.

As a further incentive the Ministry of Agriculture, Fisheries and Food have introduced grants to farmers for the 'repair and reinstatement of traditional buildings' offering a rate currently at 35% for both listed and unlisted buildings, but which must be used for agricultural purposes.

MATERIALS

Essential to the sound repair and restoration of historic buildings is the use of correct materials. In these days of mass production of building components, matching materials for particular building repairs can cause major problems, and using specially made products is often very expensive. There has been a most welcome return to the popularity of, for instance, clay products in recent years, and clay roofing tiles can now be obtained far more easily than a decade or so ago. In the case of brick, some small brickfields still produce handmade products, although the scale of production is inevitably small.

Kent County Council were recently faced with a particular problem as a result of the great storms in October 1987, when many roofs were stripped of tiles. These were of the peg tile profile, and little appropriate restoration could proceed until these tiles were once again available. The County Council took the initiative in persuading small local potteries to manufacture these tiles, and with the help of a grant from the County Council, these are now once again available for historic building restoration. In the same County, the absence of the traditional limestone used in many Kent buildings – known as Kentish Rag – was causing repairs to be carried out in imported Portland stone. However, a quarry has now been re-opened and, in an agreement with the County Council, the quarry will set aside a limited amount of the Ragstone for essential repair work. Both these examples are illustrated in this chapter.

The amount and diversity of historic building work being undertaken by County Planning Departments is impressive, particularly at a time of high building costs and limited Council budgets. The case studies given in this chapter illustrate not only the range of building work undertaken, but also the breadth of conservation skills and dedication that has been committed, of which, together with our District colleagues, we can be immensely proud.

REFERENCES

1. Buildings at risk – a sample survey (1992). *English Heritage*.
2. Building at risk grants. *English Heritage Conservation Bulletin* (1990). Issue 11 (June).
3. Annual Report (1990). Hampshire Buildings Preservation Trust Ltd.

FURTHER READING

1. *The Future of Farm Buildings*. SAVE Britain's Heritage.
2. *The Country House: To Be Or Not To Be*, SAVE Britain's Heritage.
3. *Directory of Public Sources of Grant for the Repair and Conservation of Historic Buildings* (1991) Conservation Publication, English Heritage.
4. Michell, E. (1988). *Emergency Repairs to Historic Buildings*. English Heritage.
5. Salisbury Civic Society (1991). *Traditional Farm Buildings in South Wiltshire – Their Threatened Future*. SCS.
6. Brereton, C. (1991) *The Repair of Historic Buildings – Advice, principles and methods*, English Heritage.

BERKSHIRE

PROJECT 3.1, Restoration of 29 Rose Street, Wokingham

Wokingham is an ancient market town and had a thriving silk industry in medieval times, centred on Rose Street which accommodated many timber-framed merchants' and weavers' houses. The oldest of these dates from the fourteenth century and includes, perhaps rather surprisingly, three 'Wealden' type houses of the fifteenth century. Most of the timber-framed houses were refronted in the eighteenth and nineteenth centuries. No. 29 Rose Street was refronted in the late eighteenth century and consists of two timber-framed buildings, one a hall house of the fifteenth century and the other added to it, perhaps 100 years later. This has an eighteenth-century extension at the rear. The two houses have a large seventeenth-century chimney-stack inserted between them.

The owner has a twentieth-century property adjoining No. 29 which accommodates a dress hire business. He wished to extend this business into No. 29 which had been empty for some time. The proposal was to use the first floor as residential accommodation and the ground floor as a sewing room for the repair of damaged clothing. An application was duly made to the Wokingham District Council by the owner for these uses. The architects from the Heritage Group within the Environment Branch of the County Council advise the District Councils on all applications involving listed buildings, and it was realized in this case that a worthwhile restoration could be made to the building if the owner was in agreement. He was indeed, and became very enthusiastic and co-operative.

A frame survey and record was made by the Heritage Group with the help of volunteers at weekends using photographs and measured drawings, some of the modern hardboard and plasterboard lining having been removed. Where members of the timber frame were missing, all the evidence remained through mortices and peg

No. 29 Rose Street, Wokingham. (Reproduced with kind permission of Berkshire County Council.)

holes, and so a proper restoration could be made. Drawings showing the restoration were prepared by the Heritage Group and the owner employed carpenters who worked to the drawings and with the Group Architect.

The older part of the structure was very delapidated. Two principal timber beams had been cut and partially removed some years ago causing a post to drop some 30 cm (12 in) away from the roof truss. The bottom part of this post had also been removed. This in turn had caused part of the roof and the first floor, composed of large sectioned joists, to sag dangerously in one corner. The dropped post roof and floor joists were gently eased back to a position near the original and secured. Three original diamond mullioned windows were discovered; the mullions were replaced and these windows have been left exposed. All missing timber members, including large braces and floor joists, have been replaced

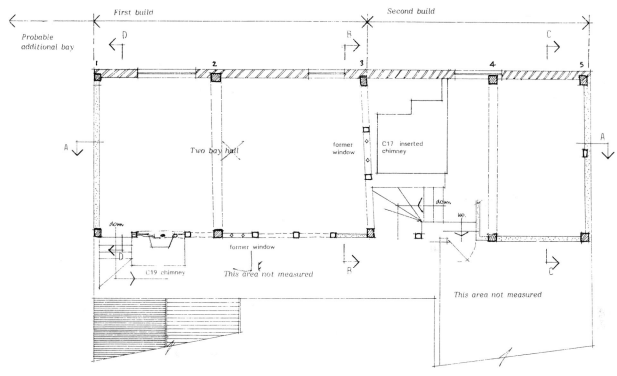

FIRST FLOOR PLAN

Nos 27 and 29 Rose Street, Wokingham. First floor plan. (Reproduced with kind permission of Berkshire County Council.)

(a)

(b)

No. 29 Rose Street, Wokingham. Centre truss before (a) and after (b) restoration with strut in roof truss replaced and the mullions replaced to an old window discovered during pre-contract survey. Note also the removal of the modern ceiling joists which enables the roof to be left exposed, thus increasing the feeling of spaciousness. (Reproduced with kind permission of Berkshire County Council.)

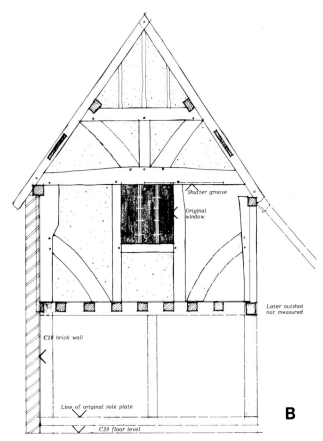

and new oak, of sizes close to the original, has been used.

The external wall facing the road which had been previously refronted in brick and contained no remains of the timber frame was left well alone, although the windows were replaced with those more compatible with the date of the refronting.

The cost of the restoration work, including services, bathroom and kitchen fittings, was £47 000, and was provided solely by the owner without any grant aid, although the County Council made a significant contribution through the services and free advice of the Architect of the Heritage Group.

The finished job shows how well such a building may be restored with an enthusiastic owner using the type of specialist advice which in this case was provided by the County Council. The owner is extremely pleased with the result and although the restoration work concerns only the interior and is not readily visible from the road, is more than willing to show anyone the work by appointment.

B

No. 29 Rose Street, Wokingham. Cross-section of centre truss. (Reproduced with kind permission of Berkshire County Council.)

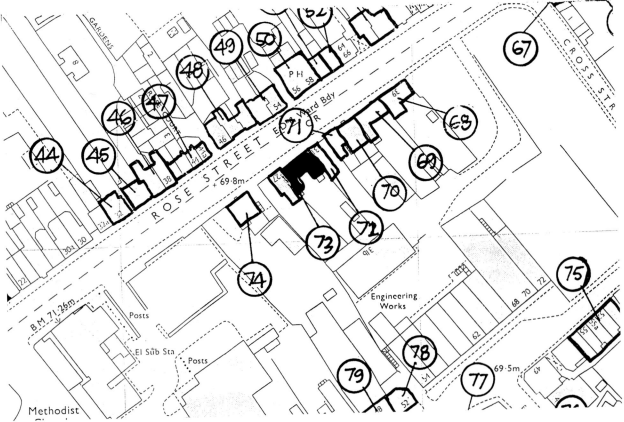

BUCKINGHAMSHIRE

PROJECT 3.2, Missenden Abbey reconstruction

Founded as an Augustinian Monastic House in 1133 and dissolved under the 1536 Act of Suppression, Missenden Abbey assumed the role of country mansion that befell many former religious houses. After extensive remodelling in the early nineteenth century the Abbey remained in the hands of the Carrington family until 1946 when the estate was purchased by Buckinghamshire County Council. In 1982 work commenced on incorporating the County Council's Management Centre into the Missenden site alongside the two other functions of Adult Education and In-Service Teacher Training. In July 1985 during refurbishment of the Abbey, fire broke out and all but destroyed the building.

The refurbishment scheme was to provide reception, dining, social and administrative accommodation for the complex to supplement a 56-bedroom residential building with associated lecture and teaching facilities nearing completion. After the fire the Council Council decided the Abbey, a Grade 1 Listed Building, should be reconstructed along guidelines closely defined by the County Architect in conjunction with English Heritage. These included the retention and repair of the surviving nineteenth-century facade, the reconstruction of at least some of the 'Strawberry Hill Gothic' plasterwork and the preservation of as much of the remaining medieval fabric as was practical. Additionally the reconstructed building was to function efficiently in its multi-use role and to be financed solely from insurance monies. The

total floor area is 1735 m^2 (2075 square yards).

To enable a rapid start on site and prevent further deterioration of the remaining fabric, the contract was in two phases, a stabilization contract and a finishing contract. To stabilize the facade a steel frame was erected within the building together with a new brick inner leaf, the nineteenth-century facade and remaining medieval flint walls being mechanically tied to both elements. The steel frame and new brick leaf were supported on a series of reinforced concrete ground beams and mass concrete pad foundations. Additionally structural works included the resin grouting of exposed flint walling and the pressure grouting of areas of the gravel-bearing strata showing signs of instability.

The elaborate plasterwork in the Garden Room and Dining Room was undoubtably the centre piece of Missenden Abbey and as such its re-creation was considered a high priority. Because the severity of the fire had destroyed all but fragments, the re-creation relied heavily on photographic evidence. In addition to the re-created ceilings, new ceilings were designed for the Entrance Hall, Lounge and Library, these being deliberately understated to act as a foil against the elaborate nineteenth-century re-creations. In the Garden Room and Dining Room a series of plaster figureheads existed above each capital and at the rib intersections. These were presumably of people some way involved in the nineteenth-century rebuilding. To continue this tradition, figureheads

Missenden Abbey. (Reproduced with kind permission of Buckingham County Council.)

of those connected with the current rebuilding have been substituted, the plasterers themselves being modelled over the two doors to the Library and Lounge.

The interior joinery is of natural ash whilst the lighting makes extensive use of low-energy lamps. The lighting design called for much careful consideration if it was to complement successfully the historical and architectural features of the building whilst avoiding the slavish use of 'traditional' fittings. This resulted in a range of modern luminaires being chosen that would not only enhance the architecture to the full but also fulfil the high functional demands placed on the lighting.

Apart from the nine sixteenth- to eighteenth-century flemish roundels now displayed in the Entrance Hall, all the remaining stained glass was lost in the fire. Following an invitation to six artists to submit designs, a commission was awarded for the design of glass in a total of 11 windows.

The external facade was considerably damaged by the fire and as a consequence was completely rerendered onto a stainless steel Riblath backing. Because this increased the overall thickness of the existing finish, it was necessary to rerun all the moulded work to maintain the original appearance.

It was considered important to retain the external appearance of the Abbey and as a con-

sequence the original roof ridge line has been retained although the roof pitch has been reduced to increase storey heights and floor thicknesses. Great care was taken to avoid roof penetrations through the roof slopes visible from the main areas of the grounds. As a consequence all services and roof lighting for the upper floors are concealed from view on the inner roof slopes. Much of the high level walling including the pinnacles and castellations was damaged beyond repair and has been replaced with reconstructed stone moulded from the remains of the original features.

Because of the importance of the surroundings to the Abbey, it was vital the hard and soft landscaping was handled sympathetically. Paving is generally riven York stone echoing the sawn York stone within the building. However, brick paving is also used to form a visual link with the brick-built residential building. The important entrance and garden fronts of the Abbey are illuminated after dark with a series of high pressure sodium units positioned to emphasize the deeply modelled stucco elevations. In addition low-level lightings using high-pressure mercury lamps illuminate the circulation areas adjoining the building.

CHESHIRE

PROJECT 3.3, Chester Rows Research Project

The Chester Rows Research Project is engaged in a study of the surviving medieval Row buildings which characterize the four main streets in Chester city centre. This unique two-tier shopping system has a line of shops at street level and another at the first floor, served by a continuous covered pedestrian gallery, called the Row.

The Project aims to make a detailed record of all the buildings surviving in the Row system, to publicize them and to improve their care and protection. The Project is jointly promoted by Cheshire County Council and Chester City Council and employs a full-time consultant architectural investigator and a fee-paid documentary researcher, tree-ring dating specialist and support staff.

The Project has shown that most surviving Row buildings retain fabric from the medieval period. The stone-vaulted undercrofts or cellars of the city make an immediate impression. They date from the late thirteenth and early fourteenth century. A remarkable range of early timber structures has been dated by the tree-ring dating method to the early thirteenth century. Later periods are just as interesting, not only in showing how individual houses were modified to meet changing social needs but also in the way the appearance and use of the Row system has changed.

The work is confirming how special the Rows of Chester are. The density of surviving medieval fabric in both stone and timber is probably unmatched in any other English city centre. Row buildings exist in isolation in other English towns, but only in Chester has the continuous system of linked galleries survived to the present day.

The discoveries of the Project have prompted the relisting of all buildings in Chester City. The

Watergate Street, Chester. A view along the Rows. (Reproduced with kind permission of Cheshire County Council.)

Watergate Street, Chester. Row walkway showing stallboard (right). (Reproduced with kind permission of Cheshire County Council.)

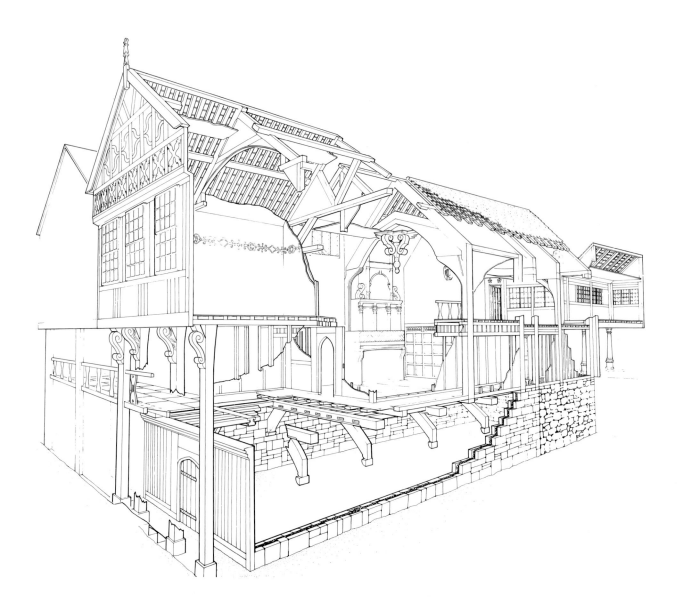

present listing description dates from 1972 and is based only on external inspection of the buildings. The relisting is being carried out on a contract basis by the Chief Conservation Officer. This will offer some protection to the buildings and ensure that planning decisions are made on an informed basis.

The Project is sponsored jointly by Cheshire County Council and Chester City Council, who provide approximately 25% of the annual budget which runs at between £20 000 and £25 000. Both Councils also provide support in kind, such as administrative and fieldwork support, stationery and photographic costs. However, most of the funding comes from outside bodies. English Heritage provide approximately 35% of the annual

Watergate Street, Chester. Perspective cutaway of Leche House (c.1725) showing the Row walkway at the front of the building, with shop and living accommodation behind. (Reproduced with kind permission of Cheshire County Council.)

budget, The Royal Commission on the Historical Monuments of England provide approximately 25%. Other sponsors over the years have included St John's House Trust, Chester (10%), Chester Civic Trust (2.5%) and private sponsors (5%).

An interim report, entitled *Watergate Street – The Rows Research Project*, published by the Chester Archaeological Society, gives further details of the work carried out so far.

CHESHIRE

PROJECT 3.4, Restoration of timber-framed buildings

Cheshire has an appreciable number of timber-framed buildings with dates ranging from the fourteenth to nineteenth centuries and proportions which are equally varied. Visitors to Cheshire look for timber-framed buildings in Chester, Nantwich and Eaton-by-Tarporley but there are few towns and villages in the County without the odd timber frame and many of the better, larger, structures are hidden away in country lanes or at the ends of long farm tracks.

The maintenance of timber frames in a comparatively damp area requires a continuous advice input from County and District Conservation Officers and such local government Grants as are available are very much in demand by the owners of such buildings.

In south Cheshire, which has the greatest density of timber buildings in the county, contractors are so familiar with restoring these buildings that they will quote with confidence, for instance £11 000 for the complete restoration of an average sized gable-end or part elevation of similar proportions. These restorations will be based on the joints and panel infilling methods illustrated in the County Council publication *Restoration and Protection Techniques*; the contractors will be listed in a companion publication *Restoration Specialists* and if the contractors are in doubt regarding the way forward they will invariably involve the County Historic Buildings Officer who was involved in both these publications.

District Council Conservation Officers and the County Conservation Unit operate as a County-wide Conservation Team, not overlapping but with the County Unit providing expertise not normally available at District Council level.

Grant finance is a problem for all local authorities but in Cheshire there are a number of Town Schemes and the grant-sharing principle is extended to embrace village Conservation Areas so that the County and District Councils match each other's offers. If a County Council listed building is subject to alteration then the appropriate District Council is consulated and in return they consult the County Conservation Unit on their Listed Building Consent matters and the designation of Conservation Areas.

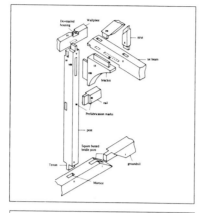

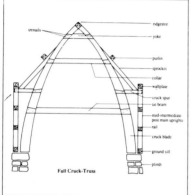

Full Cruck-Truss

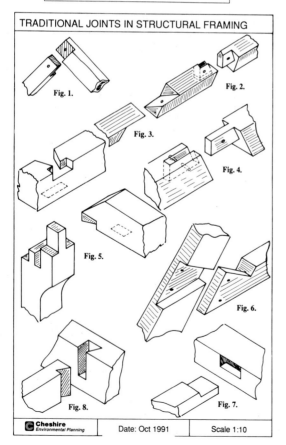

TRADITIONAL JOINTS IN STRUCTURAL FRAMING

Fig. 1.
Fig. 2.
Fig. 3.
Fig. 4.
Fig. 5.
Fig. 6.
Fig. 7.
Fig. 8.

Cheshire
Environmental Planning | Date: Oct 1991 | Scale 1:10

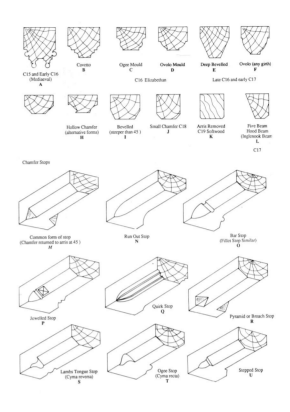

Restoration of timber-framed buildings. Examples of pages from *Restoration Techniques*. (Reproduced with kind permission of Cheshire County Council.)

CLWYD

PROJECT 3.5, Bodelwyddan Castle restoration, near St Asaph

Bodelwyddan Castle is a large, mainly Victorian castellated country house set in 81 hectares (200 acres) of parkland and woods, formerly known as Lowther College, located just off the A55 opposite Bodelwyddan's famous marble church and close to the holiday resorts of Rhyl, Abergele and Colwyn Bay. A house has existed on this site since the fifteenth century and, 200 years later, the estate was purchased by Sir William Williams, Speaker of the House of Commons in the reign of King Charles II and later Solicitor General and member of the Welsh judiciary. However, the descendants of Sir William must take credit for the considerable enlargement and embellishment which gave the Castle its present appearance.

In the early nineteenth century, the house had been 'classicized' by Sir John Hay Williams (1794–1859), but in order to keep pace with rapidly changing fashions set about 'gothicizing' the building by adding crenellations and turrets. His architects were J.A. Hansom of Hansom Cab fame, and Edward Welch, a native of Overton, Flintshire. The resulting castle has been described as 'one of the most ambitious of Hansom's houses, being wildly dramatic and owing nothing to its predecessors'. At the same time improvements were also made to the park which was enclosed by a high limestone wall with castellated gateways, still very much in evidence today.

The estate was sold in 1925, the new purchasers adapting the Castle for the use of a private girls' school from Lytham St Annes. The tenants' hall and stables were converted for use as classrooms and assembly hall and the barn into dormitories and laboratories. The transaction marked the end of the Castle's life as one of the foremost country seats in Wales, and its new role would last a further half-century until its acquisition by Clwyd County Council in 1982.

When officers of the County Council inspected the site in December 1982 they entered a scene of some dereliction and immediately set about the long task of survey and restoration of buildings and landscape setting. The Castle, a Grade II* listed stone mansion, consists of a range of buildings surrounded by an impressive stone curtain wall which is turreted and embattled, pierced by four arched gateways complete with portcullis-style gates. The principal rooms of the house, including the Williams Hall, are set in the north-east, this being the most impressive and prominent part of the Castle and enjoying the finest views over the Vale of Clwyd. The various ranges of buildings are linked by the Bailey and other smaller courtyards which together with the ancillary buildings form an extremely attractive and interesting series of spaces enticing the visitor to explore from one part to another.

New uses had to be found for the buildings comprising the complex. A Technical Vocational Education Initiative Centre (TVEI) opened in 1985 and was the first development to take place under the County Council ownership. Formed by the restoration and conversion of a range of buildings within the Castle walls and a post-war teaching block to the rear of the Castle, it provides high

(a)

(b)

Bodelwyddan Castle. (a) Exterior and (b) interior views.
(Reproduced with kind permission of Clwyd County
Council.)

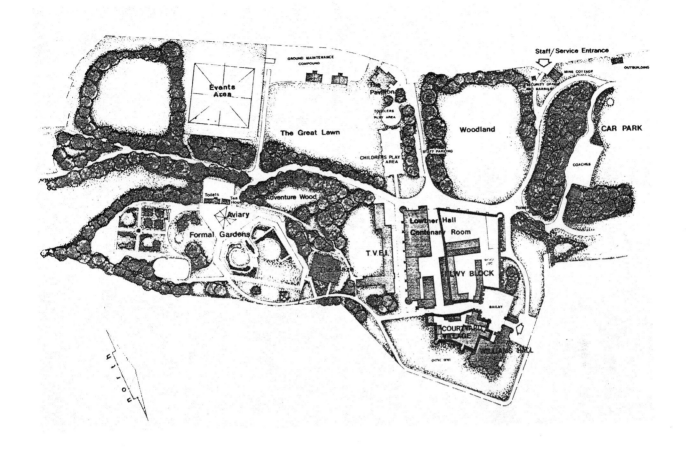

technology and computer training for 14–16 year-olds. It was funded largely by the Manpower Services Commission and is a major facility for both teachers and students. Although not yet open to the public, it is intended to establish strong links with the visual arts and heritage museum.

At about the same time, the Great Hall, formerly a builders' compound and fuel storage yard, was refurbished and fitted out. This is now a valuable local venue for conferences, concerts, lectures and a range of local events.

In 1919 the contents of the house had been sold at auction and the sale catalogue gives a clear indication of the gentry life-style enjoyed by the Williams' family. It is the re-creation of that style which the County Council has striven hard to achieve both internally and externally in the park and woodland.

The original 'state rooms' comprised an entrance hall, a linking corridor, withdrawing rooms, library and dining-rooms representing the Castle's greatest asset. At one time there were 13 principal bedrooms and a host of domestic offices including the servants' hall, joiner's shop, laundry, brew house, game larder, granary, smithy and builders yard. All had been 'institutionalized' whilst occupied by the private school. Since March 1985, the principal suite of rooms, now collectively renamed the Williams Hall, has been thoroughly and extensively restored and is now the North Wales outstation of the National Portrait Gallery. Considerable investigation and research involving the County's architects and Conservation Officer along with the specialists of the National Portrait Gallery resulted in the retention of authenticity whilst incorporating all the safeguards necessary for a building which is available for public access.

Apart from reroofing, strengthening of floors and much internal reconstruction, new environmental controls have been added together with heating, lighting, security and fire-detection installations, all of which have been specially adapted to suit the particular requirements of appearing to belong to a period residence, whilst the original kitchens have been refurbished to provide a visitors' tea and function room.

Several interesting discoveries were made during the progress of building works: a forgotten cellar, a re-used sixteenth-century pegged truss and a buried fireplace. These last two are now on view as part of the restoration. Many craftsmen and artists have been employed in the restoration of plaster mouldings, wood carving, stained glass and ceramics, together with the replacement of encaustic tiling featuring the Williams family Crest of Cross Foxes, and the total redecoration of the state rooms in the appropriate Victorian manner. The curtains and drapes were specially manufactured and the carpets were chosen from patterns held by a manufacturer who still retains chronological records spanning over two centuries.

Essentially, the Williams Hall has been prepared for two separate but complementary exhibitions. Displayed within the high Victorian setting of the refurbished ground floor state rooms are the recently restored Victorian portraits on permanent loan from the National Portrait Gallery. Negotiations with the National Portrait Gallery provided the impetus for the establishment of the Clwyd Fine Arts Trust. In association with other outside bodies, notably the National Library of Wales, the Fine Arts Trust will hold a series of annual exhibitions, in the first and second floor accommodation, of paintings, photographs and interpretative displays expanding the Victorian theme.

To the south of the Castle lies the walled garden. It is approached along a serpentine pathway which starts its journey from one of the portcullis gateways, wandering through the parkland and beside the lawns, sweeping up to the small classical portico which formerly was attached to Sir John Hay Williams' classical country house. From here the pathway leads to the formal garden designed in 1910 by Thomas Mawson and on under the pergola to the rockery and pool. To the north of the garden lies a dramatic pattern of flower beds formed by the new terracing which has been constructed to gain advantage of the views across the Vale.

Bodelwyddan Castle is now open to the public but much more has to be done. The site contains a derelict ice house which is to be restored, and lead mines dating back to the first century Roman occupation will hopefully be interpreted when the heritage museum is established. A craft village with retail outlets will add further interest for the visitor.

The restoration and refurbishment of the Williams Hall has cost approximately £1.7 million and grants were received from Cadw, Wales Tourist Board, Council of Museums in Wales and the European Regional Development Fund. Clwyd County Council is committed to the preservation of its architectural heritage and takes every opportunity to marry schemes for conservation to initiatives for cultural, leisure and commercial development.

CLWYD

PROJECT 3.6, Llangollen Baptist Chapel conversion into an Exhibition and Conference Centre

The Welsh Baptist Chapel was built in 1860, and with its imposing facade of three giant arches on pilasters beneath a pediment, and round headed windows, it has formed a significant part of the main street scene in Llangollen. However, in the early 1980s, the chapel became redundant, but it was important for this building to be retained in order to preserve the integrity of the street.

At that time Llangollen required a Centre for the fostering of European and Regional Cultures, having been chosen because of its links with Europe as the home of the International Music Eisteddfod since 1945. The main challenge in adapting the chapel for this purpose was to provide the Client with accommodation which could be utilized to suit each of the brief's requirements, whilst retaining wherever possible, the character and style of the building, which is listed Grade II.

The chapel was purchased in 1982 for £40 000 and in order to assist the relief of unemployment in the area it was decided that construction work would be undertaken by the County Construction Agency under the auspices of the Manpower Services Commission.

The new centre required a conference/performance space with seating capacity for 150 persons, and an exhibition hall housing eight display cases. A shop area was also to be provided. Clearly the conference/performance space would occupy the main body of the original chapel, with its vaulted ceiling and frieze of plaster-moulded acanthus leaves. The fabric of the main building was completely overhauled and the rear meeting rooms,

Welsh Baptist Chapel converted to Exhibition and Conference Centre, Llangollen. (Reproduced with kind permission of Clwyd County Council)

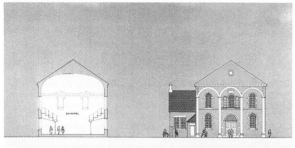

TYPICAL SECTION   ELEVATION (CASTLE STREET)

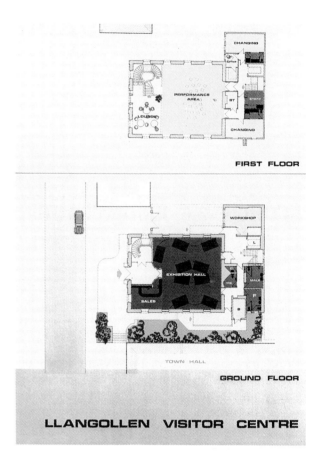

FIRST FLOOR

GROUND FLOOR

LLANGOLLEN VISITOR CENTRE

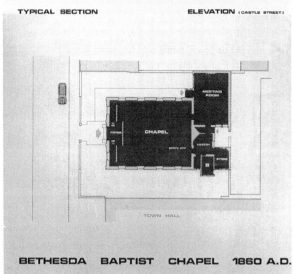

BETHESDA BAPTIST CHAPEL 1860 A.D.

vestry etc., demolished and rebuilt to accommodate the offices, changing rooms and toilets.

Both structural and Fire Officers requirements necessitated the complete removal of the timber-galleried pews and staircases, and the installation of a new first floor for these areas. This was constructed of pot and beam, spanning onto a steel frame with an *in situ* concrete mezzanine level introduced. The main brick and stone facade was cleaned and restored to its original condition, with the introduction of an entrance canopy above new glass doors. A secondary timber window frame was installed to each window in order to provide a 200 mm (7.8 in) air gap, thus greatly improving the sound-proofing and insulation of the new Conference/Performance Hall. The County Council provided the mechanical and engineering services, as well as overseeing the design and building work.

Funding for the project was provided by the Wales Tourist Board, who contributed £50 000; the EEC European Regional Development Fund, £143 000; the Manpower Services Commission (the labour element), £190 000; the Urban Programme, £60 000, and the Clwyd County Council, £76 000.

Apart from the conversion work to the building itself, considerable attention has been given to the external soft and hard landscaping, extracting the best from a restricted site and existing footpath levels. The finished design for the landscaping complements the curves of the building's facade, with smooth red pavers and exposed aggregate slabs and stonework harmonizing with the original materials.

Since the Centre opened in 1988, there has been a weekly programme of performing arts and a changing exhibition promoting regional culture in Europe. Public interest has been widespread and visitor figures are already high and improving, with a 100% increase in sales from the shop, which stocks a variety of hand-crafted goods and books with a European theme. Major conferences have been held and the facilities have been well booked for 1992.

DURHAM

PROJECT 3.7, Little Holmside Hall, near Burnhope

Little Holmside Hall lay derelict throughout the 1960s and 1970s, and despite the presence of listed building legislation, its future seemed bleak. By the 1980s the County Council and the District Council were determined that the building should be saved, with financial assistance for the new owner in undertaking its restoration.

Dating from 1668, the Hall was built for Timothy Whittingham and was extensively altered and added to in the eighteenth century. Until recently the basic L-shaped plan of a south-facing Jacobean wing and east-facing Georgian wing remained virtually intact. By 1967, when the building became included in the list of buildings of Special Architectural or Historic Interest, it had already been unusable as a farmhouse for about ten years (a replacement farmhouse had been built nearby). It was owned by the National Coal Board and was in such a severe state of deterioration, largely due to mining subsidence, that it was excluded from the farm tenancy as beyond economic repair, even for use as a farm building. (The tenant farmer was nevertheless known to have used it as a poultry house.) At the time of listing the Coal Board suggested that the property might be offered for sale as a dwelling, with the only alternative being total demolition.

Later in 1967, the Coal Board suggested that further mining subsidence could occur during the following two years; the property would, in any event, be hard to sell because the remaining 'shell' of a building would be difficult to separate from the adjoining agricultural buildings. By November 1967, the Coal Board confirmed its intention to demolish the building and by February 1968, the

County Planning Officer was writing to the Ministry for their observations, having regrettably reached the conclusion that a Building Preservation Order could not be justified. In March the Society for the Protection of Ancient Buildings, having been alerted by the Ministry to the demolition proposals, was offering to include the house on the Society's list of threatened buildings in the hope of finding a purchaser willing and able to 'put the property to right'.

Shortly afterwards, the Ministry decided that the decision in the matter should rest with the Council, which, if they agreed to the demolition, should look into the possibility of 'worthy parts' of the building – such as its handsome carved entrance door-way – being preserved, possibly by re-erection elsewhere.

In the summer of 1970, the Coal Board, because of increasing danger of falling masonry, was strongly favouring demolition before the coming winter. The County Planning Officer, feeling unable to withhold consent, suggested to the Beamish Open Air Museum that, should the building be demolished, it might acquire parts of it. The museum reluctantly had to decline this offer since it lacked the resources at the time. In November 1970, the County Planning Officer recommended to his Committee that, since restoration might be undertaken in the future, and since no alternative development of the site was being held up, consent for demolition should be withheld in view of the building's Grade II listing, and its importance and rarity in the county. Having agreed to the retention of the structure, the Coal Board now also agreed to the advertising

of the property by the Historic Buildings Bureau of the Department of the Environment and by the Society for the Protection of Ancient Buildings.

The building was eventually acquired by a local farmer, but when the DoE on the advice of the, then, Historic Buildings Council could not offer a grant, the owner declined to proceed with the restoration, estimated to be £38 000 in 1974.

By January 1977, the local authorities were reluctantly considering allowing demolition of the eighteenth-century wing, the least stable part of the structure and consent was granted for this in December of that year. A year later the same owner was still unable to finance restoration even with a demolished wing and he offered the building again to the Beamish Open-air Museum, free, who were not able to take it.

In December 1983, Derwentside District Council was exploring the possibility of serving a Section 101 Notice (Town and Country Planning Act, 1971), and in 1984, the Northern Heritage Trust was reaffirming an interest in taking the building on for restoration. However, in 1986, Little Holmside Hall was acquired by a local solicitor. In

Little Holmside Hall before restoration. (Reproduced with kind permission of Durham County Council.)

order to finance restoration of the Hall, the owner sought permission to convert some of the farm outbuildings for residential use. With the outbuildings converted the new owner undertook the restoration of the Hall which involved the demolition of the eighteenth-century wing. With considerable assistance and advice from the conservation staff of the County Planning Department, the owner was persuaded to restore the building in as authentic a way as possible. He was assisted in the costs of the restoration by a grant of £6000 each from Durham County Council and Derwentside District Council.

By December 1988, the owner was residing in the Hall, the seventeenth-century wing restored externally with some alterations to the eastside, incorporating elements of the former eighteenth-century wing.

(See Plate 7.)

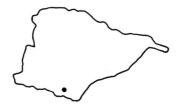

EAST SUSSEX

PROJECT 3.8, Restoration of barns at an Exceat Estate, Seven Sisters

When East Sussex County Council acquired the Exceat Estate in 1971 it not only secured the famous Seven Sisters cliffs and over 300 hectares (741 acres) of farmland but three groups of farm buildings as well. These included four large traditional flint barns and a whole range of associated buildings of varying architectural merit but all historically valuable.

With initial enthusiasm and relatively relaxed Government financial controls the County Council quickly converted one barn to the new country park centre, a focus for all visitors to the park since it opened in 1974 (costs came to a little over £20 000, less 75% grant aid). The design and conversion work has proved very successful both with visitors and with the County Council as managers; even the massive full height glass doors (giving glorious views down the Cuckmere Valley to the Channel) have caused no serious problems.

The other three barns have proved more difficult to restore and use effectively. A large flint barn and a twentieth-century brick barn were converted in the early 1980s by two local businessmen into the 'Living World' ('a spectacular and fascinating world of Natural History'). They invested their capital in the barns in return for a 25-year lease and a 5-year rent-free period. Thus, two restored barns, a fine new visitor service plus a small annual rent to plough back into the park, were obtained.

The third smaller barn in the middle of the park is being converted to a camping barn. Grant from the Countryside Commission, a donation from the Society of Sussex Downsmen and some County Council capital has funded essential repairs to the barn and some fairly spartan washing and toilet facilities in the yard (total costs about £40 000). The fitting out of the barn, including doors, bed spaces and lockers has come to a further £40 000.

This leaves the largest traditional barn, New Barn, still looking for a new use and the money to achieve it. Other buildings on the park have been converted to rangers workshops, stores, a boat-house (for canoes on the river); a farm grazier uses a large asbestos barn for his flock and has restored a small cottage for his own use (all under a special short-term tenancy).

The most pressing problem now is Exceat farmhouse, which is to be converted into 'tearooms'. Formal offers have been received from the private sector to pay for the full restoration of this listed building, plus a substantial initial payment, in return for a long lease and a short rent-free period. This will be the biggest restoration project so far.

(See Plates 8–11.)

ESSEX

PROJECT 3.9, Restoration of barns at Cressing Temple, near Witham

There has been a working farm at Cressing Temple for over 800 years. In 1137, the site was given by Queen Matilda, to the Knights Templar – the band of Knights that provided protection to the pilgrims on their way to the Holy Land, and who subsequently became a powerful and wealthy organization with estates all over Europe. The Order was disbanded in England in 1308 and their property and possessions dispersed.

Cressing Temple passed into the hands of the Knights Hospitaller who developed it as a centre for their large agricultural settlement. However, during the Peasants Revolt of 1381, the site was sacked and plundered, but during the subsequent centuries it has withstood the ravages of time such that, today, Cressing Temple is recognized as a remarkable survival of an important farm complex originating from the Middle Ages.

Two of the massive barns still survive, and rank as some of the most impressive farm structures in Britain. Both the Wheat Barn and the Barley Barn, the first built about 1220 and the latter about thirty years later, are masterpieces of timber construction, surviving today in something near to the form in which they were built by the Templars. The very size of these 'cathedral'-like structures is, indeed, awe inspiring. The Wheat Barn is over 31 m (102 ft) long, and has a width of over 13 m (43 ft), whilst the Barley Barn is nearly 37 m (121 ft) long, and slightly wider than the Wheat Barn, at over 14 m (46 ft). The ridge height is just under 17 m (56 ft), more than twice the height of the ridge of a conventional two-storey house! The

size of the timbers used and the workmanship of the joints and braces, clearly show the skill of those early carpenters, working with quite basic tools. Their work also shows the influence of similar structures that are to be found in northern Europe and Scandinavia.

Other buildings in the complex are the sixteenth-century farmhouse, the Elizabethan Court Hall granary and stables, the seventeenth-century walled garden and the eighteenth-century cart lodge, a charming thatched structure that was severely damaged in the gales of 1990. All these buildings are listed Grade II and the whole site constitutes a Scheduled Ancient Monument.

Concern for the future of the site and its buildings prompted Essex County Council to consider public ownership as the best way to safeguard the future of this internationally important site. There would be the opportunity, with public ownership, to carry out the necessary and time-consuming restoration and to undertake archaeological investigations. Public accessibility would be assured. The site was purchased in the autumn of 1987, at a cost of £300 000. Grant aid towards this figure was provided by the National Heritage Memorial Fund which offered £170 000, and English Heritage with £50 000.

Initial efforts were directed towards the necessary and immediate repairs, and a schedule was drawn up by the County Architect. Work to the barns was commenced in 1988 with repairs to the timber frame, cladding and brickwork to the Wheat Barn. Following this, attention was given to

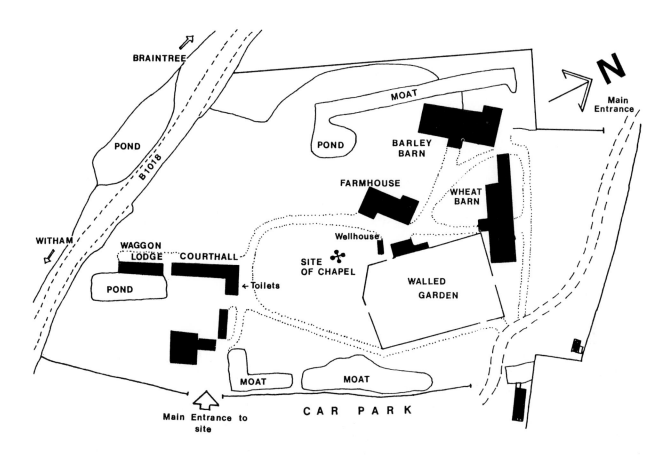

the mammoth task of retiling both barns, which suffered considerable damage during the earlier gales of 1987; great care being taken to salvage as much of the original material as possible.

The cart lodge was thatched in the autumn of 1988, using straw harvested in the adjacent field, in much the same way as would have been done centuries before. The farmhouse is typical of the area, probably dating from the sixteenth century, but it is considered that some parts of it may contain elements of the earlier 'Greate House'.

The walled garden is thought to date from the fifteenth century and excavations will be planned to establish more accurately the design of the garden. It will be reconstructed as a historic garden, probably from the period before 1600, and planted to illustrate the style and traditions, and, indeed, planting, of the time.

An overall strategy for the site's restoration, development and interpretation is slowly being implemented. It will become a centre providing a range of historical information for those whose interests cover agriculture, building conservation, archaeology, planting and the local, vernacular scene. The surrounding moats will also provide

plant and wildlife interest, while the whole complex is a virtual book in itself on the social history of the area. This is an ambitious programme and it is estimated it will take between five and twelve years to achieve.

In the immediate future it is planned that the Wheat Barn will house an exhibition on the history, architecture and archaeology of the site, and will explain the traditions of Essex and East Anglian buildings. The Barley Barn will provide space in which a whole range of artistic and social events can take place, from medieval plays, to concerts and barn dances, lectures, art displays and short-term exhibitions; its beauty as a building providing a fitting backdrop to such activities. The Courthouse will contain a meeting/lecture hall to enhance the educational potential of the complex. Open days during the summer have already attracted hundreds of visitors, and this can be expected to increase as further restorations are completed and the buildings fitted out.

The final cost of the whole project cannot, at this stage, be estimated accurately; expenditure is calculated on a yearly basis, although, obviously, there are on-going costs both of maintenance, and

for those contracts covering more than a single year. For 1991, the County Council set aside a further £60 000. A small income is beginning to be developed with the hiring out of some of the facilities and from the sales of publications.

(See Plates 12 and 13.)

Cressing Temple. The Cart Lodge being rethatched. (Reproduced with kind permission of Essex County Council.)

Cressing Temple. Interior of the Barley Barn. (Reproduced with kind permission of Essex County Council.)

GWENT

PROJECT 3.10, Nantyglo Round Towers, near Brynmawr

The Round Towers are a unique feature of historic importance and played a significant role in the tumultuous days of the early nineteenth century. They were built as a safe retreat from the nearby mansion of the ironmaster Crawshay Bailey and his family, in the event of rebellion by the workforce of Nantyglo Ironworks, which was one of the great centres of iron production in the country.

The period of 1800–1900 was one of dramatic change in the whole of the South Wales coalfield area, and the area around Nantyglo witnessed one of the largest population rises in the whole of Britain. With such population pressures, and following new industrial developments, it was inevitable that problems between ironmaster and workers and also between groups of workers, erupted into violence from time to time.

The working and living conditions of the workers were for much of the time appalling, with the level of wages rising and falling with the fluctuations in the price of iron. Row upon row of workers' houses were built as more employees were needed at the ironworks; houses that were without even the most basic sanitation. The houses were owned by the ironmaster, so if a worker was made redundant for any reason, he also lost his home. Most therefore, did not dare to rebel individually against the ironmaster.

Trade Unions were illegal, but there is a strong tradition of organized workmen's associations in South Wales. Friendly Societies were allowed by the ironmasters, so long as they remained benevolent, collecting dues to provide sickness or death benefit for their members. One of the first attempts at an organization by the workers them-

selves to protect their trades emerged in 1822, in order 'to prevent strangers from being taught the art of mining'. During the early nineteenth century many Irishmen emigrated to Wales fleeing from the potato famine in their own country. They were so desperate for jobs that they were willing to work for a lower wage than the native Welshman. The ironmasters became very clever at turning the workers against each other, employing the desperate Irish to break strikes. Threats inevitably ensued, against property and even lives in attempts to terrorize workers into stopping work.

These were the turbulent events when there was such social and industrial unrest throughout the South Wales coalfield, that brought about the construction of the Nantyglo Round Towers. Today these Towers remain as a gaunt monument to those troubled times.

The Baileys constructed a pair of fortified towers – the last private castle-type fortification to have been built in Britain. The northern tower is a two-storey building with a well ventilated cellar at the basement for the storage of food and other essential provisions in case of seige. The other floors housed the ironmaster, his family and supporters. A spiral stone staircase is set into the inside wall allowing access to the upper floor and roof area. The roof itself is unique. Cast at the works, it is formed of slotted iron 'petal' sections, interlocked and inlaid with a course of bricks. Many of the fittings and structural features are made from cast iron, reflecting the economy of the area at the time, when iron was cheaper than wood. The entrance is a solid iron door, set into a

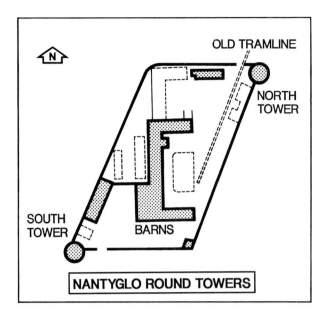

NANTYGLO ROUND TOWERS

qualified staff in the County Council's Planning Department. During these first three years, a stone mason, together with six labourers, all local, provided an enthusiastic workforce.

The total cost of the restoration completed so far has been £23 000; this figure includes a grant of £3400 from the Nantyglo and Blaina Town Council, and a grant of £3100 from the Wales Tourist Board. The remainder of the costs (£16 500) was provided by the Gwent County Council. Due to the termination of the M.S.C. Scheme, the wages of the stone mason and the cost of materials has been met by the County Council and the Nantyglo and Blaina Town Council.

Technically, the most demanding task during the restoration work was the repositioning back together the cast-iron petals of the roof, these having slumped due to approximately six tons of cement screed being added on top of the roof in recent years. Facsimile windows had to be made for both towers, matching the originals as close as possible. The south tower was consolidated and large areas of the stone walling infilled, using stone originally from the tower and found tipped in the basement.

Whilst the Round Tower complex is in private ownership, and part of a working farm, the County Council has secured an agreement with the owner to permit visitor access, and, indeed, visitors are encouraged to look over this interesting set of towers. With the increasing awareness and interest in industrial archaeology, the Round Towers are already proving to be a popular tourist attraction for the growing number of visitors to the South Wales valleys. A car park has been provided, together with interpretation facilities and publicity leaflets.

stone porch and covered by a slated canopy. In the door are two holes through which musket barrels could protrude, protected from the inside by swinging iron shutters. The walls are 1.2 m (4 ft) thick with windows narrowing sharply towards the outside for maximum protection. The south tower exists today as a ruin, having been partially demolished by blasting in the 1940s to salvage the cast iron for scrap. This tower has a third floor which was used to accommodate the private secretary to Joseph and Crawshay Bailey.

The scheme drawn up by Gwent County Council was to make the towers safe, which were in a derelict condition, and to carry out repairs to these listed Grade II structures. Work commenced in February 1986, with labour being provided under a Community Programme funded by the Manpower Services Commission (MSC) for the first three years. Supervision was provided by

(See Plate 14.)

HERTFORDSHIRE

PROJECT 3.11, Restoration of the Eleanor Cross, Waltham Cross*

Each of the 12 Eleanor Crosses erected by Edward I, between 1291 and 1294, marks an overnight stop for the funeral cortege bringing the body of his Consort, Queen Eleanor, from Harby in Nottinghamshire to Westminster Abbey. Only three of the crosses now remain on their original sites and the Waltham Cross is one of these. The others which survive are at Geddington and Northampton.

The renovation of the Cross was made possible by the opening of part of the Waltham Cross by-pass, which meant that a large proportion of the traffic that had hitherto passed through the centre of Waltham Cross was now removed. A comprehensive town centre improvement scheme could be initiated, incorporating a pedestrianization of the High Street and the area around the Cross. Up to this moment, the Cross had been at the centre of a traffic island. The enhancement scheme was proposed by Broxborne Borough Council and supported by Hertfordshire County Council, the latter undertaking the complete restoration of the Cross, as their contribution to the County Council Centenary celebrations in 1989.

The Cross is a Scheduled Ancient Monument and a Grade I Listed Building. With its intricately fashioned carving and geometric patterns, it ranks amongst the finest examples of the English Decorated style.

*This article has been derived, with acknowledgements, from an original text by Mike Daniells (Archaeologist, Hertfordshire County Council) and Cecil Rhodes (Consultant Stone Surveyor).

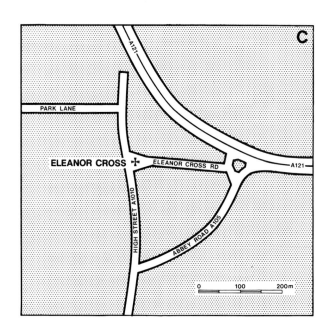

Up to the nineteenth century, only minor repair work was carried out, although it is interesting to note that as an early example of civic conservation, the Society of Antiquaries, in 1721, provided wooden posts around the Cross to prevent damage from carts and carriages. In 1833, William Clarke began work involving the major rebuilding of the Cross using Bath stone. Unfortunately the stone proved too soft and further restoration was carried out between 1887 and 1889 under the

Eleanor Cross, Waltham Cross, following the 1989 restoration, viewed from the south-east. (Reproduced with kind permission of Hertfordshire County Council.)

direction of Charles Ponting. This was a much more careful job than the 1833 work, with several pieces of the original thirteenth-century masonry being refixed back on to the Cross, which Clarke had removed. A fine wrought-iron fence around the monument was also erected.

Little work was carried out again until 1950 when the County Council removed the original statues of Queen Eleanor for safe keeping, ultimately to be housed in the Victoria and Albert Museum in 1985. In their place were installed replicas, and apart from periodic repair to the enclosing railings, little further work was carried out until the 1989 work.

Hertfordshire County Council has been both responsible for and the *de facto* owner of the Cross since around the turn of this century. The work in 1950 had been carried out at the County Council's expense, and, although it had been a thorough and careful job, atmospheric pollution, traffic damage and pigeon fouling had all contributed to a pressing need for a new restoration.

The first stage required the removal of years of accumulated droppings, dirt and general debris allowing restoration work to be assessed and specified. Approvals and consents were obtained from English Heritage and the Department of the Environment, and grant applications made. The original, exposed Caen stonework was carefully surveyed and photographed, and these photographs have now been stored in the County archives. A fundamental principle carried through all the conservation work, was that none would be done unless necessary, and stonework was only to be replaced if either the monument was in danger of further weathering or pieces were damaged or irreparably decayed.

The actual cleaning of the stonework involved hours of painstaking work under protective polythene sheets, which enshrouded the Cross. Layers of carbon and grime were softened by the controlled spraying of clean water in short bursts. Brushes, some as small as a toothbrush, were used to clean the mouldings. Where removing carbon would cause damage to the stone, these areas were only partially cleaned, effectively leaving a protective layer.

Once all the cleaning and repair work had been carried out, the whole of the stonework was strengthened and protected with lime water and a minimum amount of pigeon netting with wires was fixed to complete the restoration work; the surrounding Victorian railings were stripped of multiple layers of paint and repaired prior to being refixed and repainted.

Once the work to the monument was complete an archaeological excavation was carried out to establish the extent of the earliest foundations to this hexagonal structure. The original medieval foundations could be clearly seen alongside the footings of the once adjoining Falcon Hotel, demolished in the 1880s. This excavation was the first controlled archaeological work associated with any of the Eleanor Crosses, and revealed an unexpectedly good survival of the original foundations, which comprised a flint and limestone rubble core within an ashlar facing. This was some 1.5 m (5 ft) wider on all sides than the present plinth, and 1.5 m below the existing surface.

The total cost of the works, including the archaeological work and specialist fees was just over £62 000. The costs were borne by Hertfordshire County Council with a substantial grant of £20 000 from English Heritage.

Apart from providing an almost traffic-free setting for this national treasure, the opportunity will be taken to provide floodlighting and detailed public information. That the Cross has survived for almost 700 years on its original site is a miracle in itself, given the fate of most of the others, but its continuing survival is due to the more pedestrian virtues of constant vigilance and the dedicated skills and expertise of past generations. Certainly, it is extensively repaired – that is the price for its survival – but the medieval core of this monument to Queen Eleanor, remains as the original stone carvers and sculptors seven centuries ago envisaged it. Hertfordshire County Council has been privileged to act as its custodian for the country for future generations.

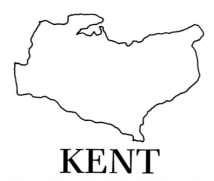

KENT

PROJECT 3.12, Peg Tile and Kent Ragstone Revival

PEG TILES

The hurricane force winds on the night of 15–16 October 1987 caused extensive damage to woodlands, trees, hedgerows and buildings throughout the County. It was estimated that between 30 and 50 timber-framed barns were destroyed. It did, however, also provide an incentive for the revival of manufacture of the hand-made plain clay tile which had ceased to be produced 30 years previously. The stories of roofs being completely stripped of tiles abound. Across the County many traditional roofs were damaged and this resulted in intense pressure on the local building trade. The price of second-hand peg tiles increased from 35p to £2 each.

The decline in brick and tile makers in Kent is well researched. In 1891 there were 150, in 1913 it had reduced to 105 and by 1938 only 64 existed. The decline accelerated after that and the last known manufacturer of handmade tiles at Staplehurst ceased production in 1954. As a result, the repair work to all traditional brick tile roofs was of necessity done with second-hand tiles acquired (sometimes illegally) from other roofs, or patched with unsympathetic mass-produced clay or concrete tiles.

It is helpful to appreciate the reason for the development of the local peg tile industry in order to understand the uniqueness that the particular product gives to Kent's buildings. The name 'peg tile' is derived from the means of fixing tiles to roof battens using round oak pegs driven into square holes (not 'square pegs into round holes'). Records show that tiles were being produced in Kent as early as the twelfth century. They had to be easily made for they were often made on-site by a travelling tile maker. Locally dug clay was used and the tiles, after drying, were fired on site. With the tile maker's skill as the only way of judging the kiln's temperature it is not surprising that a tremendous variety of colours and textures resulted. The composition of the clay was important, chalky clay produced a creamy coloured tile whilst a clay rich in iron oxides became a glowing orange. In 1477 a Royal Charter of Edward IV stated that a 'standard size of tile should be 6½ in. wide × 10½ in. deep × ⅝ in. thick' (165 × 266 × 16 mm). Today, this is the British Standard Size for plain clay tiles and modern tiles are produced to these dimensions. However the locally produced peg tile never followed these dimensions and a size of 9 × 6 in (229 × 152 mm) remained the predominant size in Kent up until the late nineteenth century when the size was increased to 10 × 6 × ½ in (254 × 152 × 13 mm). As a result of this, modern tiles cannot be used on old roofs. Nor do the modern machine-made tiles look correct since their texture and colour is not often in sympathy with the older examples. In some cases concrete tiles have been used to patch or replace old roofs and the difference is readily noticeable.

Although the different size of the modern clay tile was important, the key factor in establishing a need for a replacement hand-made tile was that none of the machine-made products had a similar variation in colour or texture or were adequately cambered to provide a suitable match on an existing peg tile roof, which gives such a characteristic appearance to many roof-scapes in the county.

Retiling with Kent peg tiles. (Reproduced with kind
permission of Kent County Council.)

Stone repairs at the Elizabethan Knole House in Sevenoaks, where patching with imported Portland stone has not been successful. (Reproduced with kind permission of Kent County Council.)

After the 1987 hurricane, a meeting was instigated by Kent County Planning Department of those interested in reviving a traditional peg tile industry in the south east of England. In May 1988, a report investigating the potential for the production of peg tiles in Kent was prepared. This report established that there would be a market for hand-made peg tiles and, as a result, the County Council agreed to contribute £10 000 for the design and construction of display stand, production of leaflets and an audiovisual presentation, for use at the County Show and other venues. By the end of 1988, and with the help of the Rural Development Commission, it became clear that there was indeed a market for newly produced peg tiles and there were manufacturers willing to produce. As a follow-up early in 1989 an opinion survey was carried out and this resulted in a Kent County Council publication *The Demand for Peg Tiles*.[1] By this time four manufacturers were producing locally hand-made clay tiles and fittings. Nearly 400 questionnaires were sent to architects, surveyors, roofing contractors, house-builders, merchants and local authorities to assess the likely demand for these tiles in the medium term. The survey also questioned the attitudes of local planning authorities on the use of hand-made tiles in relation to different types of development, from extensions to Listed Buildings to new housing estates. The results of the survey showed that during the 1980s the fortunes of clay tiles were beginning to revive. Tighter planning controls, the higher price of building land (which meant that house-builders have to build more 'expensive-looking' houses), improvement in kiln firing technology and clay-handling systems have all been factors. In Kent and Sussex the hurricane damage had increased the demand and therefore the cost of tiles. The production of new tiles became more economic as a result and the number of companies producing peg tiles is gradually rising, including the major manufacturers who have now introduced 'hand-made' Kent peg tiles to their ranges.

As a means of publicising the hand-made tile industry, Kent County Council has produced a leaflet which lists the names of the manufacturers and this is available free of charge from the County Council.[2] The process of encouraging the production of genuinely hand-made tiles using suitable clay and sympathetic manufacturing techniques is now well established. Of its nature however, it is small in scale and growing gradually as the market demands. The future of the industry depends partly on its ability to identify and satisfy a market, but also on the influence of local authorities, particularly conservation officers, for establishing a realistic approach to the use of new peg tiles on Listed Buildings, buildings in conservation areas and where relevant in new buildings. A draft guidance note on the use of old Kent tiles for repairs and new construction was produced in 1988. This was never formally agreed by the District Councils and the time has come now for a guidance note on the use of old and new peg tiles throughout the County. Such a guidance note is essential since the supply of second-hand Kent peg tiles is limited and the prices are likely to remain high when District Councils continue to insist on their reuse in any repair work. This increases the danger of unprotected buildings, such as unlisted barns or other lesser farm buildings, being stripped of roofing tiles and abandoned. It is hoped that this will be the next project for a group of Kent County Council and District Council officers.

RAGSTONE

The predominant local building stone in Kent is limestone, known locally as Kentish Rag. Many churches, bridges, houses (such as Knole House at Sevenoaks) and walls have been constructed in this material. It was also a stone much favoured by Victorian builders, particularly those designing in the 'Gothick' style. Production of Ragstone of building quality had virtually ceased, although approximately 400 000 tons a year are quarried for crushed roadstone.

Planning consent has now been granted for two new quarries to open and to produce Ragstone which will be of a quality suitable for the repair of historic buildings. Between them the two quarries should ensure adequate supplies of the stone for the next 60 years. By agreement with the quarry operators, 'lanes' of stone of a suitable architec-

tural quality will be set aside for selection by stonemasons.

Recent demonstrations by the stonemasons have shown that the newly quarried Ragstone is quite workable and suitable for the bulk of restoration work envisaged, where coursed, and sometimes, dressed stone is required. The practice, hitherto, of 'patching' stone buildings in Kent with stone imported from other parts of the country and abroad should now cease. None of them provided a suitable match, either when worked or after weathering. The illustration shows earlier stone repairs carried out at Knole House, an Elizabethan mansion in Sevenoaks, where patching with imported Portland stone has not been successful.

REFERENCES

1. Kent County Council (1989). *The Demand for Peg Tiles*. Kent C.C.
2. Kent County Council (1989). *The Revival of Kent Peg Tiles*, Rural Development Commission and Kent County Council.

LEICESTERSHIRE

PROJECT 3.13, Queniborough Dovecote

Queniborough Dovecote is located in the village of Queniborough, 11 km (7 miles) north east of Leicester. It is Grade II listed and was built in 1705 by William While. By 1985 it was in danger of becoming land-locked by new residential development, leaving it inaccessible to the public and in a considerable state of decay. In an effort to save it the County Council, in conjunction with the owners, decided that it should be relocated adjacent to a public footpath where it would easily be visible to the public. The project was undertaken using the Building Craft Unit, one of the then Community Programme Teams run by the County Council Community Programme Agency on behalf of the Manpower Services Commission. The County Council provided the day-to-day management of the project through the County Planning and Transportation Department's Conservation Team. Estimated costs for the project were around £15 000 and funding was organized jointly with the County Council matching that provided by the MSC, with contributions from Charnwood Borough Council and the owners.

The Dovecote was archaeologically dismantled, the bricks numbered and marked on record sheets, and measured drawings were made of the entire building, including all the decorative brickwork so that features could be reproduced exactly. Consequently, all the brick courses, including the spaces for 638 nestboxes, were replaced in exactly the same position as found in the original Dovecote. Any damaged bricks were replaced with hand-made bricks from the Charnwood Brick and Tile Company of Shepshed, Leicestershire. A new oak roof was constructed to the same pattern as the original and the cupola was replaced. The re-roofing was carried out using most of the original Swithland slates, laid to diminishing courses. The re-slating was the only part of the job not undertaken by the Community Programme Team but was carried out by a specialist company. Finally, new oak doors were made to replace the badly decayed originals.

The reconstruction was completed by November 1987 and opened in March 1988 by the Chairman of the County Council. The reconstruction work has generated a positive and valuable training project for the semi-skilled and unskilled labour in the Building Craft Unit who have achieved a consistently high standard of workmanship. The Dovecote does not remain a cosmetic restoration and museum piece, but has now been stocked with birds and is managed by a local resident on behalf of the owners.

The public reaction to the finished work has been very favourable with the building providing an important visual amenity. In 1988 the Dovecote received a national award when its 'impeccable craftmanship' was praised.

Queniborough Dovecote restored in new position.
(Reproduced with kind permission of Leicestershire
County Council.)

NORFOLK

PROJECT 3.14, The restoration and conversion of Melton Constable Hall, near Holt

Melton Constable Hall was built for Sir Jacob Astley to the designs of an undocumented architect – but possibly Roger Pratt. It is an important double pile house, completed in 1687. It retains most of its original features, including Baroque plaster ceilings, panelling and staircases. Adjacent to the Hall are the outbuildings and stables surrounding a courtyard. These were refaced in the early nineteenth century and have the appearance in part, of Regency terraces. In 1887, a connecting block was built linking the courtyard to the main Hall. These very extensive buildings stand within a magnificent deer park, laid out by Capability Brown; a layout which includes some garden structures, lodges and farms.

The Hall and the estate buildings had been neglected and largely unoccupied since the estate was bought by a local farmer in 1959. Norfolk County Council and North Norfolk District Council were very concerned about the deteriorating condition of the buildings in the late 1970s and tried to persuade the owner to undertake repairs. A serious outbreak of dry rot was uncovered and major repairs had to be undertaken to eradicate it; work that was carried out with the aid of a large grant from English Heritage. However, the building continued to remain empty and further deterioration took place.

The County Council's role in this project has been as an 'instigator of action'. Faced with the problem of a magnificent mansion in their county

continuing to deteriorate rapidly, and its owner unable to carry out the necessary restoration, the County Council decided, in 1986, to issue Repairs Notices, under Section 115 of the Town and

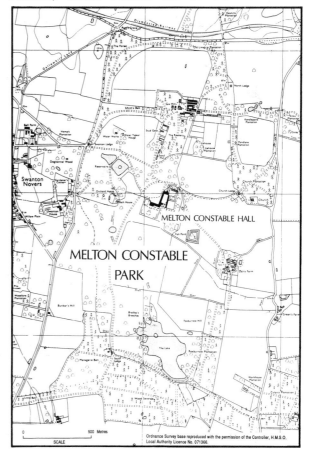

Melton Constable Hall, near Holt. (Reproduced with kind permission of Norfolk County Council.)

Country Planning Act 1971, (the Act in force at the time) which could have forced the Council to make a Compulsory Purchase Order at a cost of up to £409 000. The cost of repairs to the buildings had been estimated at over £1 million. Five Repairs Notices were issued on the Hall buildings themselves and several others on buildings in the Park.

In the event, the action taken under S.115 forced the buildings onto the market which generated a great amount of interest. The County Council issued interim policy guidelines to provide information for prospective purchasers, and the Hall was sold by tender in 1986 to a developer specializing in the rehabilitation of historic properties.

The new plans for the Hall were to convert the outbuildings into houses, to construct some new buildings in the walled garden and to repair the Hall for use as an Arts cum Conference Centre. A S.52 Agreement (now S.106, Town and Country Planning Act, 1990) was drawn up by North Norfolk District Council linking the residential conversions and new buildings to phased repairs of the main Hall.

The County Council is involved with monitoring the restoration progress, which takes the form of regular meetings with the owner and his architect. The re-leading of the flat roof has been completed to a very high standard, and repairs have begun on the west facade and the slow painstaking replacement of ashlar in the eighteenth century loggia. The stonework is probably the most difficult aspect from the technical point of view. All the window architraves are of limestone and they have cracked and shattered from the expansion of corroding iron ties. All the stone will need to be removed carefully, repaired and replaced using stainless steel ties.

Despite the incomplete repairs the Hall is now being used for concerts and private functions and an 'Arts Co-ordinator' is employed full time to organize bookings, catering, etc. Some of the residential conversions have been completed, but the proposal to build within the walled garden has been dropped, and the garden itself used for the production of organically grown fruit and vegetables.

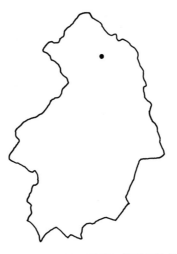

NORTHUMBERLAND

PROJECT 3.15, Restoration and rehabilitation of Belford Hall, near Alnwick

Belford Hall (a Grade I listed building) is one of James Paine's most outstanding country mansions that survives today. Constructed in 1756, and standing in its original unspoilt parkland setting, the Hall was remodelled in 1819 by John Dobson who added east and west wings and converted the rear access into the principal entrance. These alterations to this Palladian house were carried out under the instructions of its new owner, who had purchased the property in 1810. It remained in this family until the death of the last member in 1921, when it was sold together with the estate, and stripped of much of its fine furniture and fittings.

Before World War II an attempt was made to convert part of the house to flats, but the house was then requisitioned by the army and huts built all around. After the war, it was never re-occupied, and gradually fell into serious decay. The sale and theft of many of the historical features of the house, and the vandalism of many others heaped further indignities on the building, and by the mid 1980s partial collapse of some of the walls had occurred, dry rot was rife and little of the interior remained intact, including the richly decorated plasterwork.

Northumberland County Council had for many years encouraged interest in restoring the build-

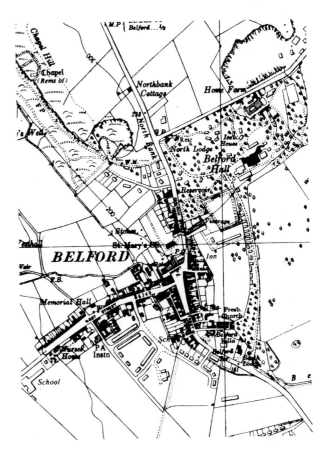

159

Belford Hall, before restoration. (Reproduced with kind permission of Northumberland County Council.)

Belford Hall, after restoration, in its parkland setting. (Reproduced with kind permission of Commander A.C. Mathews, RN.)

Belford Hall, after restoration. (Reproduced with kind permission of *Country Life*.)

ing, and after a number of abortive efforts, the breakthrough came in 1983, when the Northern Heritage Trust took on the daunting task of restoring and rehabilitating the Hall, with the full support of English Heritage. In particular, mention must be made of the tremendous enthusiasm of Phillip Deakin, chairman of the Trust's Northumberland Branch, and Neville Whittaker, Director of the Civic Trust (North East), in tackling such a mammoth undertaking. Determined to see its full restoration, it was decided that this could only be achieved economically by subdividing the mansion into 16 apartments of varying size. Commissioning a local architectural firm, the plans were prepared. The necessary garaging requirements were accommodated in a detached garage block in the form of stables sited to the rear of the hall in a manner harmonious with its setting. The sub-division of the building into flats has resulted in a restoration which, whilst creating new housing provision with modern services and facilities, has, at the same time, resulted in a faithful restoration, retaining the original character and integrity of the building. This solution has ensured the future maintenance of the building without further calls on conservation funds.

With help from English Heritage, who offered a grant of £400 000, and from Berwick upon Tweed Borough Council offering £180 000, it was clear that this was going to be an expensive restoration. As the architect was to say later, 'the project was not one for the faint-hearted, especially as the fees were not assured, but nostalgia took over and business sense was set aside'. Assembling the finance was indeed a major headache, but other contributions were received, amounting to a further £25 000. Northumberland County Council contributed the whole of its annual historic building budget to the project. Whilst these grants provided the springboard for success, perhaps the most significant contribution came from the Monuments Historic Buildings Trust, which is supported by the Sainsbury family agreeing to support and underwrite the project. The costs were high, as might be expected for such a task, with a final figure of some £1.75 million. This cost was roughly shared between those for restoration and those for the new conversion works. The apartments were priced in a range of £25 000 to £100 000 and all have been sold on long leases. A management company has been set up to maintain the house and grounds. The individual apart-

Belford Hall, after restoration, south front elevation. (Reproduced with kind permission of *Country Life*.)

ments do not have their own private gardens, as this would have been difficult to achieve satisfactorily within the overall setting of the house. The Trust however, have been able to purchase a large area of adjacent land in front of the house and this will be planted to form a park, complete with a newly formed lake.

As would be expected from a building that was in an extremely ruinous state, the amount of restoration work necessary was considerable. Virtually all flooring, internal doors, fireplaces, and windows had gone and needed replacement. Roofing, guttering and ceilings all required considerable overhaul and repair. The delicate internal plasterwork, although surviving in some areas, had to be replaced due to the presence of dry rot. Masonry also needed attention for in some places this had fallen. The general principle adopted for the stonework was to use and repair as much of the displaced stone as possible, including the Ionic capitals. Appreciation of the high standard of work should be given to the general contractor who put in many hours of unpaid work. The decorative plasterwork was carried out by a firm of craftsmen from Leeds, using moulds taken from the original ceilings.

The creation of the 16 apartments required the insertion of new doorways at ground level, and this was sensitively achieved by utilizing existing window openings. The main staircase leading to the 'piano nobile', of which little of the original metal balustrading remained when work commenced, was faithfully restored with replacement balustrades and stone steps, to the original designs.

There is no doubt that the restoration of the once derelict Belford Hall has given back to the County a Palladian mansion of immense architectural and historical significance. The work has won praise and awards from many quarters, not least from the residents, who can now enjoy the comfort of modern living standards in an historic house, set within beautiful surroundings.

NORTHUMBERLAND

PROJECT 3.16, Burncliffe Cruck Barn

Burncliffe Cruck Barn (a Grade II* listed building) is a mid eighteenth-century timbered farm building constructed in oak with rubble walling and heather-thatched roof. The north gable is, however, of brick construction and the heather thatch was covered earlier this century by corregated tin sheeting as a stop gap weather protection measure. Whilst the cladding has been reasonably successful, the building now has a number of severe defects that, if not tackled urgently, will result in irreparable damage to the original structural timbers. The defects include mild woodworm infestation and slight wet rot, thatching defects allowing water penetration, perished mortar throughout the rubble walling and rising damp threatening the feet of the cruck blades. As the barn is a unique historic remnant in the county of a medieval type of timber-framed building, its retention and full restoration have been given a high priority.

In discussions with the owners, the solution adopted has been to opt for a full restoration of the building rather than the owners' original intention of repairing the roof only. Of major significance in this respect was the decision by the owners to retain the building as a domestic garage which leaves the existing structure entirely undisturbed.

The decision to retain the building as a domestic garage, whilst entirely in keeping with conservation interests, imposed a considerable burden on the owners. Outside funding was therefore essential to get the project operational. Northumberland County Council and Tynedale District Council have given grants of £1905 and £2500, respectively, and English Heritage a grant of £5620.

The full cost of restoration works is in the order of £17 000. Roof works, including repairs to thatch and roof timbers, account for about £6000 and stonework consolidation costs amount to some £3000.

Public access to the barn will impinge on the privacy and domestic life of the owners due to the modest size of the house and the associated garden within which the barn is situated. They are, nevertheless, happy to take on board this conservation role and have in the past made the occasional visitor welcome. Neighbours have, however, expressed some concern at the prospect of people converging on the small hamlet and causing parking and traffic problems. As public access is to be on a limited basis only, this prospect is unlikely to materialize but the situation will be monitored.

Considerable care has been taken to retain both the character and original materials and detailing

Burncliffe Cruck Barn, before restoration showing cor-
rugated tin sheeting covering heather thatch. (Reproduced with kind permission of Northumberland County
Council.)

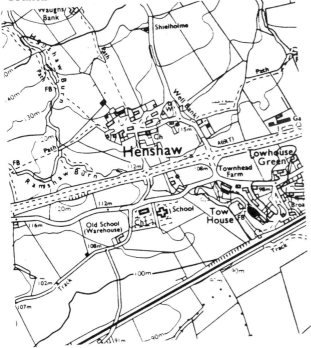

Burncliffe Cruck Barn. Interior view showing cruck construction and original rafters. (Reproduced with kind
permission of Northumberland County Council.)

of this unique building. The original oak crucks and purlins were retained in their entirety with only minimal treatment to ensure their continued structural stability and integrity. Perished common rafters were replaced with riven oak which required an extensive search to identify suitable timber and a willing seller. The walls, which were in part to be pressure-grouted, could not withstand this treatment and have been deep-bedded with a lime mortar by a skilled local stonemason and carver. Roofing repairs required specialist treatment and a Master Thatcher was engaged from the Midlands, with the necessary specialist skills, to undertake the work; suitable heather was obtained from Cumberland.

A measured drawing of the building was undertaken by the recently formed Tynedale Vernacular Building and Architectural Group.

PEMBROKESHIRE COAST NATIONAL PARK

PROJECT 3.17, Conservation of Carew Castle

Carew Castle, considered to be one of the finest fortresses in this County of castles, is built in a defensive position on the upper tidal reaches of the Milford Sound, some 6.4 km (4 miles) east of Pembroke. Although parts of the original thirteenth-century structure remain, most of the impressive building we see today is the result of considerable rebuilding during the fifteenth and sixteenth centuries, commenced by the owner, Sir John Perrot.

In 1984, the Pembrokeshire Coast National Park Authority leased Carew Castle together with around 12 hectares (30 acres) of surrounding land which contained a tidal mill, causeway and mill pond, with the aim of conserving the unique buildings, improving their setting and increasing public access and enjoyment.

Some six years into the programme, a substantial area of the castle, including major renovation and safety works, has been restored by a works team of the Park Authority that was especially set up for the purpose, and which was generously grant-aided by Cadw. The works to the castle itself have cost some £300 000 to date, of which approximately £250 000 was in the form of a grant contribution from Cadw towards the agreed 10-year complete restoration programme.

The Carew Mill and causeway, just a few hundred yards away, are also maintained and managed by the Park Authority. The four-storey Mill building has also received considerable restoration and repair, and a new visitor reception area provided in a small annex on the northern side. Apart from attention to the fabric of the Mill, the massive water-wheel, 4.9 m (16 ft) in diameter and 2 m (7 ft) wide, has also been repaired and is a spectaculer sight for the visitors. The Mill restoration works included major structural and underpinning work, as well as replacement of windows and downpipes, internal improvements, a new access and the installation of a small reception area, audiovisual room and an audio self-guide system. This has cost in the region of £100 000 with a small contribution from Cadw.

For the past four years a major archaeological excavation has been underway and valuable evidence of the early life of the Castle and its inhabitants is beginning to be assembled, sufficient to rewrite some chapters in its long history. A programme of guided walks has begun, including arrangements for school activities and special events associated with the history of the Castle. These operate during the summer when visitor numbers can be expected to exceed 35 000 – a number which is increasing as the attractiveness of the Castle and its setting is developed. A purpose-built interpretative centre is planned for the early 1990s.

Carew Castle, south and west elevations. An impressive Norman fortification on the banks of the Carew river, which together with an adjacent four-storey tidal mill are now leased and managed by the Park Authority. (Reproduced with kind permission of Pembrokeshire Coast National Park.)

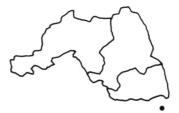

SOUTH GLAMORGAN

PROJECT 3.18, Flat Holm – conservation of an island fortress

Situated some 8 km (5 miles) south east of Cardiff, the small, low-lying island of Flat Holm is approximately 500 m (0.3 miles) in diameter and represents the outermost folds of the carboniferous limestone that forms the Mendip Hills in Somerset. This small island in the Bristol Channel, despite its relative inaccessibility, has attracted much attention over the past centuries. Following the Norman Conquest in 1066, the island came under the jurisdiction of South Wales, but, by the end of the fifteenth century, ownership had passed to the Royal Duchy of Lancaster. In 1823, following an Act of the previous year empowering the Trinity House Corporation to acquire all the remaining private lighthouses in the British Isles, Flat Holm was purchased, and over the subsequent years, as the Bristol Channel became busier with shipping from Cardiff, Newport and Bristol, the old lighthouse was raised in height and the illumination of the lantern improved.

The island was continuously farmed for many centuries, and, indeed, the farmhouse, which was rebuilt in the eighteenth century still stands. However, during the early 1860s, it was realized that Flat Holm could play an important role in forming part of a 'strategic coastal defence system for the Bristol Channel', following concern over possible attacks by the French Navy on the English Coast. This defence system would also include the neighbouring island of Steep Holm, and the rocky peninsula of Brean Down and Lavernock Point; each defensive position using a different armament system. Construction of the fortress started in 1865, and included the installa-

tion of nine, 7 in (18 cm) cannons each mounted on a collapsable form of carriage in a circular emplacement some 5.5 m (18 ft) in diameter and 3 m (10 ft) deep. Extensive stone-built barracks were also erected within close proximity of the lighthouse and lighthouse battery, to provide accommodation for the 50 soldiers needed to man the four batteries of cannons. Work on the fortifications was completed in 1869.

The increase in maritime trade from the ports along the Bristol Channel with the Continent and the Near East, gave rise to concern over the spread of infectious diseases in the ports themselves. In 1883, it was decided that the island should be used as an isolation hospital for sailors infected with cholera. The first hospital was little more than a ward established in a tent, but in 1896, a more substantial hospital was required and a new building erected for the purpose, which remained in use until 1935.

Another facet of the island's fascinating history occurred in May 1897, when Marconi came to the Bristol Channel area to continue his experiments using Hertzian waves as a basis for wireless communication; he conducted his test transmissions over water between masts on Lavernock Point and Flat Holm. During World War II, the island was again fortified with anti-aircraft guns guarding the approaches to the ports of Bristol and Cardiff from enemy action. The closed isolation hospital was reopened and used as a Naafi and cinema for soldiers manning the guns. In 1946, apart from the lighthouse and its keepers, the island was virtually abandoned and left to the mercy of the elements,

Flat Holm island. Aerial view from south. (Reproduced with kind permission of Welsh Industrial and Maritime Museum.)

with the buildings deteriorating and the vegetation growing wild. In 1975, in response to requests from local groups, South Glamorgan County Council took a 99-year lease of Flat Holm from the Corporation of Trinity House.

The lease requires the County Council to manage the island as a nature reserve, the island having been designated as a Site of Special Scientific Interest in 1972. The Council quickly recognized the very significant historical aspects which were evident on the island and resolved to provide for the conservation of these, as well as opportunities for people to visit them.

There were two basic problems to be solved: the need for regular access by boat, and the provision of both shelter and living accommodation on the island. In 1982, with considerable help from the former Manpower Services Commission, a Community Programme team was set up, and a small boat acquired. Despite considerable logistical problems, including the regular conveyancing of both men and materials to the island, the semi-

Flat Holm island. Part of Lighthouse Battery, soon after its construction, showing the R.M.L. cannon in the raised firing position. A commercial photographer visited the island to take photographs of the lighthouse for picture-postcards. One of the views he selected included the gun-pit and he persuaded the gunner to raise the cannon to add interest to his photograph. Military authorities were very displeased by this indiscretion, the photograph was suppressed and the unfortunate gunner reprimanded. (Reproduced with kind permission of South Glamorgan County Council.)

derelict island farmhouse was rebuilt to provide warden and hostel accommodation, and regular visits to the island were being made by a variety of interest groups.

Since those early beginnings, the Flat Holm Project has gained a high reputation for both its management of the nature reserve, and for its commitment to providing opportunities for visits to this interesting island. Each year some 3000 people visit Flat Holm. The Project has a full-time staff of six, including two island wardens and two boatmen, and a fully licensed purpose-designed passenger boat. This can carry 45 people or 3 tons of materials. Visitors can appreciate at first hand the chequered history that the island has witnessed over the centuries. Apart from the interest as a nature reserve, the Victorian fortifications still hold a particular fascination. The circular gun emplacements are now protected as ancient monuments and there are many remnants of the other military buildings.

The County Council spends over £140 000 per year supporting the Project, with financial help from the Countryside Council for Wales. Over the years, considerable help in kind has been donated by a number of bodies and organizations.

In a Management Plan, adopted by the South Glamorgan County Council in 1988, the Authority aims to restore and manage buildings of historic interest. Permission has been obtained recently to repair the Victorian gun emplacements and, indeed, some of the original cannons can still be

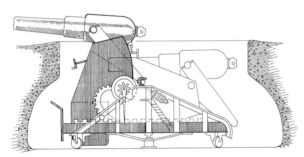

Flat Holm island. Moncrieff Carriage with 7-in R.M.L. gun. (Reproduced with kind permission of South Glamorgan County Council.)

Flat Holm island. Farmhouse Study Centre. (Reproduced with kind permission of South Glamorgan County Council.)

seen. To the historian particularly, these cannons and their carriages are of great interest. Due to the relatively low and exposed terrain of the island, the unique Moncrieff Disappearing Carriages were installed whereby, by using the recoil of the cannon after it had been fired, it was forced down into the gun pit for ease of reloading whilst, at the same time, giving the gun crew a degree of protection. A future proposal, if sufficient funds can be found, will be to build a working reconstruction of one of the original Moncrieff Disappearing Carriages and to reassemble a mounted cannon. The original Carriages have long since been removed.

The recently automated lighthouse is an obvious focal point for visitors, as is the now redundant foghorn station. Despite its state of repair, the old cholera hospital and its associated laundry building continue to arouse morbid interest. One most interesting and original feature on the island is the water catchment area, built by the Victorians in 1865. This is a large cliff-top area of unglazed ceramic tiles to collect rainwater into an underground chamber, to supply all the drinking water for those on the island. It has recently been renovated and now helps to supply treated water for the farmhouse study centre.

Future plans include the renovation of the Victorian barracks to provide study and recreation rooms, and the restoration of one of the former underground shell stores in which there will be the display of descriptive material about the fortifications, as well as providing an undercover area for visitors in periods of inclement weather.

South Glamorgan County Council has balanced the need to respect the requirements of the nature reserve with the equally important task of conserving the Victorian fortifications and the other listed structures on the island, making them available for study by the public.

STAFFORDSHIRE

PROJECT 3.19, Hamstall Hall

Hamstall Hall comprises a group of domestic and formerly agricultural buildings in Lichfield District, including the watchtower, gates and porch of the originally sixteenth-century manor house. These are scheduled as Ancient Monuments. In 1983, following acquisition of the site by its present owners, a number of barns on the site were converted to gallery and workshop use as part of the development of the site as an arts centre. The County Council was instrumental in the conversion of one of the barns to a gallery through its Community Programme Agency, which also undertook the landscaping of part of the site. Total costs of these works were in the region of £90 000, all derived from the, then, Manpower Services Commission. The problem of tackling the substantial remains of the late medieval Manor House, however, remained.

With the demise of the Community Programme it became evident that it would be necessary to look to other means of achieving further restoration work. Specifications were drawn up by architects acting for the owners, with financial assistance by English Heritage, Lichfield District Council and the County Council. In 1989 repairs to the watchtower commenced, again with financial input by the three public authorities, the County Council contributing £1000 towards the £8000 costs. In 1990 the County Council offered £5000 towards the total of £20 000 for the first phase of the repairs proper. A charitable trust has now been formed to implement these works which will

Hamstall Hall. The fifteenth-century 'watchtower' and the sixteenth-century porch are the principal remains of the original manor house. The first stages of consolidation works to the tower have been completed, and preliminary works to the porch are currently being planned. (Reproduced with kind permission of Staffordshire County Council.)

Hamstall Hall. The seventeenth-century roadside barn houses an exhibition area at first floor level, with workshop and retail areas being provided on the ground floor. The former cart entrance now provides the main access to the arts centre car park in the former farmyard. (Reproduced with kind permission of Staffordshire County Council.)

largely comprise the underpinning of the tower and its internal strengthening with a reinforced concrete frame tied to the sixteenth-century fabric. For the future, similar packages will need to be agreed each year during the term of the project, which, it is hoped, will take in the other parts of the monument. Coupled with the current work to the watchtower, the County Council will itself be undertaking the repair of the gate towers, which are in the authority's guardianship under the Ancient Monuments Acts.

The establishment of the arts centre at Hamstall Hall has created a very successful facility for both residents and visitors to Staffordshire. The consolidation of the monuments and their availability to the public will enhance the visitor appeal of the site considerably. The achievement of this success has stemmed largely from the spirit of co-operation between the relevant public bodies and owners who have shown regard not only to the commercial viability of the centre but also to its public benefits.

(See Plate 15.)

SURREY

PROJECT 3.20, Chatley Heath Semaphore Tower, near Wisley

The Chatley Heath Semaphore Tower, a Scheduled Ancient monument and Grade II listed building, was one of a chain of semaphore stations built in the aftermath of the Napoleonic wars to provide a permanent and rapid means of communication between the Admiralty in London and the Naval Dockyard at Portsmouth, a distance of some 75 miles. Not all the semaphore stations were such impressive towers; on many sites single-storey buildings were sufficient. The tower at Chatley was also the 'branching point' for another chain of semaphore stations planned to extend to the Naval dockyard at Plymouth. Several stations were built but the line was abandoned in 1830. The line to Portsmouth, however, was fully operational between 1822 and 1847 when it was superseded by the electric telegraph system associated with the development of the railway network.

The Tower itself is an impressive octagonal brick building with a two-storey attached annex. It stands some 22 m (64 ft) high and is surmounted by a 9 m (30 ft) working semaphore mast. The mast has upper and lower 'arms' able to provide sufficiently distinct outlines for the visual semaphore messages to be read from the next station several miles away.

The tower was purchased by Surrey County Council in 1965 as part of Chatley Heath adjoining the existing Wisley and Ockham open space. The combined 303 hectares (750 acres) forms part of the much larger countryside estate much of which was acquired in the 1930s as a means of preventing urban sprawl before the Green Belt was established. At the time of purchase the Tower was occupied as a residence but the occupiers were subsequently rehoused because the Tower lacked basic housing amenities. It remained empty until

Chatley Heath Semaphore Tower. (Reproduced with kind permission of Surrey County Council.)

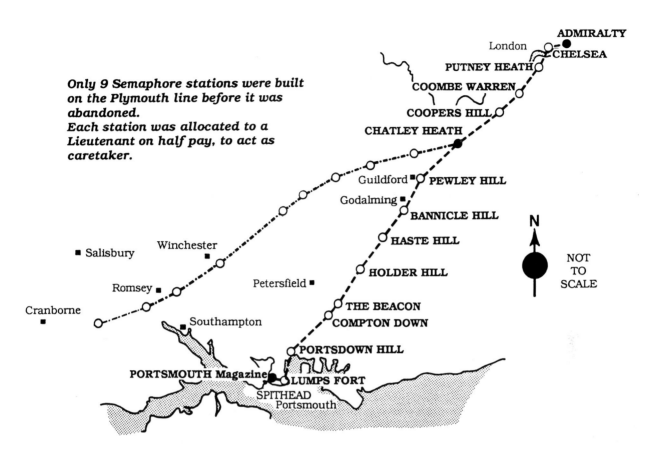

Only 9 Semaphore stations were built on the Plymouth line before it was abandoned.
Each station was allocated to a Lieutenant on half pay, to act as caretaker.

Chatley Heath Semaphore Tower. Admiralty to Portsmouth semaphore line, 1822–1847, and the uncompleted branch line to Plymouth, 1825–1831. (Reproduced with kind permission of Surrey County Council.)

August 1984 when the building was gutted by fire probably started by vandals. Some of the original semaphore equipment was able to be salvaged.

Wishing to undertake a significant and permanent project to mark the centenary of the County Council in 1989, the Surrey Historic Buildings Trust was asked to undertake a feasibility study into the possible restoration bearing in mind the Tower is as an historic building, being the best remaining example of a semaphore station, others having been demolished or converted into private residences bearing no relationship to their original purpose; that there will be a need to provide public access via interpretative displays to the spectacular views from the roof; and to provide residential accommodation for a trainee assistant ranger. A permanent residential presence on the site was deemed vital to preclude vandalism.

The County Council accepted the feasibility study findings and subsequently undertook to fund the restoration in accordance with the scheme prepared by the Trust, assisted by consultants. Specialist historic building, landscape and interpretation advice was provided by the County Planning Department. Work was started in August 1988 and was opened in July 1989.

The Tower has been restored as near to the original specification as practical. References were found which showed accurate details for much of the softwood joinery. Original etchings of the hollow pitch-pine mast enclosing the signalling arms and mechanism were found which provided sufficient information, together with the salvaged mechanism, to warrant the production by a specialist firm of a full-scale working mast some 14 m (45 ft) overall, erected as a single unit.

Since the opening in July 1989, the Tower has become a very popular attraction in Surrey. Closed to the general public in the winter, the Tower is available for visits by pre-booked groups and school parties for whom a teacher's pack has been produced. As visitors have to walk for some 20 minutes from car parks to reach the Tower the opportunity has been taken to encourage, by means of wayside panels and leaflets, visitor appreciation of the heathland and woodland on the open space.

Chatley Heath Semaphore Tower. Aspect from south-west. (Reproduced with kind permission of Surrey County Council.)

WARWICKSHIRE

PROJECT 3.21, Conversion of a Victorian school, Nuneaton

The St Nicholas' C. of E. Primary School in Vicarage Street, Nuneaton, was built in the last quarter of the nineteenth century. It closed as a Primary School when a new school was built in 1966, and most of the original building was demolished 12 years later. Although the area is not a Conservation Area, and the building was not listed, it was decided that one wing should be retained, which was used until recently by the Social Services Department as a store.

The building comprised one large and two small classrooms and externally retained considerable architectural character and detail. It possessed a proliferation of steeply pitched tiled roofs, triplets of arched windows under main gables and polychrome brickwork, including distinctive stepped motifs at the corners. This character is still in evidence on the north, east and south sides of the building, but on the west side, where part of the school had earlier been demolished, there were no features of distinction. Although parts of the structure had deteriorated badly and needed immediate repairs, the contribution the building made to the immediate street scene was such that a new use had to be found if the building stood any chance of being retained.

Such an opportunity occurred in 1987, when accommodation was being sought for an office for business support services to serve the north of the county. The old school building was an under-used, county-owned property, conveniently located by car parking and reasonably near to the centre of Nuneaton.

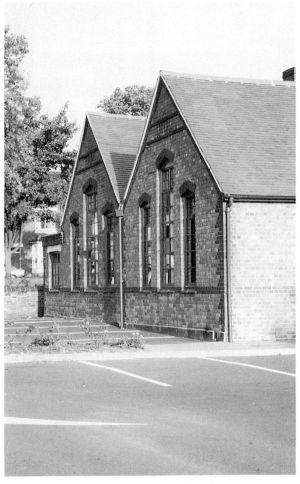

St Nicholas' School, Nuneaton. Retained portion of school, now used as a business centre. (Reproduced with kind permission of Warwickshire County Council.)

St Nicholas' School, Nuneaton. Frontage showing the rebuilt west elevation. (Reproduced with kind permission of Warwickshire County Council.)

The original brick walls have been injected with a damp-proofing membrane and have been repointed, and other structural repairs have been carried out, including rewiring and the installation of a heating system. Internally, new walls were inserted to form a main public reception area, a meeting room, four individual offices and ancilliary accommodation. A quarter of the building remained in use as a Social Services store until early 1992, and is now a training suite.

The three sides of the building which have retained their original character have been respected in the conversion works; no new window openings have been inserted and where decayed timber has been found, this has been replaced and new woodwork painted polychromatically in dark green and red. The brief required an entry frontage appropriate for an office, which aims to attract new business to Nuneaton, a 'shop window' and a sign identifying the office. These requirements entailed some departure from the style of the main elevations. The new front entrance has been formed on the 'blank' west side, and picks up the rectangularity of the window panes of the existing windows, but uses somewhat larger sizes. It attempts to echo the diagonal pattern of the existing polychrome work, but in larger scale diagonals. It achieves the appropriate impact while still complementing the character of the existing building.

The contract value was £91 945, and was financed as part of the County Council's capital programme in the financial year 1987–88.

4

ENHANCEMENT AND TOWN SCHEMES

SOMERTON.

HASKELL

PROJECTS

Drawing overleaf shows Somerton Market Place, Somerset.

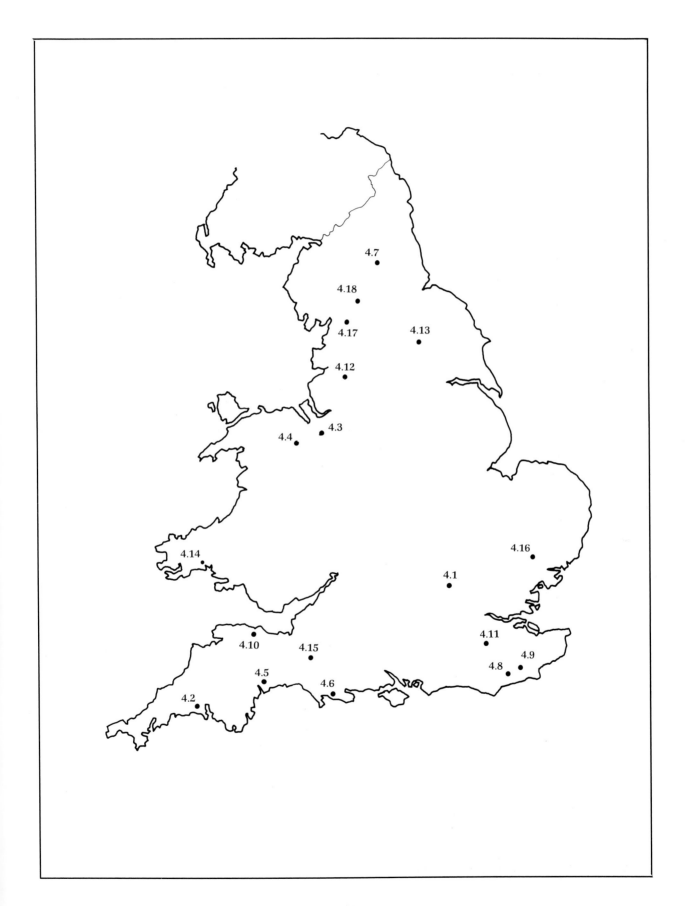

INTRODUCTION

Previous chapters have dealt principally with the care and restoration of individual sites, such as a historic building, or an industrial or archaeological feature. This chapter considers the wider conservation issues involved in promoting enhancement schemes in conservation areas. The examples shown have nearly all been carried out in conjunction with District Councils and others. For the development of this environmental awareness, the Civic Trust can largely claim responsibility and the credit. In David Smith's informative book *Amenity and Urban Planning* he states that 'the Trust soon took an interest in historic areas, especially in the improvements of streets by repainting and the replacement or repair of street furniture, paving and lighting, which culminated in the passing of Duncan Sandys' Civic Amenities Act, 1967. The original "street improvement scheme" was carried out at Magdalen Street, Norwich, in 1959, and a great many have followed since'.[1]

Durham City pedestrianization scheme, 1975. Pedestrian and vehicle access areas.

A year after the passing of the Civic Amenities Act, a scheme was completed in Norwich which was destined to set new objectives for conservation and enhancement proposals for the coming decades. This was the pedestrianization of London Street, a major achievement at the time for it indicated a more imaginative and determined approach to conservation and enhancement where previous efforts had usually been directed at repainting and the removal of 'eye-sores'. Again, in the City of Durham, the County Council's inner relief roads and bridges were completed in 1975, allowing for the closure of the historic medieval streets of the city centre to through traffic, and enabling considerable enhancement works to be undertaken.

PREPARATION OF SCHEMES

Local authorities, having designated a conservation area, have a duty to formulate proposals for preserving and enhancing the character or

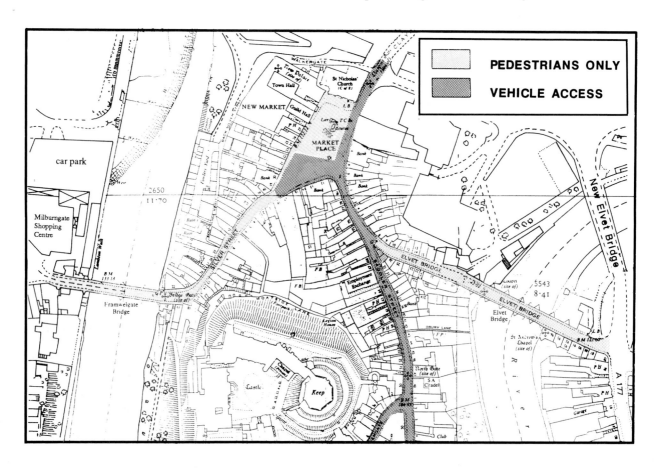

appearance of the area, and S.77 of the Planning (Listed Buildings and Conservation Areas) Act 1990, authorizes both English Heritage and the Secretary of State for Wales to offer grants or loans for the preservation or enhancement works carried out in these Areas.

To be effective, conservation policies must be fully integrated with wider planning policies and highway strategies, and incorporated into Structure and Local Plans. This will allow public debate at the plan preparation stage, as well as giving the local authorities a programme of conservation and enhancement works to be considered within the plan period. Indeed, local authorities are uniquely placed to promote environmental enhancement schemes, for many of the 'components' of the urban scene, such as the highways themselves, footpaths, car parking, street closures, surfacing, signing and lighting all fall within their responsibilities. Local authorities recognize that the conservation of the historic environment is a major planning objective in their forward plans and regard the designation of conservation areas only as the first step in a programme of ensuring such areas are protected and enhanced. Positive statements, together with clear policies for both protecting the historic features of a conservation area and formulating enhancement schemes, need to be included in local plans so that the act of designation is followed energetically by conservation action.

Local communities and Chambers of Commerce will need to be involved and be aware of enhancement proposals, for they have a valuable role to play in ensuring their success. Sometimes schemes can be programmed to coincide with reinforcing and renewal works of the Statutory Undertakers who will also be able to assist both practically and, sometimes, financially.

Enhancement schemes in conservation areas can be initiated in any number of ways. Some of the smaller, but equally effective, schemes have been put forward by Parish Councils or local amenity societies. Others emanate from local plan proposals prepared by District Councils. Again, County Councils are able to promote schemes, and where the Districts request it, carry out the design, arrange the funding and organize the work on site. In many instances substantial environmental improvements have been achieved from a comparatively small outlay especially when the costs can be shared between a number of contributors and spread over a number of years.

In order to programme this work effectively, some County Councils have prepared Environmental Management Plans for their historic areas. Kent County Council in 1986 initiated 'Improvement Action', shortened to IMPACT, which linked environmental improvement to an economic strategy. With the support of the District Councils, English Heritage and a wide range of organizations and businesses, the County set down a programme of possible environmental improvement schemes, deciding that a substantial part of these improvement activities should be concentrated in one selected area as a short-term, 3–5-year project: Gravesend was selected. The IMPACT team has now moved to Ramsgate where its principal partners are the Thanet District Council and the Civic Trust.

Similarly, Devon County Council recognized that while a great deal had been achieved to protect and enhance the important conservation areas of the County and the listed buildings within them, there was a need to examine the appearance of the centres of historic towns as a whole and a series of comprehensive environmental management plans for several towns has now been prepared.

Appreciating that the phasing of enhancement schemes may spread over many years the Dorset County Council, with the West Dorset District and the Dorchester Town Council, formed, in 1983, the Dorchester Heritage Committee. This Committee implemented a 5-year programme of enhancement work in Dorchester. A similar scheme has been set up by the East Sussex County Council, with the Hastings Borough Council, operating an urban conservation project working over a number of years. It is supported financially by English Heritage and operates independently from the Councils but is overseen by a joint committee of members.

The case studies that are included in this chapter are only a selection of the many that are being undertaken in the country to re-establish the character of our historic areas, where the buildings and their spaces can once again be dominant in the street scene and not eroded by inappropriate 'clutter', unattractive surfaces, intrusive 'wirescape', and, perhaps the biggest problem of all, the pressures of unacceptable levels of traffic, with all the resultant problems of parking and pedestrian conflict. At Lavenham, in Suffolk, for example, improvements have been made to the Market Place to enhance the setting of the surrounding historic buildings, while still respecting the need for some car parking. At Bishop Auckland, in County Durham, with the completion of the town centre relief roads and the construction of a new bus station, it was possible to undertake a scheme of pedestrianization in conjunction with the Wear Valley District Council.

At Looe, in Cornwall, a series of problems were present, including a declining fishing industry, a tightly-knit historic town attempting to absorb tourism pressures, traffic congestion on narrow streets and an abundance of unattractive advertising. At Somerton, in Somerset, again a popular town for visitors, the market place had become overrun with parked cars, which distracted from the attractive environment of the space created by the enclosure of historic buildings. A particularly interesting example of enhancement has been carried out at Wycoller, in Lancashire, where an abandoned village of seventeenth-century cottages within a Country Park has been restored and rehabilitated.

If enhancement schemes are promoted to achieve the well-being of our historic environment, then a scheme currently being undertaken by the Yorkshire Dales National Park is worth a special mention. Falling somewhere between enhancement and buildings 'at risk', the Park Authority have drawn up a Barns and Walls Conservation Scheme, not only to safeguard the dry-stone walls in this 72 sq km (27 sq miles) area of the National Park, but also to conserve the intricate pattern of traditional field barns. In this case there is little prospect of alternative uses, except that recently, in line with a growing popularity for long distance hiking, some barns may have an alternative, and beneficial use found for them as camping barns. A scheme for providing a camping barn network has been drawn up by the Youth Hostels Association in association with the Countryside Commission and the Ministry of Agriculture which, at the same time, provides an alternative use for historic, but otherwise redundant, barns. In the National Park area alone there are almost 800 barns, most of simple design with little architectural pretention, and it is 'seen as paramount that this unique landscape is conserved.'[2]

All the schemes in this chapter show how County Councils, working together with District and local Councils, and with English Heritage and Cadw are able to undertake the enhancement of our historic areas in a way that would be a re-

Totnes, Devon. Aerial view showing the medieval centre of the town, and the castle dominating the high ground. In September 1990 a fire at Eastgate (lower centre) caused much damage, and this photograph was helpful in assessing the reconstruction work. (Reproduced with kind permission of Frances Griffiths and Devon County Council.)

velation to those who first promoted the Civic Amenities Act in 1967. Fortunately, funding is now being made available in Local Authority budgets to tackle these problems, and, although never enough, can, by pooling resources, and by programming over a number of years, provide for very worthwhile schemes to be undertaken. Most importantly, enhancement schemes carried out by local authorities have often provided the encouragement and confidence for private individuals to repair and invest in their own properties.

TOWN SCHEMES

The adoption of a 'Town Scheme' is perhaps the most effective way of advancing a programme of historic building and enhancement works in conservation areas. Local Authorities are encouraged by English Heritage and Cadw to promote such schemes as they enable the restoration of buildings to be undertaken involving the owners of property and local authorities. Often with quite small sums of money contributed each year over an agreed number of years by the various contributors, and with the direction of works often delegated to the local authorities themselves, it is possible to undertake the repair of groups of listed buildings where necessary.

A Town Scheme will be centred upon a group, street or a larger area of historic buildings within a designated Conservation Area. The owner of a property, under the Town Scheme agreement, could expect to receive, at the present time, grant-aid of up to 40% of the eligible works for agreed repairs. This contribution would be shared between the local authority (20%) and English Heritage, or, in the case of Wales, Cadw. Where both a County and District are involved in a Scheme, the 20% contribution can be shared, thus making a joint involvement a financially attractive proposition. Grant-aid may also be offered for works which make a significant contribution to preserving or enhancing a conservation area. Although generally awarded towards the repair of historic buildings, grants may also be given to help meet the costs of other environmental works, such as paving and the provision of railings.

This chapter includes a number of Town Schemes, either contributed to or initiated by County Councils. At Barnard Castle, in County Durham, the County Council in 1976 was concerned at the poor state of many of the properties in the town and the untackled problems of dereliction behind the street frontage. Developing from successful schemes at both Richmond and Whitby in 1975, the North Yorkshire County Council have recently introduced their seventeenth Town Scheme at Knaresborough, where a group of houses are being restored.

Clwyd County Council, with Wrexham Maelor Borough Council and Cadw are promoting a Town Scheme at Wrexham, and with Glyndwr District Council and Cadw at Denbigh, as an economically attractive way of both stimulating and protecting the historic character of these towns. A proposal being put forward by the Pembrokeshire Coast National Park and Cadw at Tenby, with over 300 buildings of architectural or historic importance, links both an Enhancement Scheme and a Town Scheme as a means of enhancing its historic centre. In Buckinghamshire the County Council joined with Aylesbury Vale District Council and English Heritage in undertaking a Town Scheme for Buckingham, where a number of historic buildings are being repaired together with environmental improvements in the Market Place, the latter in conjunction with a local Trust, who have made financial contributions.

County Councils, through their responsibilities as the Highway authority, are often able to undertake a valuable and supportive role in enhancement proposals. Described in this chapter is a scheme in East Sussex, where the County Council, as part of its centenary celebrations, undertook, with Rother District Council and others, the refurbishment and enhancement of the street lighting in the remarkably complete medieval hill-town of Rye, one of the original Cinque Ports.

REFERENCES

1. Smith, D. (1979) *Amenity and Urban Planning*, Crosby Lockwood Staply, London.
2. Barns and Walls in the Yorkshire Dales (1989) *Conservation Bulletin*, Issue 8, June 1989, English Heritage.

FURTHER READING

1. Graham Pearce, Les Hems and Brian Hennessy (1991) *The Conservation Areas of England*, English Heritage.
2. Urban conservation studies (1989) *Conservation Bulletin*, Issue 8, June 1989, English Heritage.

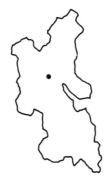

BUCKINGHAMSHIRE

PROJECT 4.1, Town Scheme Buckingham

The Town Scheme has an annual allocation, currently of £20 000, made up in the usual way by English Heritage, Aylesbury Vale District Council and the Buckinghamshire County Council. The scheme has been running since 1981, and over that period a number of buildings have been successfully repaired with the collaboration of their owners. The following three projects have recently been completed.

NO. 3 WELL STREET

The Old Meeting House was built in 1726 and altered in the early nineteenth-century although the street facade seems to incorporate original features including leaded windows. The present use, somewhat incongruously, is a garage, and consequently the chapel interior is unrecognizable, although partly intact.

The condition of the building, listed Grade II, was of considerable concern both to the Authority, and to the neighbours, who complained of the leaking roof. The garage owners were approached and asked to consider making an application under the Town Scheme to repair and renew the defective tiled and slated roof. The initial cost of this was estimated at £12 460 and a 40% grant of £4984 was offered in March 1990. Work proceeded later in the year when some interesting discoveries were made.

The first was the exposing of the original early eighteenth-century roof structure which not only proved to be a first-class specimen of carpentry, but the oak timbers were in almost perfect condition which, considering the external state of the roof, was a pleasant surprise. Nevertheless, extra costs arose, mainly from the need to replace some timbers previously renewed, and for additional leadwork. The extra cost was £5200 and a further grant of £2080 was offered.

The work was carried out to a good standard and the garage owner himself took advantage of the scaffolding to carry out a programme of replacing spalled bricks on the facade using local bricks from a nearby demolition, piecing them in with considerable skill. He has also had some of the leaded windows expertly repaired at his own expense. As a consequence, a building of great local interest, in the historic heart of the town, has an assured future and an improved appearance, a notable achievement for the Town Scheme.

CASTLE HOUSE, WEST STREET

This large Grade II* listed building has important medieval fabric behind an impressive front elevation of the early eighteenth century, the design resembling the original mansion at nearby Stowe. Faced in red brick, it has limestone dressings, which were in a very poor condition.

The present owners acquired the building from the District Council, whose predecessor, the Borough of Buckingham, had used it as offices. It had been poorly maintained, and the new owners

Buckingham Town Scheme. Castle House under repair. (Reproduced with kind permission of Buckinghamshire County Council.)

Buckingham Town Scheme. Stonework repairs to Castle House. (Reproduced with kind permission of Buckinghamshire County Council.)

set about an extensive programme of repairs and improvements.

The only item for which a grant was requested was the special repairs to the stone dressings on the facade. The quotation for this in 1986 was £10 000. Despite the Grade II* listing the building was not accepted as 'outstanding' for grant purposes by English Heritage, so the Town Scheme was the only possible source of grant. At that time the allocation was fully committed. Fortunately, however, it proved possible to provide additional funding for the scheme to make a special grant of £4000, equivalent to a year's allocation at that time.

The contributors to the Scheme all felt that the benefit of the repairs to this important and prominent building justified their action and the

Buckingham Town Scheme. The Old Chantry, Market Hill: stonework repairs to Norman doorway and medieval masonry. (Reproduced with kind permission of Buckinghamshire County Council.)

noticeable improvement which resulted has borne out this view.

THE OLD CHANTRY, MARKET HILL

This small stone building is of Norman origins, much altered, and restored in the nineteenth century by Sir Gilbert Scott, a native of Buckingham. It now belongs to the National Trust, but despite its Grade II* listing, did not qualify for grant aid from English Heritage. A scheme of specialist stonework conservation, involving lime water and shelter coats to the soft stonework surrounding the Norman doorway, was carried out in 1985. The cost was estimated at £3190 and a Town Scheme Grant of £1595 was offered. Additional repairs to the south and east walls, at a further cost of £7154 were also carried out, and a second grant of £3577 was offered in 1986.

CORNWALL

PROJECT 4.2, Looe Enhancement Scheme

Looe is a special town with several unique features. It sits at the confluence of the Looe and West Looe Rivers before they meet the sea. The Looe Valleys are a particular feature of the south coast of Cornwall. The town itself, consisting really of the twin towns of East Looe and West Looe is one of a number of settlements in Cornwall which had their origins in the medieval period and, as such, has been defined by the Cornwall Archaelogical Unit as an Historic Settlement. The boundary of the settlement closely follows the present boundary of the Conservation Area which was designated in 1973 and extended in 1987. It contains over 100 listed buildings.

The problems of Looe were diverse. Its original *raison d'être*, fishing, had declined in competition with marketing growth elsewhere, particularly Plymouth. In parallel with this decline had come an increase in the popularity of the town as a holiday resort which resulted in the usual overlay of advertisements, signs and traffic congestion in its narrow streets. The main pressure in the last 20 years or so has been as a place for retirement. The County Council sought to tackle these problems on three main fronts: the revitalization of the Port, the management of traffic and, through the Local District Council, the creation of a Town Scheme.

The Port of Looe Revitalization Project involved, at the outset, the rebuilding of the East Quay in East Looe, with the County Planning Department taking a co-ordinating role. This was followed by a new fish-handling and -marketing building on the Quay itself, built with assistance from the European Regional Development Fund. This building provides almost $929\,m^2$ ($10\,000\,ft^2$) of accommodation and, such has been its success, a similarly sized extension is being sought to provide also fish-handling units for several of the registered buyers in the market.

Pedestrianization is both desirable and necessary for the economic regeneration of Looe. A 5-year programme has been drawn up by the County Surveyor to spend some £50 000 on the pedestrianization of streets in the Town Centre of East Looe and, already, better floorscape has been introduced. Other environmental improvements are being considered throughout the Conservation Area, particularly to the main town car park and the sea front. The scenically attractive branch railway line to Looe from Liskeard has been developed as a park-and-ride facility.

Following steps to ensure the long-term viability of the immediate harbour area and to improve traffic management in the Town, the need for some form of complementary activity became apparent. Caradon District Council took this up through the preparation of the Looe Town Scheme. This commenced in 1987 and has, to date, expended some £24 000, contributing to £60 000 worth of work in the town. Further, the District Council has prepared, in consultation with the County Council, a Conservation Area Policy Document and Design Guide issued in 1988 to coincide with the preparation of an Action Plan for

Looe. Fish Market at Buller Quay. (Reproduced with kind permission of Cornwall County Coucil.)

Looe. Higher Market Street. (Reproduced with kind permission of Cornwall County Council.)

Looe, prepared by the Civic Trust's Regeneration Unit, at the invitation of the County, District and Town Councils. The Plan is, in effect, a strategy for the Town and sketches out a range of policies for the revival of Looe and its neighbouring fishing village of Polperro. It suggested that these would be best advanced through a Forum comprising the Town Council, Harbour Commission and the Town Trusts of East and West Looe. The Looe Town Forum is now in being.

Thus, the enhancement of Looe is an example of co-operation and input by many organizations within and outside the town aimed at the economic and environmental regeneration of the town. A considerable measure of success has already been achieved on both fronts and the setting up of the Looe Town Forum should ensure that further progress is made.

Looe. Buller Quay car park. (Reproduced with kind permission of Cornwall County Council.)

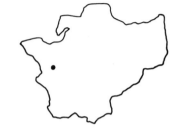

CHESHIRE

PROJECT 4.3, Pedestrianization of Chester City Centre

Chester enjoys an enviable reputation as one of a small number of historically interesting cities in Britain, and was one of four for which Central Government commissioned a townscape study by consultants in the 1960s. Apart from the problems associated with the use and occupancy of Chester's unique Row buildings (refer to Project 3.3), the study raised important issues of concern about traffic and townscape. The problem was to find ways of relieving the mounting pressures of traffic which was having an increasingly adverse effect on both buildings and the pedestrian environment, without undermining the city's economy.

For several years now, Cheshire County Council has worked in partnership with Chester City Council on a range of projects aimed at conserving and enhancing Chester's historic and architectural heritage. The restoration of historically important buildings and the construction of new public buildings have visibly improved the city's environment and allowed opportunities for archaeological study. Furthermore, traffic management measures, combined with the creation of new pedestrian spaces are all part of both Council's efforts to achieve a better street environment in Chester enabling people to enjoy and appreciate the city in greater safety. Cheshire County Council is the Highway Authority for the City Centre, whilst Chester City Council is the Local Planning Authority with a particular role in conservation and funding allocated for positive action.

Following completion of the Inner Ring Road in 1973, it became possible to introduce measures aimed at reducing the amount of traffic that needed to pass through the city centre. These were introduced gradually and involved extensive consultation with the public and local businesses. An early intention was to make the four major streets radiating from The Cross more available to the pedestrian and less accessible by motor vehicles. To this end, a phased programme of work was begun in 1981 with an experimental scheme followed by five separate interlinked phases up until 1989. In each phase of the pedestrianization over almost 10 years, the County Council, through its landscape architects in Planning, and close working links with colleagues in County Highways, acted as design and implementatation consultants to the City Council as client.

The balance between a conservation approach and the need to satisfy highway design, specification, maintenance and safety criteria was crucial to the success of each phase. This involved liaison between many officers and departments in County and City as well as the police, fire and ambulance services and a whole variety of statutory and voluntary organizations. Funding was provided by the City Council with grant assistance from English Heritage and the European Commission. To qualify for these grants it was essential that designs evolved with an emphasis on 'quality' and the use of traditional materials.

PHASES 1 AND 2: THE CROSS AND EASTGATE STREET, 1981–1983

Pedestrianization started with an 18-month experimental paving and traffic management scheme

Pedestrian Spaces
and environmental improvements

(a)

(b)

Chester. The Cross before (a) and after (b) pedestrianization and improvement. (Reproduced with kind permission of Chester County Council.)

along part of Eastgate Street. All traffic was restricted at The Cross and the roadway paved over in reclaimed York stone. The new space acted as a focus and meeting area at the junction of Chester's four primary Roman streets. The paving scheme was a demonstration of the quality to be achieved and designed to encourage public response and support for the principle of further traffic reduction and returning streets to people. Part of Eastgate Street was repaved in concrete blocks chosen to tone in with the stone buildings and to blend with York stone in later phases. Temporary movable plant containers and seats were used to experiment with narrowing the street for vehicle access.

An important constraint in Chester is the impossibility of total traffic restriction in the central streets as many of the historic buildings have no rear access, so deliveries and servicing must be made from the street. The experimental scheme was aimed at finding the right balance between traffic and people and the continued economic success of the city. There was an overwhelming public response in favour of further pedestrianiza-tion. The second phase, following the experimental period, completed the paving of Eastgate Street to link with The Cross and provided a layout for the street incorporating permanent fixed features and specially designed cast-iron furniture.

Chester Library and Bus Exchange: 1984

The development of Chester County Library and the City Bus Exchange was a joint urban renewal project involving the relocation of buses and taxis from the Town Hall frontage and Northgate Street to a site at the rear of the library. The scheme included retention and restoration of a listed Edwardian three-arched terracotta facade as the front elevation to the new library. This development enabled extensive archaeological excavations to be undertaken revealing much information on the Roman occupation.

Removal of buses and taxis allowed the creation of a new pedestrian space at the front of the library, in which the arched theme of the building was echoed in York stone and block paving, with

Chester. The Cross and Eastgate Street – streets for people. (Reproduced with kind permission of Cheshire County Council.)

Chester. Listed Edwardian three-arched terracotta facade of new library. (Reproduced with kind permission of Cheshire County Council.)

raised brick planters, street furniture and tree planting. The library and bus shelters were designed by the County Architect and the whole project co-ordinated through an inter-authority joint working group chaired by the County Council.

PHASE 3: NORTHGATE STREET, 1985

This phase extended the Eastgate Street pedestrianization into Northgate Street, towards the Town Hall Square. It involved the re-use of traditional paving materials only. Victorian granite setts, buried under tarmacadam were lifted, cleaned and relaid with low granite kerbs and York stone footways. Care was taken to consult with organizations about provision and design

of accessways across the setted street area for physically and visually handicapped people.

PHASES 4 AND 5: TOWN HALL AND FORUM FRONTAGES, 1987-1989

The removal of buses from Northgate Street allowed the creation of further pedestrian spaces to the Town Hall and Forum frontages. The Town Hall space is important for its various civic events, parades and processions, and its proximity to Chester Cathedral.

The City's ceremonial flagpole stands in an open area of York stone and granite sett paving. Lighting columns incorporating floodlights to the Victorian Town Hall facade carefully concealed behind specially designed shields, carry the City's coat of arms, and are a feature of this area.

The most recent fifth phase fronting the Forum, unites and completes the northern and eastern streets radiating from The Cross. This phase endeavoured to relate the unpopular 1960s Forum building to its setting by the use of matching brick paving integrated into the Town Hall frontage. New planting and specially designed seating together with an improved access to the Tourist Information Office have provided an attractive setting and access for wheelchairs.

The first three phases cost £126 500, whilst phases 4 and 5 cost a further £220 000. These costs were met by the City Council. The Chester County Library development was a County-funded scheme costing £1.5 million, and the adjacent pedestrian area works were seen as part of the street environment related to the pedestrianization scheme, costing £35 000. The City Bus Exchange was a jointly funded scheme costing £800 000, a figure which included the costs of the archaeological research on site.

The Chester City centre pedestrianization scheme illustrates an ambitious project, that could only proceed in the way it did, because of the decision to work closely with the City Council, and to form joint working groups and jointly share the costs. The results are clearly shown. Chester now has a pedestrianization scheme that has been recognized both nationally and internationally as one of great sympathetic and sensitive improvement to the pedestrian environment in the city centre. It gives a quality of townscape, together with other wide-ranging improvements, enabling residents and visitors alike a greater enjoyment of the city.

Following the success of this scheme, further phases of pedestrianization are being considered for the city. A policy of continuing improvement and traffic management is embraced within a recent joint County/City study and consultation document, entitled *Chester Traffic Study*.

CLWYD

PROJECT 4.4, Wrexham Town Scheme

In the early 1980s there was growing concern at the run-down appearance of the town around the commercial area close to St Giles' Church, a Grade I listed building, and the High Street. A number of key listed buildings in the conservation area were suffering from neglect. The High Street area was becoming increasingly secondary in terms of commercial activity, with problems associated with the unsympathetic adaptation of the older buildings and traffic congestion exacerbating the situation.

At the beginning of the 1980s, the Borough Council of Wrexham Maelor set up a modest fund in order to grant-aid the repair and restoration of key buildings. However, it was clear that this fund would be insufficient in its amount to persuade the private sector to tackle the backlog of neglect. Consequently Cadw was approached to secure additional funding through the concept of a Town Scheme.

In the first year of operation, the partnership was between the Borough Council and Cadw, who each contributed £5000 to the scheme. However, in subsequent years, Clwyd County Council matched the contributions of the Borough Council, and this figure was doubled in the amount offered by Cadw. The result has been that after the commencement of the Town Scheme in 1986, the Borough Council's contribution has amounted to £39 000, the County Council's, £34 000, and Cadw £73 000. In addition to this total of £146 000, the Borough Council provided other environmental Capital funding totalling a further £47 000. The number of applications to take part in the Scheme has been encouraging, reaching 13 to

date. Nine properties have been repaired, and it is clear that the worst properties in the scheme area in the vicinity of Chester Street and Yorke Street are beginning to be put forward for repair. It has been recognized that environmental problems affecting the area need to be tackled concurrently with the repair and adaptations of the buildings, not only to improve conditions in the area but also to create a climate of confidence.

Investment through Borough Council projects designed to improve the environment is also

202

beginning to have an effect on the setting of the Parish Church, which is itself undergoing a comprehensive renovation.

The owner of one of the properties adapted under the Scheme has commented that the actual grant-aid itself was marginal in so far as the viability of the project was concerned, but its award did unlock finance through bank loans and other sources. Professional advice also became available through Cadw and the local authorities, and it was these aspects that were considered critical to the success of the project.

One problem that it was hoped would have been ameliorated during the period of the Scheme was that of traffic congestion in the High Street. However, this problem continues to affect the Conservation Area and an early solution is not yet in sight.

Without doubt the Town Scheme has been an important factor in helping owners adapt and renovate buildings for present-day needs, in the oldest part of the town centre.

DEVON

PROJECT 4.5, Environmental management plans for historic towns and resorts

During the mid 1980s, Devon County Council recognized that, while a great deal had been achieved to protect and enhance the important conservation areas in the county and the listed buildings within them, there was a need to examine the appearance of the centres of historic towns as a whole, and a series of comprehensive environmental management plans for several towns have now been prepared.

The first two schemes commenced in 1986, which was designated by the County Council as Devon Conservation Year. These schemes were prepared for Totnes and Dartmouth and gave guidance on materials to be used for upgrading footway surfaces, the design of street furnishings, signs and street lighting. Programmes for the implementation of enhancement projects in the main shopping and tourist areas were included in the management plans.

It was clear from the outset that the success of the plans would depend to a large extent on consultation with the District Councils, Town Councils and local amenity groups. The County Council set up joint officer and member working groups to assist in the preparation of the management plans, and public consultation was achieved through exhibitions and meetings with local

Dartmouth. Foss Street following enhancement. (Reproduced with kind permission of Devon County Council.)

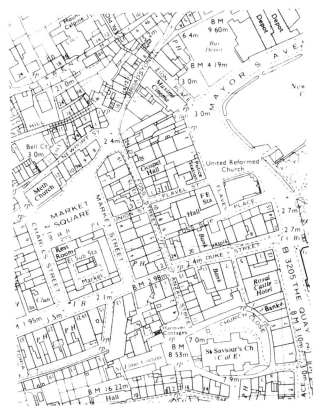

traders and private individuals.

Similar schemes have since been undertaken for Tavistock, Axminster Cullompton and Sidmouth. Whereas the earlier schemes had concentrated essentially on the enhancement of highway and footway surfaces and the replacement of unsightly street furniture, the above management plans were widened to provide a range of policies and advice on conservation including, for example, guidance on the redevelopment of shop fronts and advertisements. This involved a greater level of input into the management plans by the District Councils. The Sidmouth management plan document was a runner-up in the 'Control in Action' competition run by *Planning* newspaper.

The County Council's funding for these schemes has been obtained largely through the re-allocation of part of existing highway maintenance budgets.

One of the benefits of these management plans is that the work undertaken by the County Council has not only achieved positive environmental im-

Sidmouth. Sketch of proposed enhancement of Church Street. (Reproduced with kind permission of Devon County Council.)

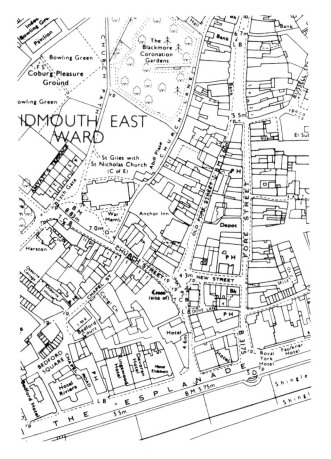

provements but has also encouraged conservation-conscious property owners to refurbish their properties, and in some cases private owners have made financial contributions towards the cost of schemes. Additional funding has been obtained from District Councils and English Heritage has also contributed to schemes in Totnes and Sidmouth. One of the most successful projects, involving a range of financial and other contributions from the County and District Councils and other agencies, is the refurbishment of the old riverside warehousing area at Totnes, known as the Plains. This scheme was the recipient of a Civic Trust Award in 1991.

The management plans and enhancement programmes for towns in Devon have been generally well received by the public, although, in a limited number of settlements, there remains an element of resistance to measures which reduce traffic and parking in town centres. However, the County Council has found that the completion of the early enhancement projects in Totnes and Dartmouth has led to demands from other towns for the preparation and implementation of similar schemes. Environmental enhancement in Devon is perceived as being of particular importance to the tourist industry.

DORSET

PROJECT 4.6, Dorchester Town Enhancement Scheme

The Dorchester Heritage Committee (originally entitled 'The Dorchester Steering Committee for Conservation, Archaeology and Landscape') was set up in May 1983 by the Dorset County, West Dorset District and Dorchester Town Councils. Its initial brief was to prepare and implement a five-year programme of environmental enhancement schemes in accordance with the policies and proposals contained in the document *Dorchester: Conservation, Archaeology and Landscape* published and approved by the County and District Councils in April 1983. The Committee consists of nine members, three members from each of the Councils, together with representatives of the Dorchester and District Chamber of Commerce, Dorchester and District Trades Council, the Dorchester Association, the Dorchester Civic Society and the Dorset Natural History and Archaeological Society. The achievements and value of this Committee during those first five years were recognized by the three parent Councils, and in 1988 it was agreed that it should continue in existence for at least another two years. This was extended for a further year in 1990.

Since the original document was prepared, significant progress has been, and is being made in achieving its objectives. This is due to the combined and individual efforts of the local authorities, developers, various organizations, traders, property owners and, not least, the Heritage Committee which can look with satisfaction at its own particular contributions. It has not only been responsible for specific improvements, but also provided a useful and influential forum for discussing and encouraging the many facets of conservation and development primarily involving other agencies which are enhancing the environmental quality and character of the historic County town.

During recent years, Dorchester has been undergoing a period of rapid change. The opening of the long-awaited bypass and the pedestrianization of Cornhill/South Street have considerably improved the environmental quality of the town's principal streets. Redevelopment has taken place, and is still taking place in most parts of the conservation area. To date, a significant proportion of this redevelopment has been residential in the form of flats – a clear indication that, unlike many towns, the centre of Dorchester is a pleasant and convenient place in which to live.

It is pleasing to note that, by and large, this redevelopment generally reflects and re-enforces the inherent historical and architectural character of the town – a good indication that the conservation policies set out in the initial document are being recognized and accepted as the way in which Dorchester should develop and adapt to change.

So far as the practical aspects of the Heritage Committee's work is concerned there has been, and still is a steady programme of improvement schemes. To date, it has been involved in 31 schemes. Some of these it has carried out itself, some in partnership with other agencies, and others have been assisted and encouraged with grant-aid.

Concern for Dorchester's archaeological heritage has also figured prominently. There is now a

Dorchester. Fordington Green enhancement by the Heritage Committee including repair and protection from vehicle erosion, new lighting, seats, litter bins, restoration of churchyard railings. Repairs to church were grant-aided by the Dorset Historic Buildings Financial Aid Scheme. (Reproduced with kind permission of Dorset County Council.)

Dorchester. Restoration of railings in High West Street, with 50% grant from the Heritage Committee. (Reproduced with kind permission of Dorset County Council.)

Dorchester. Repair and cleaning of Town Pump, Cornhill, as part of enhancement of the town's main shopping street. (Reproduced with kind permission of Dorset County Council.)

distinct awareness of the need for adequately funded and organized archaeological investigations to take place prior to redevelopment or development both within Dorchester and its surrounding area. The Heritage Committee has been particularly concerned to ensure that the town's principal archaeological monuments are appropriately managed and displayed.

The Heritage Committee has been particularly active in pursuing landscape objectives both within and on the approaches to the town. The most notable achievement to date has been progress in replanting the avenues of trees along the town approaches. Again, a number of agencies and organizations, including the Heritage Committee have been involved, and the process is now almost complete, so that in years to come this traditional feature of Dorchester will be established once again in the landscape.

Possibly the most significant feature of this aspect of conservation work is that since a very comprehensive set of policies and proposals had been produced, there was the determination to see them translated into action, and the recognition that this required a joint approach by all concerned. The Heritage Committee, formed and funded by the three Councils and including representatives from the appropriate local organizations, has proved to be an effective and efficient medium for achieving this objective.

DURHAM

PROJECT 4.7, Barnard Castle Town Scheme

Barnard Castle is a medieval town whose castle has guarded a river crossing since the eleventh Century. The main streets zigzag up the hill and round the castle and contain buildings mostly of seventeenth- and eighteenth-century origin with at least one outstanding house dating from the sixteenth century. The town was identified in a report by the Council for British Archaeology in 1965 as one of the 51 most important historic towns in Great Britain. It was designated a conservation area in 1968 and acquired 'outstanding' status when this was a prerequisite of government financial assistance.

Two main concerns led to the establishment of the Town Scheme in 1976. The first was a report highlighting the poor state of many of the properties in the town, particularly on The Bank, one of the main streets, and of growing and untackled problems of dereliction behind the street frontage. The second particular concern was the erosion of the town's character through the loss of the traditional roofing slabs which are of local riven stone.

The major dereliction was tackled in 1980 by means of a reclamation grant. A start was made on the first building under the Town Scheme in 1977. Progress was at first slow and the Scheme was not delegated. In order to provide better stimulus and a quicker response the Historic Buildings Council agreed in 1980 to assist for an initial two-year period with the salary of a part-time Conservation Officer whose main job was to promote the grants, oversee the repairs and prepare improvement schemes. A member of the former County Planning Department conservation staff was appointed, initially on a three-day a week basis. Although the Historic Buildings Council later withdrew their salary contribution, the post remains as an arrangement between the Teesdale District Council and the County Council with a member of the County Environment Department conservation staff being present in the town on two days each week.

(a)

Barnard Castle: (a) dereliction behind the street frontage. (Reproduced with kind permission of Durham County Council.)

Some of the most expensive repairs were undertaken with assistance under S.10, Town and County Planning (Amendment) Act, 1972, since the initial total fund for the Town Scheme was only £6000. This sum is now £40 000 made up of £10 000 from each local authority and £20 000 from English Heritage. The Town Scheme is now the principal funding scheme, since the number of eligible properties has expanded from 243 to 420 (though not all are in need of extensive repairs). Grants totalling £249 400 have enabled repair work to be carried out to a total of £554 880 on 75 buildings. The change from a 50% to a 40% rate of grant does not seem to have affected the take-up of grants and in the last three years all the money has been allocated.

From an initial indifference and, in a few cases, hostility to spending money in this way, there is now widespread acceptance both of the aims of

Barnard Castle: (b) after restoration. (Reproduced with kind permission of Durham County Council.)

Barnard Castle. Restoration and conversion to flats of two- and three-storey disused warehouses in Hall Street.

(Reproduced with kind permission of Durham County Council.)

the Town Scheme and the increasing expenditure needed to achieve them. No doubt this has coincided with the growth of interest and investment in tourism which the District Council is keen to promote and from which the town derives an increasing income. It has raised the level of public interest in conservation so that concern about things which appear to be contrary to good practice is also increasing.

Because the Town Scheme is so much concerned with repair work much of the expenditure does not result in significant visual change, though a general improvement in standards of maintenance is very significant. There are, however, also a number of cases in which buildings have been brought back into use or converted with the assistance of Town Scheme grants, some at key visual points in the town.

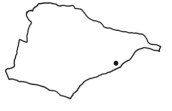

EAST SUSSEX

PROJECT 4.8, Hastings Urban Conservation Project

In the 1930s, Hastings was one of the busiest holiday resorts, chiefly due to the ease of access by rail from London. However, in the post-war period this tourist trade had steeply declined with the growth in international tourism. Whilst other British resorts were then in a similar predicament, they have been able to develop alternative economies. This was not to be achieved effectively in Hastings until recent years.

In the early 1960s the medieval Old Town, situated in a separate valley from the main town of Hastings, was suffering from a lack of investment, with a number of empty or run-down properties. Shops were closing, or only open for seasonal trading, catering for the trippers. Coach parking on the beach, side by side with the fishing fleet, did nothing to help the image. In the early months of 1964 the then County Borough Council commissioned Town Planning consultants to advise them on how this problem could be arrested and reversed, and to outline the possibilities of future development. There were many houses in the Old Town which, due to Closing Orders, became empty and fell into disrepair. The Consultants' Report, which was the first in the country to use the phrase 'conservation area', pinpointed the need to rescue these empty buildings and refurbish them. Vacant sites were to be sympathetically redeveloped. The possibility of pedestrianizing one of the shopping streets was explored, as was the provision of further public car and coach parking. In the two decades following the adoption of the Report, much work was carried out.

In the summer of 1985, Members of the East Sussex County Council's Environment Committee visited Hastings on their annual tour. They were able to see, adjacent to the present-day Hastings, the Old Town, with its narrow streets and passageways, and a fishing fleet drawn up on the shingle beach in front of the internationally known net shops. Between the two areas was the focus of the Committee's attention, the disused church of St Mary-in-the-Castle – its classical portico forms the centre-piece of one of the county's finest Regency seafront crescents of houses, designed by Joseph Kay in 1824 for the Earl of Chichester. The church had been empty for many years, and by 1985 the building was in an extreme state of dereliction.

Hastings Old Town. (Reproduced with kind permission of Hastings Urban Conservation Project.)

(a)

(b)

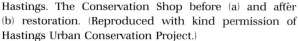

Hastings. The Conservation Shop before (a) and after (b) restoration. (Reproduced with kind permission of Hastings Urban Conservation Project.)

(a)

(b)

Hastings. Conway Court before (a) and after (b) restoration. (Reproduced with kind permission of Hastings Urban Conservation Project.)

The Committee donned hard hats to penetrate its extraordinary semi-circular interior in the form of a tiered amphitheatre, now filled both with scaffolding supporting the roof and the screech of gulls wheeling in and out through the shattered windows far above.

The visit to Hastings bore spectacular fruit, for less than a year later the newly appointed Director of the Hastings Urban Conservation Project had been set to work, setting in train perhaps the first application to a major urban area of the approach so successfully pioneered at Wirksworth, Derbyshire. The project was a joint initiative by the East Sussex County Council and Hastings Borough Council, set up initially for three years, subse-

quently extended to four and part of a fifth. A large part of the work was generously supported by English Heritage.

The aims of the project were: 1. to raise standards of maintenance, appearance and preservation of buildings and their surroundings in Hastings; 2. to work with the townspeople, involving them in the processes of conservation; 3. to bring together all those concerned with urban conservation in Hastings with those having the will, ability and skill to achieve results; 4. to convince the people of Hastings of the quality and potential of their town; 5. to secure additional resources so that all these aims can be realized.

The project operated as an independent entity with its own headquarters, 'the Conservation

Shop' in the Old Town with a 'branch office' at St Leonards. The project was overseen by a Joint Committee of elected members drawn equally from the participating authorities together with a representative from English Heritage. Salaried staff consisted of the Director and his personal assistant. The participating authorities made available their professional staff as necessary at no cost to the project.

The core funding provided by Borough and County Councils amounted to £50 000 per year from each. English Heritage has contributed approximately £20 000 per annum towards a Town Scheme in addition to contributing substantial funds to conservation schemes initiated or co-ordinated by the project. The Manpower Services Commission provided the Project with staff resources and running costs to a value of approximately £50 000 per annum under the Community Programme in 1987 and 1988. This support continued in modified form under the Employment Training Scheme. Some funds for environmental works were assembled from both the private and charitable sectors and income was generated by the sale of merchandise and by consultancy.

At the time of the Project's 'Mid Term Review' it was calculated that grant expenditure of £42 000 had generated improvement work to the value of £585 000 representing a leverage ratio of almost 14:1. Of this, HUCP-initiated schemes had generated more than £238 000, a lower but very respectable leverage ratio of 6:1.

The following schemes have been undertaken:

- *Pedestrianization of George Street* – the main shopping street in the Old Town completed in August 1987.
- *Shop front scheme* – grants of up to 40% are available for repair and enhancement of shop fronts. To date, 10 of the 21 projects receiving offers of assistance have been completed.
- *'Over the shop'* – grant scheme covering 40% of costs of conversion works of disused premises above shops was started in 1988. Two schemes have so far been supported.
- *Town Scheme* – the project was able to negotiate a Town Scheme agreement with English Heritage covering Burton's St Leonards and Pelham Crescent, which frames the Church of St Mary-on-the-Castle. Response to the scheme has been excellent, 35 properties have received an offer of grant, 28 of which have been completed.

Hastings. St Mary's in the Castle.

- *Enhancement Scheme* – covers 40% of the costs of decoration and reinstatement of architectural features in strategically located properties, was established in 1988; 23 properties have received offers of grant of which 14 have been completed.
- *Environmental Projects* – a small projects grant scheme enables HUCP to initiate and co-ordinate landscaping, heritage and conservation projects, normally by combining forces with local authority departments, voluntary bodies and the private sector; 12 projects have been completed and several others are in progress.
- *Environmental studies* – HUCP have commissioned environmental studies from consultants which can be used as a basis for targeting grant schemes. One major study on the Old Town called 'Opportunities for Action' has been completed by landscape architects and several others are in progress.

- *Environmental education* – HUCP now operates two conservation shops. It has produced a range of reports and handbooks and has organized study, days, ideas and exhibitions.

The public response has been encouraging. Budgets were beginning to be overwhelmed by applications for assistance under the various scheme headings and the project was increasingly being turned to as a medium for information and advice. Its independence allowed it to mediate and find solutions to a number of intractable problems not necessarily involving grant-aid. The project won several local and national awards for its contribution to the community and there was a great deal of media coverage.

It was envisaged from the outset that a specially established Charitable Trust would become central to the project's operation and perhaps form the medium by which the project might evolve. This has been put in hand and the Hastings Trust has now succeeded the Hastings Urban Conservation Project with its membership drawn from a wide range of interests and organizations.

The Church of St Mary-in-the-Castle is now undergoing the first stage of restoration funded by Hastings Borough Council and English Heritage. It is acknowledged that the Project's intervention in bringing together many groups concerned with the conservation of historic buildings led to a shift in attitude and appreciation of the architectural quality of this fine, and somewhat unique church, on the sea front at Hastings, and its potential use for tourism related facilities.

EAST SUSSEX

PROJECT 4.9, Renewal and enhancement of street lighting in Rye

As one of the original fortified Cinque Ports, Rye still displays its remarkable medieval character, with its narrow cobbled streets and compact urban form. Within the old town walls, and overlooking the Romney Marshes, the wealth of sixteenth-century houses is still very much in evidence, alongside Georgian buildings, making up some of the most memorable and picturesque streetscapes in Britain.

Rye remains unique with little built or changed over the past 200 years. This in itself is a conservation challange, for it demands that maintenance and repair work are carried out in sympathy with the medieval environment. Whilst the repair and restoration of historic buildings and structures are obvious areas of concern when dealing with enhancement schemes, other, perhaps less obvious, features also need attention. Street lighting has an economic life estimated at around 20–30 years. Beyond this period, equipment is costly to maintain and the level of illumination falls below recommended standards. Old systems inevitably become structurally and electrically unsafe and need replacing for reasons of public safety.

In 1987, the County Council embarked on a major programme of lighting and highway works in the citadel of Rye, at an estimated cost of £110 000. The design brief involved a detailed survey to identify important architectural and townscape features. Commemorative or symbolic carvings, inscriptions, and date plaques, for example, form part of the history of a building and were not to be obscured. Facings of weatherboarding, tile or slate hanging, mathematical tiles,

stone, brick or stucco, having qualities of their own, were to be treated with care.

A limited number of lighting columns in Rye had been in place for some 150 years, but at the turn of this century electric lighting began to replace the earlier gas and oil as the principal means of street lighting. The light fittings came in many forms, from the cast-iron column to the period style lanterns and wall brackets. Replacement cast-iron columns were manufactured by an old established foundry from a pattern taken from an original street light.

Electricity supply cables are hidden from view or have been designed to blend in with building facades; exposed equipment has been painted to match the background of individual buildings. Similarly, all reinstatement works to the public highway have been carried out with the least disturbance to residents and visitors, with only matching materials used on completion. In the High Street, light of good quality has been achieved by the introduction of the high-pressure sodium lamp.

Alongside the need to refurbish the lighting system was the need to attend to the highway itself. The majority of the narrow streets are cobbled with whitish blue boulders, believed to have come over as ballast in ships in medieval times, plying the wool trade between south-east England and Holland. It was necessary to relay partially some cobbled streets in order to accommodate new street lighting electricity mains. This work was dovetailed with schemes of improvement to other statutory services, such as British Gas, to minimize disturbance. As these streets are still subject to car and occasional lorry traffic, it was necessary to lay the existing cobbles, known locally as bouldering, on a bed of concrete in order to give a stronger base.

This scheme illustrates how the refurbishment of street lighting and highway systems can be achieved whilst at the same time, preserving and enhancing the unique character of Rye. The scheme was carried out in co-operation with the Rother District Council, the Rye Town Council, the Rye Conservation Society, and the South Eastern Electricity Board.

(See Plates 16 and 17.)

EXMOOR NATIONAL PARK

PROJECT 4.10, Lynmouth Street Enhancement Scheme, North Devon

Lynmouth, situated on the North Devon coast and within Exmoor National Park, is a popular tourist resort. Most of the village was designated as a Conservation Area in 1973. Lynmouth Street, 149 m (63 yards) in length is the main shopping street, with a variety of shops, restaurants and cafés. Until the disastrous floods of 1952, it was the only street through this part of the village. By the early 1980s it was becoming heavily used by traffic, resulting, in the summer months, in severe congestion and conflict with the many tourists.

In 1983, an experimental pedestrianization scheme for the upper part of the street was implemented, following initiatives from local people. As a result of the welcome improvement in the street environment, suggestions were made that an enhancement project for the street should be prepared and implemented on a permanent basis.

Devon County Council and the Exmoor National Park Department developed the idea and, with the co-operation of the residents and frontagers, a scheme was prepared and the work carried out in the early months of 1985. Lynmouth Street was surfaced, originally, in the ubiquitous black bitmac to the carriageway, flanked by kerbs, footways and private forecourts, some of which were in a poor state of repair, and which, because

of the gradient, gave many steps along the sides where shoppers wandered. The enhancement proposals provided for an attractive surface which unifies the street scene throughout its length, picking up the local colour of the area, as well as offering a pleasant environment to the pedestrian. Brindle paving bricks were used on the higher part of the street, whilst, on the remainder, where some vehicular access is maintained, the street is surfaced with red coloured macadam, bounded by brick channels.

The street is somewhat unusual in that the frontagers claimed the narrow 'footway' areas outside their premises as private ground, and they were used intensively for the display of goods. However, they agreed to contribute to the scheme to the value of the works carried out on their individual properties. The existing side channels were replaced by a central drainage channel, thus reducing the steps at the street edges for the benefit of the shoppers and tourists. This was not achieved without difficulty, due to the gradient of the street, threshold levels and the requirement to provide level areas outside the shops for the traditional goods display. The brick pavers were laid on a sand bed in herringbone pattern on the street, the frontages being distinguished by the

Lynmouth. Pedestrianized repaved area. (Reproduced
with kind permission of Exmoor National Park.)

Lynmouth. Pedestrianized area showing cast-iron bollards at end. (Reproduced with kind permission of Exmoor National Park.)

use of running bond with mortar joints.

Cast-iron bollards were used at either end of the traffic-free length. Where applicable, manhole covers with brick infill were used. Modern stop-cock covers were replaced with cast iron, as was a British Telecom cover. The Traffic Orders were revised to enable yellow lines to be dispensed with on the new surfaces.

Lynmouth has an exceptionally long tourist season, so the only acceptable period to carry out the works was between Christmas and Easter. The contractor started work on the £40 000 scheme in January 1985. The finance came from the Devon County Council's Highways budget, the National Park Committee and from local residents. The official opening was in early April. During the period of the works, access was maintained throughout the street.

The scheme has been well received by residents and visitors. The residents are concerned to keep up the good appearance of the street, and together with the Local Council, ensure that it continues to be maintained to a high standard. An early fear of the residents that the bricks would be spoiled by chewing gum, ice cream etc., has proved unfounded, the surface being easier to clean than the original bitmac.

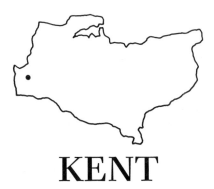

KENT

PROJECT 4.11, Westerham Enhancement Scheme

The main street in Westerham curves gently upwards, over and down a fold in the lea of the North Downs west of Sevenoaks on the county border with Surrey. Daniel Defoe knew this as a 'neat, handsome, well-built market town' with its Market Square broadening at the top of the rise above a large, sloping wedge of a town green. In 1910, the green acquired, as its focal point, a statue of General Wolfe who had spent much of his childhood in the town.

The need to renew the carriageway surface of this main street, and to repair the footways, provided the opportunity to investigate the possibility of a more widely based environmental improvement scheme for the town centre. Discussions with the Parish Council, the Westerham Society, the local Traders Association, Sevenoaks District Council and the police, resulted in the preparation of a scheme by the County Planning Department's Conservation and Design Group which incor-

porated a range of environmental and safety improvements to the principal public areas of the town. It was agreed that these should form part of the Highway Authority's contract for the structural maintenance scheme with additional funding provided by the County Council's Environment Sub-Committee, Sevenoaks District Council and Westerham Parish Council.

The scheme, carried out in April–June of 1990, following the close involvement of the above organizations in the design process, incorporated an increased width of footway and new paved areas for pedestrians in Market Square; the construction of a new parking lay-by in the approach to Market Square to compensate for spaces 'lost' in the Square; the upgrading of the quality of materials used in the footways with a combination of York stone slabs, blue/red clay pavers and ironstone setts – materials which were already present in limited quantities. The more formal qualities of

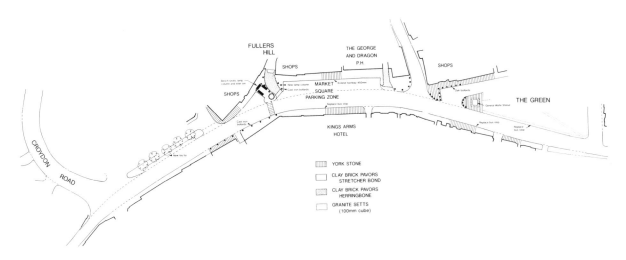

the York stone paving were used to emphasize the key, dominant buildings with the brick pavers acting to link the spaces, and granite setts have been used to form cross-overs. Improvements were also made to street furniture included the use of cast iron and oak for bollards, new cast-iron litter bins, lamp columns and bus stops, and bench seats. The carriageway was resurfaced in standard hot-rolled asphalte (HRA) wearing course with precoated chippings, while on-street parking areas were resurfaced with dark red bitumen macadam.

The total cost of the scheme was £260 000, funded by Kent County Council, Highways Sub-Committee (£208 000); Kent County Council, Environment Sub-Committee (£12 000); Sevenoaks District Council, Planning Committee (£35 000) and Westerham Parish Council (£5000).

Westerham. New parking lay-by in the approach to Market Square. (Reproduced with kind permission of Kent County Council.)

(a)

(b)

Westerham. Before (a) and after (b) upgrading of quality of materials used in the footways. (Reproduced with kind permission of Kent County Council.)

LANCASHIRE

PROJECT 4.12, Wycoller Country Park

For more than a hundred years the hamlet of Wycoller, set in a steep-sided Pennine valley near Colne northeast of Burnley, had lain deserted. The Elizabethan Hall had been abandoned by its owners in 1818; the home-based handloom industry disappeared, and finally in the 1890s the area was bought by the Borough of Colne as the site of a reservoir. Houses were left empty when leases expired and before long became ruins: by 1970 only two were still occupied.

Since before World War II, the beauty of the site and its links with Charlotte Brontë were increasingly appreciated. The ruined Hall – supposedly the model for Fearndean Manor in *Jane Eyre* – was listed in 1952 along with another house and two bridges. Attempts were made by voluntary bodies to clear the Hall's site and consolidate its walls, but these failed in the face of vandalism. The number of visitors continued nonetheless to grow, and parking and picnicking began to spoil the area.

Lancashire County Council became involved after seven more semi-derelict buildings were listed in 1970. A Conservation Area, covering the hamlet and its immediate surroundings, was designated in November 1972 and a Country Park proposed in January 1973. Within a few months the Council had bought the valley from the North Calder Water Board, which no longer wanted to flood it, and in October 1973 published a proposals report; recommendations to rehabilitate the hamlet were put into effect almost exactly as planned.

This work took nearly ten years to complete, since it was not funded separately but paid for with small contributions from annual budgets. It was a frustratingly long period for those involved, but there was time for almost every decision to be well considered and expensive mistakes were thereby avoided.

The first phase included the creation of a car park on the approach road, vehicular access to the village is now restricted to residents and disabled people. Repairs to the structure of the fine aisled barn were also undertaken, as the County Council's contribution to European Architectural Heritage Year in 1975. The second phase, between 1976 and 1978, saw improvements to the supply of water and electricity and the installation of sewers. Thereafter, houses could once more be inhabited and a small community reinstated. The cost of these services was covered by the sale of five properties (including three barns) for which the necessary planning permissions and listed building consents had already been obtained. The freeholds of the properties were kept by the County Council to ensure that the refurbishment was carried out exactly as approved.

Other buildings and the spaces around them were enhanced, for the benefit of residents and vistors alike. With financial help from the DoE, the ruins of the Hall – by now a Scheduled Ancient Monument – were consolidated at a cost of £3500, and its surroundings were improved by volunteer labour. At a further cost of £8500, the County Highway Authority repointed the old twin-arched

Wycoller Hall ruins. (Reproduced with kind permission of Lancashire County Council.)

Wycoller Cottage, packhorse bridge and ford. (Reproduced with kind permission of Lancashire County Council.)

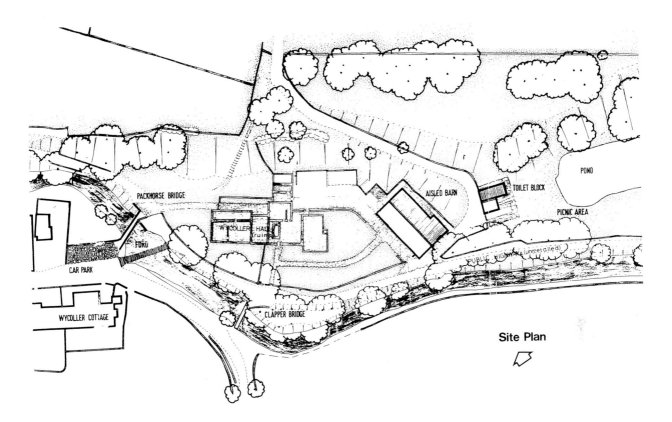

PACKHORSE BRIDGE

WYCOLLER HALL (ruin)

FORD

CAR PARK

WYCOLLER COTTAGE

CLAPPER BRIDGE

AISLED BARN

TOILET BLOCK

POND

PICNIC AREA

PUBLIC HIGHWAY (unmetalled)

Site Plan

packhorse bridge, repaired the setted roadway of the adjacent ford, and resurfaced a number of footpaths within the village.

Further work to enhance the facilities of the Country Park included the conversion of the aisled barn into an information centre at a cost of £3650, and the building of a masonry toilet block, costing £16 100, both designed by staff within the County Planning Department. A pond and picnic area have been laid out nearby, and footpaths into the surrounding countryside improved, with boundary walls being rebuilt with the aid of a £5000 grant from the Countryside Commission.

These works were finished in 1981 and received national recognition as a most significant rural project where unobtrusive rehabitation had been achieved with the greatest sensitivity and care.

In recent years work has concentrated less on the creation than on the maintenance of popular features; some leaseholders have exercised their right to buy, but restrictive covenants and the protection afforded by the designation of the conservation area have ensured that no change has been harmful. Twice in 15 months the sort of flash floods which are supposed to occur once in a century have swept through the village, causing damage and distress. Protective measures are now being designed. The challenge will be to make them also look as though 'nothing has taken place at all'.

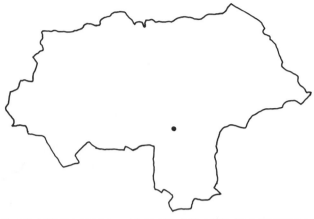

NORTH YORKSHIRE

PROJECT 4.13, Knaresborough Town Scheme

North Yorkshire County Council makes a positive contribution to conservation through financial inducements for the restoration of historic buildings. This policy is important, as the eight Districts in the County put varying emphasis on the provision of environmental grants. Assistance for the restoration of buildings is provided in two ways. Firstly, assistance may be given to selected properties within an approved Town Scheme area for repairs, provided that the works are undertaken using traditional materials and methods and lead to the architectural restoration of the property. Secondly, discretionary grants may be given under the Local Authorities (Historic Buildings) Act 1990 to encourage the restoration of buildings of architectural and historic interest located anywhere in the County. Under the 1990 Act preference is given to properties in private occupation and residential use, although other cases are judged on their merits. Grant-aid up to 25% of approved costs can be given subject to a maximum grant of £1000.

The current extensive Town Scheme programme has developed from small beginnings when Richmond and Whitby were set up in 1975. Both proved to be most successful. A further 14 projects have been launched and now operate with equal success. The most recent schemes were at Bedale and Masham, inaugurated in the summer of 1989. The full programme of 16 Town Schemes is ad-

ministered centrally by the Conservation Section of the County Planning Department although financial and administrative support is given by the District Councils. In addition to the above, in York, the City Council administers a Town Scheme to which the County Council makes a single annual payment. Further Town Schemes operate within the North York Moors National Park at Robin Hood's Bay and Staithes and within the Yorkshire Dales National Park at Settle and

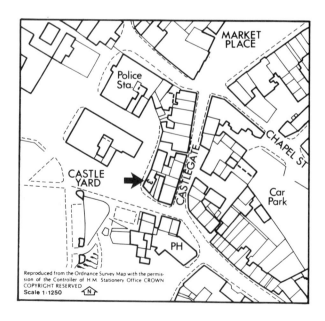

(a)

(b)

(c)

(d)

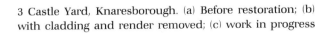

3 Castle Yard, Knaresborough. (a) Before restoration; (b) with cladding and render removed; (c) work in progress on side elevation; (d) after restoration. (Reproduced with kind permission of North Yorkshire County Council.)

Askrigg; these are administered by the respective National Park Committees of the County Council.

A typical Town Scheme project is 3 Castle Yard, Knaresborough. This is a grade II listed building occupying a prominent position adjacent to the entrance to Knaresborough Castle. An inspection carried out in 1988 showed up a number of defective items in the fabric of the building and an investigation of the obscured main elevation revealed the existence of original windows behind the steel sheet cladding.

The property was made weatherproof again by re-roofing in Welsh slates. The timber gutters, cast-iron fall pipes, leadwork etc., were all reinstated. All existing windows were repaired and over-hauled and those at first and second floor levels were replaced with new boxed sash and York sash windows. The original intention of repointing the freshly exposed masonry proved not to be viable in view of the generally poor quality of the stone and the admixture of various later materials and a decision was made to render the walls using a lime/cement/sand mix with a paint finish. The work was completed in late 1989 and represents good value both economically and in terms of townscape in this sensitive area of the town.

PEMBROKESHIRE COAST NATIONAL PARK

PROJECT 4.14, Tenby Regeneration Scheme

Described as 'the jewel in the crown' of the Pembrokeshire Coast National Park, Tenby is one of Britain's finest historic towns. Its outstanding conservation area can boast over 300 listed buildings, impressive town walls (a Scheduled monument in their own right), St Mary's Church (the largest Parish Church in Wales) and a beautiful, historical harbour.

Tenby has recently celebrated 200 years of tourism, and was developed during Victorian times as a major seaside resort, initially for the rich and influential, but later for an increasingly wider market with the advent of the railway, and, more recently, the private car. With this long-term development the town has become heavily reliant on tourism to sustain its economy. The national trend to increased overseas travel narrowed Tenby's slot in the holiday market to low-spending visitors over a reduced season, and in these tighter economic conditions the town became run down and neglected.

In 1989 a group was formed to redress these problems, called the Tenby Implementation Group (TIG). It brings together representatives from the National Park, South Pembrokeshire District Council, Dyfed County Council, Wales Tourist Board, Welsh Development Agency and Cadw, with a common aim of upgrading the town's environment, setting standards of quality in all things to complement the town's fine heritage. As a first step, the group commissioned a firm of top market consultants to research the potential of the town for tourism development. The study concluded that the key to sustaining and improving the holiday industry was to upgrade the town's environment. The strategy implemented by the group to achieve this goal has the following seven components.

HISTORIC TOWN SCHEME

Under this initiative the TIG authorities have linked to provide a 50% grant for schemes which preserve or restore the appearance of properties in the heart of the town, seen as a major step toward the regeneration of the town's many listed buildings. The scheme now has a budget of £250 000 per annum, and is heavily oversubscribed.

ENHANCEMENT PROGRAMME

The TIG Enhancement Programme is directed at shabby public areas, and projects have now been completed on some of the narrow medieval lanes, showing what can be achieved. This success has galvanized public opinion so that greater enthusiasm now greets each successive proposal as pride in the appearance of the town grows. The Enhancement Programme now has an annual budget of £250 000, 80% of which comes from the Welsh Development Agency.

COMMUNITY PROJECTS

The TIG have been keen from the outset to offer advice and financial support to grass roots initiatives. Major successes to date have included the construction of a traditional ornate Victorian Bandstand on Castle Hill, (led by a voluntary

Tenby. Oyster fountain on Tudor Square refurbished as part of the historic town scheme and undertaken by Tenby Town Council. (Reproduced with kind permission of Pembrokeshire Coast National Park.)

Tenby. Tudor Merchant's House recently enhanced with attention to signs and floorscape'. (Reproduced with kind permission of Pembrokeshire Coast National Park.)

organization), the restoration of the Dyster Memorial Fountain on Tudor Square by the Town Council, and the impressive floodlighting scheme for St Mary's Church, financed by the Tenby 200 Committee.

COMMISSIONED STUDIES

The group has approached special areas and problem topics by commissioning studies. Over the summer of 1990 it financed a study of the harbour by the Welsh School of Architecture, which produced a report and supporting artwork for proposals for enhancement. Consulting engineers

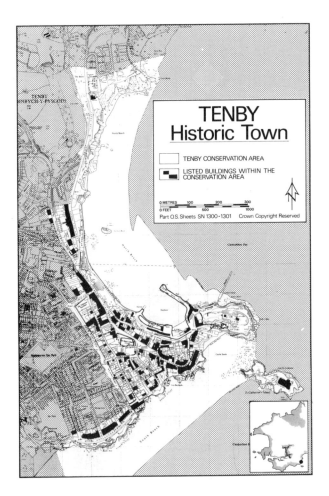

TENBY
Historic Town

TENBY CONSERVATION AREA

LISTED BUILDINGS WITHIN THE
CONSERVATION AREA

0 METRES   100   200   300
0 FEET   500   1000
Part O.S.Sheets SN 1300-1301   Crown Copyright Reserved

for three years with increasing success, and is co-ordinated by the Pembrokeshire Coast National Park with costs of just under £3000 being shared with the South Pembrokeshire District Council and the County Highway Authority. In its six weeks of operation during the 1990 season it carried over 60000 passengers, and the group were successful in attracting substantial local private sector sponsorship for the scheme. It has recently commissioned a study into overall traffic management issues for Sir Alexander Gibb and Partners.

INTERPRETATION

The Group has found that increasing public awareness and pride in the town has improved support for enhancement proposals. The National Park have produced the usual range of leaflets, and in 1990 staged an 'environment week' in the town supported by a pull-out supplement in the local paper and an exhibition in one of the shops in the town's main 'Tudor Square'. This spread the message of both environmental improvements in general and Tenby's special qualities in particular.

UPGRADING HOLIDAY ACCOMMODATION AND TOURIST FACILITIES

In 1989 a successful bid for 'Lead Initiative' funds was made to the Wales Tourist Board on behalf of Tenby (securing £1 million in special grants for the town over a three to five year period). This money is available to support the upgrading of holiday accommodation and other tourist-related projects. The common thread of the schemes, which has been to increase the quality of service and experience offered by the town, has now been widely accepted and appreciated by the community who can set any short-term inconvenience against the long-term benefits. It also presents a model of co-ordination between authorities in the pooling of skills and resources in a unified and programmed way.

have also recently carried out a study on the alternatives for providing low-tide landing facilities for the many pleasure boats, during periods when the main harbour is dry.

TRAFFIC MANAGEMENT

The walled town suffers severe traffic congestion in the summer. This has been identified as a major factor detracting from the enjoyment of the town, and efforts to reduce the problems have included small scale pedestrianization scheme, linked to enhancement schemes in the medieval lanes, a 'Permit' Scheme for vehicles in the walled town, and the operation of a free Park-and-Ride service from the Salterns Car Park to the outside of the walled town. This service has now been running

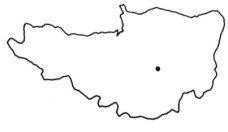

SOMERSET

PROJECT 4.15, Somerton Market Place Enhancement Scheme

The small town of Somerton, designated a Conservation Area in 1974, is situated in a commanding position overlooking the River Cary, some 16 km (10 miles) north of Yeovil. The town contains a great number of listed buildings, mainly dating from the seventeenth and eighteenth centuries. At its centre lies the Market Place, surrounded by historic buildings on three sides and, on the fourth, by the church of St Michael and All Angels. Within this space are two fine buildings, the medieval Market Hall, a two-storey structure listed as Grade II, and the seventeenth-century Market Cross, an octagonal columned stone building, listed Grade II* and a Scheduled Ancient Monument.

In 1983, the Parish Council were keen to enhance the Market Place, which was becoming overrun with parked cars, and, at the same time, to repair the Market Hall and Cross. They approached the Somerset County Council, who in line with the policies that the Councils had adopted to enhance conservation areas, agreed to undertake the work, in liaison with the Parish Council, the District Council and English Heritage. It was agreed that the enhancement works should be programmed over a period of three years,

Somerton Market Place before enhancement. (Reproduced with kind permission of Somerset County Council.)

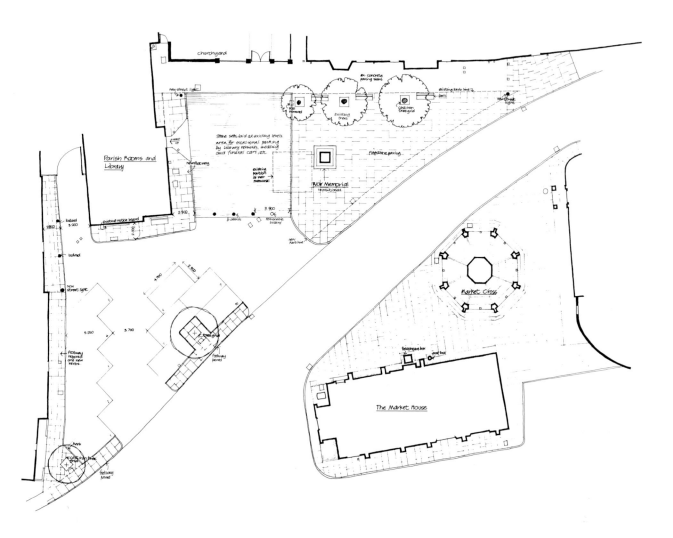

so that each contributing party could make the necessary budgeting provision, easing the costs for any one year.

In 1984, work commenced on the Market Cross, at an estimated cost of £10 000. This involved the repair, replacement and treatment of the structural timbers making up the fan-shaped roof, new lead parapet gutters, new gargoyle spouts and repairs to the lias stonework and paving. The Parish Council and English Heritage both made financial contributions to this work, the balance being met by the two local authorities.

Phase 2 entailed the structural repair and conversion of the Market Hall, again on the southern side of the Market Place, and a building that, sadly, had been neglected for many years, and showed clear signs of structural weakness in both the roof and one wall. A structural survey was carried out by the County Council as part of its investigations to use the building as a library

and meeting room. In the event, the estimated costs proved too high and the building was eventually acquired by a local business man and has now been repaired and used as an antiques showroom with offices. The environmental enhancement works in phase 2 around both the Market Hall and the Cross were, however, carried out by the County Council. These works involved the removal of the existing tarmac, and its replacement with stone slabs, setts and kerbs. Indiscriminate parking areas were removed from around these two buildings as part of the environmental enhancement works. This work was completed in 1985 at a cost of £16 000.

The final phase involved the removal of tarmac and the repaving and enhancement on the north side of the Market Place. A number of car-parking spaces were removed to enable the War Memorial to be resited on a stone-paved area in a better location relative to the church. The approach to the church was resurfaced with stone setts and a safeguarded access area to the church provided by the installation of cast-iron bollards. Street furniture was either replaced or repaired and additional trees were planted within the Market Place. The cost of these works, which were completed in 1987, was £25 000, which was met by financial contributions from the Parish Council, the South Somerset District Council, the Somerset County Council, English Heritage and local contributions.

(See Plates 18 and 19.)

COLOUR PLATES

Plate 1. Conjectural reconstruction of aisle and hall of Drayton Bassett Manor House. (Reproduced with kind permission of Staffordshire County Council.)

Plate 15. Hamstall Hall. The entrance to the arts centre restaurant housed in the former 19th Century cattle-house. The real bricks and Staffordshire clay tiles are typical of agricultural buildings in the area. (Reproduced with kind permission of Staffordshire County Council.)

Staffordshire

Plate 2. Causey Arch. (Reproduced with kind permission of Durham County Council.)

Plate 3. Killhope Wheel. (Reproduced with kind permission of Durham County Council.)

Durham

Plate 4. Bridgwater Dock restored as a Marina in 1984. The 1841 grain warehouse has been converted into flats with a quayside restaurant and pub and new housing developed alongside. (Reproduced with kind permission of Sealand Aerial Photography, Chichester.)

Plate 5. Bridgwater and Taunton Canal. Recently restored Kings Lock in use. (Reproduced with kind permission of Grand Western Horseboat Co., Tiverton.)

Somerset

Plate 6. Cefn Coed Colliery Museum, Crynant. (Reproduced with kind permission of West Glamorgan County Council.)

Plate 7. Little Holmside Hall after restoration. (Reproduced with kind permission of Durham County Council.)

Durham

Plate 8. Seven Sisters Visitors' Centre. (Reproduced with kind permission of East Sussex County Council.)

Plate 9. Exceat Estate. Farm buildings. (Reproduced with kind permission of East Sussex County Council.)

Plates 10 and 11. Seven Sisters farm buildings – prior to conversion. Top: Camping barn. Bottom: Seven Sisters Visitors' Centre. (Reproduced with kind permission of East Sussex County Council.)

East Sussex

Plate 12. Cressing Temple. Aerial view of complex showing the sixteenth-century farmhouse, walled garden and two barns located in the heart of the Essex countryside. (Reproduced with kind permission of Essex County Council.)

Plate 13. Cressing Temple. The Wheat Barn. (Reproduced with kind permission of Essex County Council.)

Essex

Plate 14. Nantyglo Round Towers. The North Tower, Roundhouse Farm. (Reproduced with kind permission of Gwent County Council.)

Plate 16. Rye. Completed lighting scheme in Mermaid Street. (Reproduced with kind permission of East Sussex County Council.)

Plate 17. Rye. Reinstating cobbles in Mermaid Street. (Reproduced with kind permission of East Sussex County Council.)

East Sussex

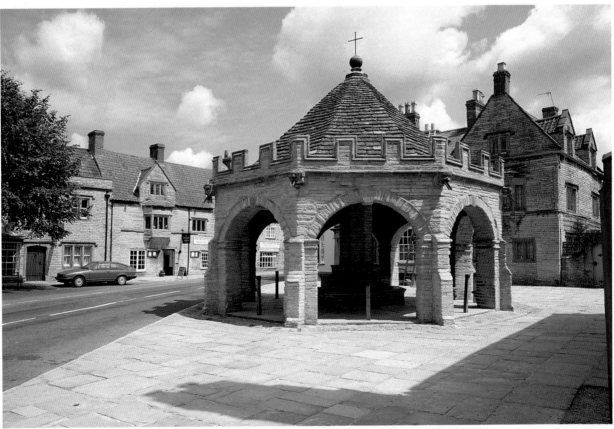

Plates 18 and 19. Somerton Market Place after enhancement. (Reproduced with kind permission of Somerset County Council.)

Somerset

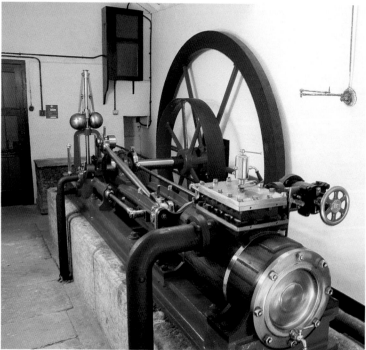

Plate 20. Parc Glynllifon. Stone bridge over River Llifon. (Reproduced with kind permission of Gwynedd County Council.)

Plate 21. Parc Glynllifon. Horizontal stationary steam engine which once drove most of the machinery in the estate workshops.
(Reproduced with kind permission of Gwynedd County Council.)

Gwynedd

Plate 22. Kirby Hall. Excavating the early seventeenth-century border beside the West Terrace. (Reproduced with kind permission of Northamptonshire County Council.)

Plate 23. Kirby Hall. Excavations in progress with Kirby Hall in the background. (Reproduced with kind permission of Northamptonshire County Council.)

Northamptonshire

Plate 24. View along newly made path towards
Amenity/Information feature in woodland. The roof
are off the old County Hall/Pump House Hotel. Al
timber was sawn in the grounds from one large Dou
Fir. (Reproduced with kind permission of Powys Co
Council.)

Plate 25. View down restored path to New County
The Victorian Gate was restored after being crushed
storm blown tree. (Reproduced with kind permissio
Powys County Council).

Powys

Plate 26. Aerial view of Hestercombe House Gardens. (Reproduced with kind permission of West Air Photography.)

Plate 27. Hestercombe House Gardens. Rill Pool looking towards the Grey Walk. (Reproduced with kind permission of Somerset County Council.)

Somerset

Plate 28. Margam Castle, Margam Park. (Reproduced with kind permission of West Glamorgan County Council.)

Plate 29. The Orangery, Margam Park. (Reproduced with kind permission of West Glamorgan County Council.)

West Glamorgan

SUFFOLK

PROJECT 4.16, Lavenham Market Place Enhancement Scheme

Some 500 years ago, Lavenham was at the centre of the prosperous East Anglian woollen cloth industry. It boasted many fine and imposing buildings, many of which still survive today. At the centre of the village, much of which was designated a Conservation Area in 1973, lies the Market Place. It is surrounded by listed buildings, the most important being the Guildhall, owned by the National Trust. Although Lavenham's woollen industry has long since declined, its outstanding collection of timber-framed houses, mostly dating from 1350 to 1650, has today made it an important and popular tourist attraction, visited by over 250 000 people a year.

This level of activity has inevitably caused both practical and environmental problems. In the Market Place conflict was evident between pedestrians and road users driving through or parking there. Although ideas to improve this situation had been considered for a number of years, it was not until 1984 that Suffolk County Council and Babergh District Council resolved to study ways in which the Market Place could be enhanced, in accordance with their agreed conservation policies. In 1986 a draft scheme was prepared for public consultation showing a reduced amount of car parking and resurfacing of the Market Place with a variety of materials. Consultation included an exhibition of the proposals. The result of this consultation indicated that some modifications would be necessary, and in 1988 a revised scheme was prepared which received support from the local community.

The basis of the revised scheme, in design terms, was threefold. Firstly, any resurfacing and accompanying details had to be in keeping with, and complement the surrounding medieval buildings and this suggested that the simplest

Lavenham Market Square. (Reproduced with kind permission of Suffolk County Council.)

Lavenham Market Square. (Reproduced with kind permission of Suffolk County Council.)

Lavenham Market Square. (Reproduced with kind permission of Suffolk County Council.)

form of surfacing would be most appropriate. Secondly, in the design of the highway verges and parking bays, painted road markings and yellow lines had to be avoided. Thirdly, traffic management schemes had to be clearly understood by the motorist so that the scheme 'read well' and was obvious to the Market Place user.

The scheme envisaged the use of pea shingle as a single material to cover the whole of the Market Place, with the carriageway and parking areas marked with strips of granite setts, thereby avoiding painted road markings. Various natural materials such as cobbles, clay pavoirs and bricks were used to define individual property boundaries. New street furniture of an appropriate style also formed part of the completed scheme.

The total cost of the scheme, including design and supervision was £14 000. This was jointly financed by Suffolk County Council and Babergh District Council, whose co-operative involvement in the design of the scheme was crucial to its ultimate success. A grant was given by English Heritage. The cost of the work to private curtilages was split 50–50 between the owners, among them the National Trust and Suffolk Preservation Society.

Advice and guidance was sought from a number of conservation agencies, including the Royal Fine Arts Commission and English Heritage, and this considerably influenced and enhanced the final scheme.

Whilst pea shingle surfacing has given some initial teething troubles, due mainly to excessively hot weather too soon after the work was done, there is every confidence that the twelve months that have elapsed since has enabled the surfacing to consolidate in a way which was originally envisaged.

YORKSHIRE DALES NATIONAL PARK

PROJECT 4.17, Village Enhancement Schemes

The settlements of the Yorkshire Dales, as they stand now, mainly date from the seventeenth and eighteenth centuries; traditional buildings were invariably built from local stone and roofed with stone slate. The landscape features of the villages were the village green, cobbled lanes and squares and the footpaths of stone flags. All of these features are now under threat. The National Park receives around 9 million visitors each year with the result that the village greens and the roadside verges leading to and from the villages, are becoming increasingly eroded due to cars parking on them. In Reeth for example on one Sunday in 1989, 600 cars were parked upon the green. Other smaller villages with no green often have up to forty cars parked on the verges at either end of the settlement.

The problem of the lanes in the villages is different in that, since the ownership of the land is often uncertain, no-one, to date, has accepted responsibility for the maintenance of the lanes. As a result *ad hoc* patching with tar or concrete has taken place. Such repairs not only adversely affect the character of these villages, but also often destroy what remains of the original cobbled surface. Flagged footpaths too are under threat. The increase in heavy lorries has resulted in stone paving slabs, adjacent to the highway, breaking as a result of lorries driving over them whilst passing parked vehicles, or delivery vehicles parking partially on the flags whilst unloading.

In order to counter the above problems the National Park Authority embarked upon a programme of enhancement works to ensure that the traditional landscape features in the villages were protected. To that end schemes were drawn up to cover major footpath works in some of the villages which had been designated, or were about to be designated, Conservation Areas. Such schemes were prepared for the villages of Askrigg, Sedbergh and Grassington. In the case of the edges of village greens suffering from incremental erosion by traffic and subsequent tarmacking by the Highway Authority, the National Park Authority has assisted with the cost of kerbing with granite setts, but only in those areas under threat. In such cases the Highway Authority has usually contributed 50% of the cost, the Parish Council 25% and the National Park Authority the balance.

In certain villages, such as Muker, Hawes and Horton-in-Ribblesdale, where suitable land has been made available, the National Park Authority has contributed towards the cost of enhancement works to new car parks, such as the provision of

(a)

(b)

Grassington. Chamber End Fold before (a) and after (b) enhancement works. (Reproduced with kind permission of Yorkshire Dales National Park.)

(a)

(b)

Malham. Kerbing and cobbling before (a) and after (b)
enhancement works. (Reproduced with kind permission
of Yorkshire Dales National Park.)

Sedbergh. Main Street resurfacing before (a) and after (b) enhancement works. (Reproduced with kind permission of Yorkshire Dales National Park.)

drystone wall boundaries which help to reduce the visual impact of such developments. In the case of a major road or footpath works, such as in Sedbergh and Askrigg, where the land ownership is unclear, English Heritage has, to date, contributed 25% of the enhancement costs with the National Park Authority providing the balance. In some instances the Highway Authority has also contributed.

A further category of enhancement works with which the National Park Authority is involved, is undergrounding of overhead wires. This, however, is a very expensive undertaking and invariably has a long lead-in time. However, in Dent for example, the undergrounding of certain unsightly overhead wires has, after several years, been successfully achieved. In association with this aspect of Village Enhancement Works it has, in the past, been possible to assist with the provision of appropriate traditional street lighting to replace existing or proposed standard steel lamp posts. Such works have been carried out in Sedbergh and it is hoped a similar exercise can be carried out in Askrigg in the near future.

The final category of enhancement works the National Park Authority is keen to encourage is the removal of eyesores, whether they be the removal of a clutter of signs or by assisting with the costs of repainting inappropriately coloured farm buildings in villages. Such repainting works have been carried out in Malham and Thoralby.

The National Park Authority has a 1992/93 budget for village enhancement works amounting to £50 000.

YORKSHIRE DALES NATIONAL PARK

PROJECT 4.18, Barns and Walls Conservation Scheme

The traditional farming landscape of the Yorkshire Dales is one of the most distinctive in Western Europe. Its special features are the intricate network of drystone walls, hay meadows and stone field barns. The walls are particularly impressive, criss-crossing the valley floors and extending up onto the higher ground. The landscape produced is both beautiful and of great historical interest.

The effort exerted in building the thousands of kilometres of drystone walls must have been colossal. Walls were chosen to mark field boundaries partly because of the local abundance of stone and they vary in age. There are some faint remnants, really just lines of scattered stones, that could date back as far as the Bronze Age, but most of the walls visible today are much younger. Those in the village centres and around the old homesteads form small, often irregular enclosures. Many of these walls have been rebuilt and realigned over the years. The villages are surrounded by larger, more rectangular fields bounded by walls dating from the sixteenth or seventeenth century onwards. Farther out on the higher ground many of the huge plots were enclosed at the time of the Parliamentary Enclosure Acts in the late eighteenth and early nineteenth centuries.

Reinforcing this pattern of walls, isolated stone barns (also known as laithes) stand in many of the lower fields all over the National Park. Swaledale is particularly well endowed with them – within a 1 km (0.6 mile) radius of the village of Muker there are about sixty. Field barns were originally built to provide winter housing for small numbers of cattle and the earliest surviving ones were probably constructed as long ago as the seventeenth century. However, this traditional man-made landscape is under threat. Changes in farming practice since the last war have introduced in-line milking, silage making and amalgamation of farm holdings. As a result a gradual decay of the barns and walls and the historic landscape has begun to occur. The survival of field barns and drystone walls is essential if the special character of the National Park is not to be lost. To help the repair of traditional barns and walls the Yorkshire Dales National Park Committee introduced the Barns and Walls Conservation Scheme in 1989 to assist farmers and other landowners with the cost of repairs.

All dry stone walls and traditional barns within the Scheme area of 72 sq. km (27 sq. miles) are considered for the scheme. For both walls and barns, 80% of approved costs will be paid. The applicant's contribution of the remaining 20%

Yorkshire Dales National Park Barns and Walls Conservation Scheme. An example of barns at risk, Angram.

(Reproduced with kind permission of Yorkshire Dales National Park.)

could be in cash, labour or materials. There is no maximum or minimum size of grant although the total funds available in any year are finite. It is intended that structures will be restored to a condition that will ensure their survival for the foreseeable future. Works therefore provide long-term repair rather than short-term 'first-aid'. They should use suitable traditional materials from a specified source and be to a satisfactory standard of workmanship. The grants are aimed at keeping the structures in their traditional form. Alterations or additions are not, therefore, assisted.

The Barns and Walls Conservation Scheme dovetails into the MAFF 'Farm and Conservation Grant Scheme'. Where works are eligible for MAFF grant the National Park scheme will 'top up' the Minstry rate to 80%. If the works are not eligible, the National Park Authority can offer the full 80%. Works on barns and walls which are covered by Environmentally Sensitive Area (ESA)

agreements will not be offered a grant unless unforeseen structural problems arise requiring works more significant than the routine maintenance envisaged in the agreement. Any farmer interested in applying for a grant under the Barns and Walls Conservation Scheme can contact the Barns and Walls Project Officer at the National Park Office at Bainbridge. An application form asks about the proposed work and its estimated cost must be completed and returned to the National Park Office, a visit is the arranged to discuss the proposals. Applications on minor works are dealt with almost immediately; those involving works costing more than £2000 take a little longer. Every effort is taken to make sure the scheme's operation is as simple and straightforward as possible and delay is kept to a minimum.

The area of Upper Swaledale and Arkengarthdale to which the scheme applies has been designated a Conservation Area. (Local settlements are not included in the Conservation Area.) This has enabled English Heritage, which has been keen to support the Scheme, to put money into it and designation has strengthened the case put to the European Commission for funding. Richmondshire District Council and the Countryside Commission also financially assist the scheme. The Conservation Area Status introduces several legal requirements, but the National Park Authority will, as far as possible, mimimize the burden these place on those living in the area.

The scheme is funded jointly by the Yorkshire Dales National Park, English Heritage, Richmondshire District Council and the Countryside Commission. This year's Barns and Walls Conservation Scheme budget amounts to £104 000 which, after making allowance for the input from MAFF (35% for barns and 50% for walls) and the owner's contribution of 20%, assisted with around £195 000 worth of work. It is hoped that next year's budget will amount to £150 000 which should assist around £250 000 worth of repairs. So far, grants towards 60 barns and over 3 km of walling have been approved.

5

BUILDING PRESERVATION
TRUSTS

PROJECTS

Drawing overleaf shows Church Street, Calne, Wiltshire.

INTRODUCTION

As has already been said, historic buildings are an essential part of the character and appearance of both our towns and country, and much of this derives from the uniqueness and variety of the buildings themselves. A high proportion of these buildings are often well looked after and maintained by their owners, and in some cases, the financial burden that falls upon them can be helped by grant-aid from the local authorities and English Heritage (or Cadw) in particular cases. It is perhaps a measure of the public interest in these buildings, that so many of their owners are prepared to keep them in good order.

Sadly, however, a minority of listed buildings are at risk for a variety of social and economic reasons, leading to neglect, decay, redundancy and even the threat of demolition. It is often difficult to assess the exact numbers at any one time in a county, but recent initiatives by English Heritage and Cadw requiring local authorities to keep an updated register of 'buildings at risk' will go some way to ensure that buildings that need urgent attention are highlighted. This is briefly dealt with in Chapter 3.

All historic buildings form part of our heritage, and if that heritage is to be saved, then this generation must play its part. For a number of reasons, regrettably, an owner may not or cannot undertake the, often, costly exercise of repairing a listed building that is becoming neglected. Local authorities, whilst empowered to acquire a building in these circumstances – following the serving of a Repairs Notice – are often extremely reluctant to take such a course, constrained, as many are today, by public expenditure limits.

Other avenues will need to be explored. One option that has a reasonable chance of effectively saving a building at risk, is where there is co-operation between the owner, local authorities and voluntary societies. If an owner can be persuaded to sell the building, the two major problems that then need to be overcome are the raising of the necessary money, both to acquire and to restore, and finding a suitable new use. One of the most successful developments in recent years has been the emergence of County Historic Building Trusts to undertake the repair and restoration of these buildings. The setting up of a Trust, independent from the local authorities, but supported by them and many other sections of the community interested in building preservation, can provide an effective answer and act as a 'long stop' to save buildings that might otherwise be lost.

Building Preservation Trusts, although they can and have taken many forms, are all basically registered Charities whose sole purpose is the preservation of buildings of architectural or historic interest within a particular town, district or county. In most cases they take the form of a Company limited by guarantee. Building Preservation Trusts are not a new concept; the Bath Preservation Trust dates back to 1934. Many counties have now established a County Buildings Preservation Trust and the following examples indicate the range of buildings restored.

Hertfordshire Building Preservation Trust Ltd was set up in 1963, having just celebrated its Silver Jubilee, and during this period has restored over a dozen properties – a magnificent achievement. The Hereford and Worcester Buildings Preservation Trust, set up in 1965 at the instigation of the, then, Worcestershire County Council, has devoted itself to 'rescuing worthy buildings in special danger', which, although they may not in themselves possess particular merit, contribute to the 'streetscape' and character of the town or district. The example illustrated of the scheme at Ledbury is an ambitious project that has recently been completed and indicates very well the scope of restoration schemes that can be undertaken by Historic Building Trusts. In Wales, the Clwyd County Council are currently launching a Clwyd Historic Buildings Preservation Trust, alarmed that many buildings of architectural and historic value within the county, from country houses to chapels, farmhouses to workers' terraces, barns to railway stations, were amongst over 150 properties demolished during the last few decades. The Clwyd County Council provides a continuing professional input with conservation staff advising the Trust, and now a few buildings in the county, that were once 'at risk', have been saved by individual effort and determination.

It is because of the loss, and decay of so many fine buildings up and down the country, that Building Preservation Trusts have an important role to play, being able to concentrate on long-term programmes of rescue, restoration, rehabilitation and resale, that might well be beyond the scope of local authorities.

HOW DOES A TRUST FUNCTION?

To achieve the object of preserving historic buildings, a Trust operates on a 'buy, repair, sell and buy again' principle, known as a revolving fund. This continuous cycle enables a Trust to undertake a sequence of conservation work in a rolling programme. As will be well known to any Trust member, the programme of building restoration is very rarely smooth, and delays and frustrations can occur at any time. Therefore, some Trusts have taken the precaution of undertaking, perhaps, two restoration projects together, so that progress can be maintained, and the essential 'turn round' of capital achieved.

A Trust can acquire properties in a variety of ways. They may be bought by the Trust or accepted from a local authority, possibly following compulsory purchase. An appropriate building may come to a Trust as a gift or legacy. In the majority of cases, as a building has often been out of use for some time, new uses must be found. Therefore, following the repair, and, if necessary, the conversion of the building to new uses, the Trust will sell, or occasionally lease the property on the open market, subject to covenants to secure its continued care and protection. All profits that accrue from sales or leases are ploughed back into the Trust's funds for the next project. It goes without saying that the state of the development market plays a most significant role in deciding either when to purchase or sell. There will be little point in bidding against developers in boom times, as the limited resources of a Trust will rarely outbid those of a developer. Conversely the sale should not be arranged at times of depressed market prices, otherwise the profit, so necessary for future projects, will not materialize. The ideal property is likely to be the one where there is little or no interest from the private market.

HOW IS A TRUST FINANCED?

Trusts will need to have working capital at the outset in order to undertake a restoration project. In most instances the initial funding has been made available by the local authorities themselves. This varies from Trust to Trust, where in some instances a Trust has financial support from the County Council, to others where the District Council has also been involved, or even several District Councils within a County. In Hertford-shire, for example, the Trust is sponsored by the 10 District Councils, as well as the County Council. The Somerset Building Preservation Trust was launched after an agreement had been given by the County Council and all five Districts to provide initial funding.

To help finance the repair of historic buildings, the Trust can apply for grant assistance, from both the local authority and English Heritage, and, in the case of Wales, the Secretary of State. Additionally there is the Architectural Heritage Fund, which is jointly administered by the Department of the Environment and the Civic Trust, and offers cheap working capital in the form of a loan repayable after two years out of the proceeds of sale. This funding is offered up to a maximum of 50% of the total cost of the project, and is often a most valuable source of ready finance to initiate restoration.

Some Trusts have had recourse to other Charities. At Essex, their revolving fund scheme is assisted with an interest-free private loan. Most certainly commercial organizations should be invited and, indeed, expected to undertake sponsorship, and there can be valuable income derived from private membership subscriptions and donations. Many members of the public support the preservation aims of these Trusts, and are prepared, very often, to make admirable efforts at fund raising for a particular cause.

With the growing number and popularity of Building Preservation Trusts, an Association of Preservation Trusts was formed in 1990, under the guidance of the Architectural Heritage Fund. In this way there could be a central source to contribute advice and experience to those who, for particular reasons, are having difficulties in progressing a restoration project.

The examples that follow indicate the enormous variety of restoration projects undertaken and seen through to a successful conclusion. As the Chairman of the Hertfordshire Building Preservation Trust remarked, in his Annual Report of 1988:

> The Trust took most of these buildings on because the normal processes of development had condemned them as unprofitable and hopeless cases. Remember too that for every restoration job done there were several hard fought battles for other worthwhile buildings – some won, some lost. And this was done on a shoestring by a charity. There is good reason for pride in the record and for celebration.

BUCKINGHAMSHIRE

PROJECT 5.1, Historic Buildings Trust: three projects

The Buckinghamshire Historic Buildings Trust Ltd was set up in 1983 by the County Council in succession to its own 'Revolving Heritage Fund'. The Board of Management consists of ten members. Two are County Councillors, two appointed by the County Council, three appointed by the District Councils, two by the County's Amenity Societies and one by the Bucks Archaeological Society. Initial funding came from the County Council who transferred the sum of £100 000 to the Trust. The following Schemes have recently been undertaken by the Trust.

49 HIGH STREET, AMERSHAM

49 High Street is the major part of a fifteenth-century timber-framed open hall house, altered in the sixteenth century by the insertion of a chimney and floor in the open hall. Neglected for many years by a reclusive owner, it came onto the market in 1984 and presented a unique opportunity to preserve a small medieval town house from the inevitable modernization schemes associated with residential use.

The Amersham Society were keen to acquire the building as a museum of local history but had no funds for the purpose. The Historic Buildings Trust therefore agreed to bid for the property in a sealed bid auction, in which it was successful, paying just over £65 000. By the end of 1984, the Amersham Society, who had launched an appeal, was able to acquire the building by reimbursing

the Trust, although the latter also made a grant of £3000 towards the cost of acquisition and repair, as did Chiltern District Council. Since then the Society has been slowly repairing the building and adapting it as a museum, which was formally opened in March 1991.

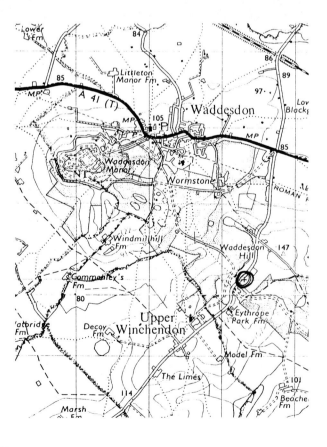

49 High Street, Amersham, Buckinghamshire, before repair. (Reproduced with kind permission of Buckinghamshire County Council.)

WADDESDON HILL STRICT BAPTIST CHAPEL

Built in 1798, this small wayside chapel stands isolated in open countryside near the small village of Upper Winchendon. Its original congregation came from throughout the surrounding area and it stands in a walled graveyard with a stable building in one corner. The Trustees were hoping to transfer the redundant chapel for a nominal figure to the Friends of Friendless Churches, a charity who take over redundant churches to preserve them intact. This was to be their first non-Anglican project, but before the transfer could take place, the Charity Commission intervened and insisted that the property should be sold for its full value.

This opened up the possibility of a residential conversion, which however 'sympathetic', would have destroyed the uniquely rural non-conformist atmosphere of the chapel. The application was eventually refused and, after long delays, its transfer to the Friends seemed possible again.

By this time the Historic Buildings Trust had taken an interest in the case. It helped in various ways, paying for new security measures, arranging meetings between interested parties (including a group of descendants of the chapel's founding families), putting the Friends in touch with a suitable local architect, carrying out the conveyancing on behalf of the two charitable bodies and finally making a grant of £3500 to cover half the acquisition cost. Having achieved the transfer of the chapel, the Trust was gratified to see the Friends proceed with full repairs, obtaining grants from English Heritage and the County Council. The chapel is now in a good state of preservation and may be viewed by the public on application.

(a)

(b)

Waddesdon Hill Strict Baptist Chapel before (a) and after
(b) restoration. (Reproduced with kind permission of
Buckinghamshire County Council.)

STOWE GARDEN BUILDINGS TRUST

The garden buildings at Stowe are probably the most important collection of such buildings in the country, erected during the first part of the eighteenth century by Viscount Cobham and his successor, Lord Temple, as they developed the great garden at Stowe and created the most celebrated example of that uniquely English art form of naturalistic landscape gardening.

Although the public school, which has owned Stowe since 1923, did its best with grants to keep these buildings in repair, their future was still in doubt in the early 1980s and some of the most important, such as William Kent's beautiful Temple of Ancient Virtue were in need of very large sums for repair.

In 1987 the Buckinghamshire Historic Buildings Trust played a significant role by making one of the first financial contributions to the new Stowe Garden Buildings Trust, a grant of £3000 specifically aimed at enabling repairs to the Temple of Ancient Virtue to be started. The launching of this new Trust and its fund-raising campaign led to the decision by an anonymous benefactor to make a gift of £1 000 000 on condition the School transferred the gardens and buildings to the National Trust. After much negotiation this was achieved and the whole future of these remarkable structures now seems assured. The County Trust is therefore proud of its small but timely involvement in these events.

CORNWALL

PROJECT 5.2, Cornwall Buildings Preservation Trust: The Butter Market, Tywardreath

There are many buildings in Cornwall which are important to the town or village scene and should be retained as part of the county's heritage. Some 7000 of these are listed by the Department of the Environment as being of special architectural or historic interest, others are not listed but many are within the 75 conservation areas in the county. Listing is not, however, a means in itself of preserving a building and, year by year, some of them fall into disrepair. Most are restored by new owners or put to new uses but, occasionally, there is need for someone to step in when, for some reason, sufficient private funds are not available. This is why the Cornwall Buildings Preservation Trust came into being. The Trust is a non-profit making company, limited by guarantee and registered as a Charity. Its object is to secure the preservation of buildings of quality and of any period in Cornwall and the Isles of Scilly, whether in towns or villages.

The County Council encouraged the formation of the Trust and, on its establishment in 1973–74, made an initial grant of £10 000. This has been used as a revolving fund to buy, restore and then sell properties. The sales, together with subscriptions and donations from members (who include Local Authority and Old Cornwall Societies), and interest from the investment of funds when not in use for a scheme, have enabled the Trust to increase its capital and take on larger projects. The County Council also helps the Trust by making available a 'rolling' loan of £50 000 at a favourable rate of interest for approved schemes. Further useful financial assistance has come from District Council improvement grants and from grants by the Department of the Environment.

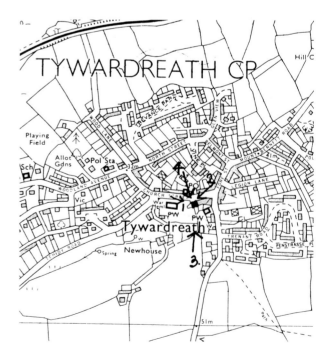

258

(a)

(b)

The Butter Market, Tywardreath before (a) and after (b) restoration. (Reproduced with kind permission of Cornwall County Council.)

THE BUTTER MARKET, TYWARDREATH

In 1977 the building now known as The Butter Market was lying empty and semi-derelict and was clearly an eyesore in the Conservation Area of Tywardreath, near St Austell. It had been built as a police station but had more recently been used by the County Council as temporary accommodation for the homeless. The Cornwall Buildings Preservation Trust bought it from the County Council for £1500 and prepared a scheme for its conversion into three flats.

At that time, the Trust only had capital to the extent of £13 500 and were also involved in the restoration of the Rashleigh Cottages, at a cost of £75 000. The cost of conversion was £38 000 but with interest on a loan of £15 000 from the Architectural Heritage Fund and other costs, the total spending amounted to £41 300. Improvement grants brought in £7950 and a Section 10 conservation grant £5000. Happily the sale of the flats (at prices markedly higher than a conservative valuation had suggested) realized £35 000 leaving a profit to the Trust in excess of £6000.

The building is quite an important architectural feature of the village centre and its loss and the possible redevelopment of the site would almost certainly have meant a deterioration of the architectural character of the village. The building was not suited for use as a single dwelling and since grants were not available for speculative development, its conversion for sale by developers other than the Trust would not have been financially viable. The structure would probably have deteriorated further and demolition would have been inevitable.

The Trust's investment paid a second dividend. The Village Silver Jubilee Committee put £500 remaining from their funds towards the cost of laying out a small area of waste land between the Butter Market and the road as an amenity area, paved with local setts, and with seats, shrubs and flower beds.

DERBYSHIRE

PROJECT 5.3, Restoration of 20–26 High Street, Whitwell

Derbyshire County Council's Design and Conservation Group keeps a 'Register of Threatened Buildings' and has done since 1972. These are nearly all listed buildings threatened by neglect for it was neglect that was perceived as the major threat to our built heritage in the 1960s to 1980s. Experience in Derbyshire is showing that another, more insidious, threat is emerging as a major danger in the 1990s – unsympathetic alterations.

The County Council's first 'in-house' historic building repair project – the rehabilitation of four houses in Whitwell – addressed this problem. The Derbyshire village of Whitwell, lying a few miles south west of Worksop, is a conservation area, the statutory definition of which is 'an area of special architectural or historic interest, the character or appearance of which it is desirable to preserve or enhance'. Most Whitwellians would probably describe themselves as conservationists, interested in preserving their village's special character and enhancing its appearance, and yet the traditional character of Whitwell, and villages like it across the country, is being gradually eroded, not so much by dereliction and demolition, but by the creeping effects of misguided alterations. It requires a good deal of knowledge to identify correct materials for replacing old building parts, and it is difficult for authorities to preserve the character of villages such as Whitwell. Derbyshire County Council decided that a solution would be to set up a self-financing, 'revolving' repair scheme,

whereby the money derived from one successfully completed restoration project is used to finance the next. The idea was double-edged: not only would eyesores be obliterated and buildings be restored in sensitive areas, but the council would be seen to be practising what they preached with regard to correct building methods and conservation practice.

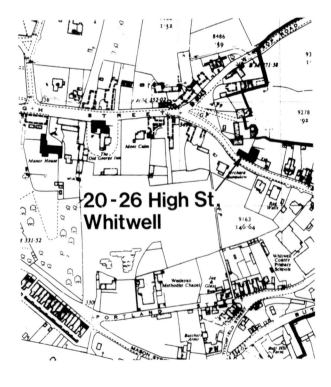

260

DERBYSHIRE
County Council
Supports Nuclear Free Zones

20-26 High Street, Whitwell

18

26 24 20

22

Greenway

High Street

pergola

28

Key

- - - - Fences

Magnesian limestone pavings

Crushed magnesian limestone

Top soil / lawns

Car parking area

Flower bed

Vehicular & pedestrian access

Pedestrian access

The object was to target an area already identified by the Planning Department at District as well as County level as being in need of attention and then to find an archetypal building or group of buildings to restore. The more prominent their position, and the more run-down their appearance, the better. The buildings at 20–26 High Street, Whitwell, fitted the bill perfectly. Their condition at the outset was 'spectacularly grotty'. They had been on the market for several years and their predicament seemed intractable.

A shift in the traditional village centre had left the old High Street blighted and run down. Whitwell's main industry, the colliery, had shut down a few years before, radically altering the village's economic and social life. Numbers 20–26 had survived the changes, but only just. The street side buildings (20–22) had suffered particularly badly from successive alterations: from private house to chapel; from chapel to shop and from one shop to two shops – each change resulting in the loss of original fabric and the accretion of another layer of material. The deeds for the properties revealed that numbers 20–22 had their origins in the late seventeenth century. All that survives from this period, however, is the huge

projecting stone plinth on which the present-day building stands. The two three-storey houses at the rear date from the early to mid nineteenth century and have always been in residential use.

Numbers 20–22 flank the street, bordered by a narrow pavement, and numbers 24–26 stand in a small courtyard behind. They are typical undemonstrative village buildings, quietly appealing now in their newly restored condition but jarringly out of harmony with their surroundings in the previous incarnation as empty and derelict eyesores. Those features that made the part of the village's context – magnesian limestone walls, Yorkshire sliding sash windows, pantile and plain tiled roofs – had been obscured by years of neglect and inappropriate alteration. The purpose of the restoration was simple: to show how the process can be reversed. The buildings facing the street had been covered in a flat render of uniform greyness; the render was in poor condition because of rising damp and leaking gutters.

The courtyard buildings were in marginally better condition, largely through not having been altered. The properties did, however, need reroofing and the joinery, pointing and gutters were defective. There were, of course, numerous unforeseen problems. Underneath the eaves of the street frontage, the top part of the wall had been constructed from brick in order to raise the roof. To compensate for the difference in thickness, two thin skins of brick running along the top of the wall had been used, with an (18 in) cavity in between 'braced' with laths that had almost completely rotted away. The County Architect commented that it was a miracle that the roof had not collapsed.

If the building were to remain rendered, rebuilding the wall would have been no problem, but since part of the scheme was to reveal the attractiveness of the local stone, replacement stone had to be found in large quantities. After weeks of searching for magnesian limestone of a similar colour (the stones are a beautiful subtle mix of buffs and pinks) appropriate material was bought from a demolition contractor.

Apart from unpleasant discoveries such as the eccentric wall structure, the course of the rest of the work was relatively straightforward: reroofing; repointing (where necessary); repairing joinery; installation of services; interior finishing and external landscaping. One of the main tasks of the latter was rationalizing the garden boundaries and making provision for car parking. Local vernacular

(a)

(b)

(c)

(d)

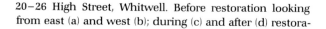

20–26 High Street, Whitwell. Before restoration looking from east (a) and west (b); during (c) and after (d) restoration. (Reproduced with kind permission of Derbyshire County Council.)

paving and detailing was used. It was the County Council's awareness of the absolutely central importance of doing these simple jobs correctly with suitable materials that led to the production of a series of step-by-step leaflets in conjunction with the work on the Whitwell project. Although the leaflets have specific relevance in Whitwell and other Derbyshire villages where similar materials are used, they are valuable as an easily assimilable account of good building practice for the rest of the County.

The first of these leaflets gives a basic outline of the individual tasks involved in the Whitwell project. The second is a guide to the sources of grants available to owners of old buildings and provides an explanation of the law in regard to planning permission. The rest of the leaflets give fairly detailed technical advice about the repair of roofs, walls, windows, doors, services, interior and external walls and a list of useful addresses.

The public's response, both locally and further afield, has been encouraging. The houses were open, on completion, as 'show houses' (Fig. 5.4d) and were visited from as far afield as Essex and Liverpool. Comments in the visitors' book clearly showed how pleased the locals were with the scheme and 18 months of hard evidence, in the form of schemes which follow the advice given, is emerging. Crucial to this success is the availability of grant-aid, both from English Heritage and the County Council.

DEVON

PROJECT 5.4, Historic Buildings Trust

The Devon Historic Buildings Trust was formed in 1973 as a joint initiative by the Devon Conservation Forum and the Devon County Council. It seeks to acquire buildings of historic or architectural merit which might otherwise be demolished or allowed to collapse, to restore them for appropriate uses and to resell them on the open market. The proceeds are then available for the acquisition and restoration of further properties. This revolving fund principle is common to the majority of Historic Building Trusts operating elsewhere in the country. In Devon, the fund was established by an initial grant of £25 000 from the County Council and a further £5000 from other local authorities. As a result of this continuing support from public authorities, supplemented by private and commercial donations, and by careful stewardship, the fund quadrupled in the Trust's first 10 years of operation. The County Council has provided most of the professional input to the various projects undertaken by the Trust in the past, but the Trust is likely to assume a much greater degree of independence in the future.

The Trusts 'track record' over the past 18 years has shown its willingness to undertake the restoration of a diverse number of properties, both in character and scale, although all are relatively modest structures in themselves. Collectively they

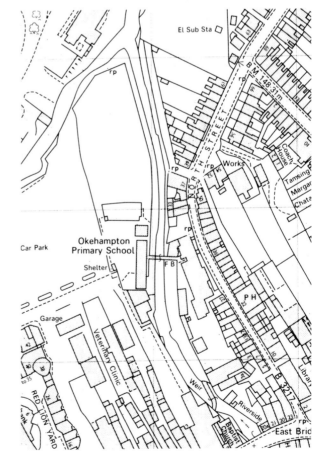

form a vital part of our heritage and both the resident population and the numerous visitors to Devon would be the poorer had they not been saved.

Since 1973, an average of one house per year has been refurbished. The latest of these include the renovation of an old mill building at Okehampton, and the Vestry at Sandford, near Crediton. In earlier years, the Trust has successfully restored a number of important buildings, including a group of three derelict cottages at South Molton, two unoccupied and deteriorating cottages in the centre of the Conservation Area at Ottery St Mary, and probably the most ambitious to date, the restoration of the near derelict 38, Holloway Street, Exeter.

OLD MILL, OKEHAMPTON

The Old Mill is an early nineteenth-century structure which included, within it, remains of an earlier seventeenth-century property. Various accretions had been added from time to time and it was in a state of collapse when it was purchased from the County Council after it was declared surplus to road widening proposals.

The transfer, which followed a public inquiry about its possible demolition, allowed plans to be drawn up and work to be undertaken at a cost of about £150 000 to convert the building into two separate dwellings. The larger of these has since been sold for £110 000 to the Nature Conservancy Council (English Nature) for use as offices, while the smaller, two-bedroom house has yet to be sold.

The conversion has ensured that the whole street has benefited, and the terraced late-Victorian buildings that front it have become more attractive to buyers. It is hoped that the sale of the remaining dwelling will result in a minimal profit. The Old Mill has been listed as a Grade II building of architectural and historic interest.

38 HOLLOWAY STREET, EXETER

The building that is known today as the Elizabethan house, in Holloway Street, is all that remains of Larkbeare House, which was replaced about 1870 by the nearby Judges' residence, the present Larkbeare. The original house was late medieval and its history is closely allied to the rise and fall

Old Mill, Okehampton, following restoration. (Reproduced with kind permission of Devon County Council.)

of Exeter's leading merchant families associated with the woollen trade in the fifteenth century.

In recent years the building had unfortunately become empty and in a very poor condition. Ultimately, a 'dangerous structure' Notice was served on the building and a public inquiry was held in the Spring of 1977. The Department of the Environment and Exeter City Council won their case for restoration against the owner's wishes for demolition. The owners, an international Petrochemical company, accepted this decision and offered to sell the property to the Devon Historic Buildings Trust for the sum of £1, and to make a gift towards the restoration fund.

The Trust commissioned its architect to examine the property, to report and make recommendations for conversion to a two-bedroom dwelling unit. The architect's first visit was alarming. The front wall to the street elevation was in imminent

(a)

(b)

38 Holloway Street, Exeter. Artist's impression (a) and interior details (b). (Reproduced with kind permission of Devon County Council.)

danger of collapse and with a constant stream of heavy traffic and pedestrians passing by, the probability of serious consequences was extremely high. Clearly there was need for urgent action. A contract was drawn up quickly for the restoration of the building, and the Trust assumed responsibility for the building in April 1979.

It was realized from the start that the Trust could not escape making a loss on this particular project, but the building was listed Grade II, and the City Council recognized its substantial townscape value, its local history connections and its relevance for future plans for improving the de-

caying Holloway Street area. Thus, with active encouragement and considerable financial support from the City Council, the Trust agreed to accept the challenge.

The inclusion of this building, from the very many examples available that the Trust have restored, is because it represents an all too familiar situation occuring in many urban streets, where a fine building presents apparently insuperable problems of repair such that demolition appears the only alternative. The streetscape suffers as a result, for no matter how fine a replacement building is, it cannot provide either the continuity of the historical street scene or the local significance of the original. With often high site values for these urban properties, it is always going to be an uphill task for a Trust to be able assemble a restoration package that, at the end of the day, provides them with not only a restored building, but also some degree of profit. In the case of 38 Holloway Street, the great advantage was the virtual donation of the building to the Trust, albeit a building that needed considerable works carried out on it. However, the result, now that the works have been completed, is an extremely interesting dwelling unit, containing several features of great historic interest.

ESSEX

PROJECT 5.5, The Revolving Funding Programme: three projects

The Essex County Council Revolving Funding Programme was formed in response to concern regarding the condition of some of Essex's historic buildings. Generally it is the small unobtrusive properties which play a vital role in the urban environment, and large visually impressive but commercially obsolete buildings such as barns and maltings which are particularly at risk from neglect. Many are regarded by owners and agents alike as uneconomic for private investment and therefore the problem is not resolved by the market.

Carefully planned capital investment enables the County Council to intervene in order to purchase and restore buildings at risk. The programme aims to recover or increase its capital from the sale of completed projects in order to maintain or even expand the operation. Since 1970 nine projects have been completed. The successful operation of the fund is achieved through the co-operation and skill of various County Council departments. Problem buildings are identified through field work and the update of registers of the buildings most at risk. When a suitable building has been selected, the County Architect is briefed to prepare a scheme and costs, based upon considerations of its most effective future uses, and repairs necessary to maximize its chances of survival.

The availability of grant-aid is vital. Of the original £25 000, £10 000 was loaned interest free by the Pilgrim Trust, a private Charity who award grants for amongst other things, the restoration of historic properties, and studies connected with conservation issues. The remainder is generated from the Council's own funds and from grant assistance provided by English Heritage. Without grant assistance from these bodies the Revolving Fund projects would (with the exception of one) all have recorded a loss.

The Fund has not only saved specific buildings, it can also claim other beneficial effects. First the renovation of a building could have a 'knock-on' effect, encouraging other owners in the area to bring their own buildings up to a better standard of repair. Secondly, interest shown by the County Council in a derelict building has tended to act as a catalyst to the owners themselves or possible purchasers. Thirdly, the Fund has set an example of how restoration can be well done by setting standards for others to see and follow.

20–36 EAST STREET, COGGESHALL

This was the first project undertaken through the Revolving Funding Programme and set a precedent for the eight schemes that followed. The site consisted of nine cottages, five of which dated from the sixteenth century. They are in a conservation area and are particularly important to the street scene. These cottages were converted into three houses and the remaining nineteenth-century cottages at the rear of the site were demolished to make way for gardens and garaging.

(a)

(b)

20–36 East Street, Coggeshall before (a) and after (b)
restoration. (Reproduced with kind permission of Essex
County Council.)

The profit from their sale provided the basis for establishing the Revolving Funding.

3–5 SOUTH STREET, MANNINGTREE

This impressive early sixteenth-century timber-framed building, known locally as The Old Coffee Shop, occupies a prime site in the centre of this attractive market town. It is thought that it was probably the Guild Hall and local tales suggest that the Manningtree Witches were detained here before being hanged on South Street Green. Samuel Pepys was also said to have used the building as a base for collecting river tolls. In the nineteenth century it was converted into two shops. Essex County Council bought the building through the Revolving Funding Programme when it was threatened with demolition to make way for a redevelopment scheme. It was renovated and first sold as an antique shop with a flat above it, before being turned into a restaurant.

34–36 HEAD STREET, HALSTEAD

This small attractive market town has in the past suffered from a depressed property market leading to the deterioration of some of its buildings. Essex County Council purchased three adjoining properties in Head Street, all Grade II listed. They were not eligible for a grant from the Department of the Environment but the Council was able to negotiate a Civic Trust grant. This project raised the status of the area, encouraging many owners to embark on private refurbishment schemes of buildings which had been vacant for some time.

3–5 South Street, Manningtree before (a) and after (b) restoration. (Reproduced with kind permission of Essex County Council.)

HAMPSHIRE

PROJECT 5.6, Buildings Preservation Trust projects

Hampshire Buildings Preservation Trust was formed in 1976 as one of Hampshire County Council's contributions to European Architectural Heritage Year. The Trust was set up with an initial grant of £100 000 from the County Council. In addition over the years it has received additional capital from the authority and its working capital has also been augmented by monies from Hampshire's District Councils. The Trust is run by a Board of Management comprising members of the County and District Councils together with representatives of professional, academic interests Amenity Societies. The constitution of the Trust envisages a role that embraces a wide range of functions. In practice certain key activities have emerged as a result of the Trust's responses to the problems and opportunities presented by Hampshire's built heritage.

11/15 CHANTRY STREET, ANDOVER

The Trust has promoted the cause of buildings under threat of demolition or at risk from unsympathetic treatment from owners or developers. In these situations the Trust relies on its close working relationship with the Districts and their conservation and planning staff. Over the years the Trust has been able to underwrite the actions of the District Councils when exercising Listed Building and Conservation Area control as Local Planning Authorities, so that if necessary a property can be purchased and restored in an appropriate manner. Such schemes provide part of the financial basis for the Trusts revolving fund.

A good example of the many buildings that have been dealt with in this way is 11/15 Chantry Street, Andover. Here the Trust has undertaken the restoration, conversion and resale of a pair of Grade II listed medieval cottages that survived the redevelopment of the town centre in the 1960s and 1970s. In the course of the scheme, the Trust was able to uncover much that was of archaeological and historical importance. In this connection it enlisted the help of Winchester City Museum's Curator who was able to confirm that the structure was in fact a mid fifteenth-century timber-framed hall house of the Wealden type. The help of a

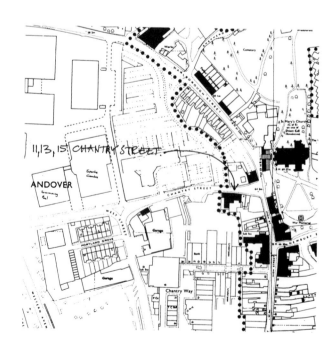

(a)

(b)

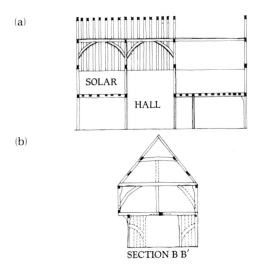

11/15 Chantry Street, Andover. Section (a) and cross-section (b) of Wealden-type hall house.

11/15 Chantry Street, Andover. Fireplace and decorative early seventeenth-century plaster ceiling. (Photograph by Garrick Palmer. Reproduced with kind permission of Hampshire Buildings Preservation Trust, Hampshire County Council.)

specialist conservator was also an important factor in the overall success of the scheme. The meticulous restoration of fine seventeenth-century decorative plaster ceilings and wall panels has added greatly to the attractive interiors. The building costs of the scheme totalled approximately £84 000 and assistance was received from Test Valley District Council, Hampshire County Council, English Heritage and the Architectural Heritage Fund. As a result a pair of two-bedroom houses was added to the towns housing stock. The Trust's involvement has also ensured the retention of an attractive and historic corner of this important Hampshire town.

SILK MILL AND BURSLEDON WINDMILL

A second circumstance in which the Trust, in liaison with the respective District and County Council and other agencies, has intervened, is where buildings are at risk but have failed to attract the attention of purchasers because they do not fit into any clearly definable niche in the property market. Two such buildings falling into this category are the Silk Mill at Whitchurch in the norther part of the County and Bursledon Windmill situated close to the River Hamble in South Hampshire.

In the former case, the long-established firm of Ede and Ravenscroft famous for their professional and academic gowns and silks found that they were unable to continue their business on a sound economic footing at the Whitchurch Mill. This is the last remaining working Silk Mill in Britain. The Trust stepped in and acquired buildings, machinery and goodwill as a going concern. A separate trading company was established to oversee the continued production of silk at the site. Meanwhile a full-scale restoration of the mill, its machinery and outbuildings has been undertaken. A visitor centre with tea rooms and a shop has been established. As a result of the action of the Preservation Trust this small but historic town has an attractive 'low-energy' textile operation, providing local employment and making its own low-key contribution to the prosperity through the employment of its workforce and the spin-off effect to the local economy of its tourist attraction.

The second example, a Grade II* Listed Building, is Bursledon Windmill, a scheme which has occupied the Trust for some years now. When acquired by the Trust in 1978, this building had been abandoned for nearly a century, and presented problems of damp penetration, decay and general neglect. Its wooden machinery, however, was of great importance, being an unusual and rare survival from the early nineteenth century. This was still retained *in situ* and was capable of

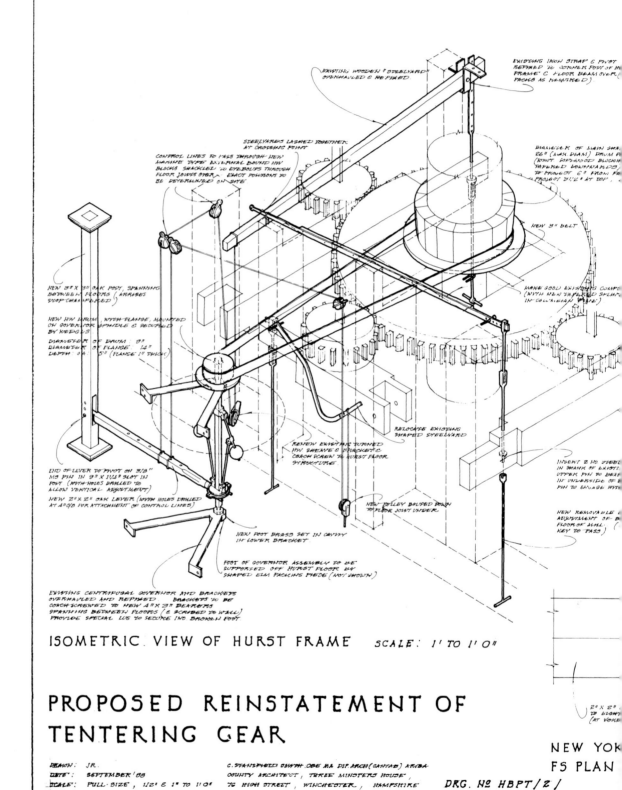

EXISTING WOODEN "STEELYARD"
OVERHAULED & REFIXED

EXISTING IRON STRAP & PIVOT
REFIXED TO CORNER POST OF H
FRAME C FLOOR BEAM OVER (
PACKED AS REQUIRED)

STEELYARDS LASHED TOGETHER
AT CROSSING POINT

CONTROL LINES TO PASS THROUGH NEW
HANGING "EYES" ON FINIAL BOUND HW
BLOCKS SHACKLED TO EYEBOLTS THROUGH
FLOOR JOISTS OVER. EXACT POSITIONS TO
BE DETERMINED ON SITE

DIAMETER OF MAIN SHA
26" (MAX. DIAM.) DRUM F
(KNOT SOFTWOOD DRUM
TAPERED DOWNWARDS
TO PROVIDE 6" FROM F
PROJECT 3½" AT TOP

NEW 9" BELT

NEW 3" X 3" OAK POST, SPANNING
BETWEEN FLOORS (ARRISES
STOP CHAMFERED)

NEW HW DRUM, WITH FLANGE, MOUNTED
ON GOVERNOR SPINDLE & PROOFED
BY WEDGES

DIAMETER OF DRUM: 9"
DIAMETER OF FLANGE: 14"
DEPTH: 4½"→5" (FLANGE 1" THICK)

MAKE GOOD EXISTING COMP
(WITH NEW TAPERED SPLIN
IN COLUMBIAN PINE)

RELOCATE EXISTING
SHAPED STEELYARD

RENEW EXISTING TURNED
HW SHEAVE & U BRACKET &
COACH SCREW TO HURST FLOOR
STRUCTURE

INSERT 2 NO STEEL
IN SHANK OF EXISTI
UPPER PIN TO ENGA
IN UNDERSIDE OF B
PIN TO ENGAGE WITH

END OF LEVER TO PIVOT ON 3/8"
MS PIN IN 9" X 1½" SLOT IN
POST (WITH HOLES DRILLED TO
ALLOW VERTICAL ADJUSTMENT)

NEW 2" X 2" OAK LEVER (WITH HOLES DRILLED
AT ANGLE FOR ATTACHMENT OF CONTROL LINES)

NEW PULLEY BOLTED DOWN
TO FLOOR JOIST UNDER

NEW REMOVABLE
ADJUSTMENT OF B
FLOOR OF WALL
KEY TO PASS)

NEW FOOT BRASS SET IN CAVITY
IN LOWER BRACKET

FOOT OF GOVERNOR ASSEMBLY TO BE
SUPPORTED OFF HURST FLOOR BY
SHAPED ELM PACKING PIECE (NOT SHOWN)

EXISTING CENTRIFUGAL GOVERNOR AND BRACKETS
OVERHAULED AND REFIXED   BRACKETS TO BE
COACH SCREWED TO NEW 4" X 3" BEARERS
SPANNING BETWEEN FLOORS (& SCRIBED TO WALL)
PROVIDE SPECIAL LUG TO SECURE INTO BROKEN FOOT

ISOMETRIC VIEW OF HURST FRAME   SCALE: 1' TO 1' 0"

PROPOSED REINSTATEMENT OF
TENTERING GEAR

2" X 2"
TO LIGHTE
(AT YOKE

NEW YOK
F5 PLAN

DRAWN: JR.
DATE: SEPTEMBER '88
SCALE: FULL SIZE, 1½' & 1" TO 1' 0"

C. STANSFIELD DIP.TP. OBE MA DIP. ARCH (CANTAB) ARIBA
COUNTY ARCHITECT, THREE MINSTERS HOUSE,
76 HIGH STREET, WINCHESTER, HAMPSHIRE

DRG. N° HBPT/2/

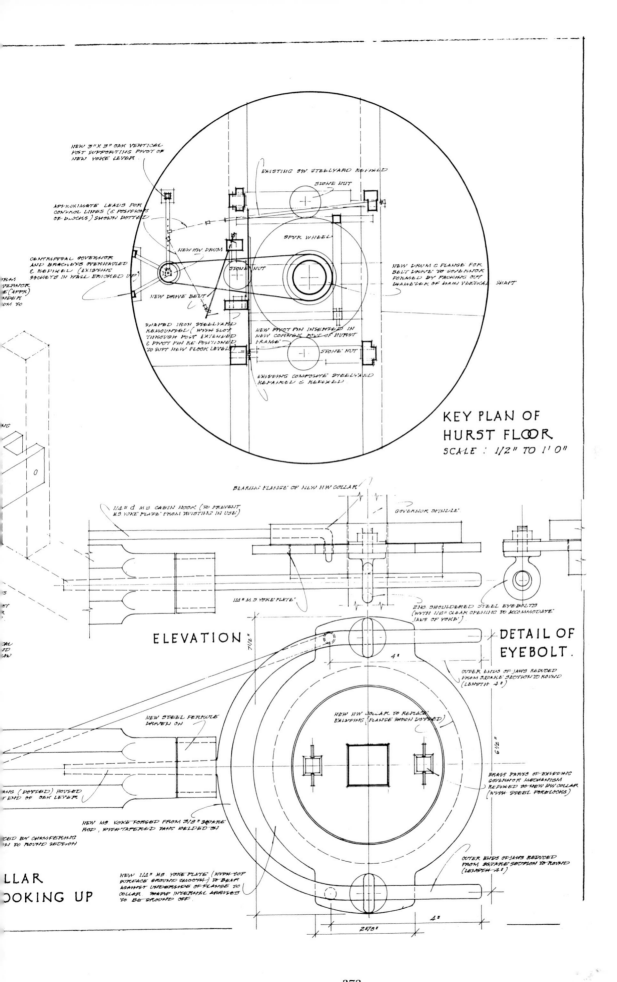

NEW 3"X 3" OAK VERTICAL
POST SUPPORTING PIVOT OF
NEW YOKE LEVER

EXISTING 3W STEELYARD REFIXED

STONE NUT

APPROXIMATE LEADS FOR
CONTROL LINES (6 POSITIONS
OF BLOCKS) SHOWN DOTTED

NEW HW DRUM

SPUR WHEEL

CENTRIFUGAL GOVERNOR
AND BRACKETS OVERHAULED
& REFIXED (EXISTING
SOCKETS IN WALL BRICKED UP)

NEW DRUM & FLANGE FOR
BELT DRIVE TO GOVERNOR
FORMED BY PACKING OUT
LHAWLECK OF MAIN VERTICAL SHAFT

STONE NUT

NEW DRIVE BELT

SHAPED IRON STEELYARD
REMOUNTED (WITH SLOT
THROUGH POST EXTENDED
& PIVOT PIN RE-POSITIONED
TO SUIT NEW FLOOR LEVELS)

NEW PIVOT PIN INSERTED IN
NEW CORBELL BOX OF HURST
FRAME

STONE NUT

EXISTING COMPOSITE STEELYARD
REPAIRED & REFIXED

KEY PLAN OF
HURST FLOOR
SCALE : 1/2" TO 1' 0"

BEARING FLANGE OF NEW HW COLLAR

GOVERNOR SPINDLE

1¼" d M.S CABIN HOOK (TO PREVENT
M.S YOKE PLATE FROM WHISTLING IN USE)

1¼" M.S YOKE PLATE

2ND SHOULDERED STEEL EYEBOLTS
(WITH 1/2" CLEAR OPENING TO ACCOMMODATE
JAWS OF YOKE)

ELEVATION

DETAIL OF
EYEBOLT.

OUTER ENDS OF JAWS REDUCED
FROM SQUARE SECTION TO ROUND
(LENGTH 4")

NEW STEEL FERRULE
DRIVEN ON

NEW HW COLLAR TO REPLACE
EXISTING (FLANGE SHOWN DOTTED)

BRASS PAWS OF EXISTING
GOVERNOR MECHANISM
REFIXED TO NEW HW COLLAR
(WITH STEEL FORELOCKS)

NEW M.S YOKE FORGED FROM 3/8" SQUARE
ROD, WITH TAPERED TAIL WELDED ON

NEW 1¼" M.S YOKE PLATE (WITH TOP
SURFACE GROUND SMOOTH) TO BEAR
AGAINST UNDERSIDE OF FLANGE TO
COLLAR SHARP INTERNAL ARRISES
TO BE GROUND OFF

OUTER ENDS OF JAWS REDUCED
FROM SQUARE SECTION TO ROUND
(LENGTH 4")

LLAR

OOKING UP

2⅝"

4"

11/15 Chantry Street, Andover. Exterior view. (Photograph by Garrick Palmer. Reproduced with kind permission of Hampshire Buildings Preservation Trust, Hampshire County Council.)

repair. The whole operation cost over £200 000, with financial support being obtained from the County Council. Specialist help was enlisted to deal with the restoration of the mill's working elements (Figs. 5.13, 5.14). Expert architectural advice from the architects department of the County Council and the work of volunteer groups such as the Hampshire Mills Group were two of the ingredients which assured the ultimate success of the venture. The sails were finally hoisted in 1990. Management of the project has been handed on to Eastleigh Borough Council who will promote the presentation and educational functions of what is now the only fully working tower wind-mill in Hampshire.

In October 1987 the County, along with other parts of southern England, experienced excep-

tionally strong winds. While the high winds cut a swathe of destruction through much of Hampshire's woodland, the storm left a small bonus in its wake as some kind of compensation for its havoc. This was the quantity of wind-blown oak. The Trust in co-operation with the County Council seized the initiative. As a result a store of appropriate timber has been laid down to season. This will be utilized for the Trusts own schemes and those of other agencies as circumstances make it appropriate.

Another example of the kind of broad-front approach adopted by the Trust is in the field of publications. As mentioned earlier considerable assistance was received from the Curator of Winchester City Museum in the work of survey and analysis at the Chantry Street site. Following

Bursledon Windmill. (Reproduced with kind permission of Hampshire County Council.)

on from this the Trust was able to assist with the publication of a record of the archaeological work undertaken by the Curator and a team of helpers from the Hampshire Field Club. Based on the team's survey notes and drawings, the result is a handsomly illustrated volume entitled *Medieval Hall Houses*. The publication goes some way to increase knowledge about the County's small but significant stock of vernacular buildings of this very important building type.

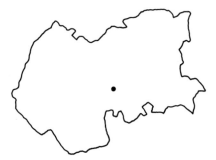

HEREFORD and WORCESTER

PROJECT 5.7, The County of Hereford and Worcester Building Preservation Trust, the Ledbury Project

The County of Hereford and Worcester Building Preservation Trust Ltd was established in 1965, at the time when the conservation movement was beginning in the UK, when there was a growing awareness of the loss of older buildings due to new development pressures. Several Worcestershire county councillors and other concerned people were taking a serious interest in the need to protect and care for such buildings throughout Worcestershire, and decided to establish a Trust that would actually take on the restoration of certain important older buildings that were at risk, and which for various reasons were falling into decay. The former Worcestershire County Council set up a fund of £5000 to start the work, with a Board of Directors, and with the County Planning Officer at the time and his staff taking a keen interest in this initiative. Some of the District Councils offered help, and had representation on the Board, as at present.

Since then, several buildings within the County have either been restored by the Trust, or have been the catalyst for such restoration, by suggesting ways and means of carrying out the work, by bringing the appropriate people together. Work has always been carried out on a revolving fund basis.

At the time of local government reorganization in 1974, the Trust became known as the County of Hereford and Worcester Building Preservation Trust Ltd. It is registered as a Charity, affiliated to the Civic Trust, and with the directors serving in a

voluntary capacity, with a secretary and treasurer. There is an Executive Committee of 10 directors who meet at six-weekly intervals. In addition to the financial contribution made to the Trust by the Hereford and Worcester County Council, their Planning Department's conservation officer offers professional advice and guidance at meetings. In

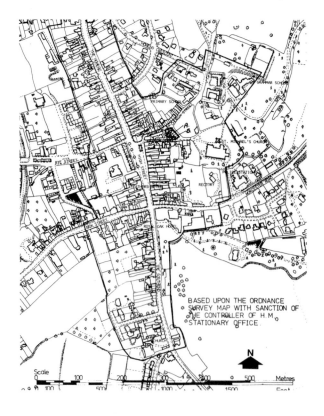

Ledbury Project. 1. Parish Church; 2. Courtyard; 3. Rutherglen; 4. Sergeant's House; 5. Magistrates' Court; 6. Heritage Centre; 7. Church Lane; 8. Abbot's Lodge; 9. The Walled Garden.

Ledbury Project. Rutherglen main elevation from south east before restoration. (Reproduced with kind permission of Herefordshire and Worcester Buildings Preservation Trust.)

1982, the Trust had its first opportunity to purchase a property and undertake a restoration scheme.

A group of prominent listed buildings, one of which is listed Grade II*, lay derelict in the centre of the fine old market town of Ledbury: the former magistrates court, police inspector's house, the 'Sergeant's House' and adjoining cottage, a coach house, which originally stored Ledbury's first horse-drawn fire engine, and a block of police cells. These buildings were owned by the Malvern Hills District Council, whose plans to demolish all but the police inspector's house for new houses, were dismissed by the Secretary of State for the Environment. These buildings were offered to the Trust for £2000, and after some heart searching at the size of such an undertaking, estimated at £450 000, at 1983 prices, decided to accept the offer and go ahead, with £40 000 in its reserves at that time.

Designs were prepared for conversion of the buildings into six houses, with a rear courtyard, all facing on to the fine old half-timbered Heritage Centre. The various statutory permissions were obtained, with fund-raising proceeding concurrently. A loan from the Architectural Heritage Fund was negotiated for £150 000, now fully repaid, and a grant of £80 000 from English Heritage. Several housing grants were offered by the Malvern Hills

District Council, and also a grant of £5500 from the County Council. A wide, and quite successful, search was made for funding bodies, and gradually the funds built up, although the Trust did not retain a professional fund raiser. A public appeal was launched within the Ledbury district, and various local organizations helped. As much publicity as possible was generated, including talks to local organizations. The Trust used every opportunity to generate confidence, as there was always the feeling of being 'outsiders', and the difficulty of operating on a county-wide basis as opposed to a specific town. Co-operation with local councillors and townspeople was considered essential.

Contract drawings, and documentation were prepared, tenders sought and a contract let to a building contractor from Malvern. An 80-week contract was agreed for the sum of £330 000, in mid 1986. The site foreman appointed was not only a skilled craftsman, but full of enthusiasm, and an excellent leader of the work force.

Extensive areas of wet rot had developed over the years, due to the absence of rainwater gutters, down-pipes, and many roof tiles and flashings. As stripping out continued, much dry rot and areas affected by death-watch beetle in one of the buildings were encountered. Later 'improvements', such as unsupported load-bearing partitions, had

Ledbury Project. Magistrates' Court. Interior in 1986 prior to conversion to three town houses. (Reproduced with kind permission of Herefordshire and Worcester Buildings Preservation Trust.)

Ledbury Project. Rutherglen interior showing raised cruck roof trusses dating from 1740. (Reproduced with kind permission of Herefordshire and Worcester Buildings Preservation Trust.)

Ledbury Project. Rutherglen main elevation from south east after restoration. (Reproduced with kind permission of Herefordshire and Worcester Buildings Preservation Trust.)

caused deflections in the most interesting internal structure, and near collapse in some areas. The old external walls had been built on stone foundations, which had to be underpinned with concrete. The buildings are examples of that interesting traditional period when timber-framed buildings were faced with Georgian facades.

Building work and fund-raising continued concurrently. Fortunately, the 1986/87 winter was reasonably good for building, so that the project was satisfactorily completed in the spring of 1988. The opening ceremony was attended by all the District Council representatives, the County Council, and representatives of the funding bodies, with the official opening by Lord Montague of Beaulieu, the then President of English Heritage. The six houses provided in the scheme were all successfully sold, providing capital to reinvest in further projects.

This search for further projects has resulted in various possibilities, including a Pump Room and Baths at Tenbury Wells, built in the 1850s following the discovery of health waters. The Trust has recently obtained the necessary consents for the restoration and conversion of a medieval Hall house to two dwellings at Bewdley, and is currently negotiating to purchase. A further possibility is at Redditch, a joint exercise with the Borough Council, to help restore a complex of farm buildings as a fishing heritage centre. The limiting factor is the need to be able to sell on the finished project, so that the restoration of non-profit making structures, such as ancient bridges, of which there are many in the County, can be undertaken.

Whilst over recent years the availability of buildings to restore has become more limited, over recent weeks, due to shortage of finance and the economic situation, there appears to be an increasing number of possibilities. The criterion is always that the buildings are 'at risk'.

HERTFORDSHIRE

PROJECT 5.8, The Forge, Much Hadham

The Hertfordshire Building Preservation Trust was established by the Hertfordshire County Council in 1963, after some members had expressed concern at the fate of some historic buildings in the County, which would be lost unless they could be rescued and restored. The Trust was incorporated as a private company, limited by guarantee and subsequently registered with the Charity Commissioners. It was intended in those early years that the Trust's activities should complement the work of the local authorities in the county, and since 1974, following local government reorganization, the Trust has worked alongside the County Council and the 10 District Councils, encouraging the role of the private sector in the renovation of historic buildings, within the constraints imposed by the necessity to preserve and enhance the character of these buildings.

The Trust has now been in existence for over 25 years, and during this time, has undertaken, on a revolving fund basis the restoration of dozens of historic buildings that were under threat, neglected or 'at risk'. Hertfordshire County Council has given the Trust, not only technical and professional advice, but, until recently – with the appointment of a part-time Executive Secretary – all the important administrative and secretarial support. The availability of skilled staff, both professional and craftsmen, is, indeed, very limited and the County Council and the Trust, faced with this problem, and the shortage of financial resources to cope with an ever increasing workload, sought new ways of tackling this problem.

The Forge, Much Hadham. Mr Page, the last blacksmith, who died in 1983 in his 91st year.

(a)

(b)

The Forge, Much Hadham. Exterior view before (a) and after (b) restoration. (Reproduced with kind permission of Hertfordshire County Council.)

The County Planning and Estates Department of the County Council undertook an arrangement whereby it would work more closely with the Trust. It seconded its specialist team dealing with design and conservation matters to the Trust for an initial period of three years. Arrangements have been made by the Trust to offer specialist advice to all District and Borough Councils on a half day per week basis. Any time over and above this will be charged by the Trust by agreement. In the longer term, it is hoped that a larger conservation team will enable specialists to be recruited, or combined, in a range of architectural and constructional skills to offer an added service to the Districts. An archaeological service could also be provided to the District Councils, based upon the information contained in the Sites and Monuments Record held in County Hall and administered separately by the County Archaeological Officer. The Trust, through this consultancy service, is able to offer advice on planning and listed building applications, particularly in conservation areas, and on historic buildings and grant-aid for repair work. A set of leaflets, which forms the Hertfordshire Conservation File, has been prepared to assist owners of properties, architects, builders, surveyors and others involved in good conservation practice.

Whilst the Trust, over the years, has, in the main, concentrated on domestic dwellings, it is also prepared to consider other worthy buildings.

Recently their attention was drawn to the imminent closure of the Old Forge at Much Hadham. One family had owned the Forge since 1811, and with the death of the last blacksmith of the family line in 1983, the opportunity afforded itself to save a fine building, and its forge as a valuable village feature, and to use this restoration in order to promote the theme of educational and training possibilities allied to the heritage concept.

With help from the Museum's Development Officer for Hertfordshire, the curator of the Cambridge Folk Museum and a small workforce supplied by Community Rural Aid Ltd, work began in 1987. The work on restoring not only the forge to working order but also the building itself is now completed and included in the restoration is a shop and information/display area as well as the Farriers Shop and Bellows Room being retained. The public, along with schoolgroups, will have the opportunity of seeing metal goods being made and horses being shod; a common enough site in many villages not so many years ago, but a rarity in these days of 'high tec'.

The cost of the project amounted to £79 000, which was grant-aided by a contribution of £1000 from the County Council and £2000 from the East Herts District Council. A sum of nearly £41 000, however, was raised by donations – a significant figure which greatly assisted the Trust in its ability to complete the repair and restoration work satisfactorily. In the early days of the work, the Manpower Services Commission, through their Community Programme, funded the workforce, but this was subsequently withdrawn, with the demise of the Scheme nationally.

(a)

The Forge, Much Hadham. Interior view before (a) and after (b) restoration. (Reproduced with kind permission of Hertfordshire County Council.)

(b)

KENT

PROJECT 5.9, 79/80 High Street, Gravesend

These two early eighteenth-century houses stand at the northern end of the High Street, a few yards from the original pier at which passengers would take the ferry across the Thames to Tilbury. They had been built soon after a disastrous fire which swept through the town in 1727, and were two of only a handful to survive a further six fires between 1731 and 1857. Converted to shops at an early date, the three-storey, timber-framed and weather-boarded buildings functioned happily until the 1970s, when large-scale shopping redevelopments elsewhere in the town, a ring road and the resiting of the ferry terminal deprived the northern end of the High Street of its trade and the buildings went into decay. By 1984, serious doubts were being expressed about their survival, with No. 79 having a narrow escape from fire and No. 80 showing signs of sliding away towards the site of a demolished building next door, where unsightly raking shores were erected. Local fire chiefs called for the buildings to be demolished as a death trap, and they were very nearly to be proved right.

Fortunately, the plight of the High Street, and the fire in No. 79, galvanized Gravesham Borough Council into action. With all-party support, a team of members and officers met all property owners in the street and encouraged them to repair their buildings. The Kent Building Preservation Trust had already identified the buildings as a high priority and a partnership was soon forged with Gravesham, in which Gravesham funded the purchase of 79 and 80 by the Trust on the basis of a loan, convertible on completion of repairs into a grant.

It took nearly four years to come up with a viable scheme, to obtain funding for it and start on site, although internal stripping and tidying was carried out free by Manpower Services. Residential/shop reinstatement was soon discovered to be uneconomic by a very large measure, and a reluctant decision was made to convert the buildings to offices, although even this seemed to be uneconomic, according to early pessimistic cost assumptions (over £200 000) and a cautious valuation (about £100 000).

The process then became one of narrowing the gap to the point where the Architectural Heritage Fund, English Heritage, Gravesham Borough Council and KBPT's own Bank were satisfied that the project would cover its costs. Further investigations suggested that the condition of the buildings was not as bad as first feared; the AHF valuation began to rise. Eventually both settled at £150 000, leaving only the cost of fees, VAT etc., to be bridged by grant.

The final costs were met by a loan of £130 000 from the Architectural Heritage Fund, and English Heritage offered a £50 000 grant under the provisions of S.3A of the Historic Buildings and Ancient Monuments Act 1953, for the repair and maintenance of buildings of outstanding architectural or historic interest. Gravesham Borough Council offered £21 500, and Kent County Council (Impact Scheme) £15 000, and over £4000 was raised by contributions from other Trusts. Emboldened, KBPT went out to tender, only to find that the lowest tender was £190 000. Fortunately, the property boom was by then taking off, and work started with the help of an additional

(a)

(b)

79/80 High Street, Gravesend before (a) and after (b) restoration. (Reproduced with kind permission of Alan Fuller.)

£30 000 loan from AHF, and a top-up loan of £15 000 from the 'Impact' scheme, a joint initiative of Kent County Council and Gravesham, to concentrate grant money in one place, where the 'impact' would be most dramatic.

Once work started, the picture darkened somewhat as unforseen structural problems emerged. The chimney stack of No. 80 was found to be exerting a heavier than expected load on the structure and appeared unstable. A steel frame was devised and cleverly inserted into the timber frame of the building to take the load. A large number of elements of the timber frame needed replacement and floor loadings were increased. Fire precaution work was extensive, with plasterboard inserted behind the panelling, which was carefully removed and refixed.

The building was sold virtually within weeks of its completion, at a price in excess of its valuation price. Then disaster struck. The adjacent three buildings of similar date (including a fine panelled house which Gravesham had decided to repair itself) were burnt down in the middle of the night. Only the fire precautions saved Nos 79/80 from the same fate. As it was, a falling chimney stack and waterlogging damaged No. 79 extensively, although No. 80 was unharmed. The new owners, who provide small serviced office space, had to repair the building again, with the help of the Trust's structural engineer. Plans are being made to rebuild the adjacent buildings in sympathetic style, so that the High Street once again provides the atmosphere it once had. Although the results were not quite what the Kent Building Preservation Trust had hoped, the project did at least save part of the townscape from Gravesend's traditional scourge of fire.

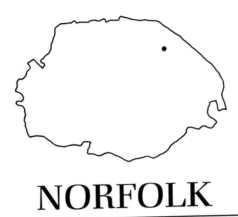

NORFOLK

PROJECT 5.10, Revolving Fund Schemes

In 1974, the new County Council and the Norfolk Society were concerned at the number of redundant historic listed buildings, throughout the county. Most had lain empty for several years with no attempt by the private sector to undertake their repair. The Norfolk Historic Buildings Trust was established in January 1977, as a partnership between the County Council and the Norfolk Society. There are 30 members, nine of whom form the Board of Directors. The Trust commenced work with the benefit of annual 'pump-priming' contributions from the County Council of £10 000.

Numbers 34 and 36 Vicarage Street, North Walsham, were the first properties to be taken on. Bought for just over £10 000 in 1978, the Trust repaired and converted them into four town houses at a cost of some £140 000 (Fig. 5.25). The houses were sold and the money ploughed back into the Trust's revolving fund. The County Council made available a loan of some £38 000, although not all of this was taken up. The Trust broke even on this project. Two projects have followed Compulsory Purchase action by Local Authorities. The first was at Beeston Beegis, where the County Council bought a Grade I listed farmhouse for £30 000 and passed it on for restoration to the Trust for the same amount. The Trust incurred a loss of some £2680 on this project. The second was at Foulsham, where the District Council acted and sold the property to the Trust, together with the building next door, a former public house. The cost of acquisition was £42 500

for the two properties, and their repair and conversion cost was £70 000. Following sale of the properties, the Trust made a loss of £2760. The two other revolving-fund schemes have been completed, both of which showed significant deficits: £9117 and £20 390.

The work of the Trust is appreciated by Parish Councils and local amenity societies and, of course, by the new owners and occupiers of the refurbished properties. The support of Trust to the work of the District and County Councils is also evident, particularly where compulsory purchase of historic buildings at risk is the only course left if they are to be saved.

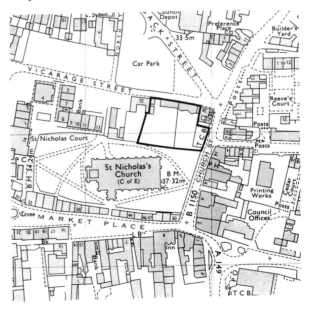

(a)

(b)

34–36 Vicarage Street, North Walsham. Street frontage (a) and garden frontage (b) before restoration. (Reproduced with kind permission of Norfolk County Council.)

34–36 Vicarage Street, North Walsham, after restoration. (Reproduced with kind permission of Norfolk County Council.)

SURREY

PROJECT 5.11, Historic Buildings Trust, 8a and b East Street, Farnham

The Trust was set up by the Surrey County Council in 1980 with a substantial financial input to help protect the county's historic heritage. The aims and objectives of the Trust are four-fold: to buy and renovate threatened historic buildings and then sell them, with the proceeds being recycled into a revolving fund to undertake further projects; to give financial support to local planning authorities to enable them to serve repair notices on owners of threatened historic buildings; to provide expert advice and encouragement to owners, or prospective owners of historic buildings; and to make small grants to owners for the repair of their buildings. County Council representatives serve with other community and amenity representatives on the Board of Management and the County Council officers provide much of the preliminary professional guidance.

The Trust has been directly involved with four restoration/conversion projects during its first 10 years of operation. These have been funded, using the limited finance of the Trust, on a revolving fund basis. Two of the schemes, including the Chatley Semaphore Tower (which is described in greater detail in Chapter 4), have been undertaken in association with the County Council. One scheme was dealt with by a local Trust, whilst further schemes are under consideration.

The first restoration project, 8a and b East Street, Farnham, was completed in 1983. The works involved the restoration and conversion of the first floor to offices of this town-centre building which, although dating from the late sixteenth century, had been the subject of much alteration over the years. A second project, at North Lodge, Chertsey, was a building situated at the edge of a Health Authority site, which was purchased and resold with the benefit of a detailed design and specification for its restoration and extension. The Trust also advised on the restoration of The Summerhouse at Godalming, a small structure owned by a local Trust.

The projects undertaken with the County Council were greatly advanced by the Trust's enthusiasm and willingness to be involved with the survey and feasibility studies which facilitated positive decisions by the County Council. The County has a generally bouyant property market which leaves a low level of need for intervention in respect of neglected properties. The Trust has, therefore, operated flexibly, using its ability to encourage and assist.

The Trust has recently published a book by Roderick Gradidge entitled *The Surrey Style* which explores the evolution of historic domestic building in the County, culminating in the richly prolific years of 1880–1930, involving the works of CFA Voysey, Ralph Nevill, Edwin Lutyens and Harold Falkner.

To celebrate its 10th anniversary in 1990, the Trust initiated an annual award scheme. Open to private owners, civic and amenity societies, commercial owners and local and national government in Surrey, the 1990 Award was awarded to the restoration work at Stoke Mill, Guildford, as the best adaptation of an old building to new uses, whilst preserving its original character.

8a and 8b East Street, Farnham. (Reproduced with kind permission of Surrey County Council.)

WILTSHIRE

PROJECT 5.12, Church Street, Calne

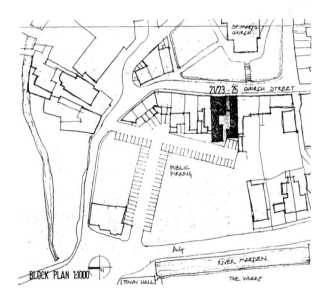

BLOCK PLAN 1:1000

Calne is a market town of some 11 000 people and much of its livelihood up to the early 1980s derived from the local Harris factories, who were in the business of bacon-curing and sausage-making on a national scale. Following acquisition and company reorganization, the 200-year-old Harris business was closed in 1983, leaving the town not only with the problem of unemployment but also with a number of empty and decaying properties. There were 2.4 hectares (6 acres) of factory buildings in the centre of the town which were acquired by North Wiltshire District Council, and demolition of the buildings began in 1985.

In June 1986 the Calne Development Project Trust was set up, initially with a life of three years, through the generous and imaginative sponsorship of Wiltshire County Council, North Wiltshire District Council and Calne Town Council. Their annual contribution towards the administration costs of 50% (£20 000) attracted an offer of 25% (£10 000) from English Heritage, so leaving the Project itself to raise the balance of 25%. The Project is a registered Charity, is independent of the local authorities and is governed by an Executive Committee on which the sponsoring authorities are represented.

In 1986 the Wiltshire Historic Buildings Trust, which had existed since 1967 and had successfully undertaken a range of property restorations, was approached by the Calne Project with a view to carrying out a rehabilitation scheme in Church Street. Many of the buildings in Church Street

had been acquired by the business so that the factory buildings could be extended over the rear gardens of the properties, and a number of these buildings had fallen into disrepair. The regeneration of the buildings in Church Street was seen as an essential part of the improvement of the town centre. Following on from a Calne Project feasibility study, the Trust agreed to carry out a three-phase rehabilitation scheme and acquired the first phase buildings Nos 7, 9 and 11 in 1987, and architects were appointed.

Phase 1 comprised 7, 9 and 11 Church Street, with retail use on the ground floor of each, storage on the first floor of the smallest shop, No. 7, and

289

(a)

(b)

Nos 7, 9 and 11 Church Street, Calne before (a) and after
(b) restoration. (Reproduced with kind permission of
Wiltshire County Council.)

(a)

(b)

No. 13 Church Street, Calne before (a) and after (b) restoration. (Reproduced with kind permission of Wiltshire County Council.)

Nos 13 and 15 Church Street, Calne after restoration. (Reproduced with kind permission of Wiltshire County Council.)

self-contained flats above Nos 9 and 11. Externally, redundant rear additions were removed and the area rationalized with new wings to give storage for the shops together with delivery yards. Work started in March 1988 and was completed in February 1989 at a cost of £159 000.

The second phase of the work included Nos 13 and 15. It was considered important that, for historical reference, as the shop at No. 13 had formerly been the retail outlet for the factory, its 1930s bronze and marble shop front, although in an advanced state of deterioration, should be retained and refurbished. On completion this phase provided two shops with one maisonette. Work started in June 1989 and finished in May 1990 and the total cost was £186 500.

Work started in June 1990 on Nos 21, 23 and 25 and is the final phase of this project. Construction works are in progress and a previously unknown timber-framed structure has been exposed. Work involves the rationalization of the original structure with removal of more recent alterations and additions. The scheme provides for two retail units on the Church Street frontage, with a

passage-way to a courtyard at the rear which is surrounded by three further retail units. This area will have access from the new public car park to the rear of the site. On the upper floors, provision is made for three self-contained flats. Again, the original features are being retained and new work designed to reflect the quality and craftsmanship of the original. Work finished early in 1992 at a cost of approximately £400 000.

Finance for the work has been from the Trust's resources supplemented by conservation grants from English Heritage and housing grants from North Wiltshire District Council. All of the completed properties have been sold, thus contributing to the aims of bringing life back into the street and also allowing the Trust to fulfil its objectives as a revolving fund. The Wiltshire Historic Buildings Trust Ltd is a non-profit making company limited by guarantee which has been registered as a Charity for the sole purpose of preserving buildings of architectural and historic interest in the county. The Trust receives financial, administrative and technical support from the County Council.

6

HISTORIC PARKS AND GARDENS

HASKELL

PROJECTS

Drawing overleaf shows Hestercombe House Gardens, Somerset.

INTRODUCTION

In recent years there has been a growing realization that, as a nation, we ought to take more care in protecting historic parks and gardens. Conservation Area legislation has been available to Local Planning Authorities since the Civic Amenities Act 1967, while the statutory protection of buildings of architectural or historic interest dates back nearly half a century to the Town and Country Planning Act 1947. The first State action for the preservation of archaeological sites more than doubles that time, owing its origins to the Ancient Monuments Act of 1882, but, for historic parks and gardens, no special facilities have been available in planning law other than the limited provisions of Tree Preservation Orders.

However, a long process of quiet persuasion by bodies such as the Garden History Society and the National Council for the Conservation of Plants and Gardens (NCCPG) has directed attention towards what has seemed to be a gap in our conservation legislation. For a nation blessed with such an outstanding heritage of parks and gardens, many of which have international acclaim, this shortcoming seems hard to explain. This situation has now been remedied to a certain extent by the provisions of the National Heritage Act 1983, the Act which set up the Historic Buildings and Monuments Commission ('English Heritage') and which includes some important advances in the protection of historic parks and gardens.

REGISTERS OF GARDENS

The most important extension of activity brought about by the 1983 Act is the authority given to English Heritage to prepare a 'Register of gardens and other land of historic interest'. There was wide consultation to provide information about sites which might be candidates for inclusion in the Register and a key role was taken by the Centre for the Conservation of Historic Parks and Gardens at the University of York. The work at York formed part of the National Survey and Inventory of Gardens and Parks of Historic Interest, intended to be more extensive than the Register. The Registers have now been published in sections on a County basis between 1984 and 1988.

In Wales, there is no such Register of small landscapes of cultural, aesthetic or historic importance. This has prompted the International Council on Monuments and Sites (ICOMOS) to take the initiative in proposing that a register would identify landscape sites important to the National Heritage of Wales. Sites would include Victorian and Edwardian reservoirs, designed landscapes including parks and gardens, small islands of particular character and historic landscapes of a specific development period such as Celtic, Monastic or nineteenth-century industrial, and specific landscapes, such as Portmeirion. The register would have no legal status and inclusion in it would not bring any statutory responsibilities on the owners. However, its purpose would be to inform owners, local authorities, statutory bodies and the public of the importance of these sites in order to better protect them against destruction, development and decay which might otherwise take place through ignorance of their worth. The inventory would be compiled by consultants working on a county by county basis over a four-year period, with costs being shared between Cadw, the private owners and the Welsh Counties. The survey is now under way with Gwent being the first county to be surveyed.

While the Registers for England and Wales are a most important step forward in the protection of designed historic landscapes, they do have their limitations. No new statutory planning controls are imposed, such as exist for other aspects of environmental heritage protection. Their main purpose is to serve as a notification to owners, Local Planning Authorities and government agencies of all kinds, that a park or garden is of historical interest, so that whenever development is proposed or conservation measures and grant aid become available, due consideration can be given to the special merit of the site. The existence of the Register should, however, put an end to such situations as a new road being proposed across an historic park, or a housing scheme being given planning permission on the site of an historic garden, because neither owner nor local authority realized the special significance of the place.

Castle Tor, Torquay. These 1920s gardens are listed Grade II and are included in Devon's register of Historic Parks and Gardens as a Grade II item.

GARDEN TRUSTS

Partly as a result of the limitations brought about by any new legislation on the subject, local organizations have been set up to preserve and restore parks and gardens of historic value. This most exciting initiative towards garden conservation in the country has taken different forms, with different terms of reference and priorities, but typically it is a county-based Trust, having close relations with a County Council. Each Trust has developed in its own way, benefiting from the experiences of others already established, to meet the perceived needs of its own county, by maximizing the particular talents and other resources available locally. They all share the view that only local activity could halt and reverse the process of neglect and dereliction highlighted during the Register survey period. In most instances, County Councils have been willing partners in the establishment of the County Trusts, recognizing the enormous potential of local 'amateur' expertise to assist County conservation and landscape officers in their expanded roles. County Council help and advice in the legal procedures of adopting a Constitution, achieving Charitable and limited liability status, have proved invaluable, as have the more tangible provisions of meeting-place facilities, secretarial support and inaugural and project grants.

The earliest Trusts to be established were almost an entirely southern counties phenomenon, with Sussex, Hampshire, Avon, Wiltshire and Devon setting the pace and creating the model and precedent for others to follow. In some ways the Sussex Historic Gardens Trust stands apart from the rest, not only because it was the first to be founded in 1982, but also by the inclusion of 'historic' in its name. Most Trusts subsequently have preferred to omit this reference, to widen their potential for involvement in modern gardens, including the enormous education value of school grounds. The Hampshire Gardens Trust followed in 1984, in many ways creating the 'model' for others, particularly with regard to the extremely close co-operation with the County Council, already renowned for its work in the field of nature conservation. The Trust's 'Pleasure Grounds' exhibition at the Southampton City Art Gallery in 1987 brought together pictures, artefacts and archive material relating to Hampshire gardens from all over the country. It succeeded in creating a national audience, as well as informing the people in the County of the interests and activities of the Trust.

The Avon Gardens Trust grew out of the Avon County Community Environment Scheme and has managed to carry out a considerable amount of practical survey and repair work under the Manpower Services Commission provisions. Changing government policies in this area, however, have proved a considerable problem and have resulted in a major cutback in the Trust's activities. In a County where the pressure on land for development is very high, the Trust takes an active part in planning negotiations with developers, local authorities and conservation societies. The Wiltshire Gardens Trust, in contrast to most other County Trusts, has not benefited from a partnership role with its County Council but, instead, has grown out of the County's branch of the NCCPG. This has resulted in a strong priority being given to historic gardens surveys and lays considerable emphasis on the importance of gardens with exceptional plants. For each garden in the survey programme, the modern visual record is matched to site plans and other documentary evidence discovered and collated in the archive search.

The Devon Gardens Trust, launched in Spring 1988, has witnessed the differing priorities of its near neighbours in Hampshire, Avon and Wiltshire and has tailored its terms of reference to adopt aspects of all three, at a scale of activity appropriate to its resources. The emphasis, however, is on developing close relationships with the County's 10 District Councils, seen as the lifeline to collaboration on development, grants and restoration projects.

The last two to three years have seen sufficient County Gardens Trusts established or mooted to warrant co-operation on regional and national levels. A liaison meeting at Urchfont Manor in Wiltshire, in 1987, was the first of a regular cycle of meetings for the south-west Trusts, and provided the trigger for Devon, Cornwall, Dorset and Somerset to seek their own County Trusts. The first National Gardens Trusts seminar was held at Weston Park, on the borders of Staffordshire and Shropshire in 1988, attracting representatives from all over the country. Part of its brief was to spread the message to the midland and northern counties of England. With Norfolk, Kent, Dorset, Cornwall, Yorkshire, Essex, Derbyshire, South Staffordshire (a District Council initiative), Isle of Wight, Hertfordshire, Northamptonshire, Surrey, Somerset and Wales all now established or in the process of doing so, pressure for an Association of Gardens Trusts became irresistible and was formally set up early in 1990.

Garden Trusts terms of reference

Although it was the national Register of parks and gardens of English Heritage that gave the initial impetus towards the founding of Gardens Trusts, their activities have developed well beyond the monitoring of threats to a rather limited list of sites of national importance. In some form or another, all Gardens Trusts have adopted four major terms of reference, albeit with differing emphases.

- Firstly, a programme of surveys, not only to discover gardens of regional or county importance, some of which may be eligible for additions to the Register, but also to create a modern data-base of archive material; the surveys, therefore, are both on-site and in Record Offices, Reference Libraries etc.
- Secondly, to be vigilant in the planning process so that sites worthy of protection are not lost through inappropriate development or ignorance. This involves close co-operation with conservation and planning officers of County and District Councils and requires the Trusts to attain a reputation for having a reliable judgement on the importance of historic designed landscapes. County Councils are currently framing policies in their Structure Plans to ensure the proper recognition of their historic parks and gardens.

- Thirdly, Trusts must be able to offer practical assistance on projects of restoration and repair. In the early years of a Trust's existence, this is most likely to be in the form of advice rather than grant-aid, so that the opportunity for a project can be recognized and the site owner be encouraged to take the appropriate steps to ensure a worthwhile and beneficial result.
- Finally, the educational role of Gardens Trusts cannot be overstressed; indeed, the Charity Commissioners will see it as an essential element of its Constitution if charitable status is to be sought. Education, in its widest meaning, will include a close liaison with local schools so that future generations will develop an understanding of the historical importance of our landscape heritage, but also the educational opportunities in a school's outdoor environment. It will also involve programmes of talks and lectures for members of the public, exhibitions, demonstrations and publications, so that the message can be imparted to an increasingly interested, aware and concerned public. Trusts are assisted in all of these aims by the quality, enthusiasm and numerical strength of its members. All strive to attract membership in a competitive market, but each Trust has its own story to tell of how an unknown local 'expert' has surfaced and been 'discovered'.

Garden Trusts – examples of projects

Although the Gardens Trust movement is in its infancy, valuable inputs have been made to several important projects of research, archaeological investigation, enhancement, repair and restoration. These have included works on the parks and gardens themselves, as well as the Listed Building structures within them. A project of this type is the restoration of the great Orangery at Margam Park in West Glamorgan, the largest and, arguably, one of the most beautiful in Britain. At Great Dixter at Northiam in East Sussex, the timber-framed medieval Yeoman's House – restored earlier this century by Lutyens – forms the backdrop to some magnificently laid-out gardens, including vernacular farm buildings which have benefited from a restoration project, with grant aid under the provisions of the Local Authorities (Historic Buildings) Act 1962 and storm damage insurance.

Brickwall School, also at Northiam, was an early beneficiary of Garden Trust involvement in garden restoration, which included a new feature of the topiary chess garden. A major scheme, that benefited from the provisions of the MSC Community Programme, was Parc Glynllifon, near the historic town of Caernarfon in Gwynedd. Here, an abandoned historic garden, with many architectural and landscape historic features, has been carefully restored and a visitor centre built at a total cost of nearly £1 500 000.

For the restoration project at Wrest Park, at Silsoe in Bedfordshire, archaeological techniques were an integral aspect of the scheme, when drought stress marks in the garden lawns revealed the position of the old house. Similar archaeological work to the gardens at Kirby Hall in Northamptonshire shows how it is possible to reveal and understand the great gardens of the past. The amazing Mellor's Garden, in Cheshire, was rediscovered in the course of a Listed Building survey and has now been restored meticulously, while the Hampshire Gardens Trust has been active in the research and restoration of garden projects at Tylney Hall and Marshcourt. Each of these has its story to tell, as can be seen in the detailed case studies that follow.

Some of our historic parklands, however, are increasingly falling prey to the growing threats of commercial leisure developments, such as new golf centres. Currently County and District Councils are endeavouring to formulate strategic policies to both control and restrict this form of development that can often irreparably damage the intrinsic landscape qualities of a parkland. English Heritage, equally concerned at the effect of these developments, is publishing policy guidance on the subject.

At a time when conservation issues are to the forefront in environmental concern, the Gardens Trust movement seems unlikely to founder in public apathy. Indeed, *This Common Inheritance*[1] gives deservedly special mention to Garden Trusts in The Heritage chapter: 'County garden trusts continue to flourish and the Government welcomes the valuable work they do in protecting our gardens'.

For those who wish guidance and, indeed, further information, both the Garden History Society, and the Inspector of Historic Parks and Gardens at English Heritage, are able to help.

I am grateful to Mr David Richardson, a conservation officer with Devon County Council, and Secretary to the Devon Gardens Trust, for providing much of this test.

BEDFORDSHIRE

PROJECT 6.1, Wrest Park, Silsoe

Wrest Park, in the centre of Bedfordshire's green-sand ridge, lies on a low knoll of Oxford clay just east of the present village of Silsoe. The estate has been in existence probably since the Domesday survey in 1086, but the present interest of the site is its nineteenth-century house set amongst gardens which were laid out in the early 1700s. These replaced a medieval house, completely lost from view. The gardens at Wrest Park suffered from neglect during the years of World War II and for some time after, but are being restored. The house is presently in the care of English Heritage.

The restoration which will take nearly fifteen years to complete is based partly on surviving areas of garden together with maps drawn in the early 1700s by Kip and Roque. The plans were not altogether consistent with evidence from the present gardens as over the years some reorientation of the paths, tree panels and canals had taken place. Nevertheless, sufficient remained of the early eighteenth-century garden for English Heritage to consider restoring some areas close to the original.

Archaeological techniques, which have proved useful in some other major gardens, were considered applicable in order to achieve accuracy in form and dating, and archaeology is now an integral part of the restoration scheme. First the site was examined on the ground in comparison with the early map evidence and the latest survey by the Public Services Agency. At this stage precise objectives could be defined. These were related to the alignment of paths, the erosion of canals and the position of the old house which had been demolished in 1826.

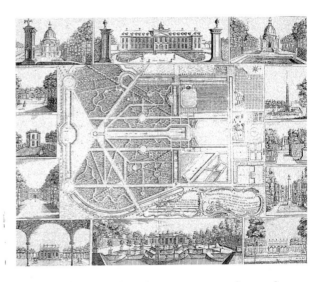

Wrest Park restoration aims to recreate the gardens as they appeared in the early eighteenth century. This garden was drawn by John Rocque twice – once in 1735 and again in 1737. (Reproduced with kind permission of Bedfordshire County Council.)

In 1989 the position of the old house, hitherto only known approximately, was recorded by surveying parched areas in the garden lawns. These had appeared above the demolished remains of the old house as the grass dried during the hot dry summer, where the stony remains of the structure were close to the surface. By comparing the lines of parching with plans of the house drawn without scales from earlier descriptions, the precise position of the medieval and

Wrest Park. A general view showing the upper garden. Once this was the site of the old house which was demolished in the 1820s. (Reproduced with kind permission of Bedfordshire County Council.)

eighteenth-century house was mapped. Many of the internal architectural features were located and better defined. Earlier in 1988 and in 1989 the canals were emptied so that the silt could be cleared. This presented an opportunity to examine where the most westerly lake, the Leg O'Mutton, had been extended into the floor of the amphitheatre to the south. It was a situation in which archaeology was to directly affect the restoration. Following the definition of erosion patterns, revetting and construction levels under the amphitheatre bank, the lake was restored to its 1735 shape. The precise dimensions were derived from the archaeological work.

Similar levels of silt had accumulated in the central 'Long Canal' and during their excavation the base of a statue was recorded, an otherwise unknown garden ornament.

The most extensive area of work was with path orientation. These are important because vistas, alignments and secret or hidden nooks are an important component in the garden. Sections were cut across existing paths to identify the type of surfacing, the alignment and if possible the date they were laid. The results suggested that paths of orange sand and stone were juxtaposed with those of grass, a technique more familiar in smaller more ornate French gardens of a slightly earlier period.

The cost of the work over the last three years has been in the order of £21 000 and has been met in full by the Properties in Care, Midlands Division of English Heritage. The Archaeology Service which is part of Bedfordshire County Council Planning Department's Conservation and Archaeology Section carried out the work, liaising closely with the County's Record Office on documentary research. The restoration works were carried out by English Heritage's consultants.

There were a number of technical problems. Firstly the garden is open to the general public during the summer months. Since most archaeological trenches are unsightly and can be dangerous, excavation was timed not to intrude on the open season. It was also carefully programmed to allow restoration works to take place in stages so that the garden had time to recover most of its aesthetic values.

At times the task was awkward, with the need to work around fallen trees, and at times hazardous when taking deep cuttings through the artificial banks of the amphitheatre. The most difficult problems of all, however, arose with the lakes. Parts of the silts had to be coffered to keep out the water, and the only way to get to the areas of investigation was to wade through thigh-high reeking mud!

The programme of works, the restoration and archaeological work was designed to achieve two goals: to enhance the gardens for the pleasure of the public and to increase our understanding of the development of gardens in a period of English history when the estate garden was as much a statement of power by the owner and designer as a place of recreation and beauty. The restoration and garden archaeology aspects form a part of a small standing exhibition mounted by English Heritage, a demonstration of the value of the project in their eyes. In addition English Heritage held a national seminar in 1989 on the problems and potential of garden archaeology at Wrest Park, using the local work as a pivotal demonstration of the essential role archaeological techniques can play in the authentic restoration of one of the most pleasurable aspects of our English heritage.

CHESHIRE

PROJECT 6.2, Mellor's Garden, Rainow

Within 0.8 hectares (2 acres) of a small Pennine valley, James Mellor (1796–1891) devoted the last fifty years of his life to creating a garden to illustrate the religious teachings of Emanuel Swedenborg (1688–1772), a Swede, who was one of the most important intellectual figures of the eighteenth century. Swedenborg was not only a pure scientist whose many discoveries were well in advance of his time, but he was interested in physiology and is well known today for his philosophical writings, believing in the correspondence of the natural and spiritual world. It

was this that consumed James Mellor, who undertook the allegories of Pilgrim's Progress to highlight the aspects of Swedenborg's Christian teachings, producing the many layers of meaning in a physical form in his garden.

The garden consists of a network of paths, steps, waterfeatures and other devices which can be used to illustrate to visitors today, all the major

Mellor's Gardens, Rainow, showing Christian's progress through the allegorical garden. (Reproduced with kind permission of Cheshire County Council.)

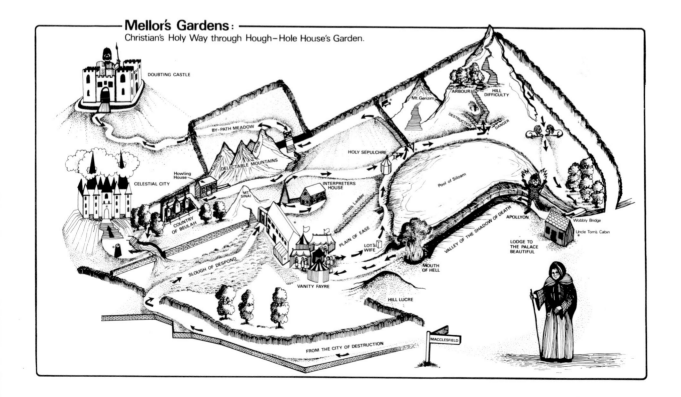

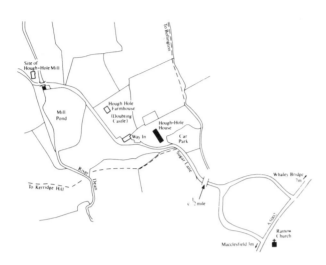

Mellor's Gardens, Rainow. General view. (Reproduced with kind permission of Cheshire County Council.)

incidents in Bunyan's book. They, too, can follow the route from the City of Destruction to the Celestial City, and learn the lessons that Christian learnt on his journey. Also included in the gardens are the Delectable Mountains, the Valley of the Shadow of Death, Vanity Fayre and the Slough of Despond.

In addition, Mellor added an episode from Uncle Tom's Cabin, and a range of stone inscriptions containing religious quotations, carved by himself. The garden is structured by the route corresponding to the Pilgrims Progress, although other elements are interwoven. Most parts of the garden had Biblical names: for instance, the mill pond was called the Pool of Siloam, and the overflowing stream the River Jordan. The summerhouse was Bethel.

The garden planting also carried on the theme of Biblical names, and those plants and flowers and trees that are mentioned in the Bible have been used, bearing in mind the climatic differences between the Near East and the hills of Cheshire, in which case the nearest practical equivalent was considered. The Bible mentions a surprising range of plants which may be used by the gardener, and some of the trees planted

by James Mellor have quite possibly survived. Apple, ash, pine, willow, oak and sycamore trees are all to be found in the Old Testament. Whilst it will be impossible to recreate the original scheme, it is still feasible to add new plants which fit the spirit of what was originally intended.

The potential of the garden was discovered and researched by a previous Principal Archaeologist in Cheshire County Council, during the listed building resurvey of the county. By a detailed study of the surviving remains, and the few documentary sources then known, he rediscovered the route through the garden.

The owners of the garden undertook the hard work of reconstruction, with only minimal grant aid. After a gap of 93 years since James Mellor's guided trips around the garden ceased, the garden was reopened for visitors in 1984. The County Council have published an illustrated guidebook, now in its second edition, and the gardens are open to booked parties, and on four open days per annum. The garden is one of several historic gardens in Cheshire 'rediscovered' and interpreted by the Council's conservation unit staff since 1974.

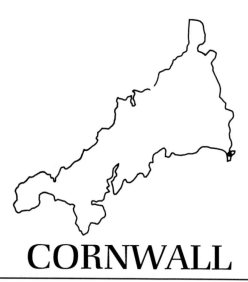

CORNWALL

PROJECT 6.3, Mount Edgcumbe Country Park

Mount Edgcumbe, the home of the Earls of Mount Edgcumbe, was bought jointly by the Plymouth City Council and Cornwall County Council as a Country Park in 1971. The original owners had sought redevelopment of parts of the parkland in the late 1960s but this had been turned down by the Local Authorities. Eventually, it was offered to Plymouth City Council for a recreational area as the inhabitants of Plymouth had long been able to use the park and the City Council were known to be anxious to buy it if possible. The purchase completed by the Joint Authority comprised a total land holding of 350 hectares (865 acres) at the tip of the Rame peninsula. The area can be neatly divided into two – the old landscape park as created by the Mount Edgcumbe family which covers 160 hectares (395 acres) on the portion of the peninsula coast facing Plymouth and, broken only by the twin villages of Cawsand and Kingsand, the coastal strip with steeply sloping woods, scrubland and fields stretching for 11 km (7 miles) westward around the south coast of Cornwall. Within the Country Park are 30.7 hectares (76 acres) of ornamental gardens together with a number of buildings, of which 50 are listed Grade II and six Grade II*.

At this time the historical significance of Mount Edgcumbe was little recognized. The grounds were totally neglected and overgrown and the park had been used extensively by American and Canadian troops during the war. Therefore, the Authorities' main aim was to open up the park for the public, to make the flower gardens as attractive as possible, create footpath systems and recreational areas and, at the same time, remove the worst examples of the war-time structures. At this time the house and its immediate gardens of 8 hectares (20 acres) were retained by the Earl of Mount Edgcumbe for his own use. Expertise was to be supplied by the County Council and the City Council, with wardens and garden staff appointed to the estate under a management team of officers from the Parks, Estates and Planning Departments of the two Authorities. The budget was split between the two Authorities and grant-aid was sought from the Countryside Commission, for development works for putting in such items as car parks and other recreational facilities, and the Inspectorate of Ancient Monuments and Historic Buildings for the reinstatement of the garden buildings. These had various listings but were accepted as being of prime significance as they were a group of listed buildings within a unified area.

The park and gardens were not considered to be of any historic importance as no records existed of any of the famous landscape improvers visiting the site and in fact records were scarce as the house had been burnt down during the war. Therefore, for the first 10 years of their purchase the Joint Authority concentrated on recovering the park and gardens from the decades of neglect and

Mount Edgcumbe Country Park. The house and Earl's
Garden. (Reproduced with kind permission of Cornwall
County Council.)

Mount Edgcumbe Country Park. The English Garden
House. (Reproduced with kind permission of Cornwall
County Council.)

making it an attractive place to visit. The place was becoming more like an urban park which some of the members and officers felt was the wrong approach but then were hampered in their desire to change things with this lack of records.

However, in the early 1980s the College of St Mark and St John carried out a project on the park and gathered together as much information as possible that they could find within local record offices and from the existing family. This resulted in a very successful enterprise that produced a wealth of historical information about the park. This was put together to form the basis of a visitors' exhibition and a guide to the Country Park. The most significant fact that emerged was that Mount Edgcumbe had been as famous in the eighteenth and nineteenth centuries as Stourhead and Stowe. The great and famous had visited it, written about it and had admired its scenic splendours. This was the catalyst that started a radical rethink by the Authority as to the approach for the development for the Country Park. It could no longer be regarded as a municipal park within an odd landscape but a famous although forgotten park and garden.

It was decided to ask the Garden History Society for advice; their Secretary was invited to visit the site. The Society appreciated that Mount Edgcumbe was of prime importance as an historic park and garden and unknown to the Joint Authority, it had been recommended for Grade 1 status for the Register of Parks and Gardens then being prepared. The Garden History Society undertook to write a report on Mount Edgcumbe putting it into historical context as a first step towards developing a Restoration and Management Plan. To provide on-site information for the Garden History Society and to carry out a survey of the park, the Joint Authority set up a survey team with the help of the Manpower Services Commission, which ran for two years and provided a wealth of detail about the Country Park. The keen interest of the Garden History Society underlined to the Joint Authority the status of Mount Edgcumbe as an historic garden, and it was decided to embark on a restoration programme.

The restoration is now proceeding in three distinct areas: the buildings, the parklands and the gardens themselves. Building restoration is the responsibility of the County Architect, whilst the preparation and implementation of the plans to restore the parklands and gardens is the responsibility of the County Planning Officer. After an

Mount Edgcumbe Country Park. Thompson's Seat. (Reproduced with kind permission of Cornwall County Council.)

Mount Edgcumbe Country Park. The Orangery. (Reproduced with kind permission of Cornwall County Council.)

Mount Edgcumbe Country Park. The French Garden House. (Reproduced with kind permission of Cornwall County Council.)

extensive survey of their condition the ornamental buildings are being restored to their original splendour. Funding is from the resources of the Joint Authorities with grant-aid from English Heritage. One of the more interesting of these buildings is the Shell Seat, where specialists have been employed to reslate the outside of the dome and restore the decorative shell and spar work interior. English Heritage considered this building to be of special historic interest and eventually proposed a grant offer of 40% of the costs. This so fired the imagination of the Friends of Mount Edgcumbe that they also raised money towards the project and were able to supply a further 20% of the final costs. In turn this allowed the Joint Authority to extend its restoration programme by having seven fifteenth-century urns replaced in another part of the garden.

In a similar manner, in the light of the Garden History Society's report, the parkland was surveyed and a plan prepared, indicating the significant plantations and views. The planting plan for the restoration of the parkland was then prepared with a five-year planting programme. Countryside Commission grant-aid was sought for this scheme.

Within the gardens the problem that faced the Joint Authority was that the park was continuously open to the public and the restoration programme would initially reduce the attractiveness that it currently possessed. The gardens consist of a series of individual Reptonesque gardens and it was decided to put in two new gardens, expanding the theme, so that there would be something for the public to look at whilst work progressed elsewhere. The two new gardens have been started on land which for years has been a waste and dumping ground. With their establishment the existing gardens can now be refurbished to bring them up to the required standard. Concurrently other sections of the garden have also been restored including the Edwardian flower lawn beside the main house. This was totally dug up and replanted to the original design as determined from old photographs which were made available to the Joint Authority. It has been greatly admired and will be further enhanced by the return of the urns.

Each year, as finances permit, a further stage of the restoration is carried out. With it comes the horrendous problems of maintenance as extra areas are taken in and standards are set higher for not only the restored areas, but the adjacent areas of the existing landscape. The restoration is to be set within the framework of the general requirements of the Country Park and therefore by necessity has to continue at a pace determined by the availability of finance from the resources of the Joint Authority.

As far as the buildings in the park are concerned, there was a considerable backlog of neglect when the County Council took over responsibility for the Country Park in 1972. The damage inflicted on the structures during World War II, coupled with the poor quality of both craftsmanship and materials available in the 1940s and 1950s, meant that much work had to be done. The policy of the Joint Authority, with regard to the listed buildings now under its control was dictated by the need to undertake the most urgent repairs in order to ensure the retention of the very wide range of buildings and structures within the Park.

The Joint Authority has followed a two-stage policy. Firstly, to survey the structural soundness of each building and to ensure all buildings are structurally sound and wind- and waterproof. Only after this initial stage has been achieved has attention been directed to the second stage, the applications of decorative detail. Responsibility for implementing this policy lies with the County Architect. By the end of 1990, the English Garden House, Cremyll Lodge, the French Garden House, Thompson's Seat and the Orangery had had major work carried out on them.

Other buildings in the Park, e.g. Milton's Temple, have been the subject of temporary repairs to prevent further degradation of the structure and materials. Very little work at the second stage, i.e. as applied decorative detail, has been undertaken as it was considered that this would divert scarce financial resources away from the fundamental work of ensuring that all listed buildings were sound and free from further damage from the elements.

Restoration of this historic park is inevitably of a long-term nature, but enough work has already been carried out to provide a sound basis for future restoration projects to bring the grounds back as near as possible to their former glory.

EAST SUSSEX

PROJECT 6.4, Brickwall School and Great Dixter, Northiam

The gardens at Brickwall School and Great Dixter are both situated in Northiam, some 16 km (10 miles) north of Hastings, and illustrate East Sussex County Council's participation with a Garden Trust in two major fields of conservation: historic garden architecture and vernacular farm buildings.

The late 1970s saw an increasing awareness of the deteriorating state of many of the county's historic parks and gardens. Whilst a few, in National Trust and Government ownership, were well maintained and patronized, there were many more in private or institutional ownership – equally deserving of attention – which were suffering from decay or even heading towards oblivion due to declining fortunes and tightening budgets.

The association of such gardens with listed historic houses only aggravated the situation: the main house had to come first and its maintenance very often drained financial resources to an extent where little or nothing was left over for repairing garden features such as temples, gazebos and terracing, the proper restoration of which was often in itself a major expense.

County conservation budgets would never be large enough to tackle these problems directly, but the County Council had a staff of landscape architects, architects, forestry officers, technicians and students capable of research, design and site work in the promotion of historic garden restoration and maintenance, so the need was to use this human resource in conjunction with extra funding from national and government sources through grants and from the private sector. Unskilled, but closely supervised, labour was available through the Manpower Services Commission.

BRICKWALL SCHOOL

Brickwall School is the home of the distinguished naval family of Frewen. This Grade I listed house has for some years now been a school and although well maintained, new ancilliary classrooms, a swimming pool and school equipment had to take precedence over the repair of features in the ground such as the moulded brick gate piers, or repointing the high brick garden wall from which the house had taken its name.

Brickwall School, Northiam. Front view through the gate screen. (Reproduced with kind permission of East Sussex County Council.)

Brickwall School, Northiam. Chess garden. (Reproduced
with kind permission of East Sussex County Council.)

Brickwall School, Northiam. Aerial view. (Reproduced
with kind permission of Rother District Council.)

The school governors were anxious to help so far as their more immediate priorities allowed. Fortunately, one of their governors, an American, was an enthusiast in the fields of gardening and British history. The County Council's chief landscape architect at the time, in his search for external funding, was able to tap this enthusiasm with the result that the Historic Gardens Trust (Sussex) was founded with the American benefactor as chairman. It was the latter's private funding which underwrote the Trust in its subsequent restoration activities all over Sussex.

Brickwall was among the first to benefit. County Council staff from the Planning department drew up schedules of repair for both hard and soft landscape elements. To put Brickwall and the Trust's work 'on the map', it was decided to restore the Elizabethan walled garden with a bowling alley, and its eighteenth-century topiary as far as available records would permit. These records were vague and scant, so the decision was taken to create a new element much in the spirit of an Elizabethan garden, to relate to the few surviving features in a convincing manner, and enhance the setting of the listed house. This new feature was to be a topiary chess garden. The design consisted of a grid of brick paviors forming the 'chess board', with black and white types of roadstone chips used as fillings to form the squares. A full chess set was placed on the board in positions that, in an actual game, might be adopted before any pieces were taken. The pieces were constructed of a light lattice of steel strips and painted black or white to designs of chessmen provided by the Planning department staff. These open pieces had planted within them green yews for the 'black' set and golden yews for the 'white' set. When mature the yews will be clipped to take up the shape of the chess piece itself. The chess garden is open to the public during school holidays. Job creation teams provided by the Manpower Services Commission carried out the whole of this work on site and in a Hastings workshop under the supervision of their own staff and County staff.

The wall and the brick steps leading to the Park were repaired mainly by school staff while a Sussex blacksmith made new iron gates of a more appropriate design than the old ones, embodying anchors symbolizing the Frewen's naval connection.

Alongside the building work, new planting and tree surgery was undertaken on the 'soft' landscaping side which included the restoration of yew

Great Dixter, Northiam. Nathaniel Lloyds' herbaceous border. (Reproduced with kind permission of East Sussex County Council.)

Great Dixter, Northiam. Barn and triple-oast-houses. (Reproduced with kind permission of East Sussex County Council.)

Great Dixter, Northiam. Entrance front and lilypond. (Reproduced with kind permission of East Sussex County Council.)

groups and hedges, and beds of lavender bordering the 'chess-board'.

The core of the chess garden was completed in 1982. As a 'built' item, only the materials had to be purchased, the job creation scheme providing the labour. The bricks cost £1350, the chess pieces nearly £500, and the yew trees and lavender nearly £100. The total of just over £1900 was shared: the school, supported by their American governor through the Historic Gardens Trust (Sussex), gave £1454 and the County Council, from its Historic Parks and Gardens budget, gave £460 and, of course, professional staff time and expertise.

From the point of future maintenance, this was a consideration that the school placed quite highly. The chippings forming the chess board squares were laid over black plastic sheeting which was perforated for drainage. This is intended to inhibit and possibly prevent weed growth on the square. Seven years exposure, with minimal attention from the school gardeners, has left them as clean as new.

GREAT DIXTER

Great Dixter is another Grade I listed house, situated at the northern end of Northiam. The main house, a half-timbered, unaisled great hall, dating from 1466, was refashioned by Sir Edwin Lutyens for Nathaniel Lloyd in 1910. The magnificent gardens are in capable private hands and are open to the public. However, the maintenance of these gardens was burdened with many vernacular farm buildings of some importance, both historically and visually. Considerable repairs were necessary.

The triple-square-kiln oast-house and its stowage are integral with the structure of the larger of the two barns, the timber frame of which was structurally weak and with a deteriorating roof. Whilst the owner had negotiated a grant from English Heritage towards the cost of the main structural repairs and reroofing, the replacement of the three oast-house cowls had to be considered more of a desirable luxury. One cowl had collapsed, one was hanging at an angle, and only one was in position, and that was rotten. The oast-house and its cowls formed an attractive and dramatic backdrop to an important section of the topiary garden and played an important visual role in the wider landscape of Northiam parish.

The County Council's historic buildings budget offered a grant under the provisions of the Local Authorities (Historic Buildings) Act 1962, to assist the owner, and County Council staff from the planning department gave technical advice on the design of the new cowls. They liaised with a local firm who made the cowls from glass-reinforced plastic (GRP) and fitted them.

The cost of the main barn repairs were estimated to be over £53 000 towards which a 40% grant of £21 298 was offered by English Heritage. The balance was paid from estate funds and insurances (there was a storm damage element).

The three oast-house cowls cost a total of £2570. They were moulded around authentic wooden cowls. Depressions due to wood grain, nails, etc., are therefore reproduced. This, together with the 'eggshell' sheen of the glass-fibre surface finish gives a convincing impression of slightly weathered painted wood. English Heritage would not grant-aid synthetic materials such as glass fibre, but agreed not to let its use prejudice their grant to the main structure. Hence grant-aid for the cowls was left to the local authorities, the County Council giving £1000 and Rother District Council £500, totalling a grant offer of over 50%. Work was completed early in 1990.

The buildings that needed urgent attention were two barns and an oast-house, which together formed two sides of a sunken courtyard garden (once the barnyard) and were survivors from Dixter's agricultural past. Garden and buildings are mutually supportive in the overall visual scheme.

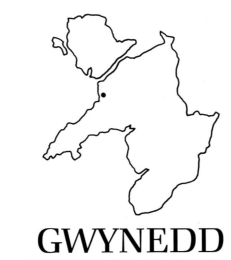

GWYNEDD

PROJECT 6.5, Parc Glynllifon

Glynllifon is a large Victorian country house standing in extensive grounds, 9.7 km (6 miles) from Caernarfon and just outside the Snowdonia National Park. Both the house and grounds are owned by Gwynedd County Council. For some 30 years, the 324-hectare (800-acre) estate of Plas Glynllifon has been run as an agricultural college. There was no public access and the grounds, together with various landscape features and buildings, not important to the needs of the college, had unfortunately been abandoned to the ravages of nature. The former estate workshops were in private ownership forming an 'island' in the site. Recently the County Council has considered extending the educational and recreational value that this park, when restored, could provide for the region, which, in this part of Wales, experiences increasing numbers of visitors each year.

A report was initially prepared by the County Council's Planning Department which indicated how public access could be introduced into the estate grounds as well as indicating which landscape features and areas within the park would be of greater interest to the visiting public. The long-term aim is to create an innovative centre for those interested in nature, the countryside, the history and heritage of Gwynedd and of Wales, art and literature, as well as serving as an educational resource for the county. This report was adopted as a basis for the development of a Country Park.

Work started in 1985, with a three-year M.S.C. community programme scheme which tackled the clearance of undergrowth and the construction of footpaths. Some 13 km (8 miles) of footpaths now exist. As the general clearance work was completed, work started on the restoration of the landscape features which originally adorned the Victorian gardens. These included fountains, waterfalls, cascades, an arboretum, a knot garden, fernery, caves, otter pool, miniature water mill, grottos, a hermitage and bridges, both of cast-iron and stone. Restoration works were also undertaken to Fort Williamsbourg, built to house and train Lord Newborough's militia at the time of the Napoleonic Wars.

All the buildings of the park are listed Grade II* or II. The estate workshops have now been purchased by the County Council and now form the Visitor Centre, having been restored to a very high standard. Some new buildings and extensions have been added which have been designed to be in character with the originals. The former trades have been reintroduced into the workshops, together with interpretation and exhibitions. What was probably the first private gas plant in Wales has been researched by the local Archaeological Trust and restoration and interpretation is being sponsored commercially. The boiler house and steam engine have been restored by the well-

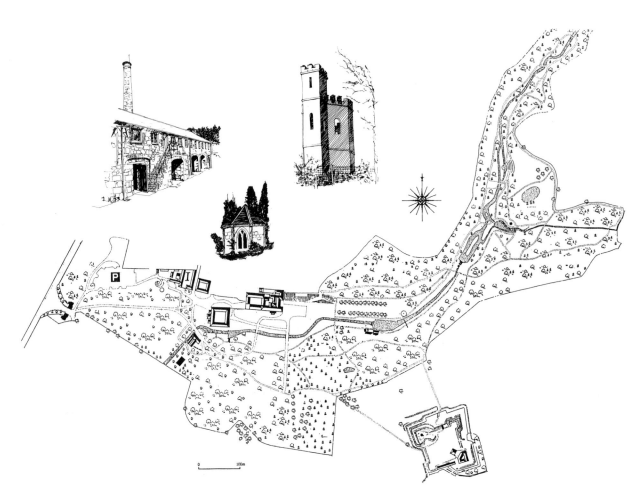

known and enthusiastic professional Fred Dibnah.

The spirit of the works undertaken by their Victorian Lordships over a hundred years ago, is being followed today with a unique programme of landscape sculpture projects being developed to interpret aspects of Welsh literature. A children's mountain, grotto, story-telling Druids circle and an amphitheatre for live performances have so far been developed. As part of the educational theme adopted for the Park, a Writers of Gwynedd project is being undertaken, as a partnership between Gwynedd County Council and Artworks Wales, formerly the Welsh Sculpture Trust, with sponsorship from the Welsh Arts Council and the North Wales Arts Association for parts of the venture.

By 1994 it is planned that the former corn mill and power house will have been restored providing accommodation for interpretation, agricultural display, design studies and workshop space. When complete the project will have involved around 200 separate contracts ranging from quite small works to the major reconstructions. The project has been managed by the County

Planning Department throughout but much of its success is attributable to major contributions from several other County Council departments.

The costs of this restoration project, which has been developed incrementally, was initially restricted to a relatively small budget. The project costs were re-evaluated when the estate workshops were acquired and this now represents a substantial investment. The costs can be summarized as follows: land acquisition £18 000; Visitor Centre and tearoom £926 000; public access, features, carpark and toilets £133 000 (this figure excludes M.S.C. Community Programme Labour costs); services £51 000; landscape sculpture £38 000; mill, power house and museum £300 000 making a total of £1 466 000.

The labour costs for the early works were provided through the M.S.C. Community Programme with the County Council meeting the cost of materials and hire of plant with grant-aid from the Countryside Commission. More recent works have been financed by the County Council with grant-aid from the Welsh Development Agency.

Glynllifon Hall. (Reproduced with kind permission of Gwynedd County Council.)

Parc Glynllifon. Children's mountain and hollow. (Reproduced with kind permission of Gwynedd County Council.)

The whole project is in the Councils' Integrated Operations Programme with grants received from the European Regional Development Fund, which assists in the implementation of such projects for the benefit of a comparatively deprived remote rural area. The Sculpture projects have all been sponsored from the private sector to at least 50% of cost.

The restoration of the water features proved difficult. Although the original reservoirs were dredged and new valves and sluices fitted, it has become very difficult to provide adequate supplies of water for all the features. This is probably explained by land drainage works undertaken on adjoining agricultural land which have diverted surface water away into other watercourses. The public response has been most encouraging, with virtually no criticism. The most commonly heard comment is that the park now has 'a special magic all of its own – it's unique'. It is firmly anticipated that within the next year or two over 100 000 visitors will come to Glynllifon.

(See Plates 20 and 21.)

HAMPSHIRE

PROJECT 6.6, Tylney Hall near Hook, and Marshcourt, near Stockbridge

The Hampshire Gardens Trust was officially launched in June 1984, two years after the concept of an independent charitable Trust to assist in the conservation of historic parks and gardens was first publicized at a conference organized by Hampshire County Council. The Trust's first objective is to promote an appreciation and understanding by as large an audience as possible of the parks, gardens and designed landscapes in Hampshire, their educational value in terms of works of art, their historic associations, horticultural and arboricultural qualities and their architectural, scenic and nature conservation potential.

The Trust's second objective is to preserve, enhance and recreate for the education and enjoyment of the public, parks, gardens and other designed landscapes in Hampshire. This has been summarized in 1990 in *Help Care for Hampshire's Gardens and Parks at Risk from Neglect or Development* (Annual Report for the Year, 1989).

In assisting the planning process in Hampshire, the Trust seeks to promote an understanding between owners, local authorities, government departments and other organizations in attempting to achieve its aims. In this sense, the Trust plays an enabling role in addition to its primary research role. It has been strongly supported in this work by Hampshire County Council committees and departments, including financially, with the establishment of a capital fund for the Trust by two grants of £15 000 and £25 000. Funding has also been found to support some of its major projects, e.g. the Petersfield Physic Garden.

As an enabler, the Trust has played a crucial role in Hampshire, in the important gardens at Tylney Hall, near Hook and at Marshcourt, near Stockbridge.

TYLNEY HALL, NEAR HOOK

Tylney Hall was one of the earliest sites to be surveyed when Hampshire County Council began its countywide survey of historic parks and gardens. Research by the Trust revealed that Tylney Hall was part of an early seventeenth-century designed landscape and that, more recently, several famous arts and crafts designers had contributed to the gardens. In particular, Robert Weir Schultz's formal gardens, some designed in partnership with Gertrude Jekyll, were recognized as of national importance.

When the property, which was originally owned and run as a special school by the London Borough of Brent, was put on the market, a Draft Policy Statement was drawn up by Hart District Council. After consultation with Hampshire County Council in April 1984, it was universally recognized that a change of use would be necessary to prevent further decay of the site and to enable restoration to take place. As the activities of the Trust were gaining momentum just prior to their launch, they, too, were consulted on the Draft Policy Statement. This was the start of a fruitful liaison between the authorities and the Trust, resulting in continued research into the historic landscape of

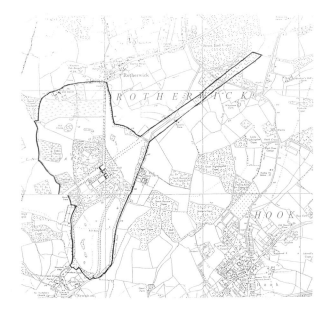

Tylney Hall and the recognition of its importance nationally when it achieved a Grade II* status on the English Heritage register of Parks and Gardens of Special Historic Interest.

By the end of 1984, Tylney Hall had been purchased by a hotel company and the Trust's liaison now included the company's consultant architects. Through the research carried out by the Trust and the support of Hampshire County Council, the value of Tylney Hall's historic landscape was recognized by the new owners and their architects, who all agreed that a master plan was required for its restoration. As a result, consultant landscape architects were commissioned on the recommendation of the Trust, and in the summer of 1985, were requested to prepare a landscape master plan with grant-aid from Hampshire County Council.

Tylney Hall. Jekyll's water garden restored in 1987. (Photograph by K. Bilikowski. Reproduced with kind permission of Hampshire County Council.)

Tylney Hall. Italian garden terrace restored with new planting in 1988. (Photograph by S.J. Hocking. Reproduced with kind permission of Hampshire County Council.)

Marshcourt. Aerial view of house and gardens. (Photograph by E.N. Lane. Reproduced with kind permission of Hampshire County Council.)

In October 1985, a Section 52 agreement was signed (under the Town and Country Planning Act 1971, provisions then in force) requiring the owner to produce a master plan for the historic landscape. This document also formed the basis of a Section 52 Agreement (now Section 106 of the Town and Country Planning Act 1990), signed by the owner with Hart District Council for the restoration programme of Tylney Hall's unusual and important Edwardian kitchen gardens and the rest of the estate. Whilst developments continued with the hotel conversions, progress was made in restoration of the gardens.

Inevitably conflicts arose over building extensions and the garden restoration. Continuous liaison between the Trust, Hampshire County Council, the consultant landscape architect, the hotel architects and the District Council enabled some of these to be satisfactorily resolved. By 1988, many of the most important aspects of the master plan had been completed and Tylney Hall Hotel held an 'open day' for the Trust to view their achievements. In terms of conservation of historic landscapes, the Section 106 procedure was shown to be an essential part of the planning process in a case like Tylney Hall.

MARSHCOURT, NEAR STOCKBRIDGE

Marshcourt is a Grade I house designed in 1901 by Sir Edwin Lutyens for Herbert Johnson. Sited on the spur of a hill overlooking the River Test, the gardens form a united and integral architectural design. The gardens are Grade II* on the English Heritage register of Parks and Gardens of Special Historic Interest; the individual garden features themselves are statutorily protected as listed buildings in their own right. Marshcourt is not only important for its house but also its setting: the Lutyens and Jekyll partnership has produced one of the most outstanding arts and crafts gardens in Hampshire.

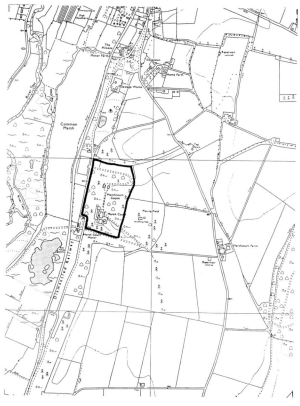

Hampshire County Council, through its own Historic Buildings Bureau, and with English Heritage and the Test Valley Borough Council, have been involved since 1976 in helping the owners of Marshcourt to restore the building. As it was then an established school and not a site where extensive redevelopment was planned, the use of Section 106 Agreements (Town and County Planning Act 1990,) was not feasible for the gardens, although statutory procedures were available to secure the repair of the listed architecture.

As part of Hampshire County Council's historic parks and gardens survey, Marshcourt was visited in the summer of 1981. A report on the garden architecture revealed the need for extensive repairs. As a result, in August and September of 1983 exploratory meetings were held with all the major parties involved, with the Trust encouraging local societies and groups such as the

Marshcourt. Italian sunken garden (without the original hippocampi) in 1983. (Photograph by E.N. Lane. Reproduced with kind permission of Hampshire County Council.)

Marshcourt. Pergola today. (Photograph by E.N. Lane. Reproduced with kind peermission of Hampshire County Council.)

Lutyens Trust to become involved in the garden restoration.

The turning point was the 14 October 1983 when a public meeting was held and the 'Friends of Marshcourt' was formed because of the interest shown. The Friends soon became active, holding fund-raising events and forming regular working parties of volunteers to help with various projects at Marshcourt. At the same time a repairs programme was established for the garden architecture, using the stonemasons from Salisbury Cathedral, supervised by the County Council's Historic Buildings Bureau.

The Trust approached both Jane Brown, a specialist in Arts and Crafts gardens from the Lutyens Trust, and Madeleine Pickthorne who had also been involved in the restoration of the gardens at Hestercombe, in Somerset; another product of the Lutyens and Jekyll partnership. A description of the gardens at Hestercombe also appears in this chapter (Project 6.10). With their help, the restoration project began to take shape under the auspices of the Trust.

With an enthusiastic and co-operative owner, Marshcourt was to be the Trust's first major project for which it gave substantial grant for the restoration of the garden architecture. In order to safeguard the long-term public benefit of the grant, a legal agreement was reached with the owner on the conditions of the Trust's grant-aid. These included arrangements for public access and maintenance of grant-aided work. Marshcourt was used as a school, up to July 1989, but that has now closed and is up for sale. No new owner has yet come forward whose proposals would not involve additional buildings, which would disrupt the fine design of the building, as well as affecting the formal gardens. The Trust is continuing its committment to Marshcourt and is monitoring the situation.

NORTHAMPTONSHIRE

PROJECT 6.7, Kirby Hall

The formal gardens at Kirby Hall, Northamptonshire (Site plan: Project 6.7), were among the finest and best known in seventeenth-century England, but the abandonment and decay which eventually left the great Elizabethan house in ruins also impoverished its surroundings, so that it is difficult to envisage their original splendour. The form of the Great Garden, which lay parallel to the house and overlooked other gardens extending onto a hillslope beyond the local brook, was largely determined by pioneer work of garden archaeology undertaken by H.M. Office of Works after guardianship of the property in 1930. New investigation, however, has shown that while the overall scheme of paths and rectangular plots was based on a rediscovered design, the interpretation of details was incorrect, having confused features of different periods.

Large-scale excavation by the Northamptonshire Archaeology Unit, a branch of the County Planning and Transportation Department, was commissioned by English Heritage with the intention of establishing the evolution of the gardens and recreating the effect of their late seventeenth-century appearance in order to enhance the effect of the monument upon today's visitor. Work carried out between 1987–1990 has both provided an understanding of the former setting of the house and helped to identify the constraints upon different methods of presenting its environs.

As originally laid out in the early seventeenth century, the Great Garden formed a rectangular enclosure with terraces around two sides and free-

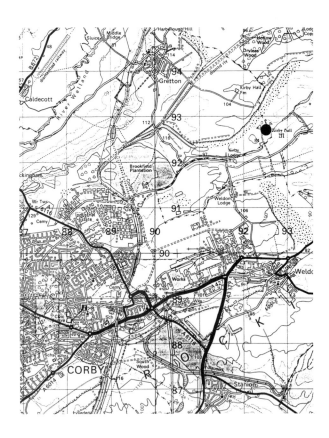

standing walls elsewhere. A stone balustrade surmounted the brick walls which formed the inner edge of each terrace beside a soil border. Steps led to the top of the West Terrace from an arch at the centre, directly opposite the doorway from the house. Statues and arbours existed at various points around the perimeter. The garden itself appears to have been divided into the arrangement of plots and broad walks which were reconstructed in the 1930s. The original boundaries seem to have been dwarf hedges, however, rather than stone kerbs; within each, a plate-bande, or border, enclosed a clear expanse of grass containing a statue at the centre.

Contemporary documents and recent archaeological discoveries attest to a major remodelling of the Great Garden towards the close of the seventeenth century. Parts of its original enclosing walls were demolished to create wider views and architectural features were relocated. The West Terrace was altered to form a turf bank with a gradient at either side of approximately 1 in 2. While the width across the top of the terrace was shortened, its base covered a much greater area, so that within the garden the new slope encroached onto the existing path. The previous arrangement of four plots was retained but their surfaces were heightened prior to the introduction of cutwork-designs.

The later history of the garden is poorly documented. Sketches of the Hall made in 1825 suggest that the Great Garden was largely abandoned at the time and its former parterres appear to have been grassed over and may already have been incorporated into surrounding 'parkland'. The area presumably remained as pasture for grazing until the archaeological investigation of the present century disclosed its former history.

Despite the low yield of artefacts from the garden, the investigation has clearly demonstrated how the disciplined application of the principles of archaeological stratigraphy can elucidate such unpromising material as garden parterres. The project has engendered widespread interest and many organizations, including horticultural societies as well as archaeological groups, have visited Kirby Hall to be guided through the project. The work has also been featured in radio broadcasts and was the subject of a television documentary film.

An important initiative has been the development by the Archaeology Unit's Education Officer of a related schools' project. By looking to the Great Garden itself and combining its investigation with other studies such as the surface examination of an adjacent abandoned village, searching relevant air photographs and plans of the house and garden which reach back to Tudor times, and by examining extracts from contemporary correspondence and other writings, chil-

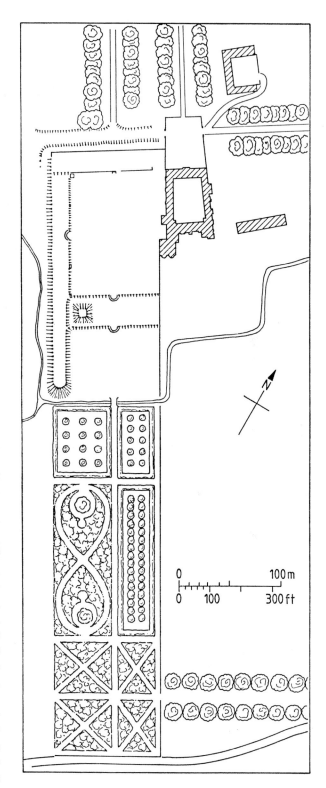

Kirby Hall Gardens in c.1700. Archaeology has revealed important details of the Great Garden immediately beside the house. (Reproduced with kind permission of Northamptonshire County Council.)

dren can begin to appreciate the purpose and processes of major changes in the Northamptonshire landscape.

Recently, the County Council has become involved in the formation of a County Gardens Trust. Such a body will ensure that local period-gardens and related landscapes are not only defined and described comprehensively, but that they are also safeguarded for the future.

(See Plates 22 and 23.)

Kirby Hall. Site of former gateway and steps leading to the top of the West Terrace. The statues of the Rape of the Sabine was introduced in the 1930s. (Reproduced with kind permission of Northamptonshire County Council.)

PEMBROKESHIRE COAST NATIONAL PARK

PROJECT 6.8, Upton Castle Gardens

Situated a short distance from Carew Castle, Upton Castle is another of the fortified Norman sites built around the shores of Milford Haven, just east of Cosheston. Located in the Daugleddau sector of the Pembrokeshire Coast National Park, lies this imposing castle, which is still privately owned. The Park Authority, however, have taken over the management of the 14 hectares (35 acres) of attractive grounds and made them available to the public. This Management Agreement was drawn up in 1975 and was one of the very first undertaken by the new Park Authorities after they assumed fuller powers following Local Government reorganization in 1974, and pioneered a new concept in land management schemes. Under the terms of the Agreement, the Park Authority maintains the grounds and carries out essential works to preserve and enhance the natural beauty of the area, in return for access to be provided for the public and opportunities given for quiet enjoyment. The agreement has just been renewed for a further period.

The grounds stretch down to the banks of the Carew River and contain a remarkable collection of over 250 species of trees and shrubs, many of them exotic species from all over the world, planted by the owner's family since the 1930s. The grounds are very much at their best in spring and early summer.

The restoration works that have been necessary include the provision of all-weather footpaths and repairs to certain structures, including a medieval chapel, a swimming pool and flights of steps in the grounds. The principle behind these restorations is to attempt to recreate these historic gardens into something near to their original design and splendour.

These works have cost an estimated £16 000 to £20 000 per year. On top of this, much of the initial work was undertaken using the M.S.C. Job Creation scheme utilizing unemployed young people mainly from the Pembroke Dock area.

A large car park and picnic area has also been provided near to the entrance to the gardens, together with toilets and a site notice board. The grounds are open weekdays from March to early November.

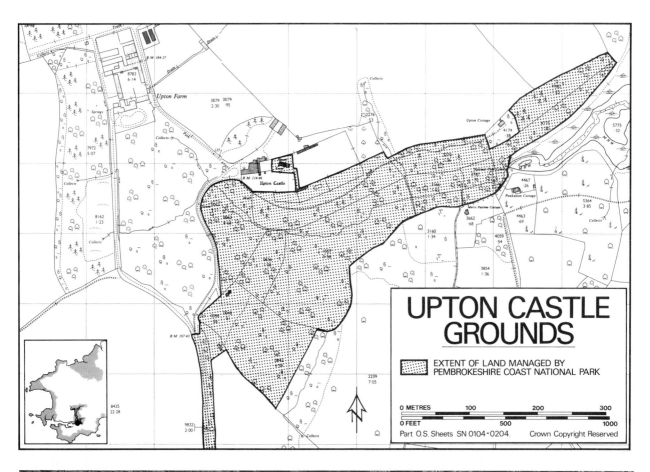

Upton Castle. Aerial view of grounds and castle. (Reproduced with kind permission of Pembrokeshire Coast National Park.)

Upton Castle. Grounds consist of both formal and informal areas and include a substantial variety of native and exotic species. (Reproduced with kind permission of Pembrokeshire Coast National Park.)

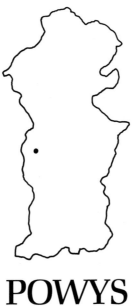

POWYS

PROJECT 6.9, Llandrindod Wells Victorian spa grounds

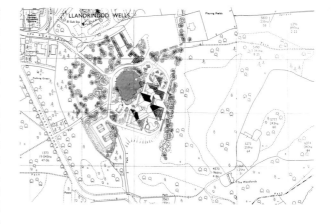

Llandrindod Wells does not appear on any map of Roman Britain, although it was reputed to have been one of their largest training encampments in Western Europe, making extensive use of the rich mineral waters of the region. Records exist which show that the presence of these waters was recognized through subsequent centuries, although it appears that no permanent settlement was established until the late eighteenth century when the spa water began to feature as an attraction to travellers of the day. It was the Victorians, continuing the traditions set down during the Regency period, who established Llandrindod Wells as a spa town, catering for those who wished to 'take the waters'. The coming of the railway greatly helped in ensuring that the town was able to capitalize on the commercial prosperity and development associated with the spa. It was built almost entirely during the Victorian period, and as little development followed in later years, it remains today largely unspoilt and showing clearly the original planning concepts of the day. The town is now designated a conservation area.

Spa towns, and Llandrindod Wells is no exception, contained many fine hotels and hydros to accommodate the large numbers who regularly visited the towns. Associated with these hotels would be the promenading areas designed and planted with typical Victorian fervour to parallel the 'healthy' taking of the waters.

One such prominent hotel in Llandrindod Wells that had its own extensive grounds was the Pump House Hotel – a name derived from the fashion of the day to pump the mineral waters from their source to wells and faucets in grand rooms within the hotel itself for the residents to take as part of their treatment. The large promenading areas were adjacent to the Hotel, in its parkland, and

New County Hall Council Offices set in the landscaped spa grounds.

provided a necessary ingredient to the treatment – exercise and relaxation.

However, with the decline in the popularity of this form of treatment during the early decades of this century, the Hotel became underused, as did many others in the town. The two war periods saw a brief respite, when they were used for convalescence for soldiers, but eventually the Pump House Hotel was taken over as a school for handicapped children. In 1974, on Local Government reorganization, the Powys County Council took over the, by then, neglected, estate as its headquarters.

In the late 1970s it was realized that the original Victorian building was becoming extremely unsafe, and was demolished upon completion of the construction of the new County Council offices in 1990. At the same time the surrounding parkland environment needed considerable attention. The indigenous oak woodland, covering nearly 6.4 hectares (15 acres), was, in its heyday, heavily

planted, with paths created to form promenades and circular walks. It was clear that a fairly robust strategy of both rejuvenation and restoration would be necessary. The main elements of this work included:

- The amenity woodlands to the front of the new County offices should have substantial felling (there had been storm damage in recent years) and be replanted in a way that is compatible with the original Victorian design.
- The parkland which contained many old oaks and is a backdrop to the new offices, should be restored using indigenous species (storm damage has also occured here).
- The recreational 'promenades' should be restored and enhanced as an asset for the general public.
- There should be an interpretive/information feature constructed to show, not only the development of the spa and its waters, but also the woodland, wildlife and environmental aspects.
- Special features should be incorporated within the planting, such as the display of ferns – a popular Victorian theme for landscaped gardens. (Fortunately, there already exits a list of all species within a 3 km (2-mile) radius of the woodlands, dated 1896).

From the evidence of the majority of the trees felled, it seems that the Victorian planting occurred about 100 years ago (when the main part of the Hotel was constructed). Today, with the new planting underway, the opportunity has presented itself to create a new landscape repeated after these 100 years.

The net cost of the woodland work, after Countryside Commission grant for the amenity woodlands in the front of the new offices, about 2.4 hectares (6 acres) in extent, and Forestry Commission grant for the woodlands to the rear, is estimated at £3000. Much of the felled wood is being converted on site to be used on other locations within the estate, or for other County Council uses. Some timber is going to local craftsmen and a reasonable volume into the trade. The interpretive/information feature, which will be made entirely from one 106-year-old Douglas fir from the site, will cost an estimated £14 000.

(See Plates 24 and 25.)

SOMERSET

PROJECT 6.10, Hestercombe House Gardens

Whilst Hestercombe house was originally a seventeenth-century structure, it had been largely remodelled in mid Victorian times. It is situated on the southern slopes of the Quantock Hills, 6.4 km (4 miles) north of Taunton, close to the village of Cheddon Fitzpaine. The house possesses little architectural distinction but the gardens are of national, and indeed international, acclaim.

In 1903, the Honourable E.W. Portman commissioned Edwin Lutyens to design a garden on the sloping land immediately to the south of the existing house. Lutyens proposed a large sunken garden (called 'a plat'), cut and filled to the slope with raised walkways on all four sides. Stone-built garden features such as a pergola walk, rotunda, niches, a Dutch garden and orangery, with the restrained use of flowing water, combined to produce an Italianate garden of classic Edwardian elegance. Lutyens asked Gertrude Jekyll to provide the planting in this very architectural garden, which Christopher Hussey was later to describe as the culmination of the Lutyens and Jekyll partnership. Another commentator of the time, Harold Nicholson, observed: 'Under the influence of Miss Jekyll, [Lutyens] brought his architecture tumbling down into the garden'.[1]

The Crown Commissioners acquired the property as part of the death duties from the Portman family, by which time the gardens had been badly neglected. After several years of leasing the property from the Crown Commissioners, the Somerset County Council purchased the house and garden in 1977.

The County Council were determined to restore the gardens to their original designs wherever possible. Considerable information was available: *Country Life* magazine had published extensive articles in 1908, shortly after its completion, and again 20 years later, probably at the height of its maturity. These articles were descriptive and illustrated with excellent photographs. Some plans were found at Hestercombe and others were located as far away as the University of Berkley, California.

Research into the project was commenced in 1970; the nearby Cannington College of Agriculture and Horticulture advised on plants and suitable substitutions, and the Architects Department of the County Council researched, produced drawings and proposals and gave day-to-day advice as work proceeded.

A survey of the condition of the garden was prepared, assessing the work required and the quality of the existing features. Being built on sloping ground, Hestercombe relies on walls, steps, balustrades and paving to reinforce the difference in levels and qualities of spaces. The pavings and timbers of the pergola were in poor condition. Due to the cut and fill, half the garden is on made-up ground and subsidence of the paving was a problem. Considering the earthworks were carried out using manual labour, and horse and cart, it is remarkable that the settlement has been no worse.

The first few years were devoted to restoring planting, and the Council set aside £750 per year for this. However, as stone walls and paving have deteriorated it was obvious that additional finance would be required from other sources. After several years of negotiations, English Heritage

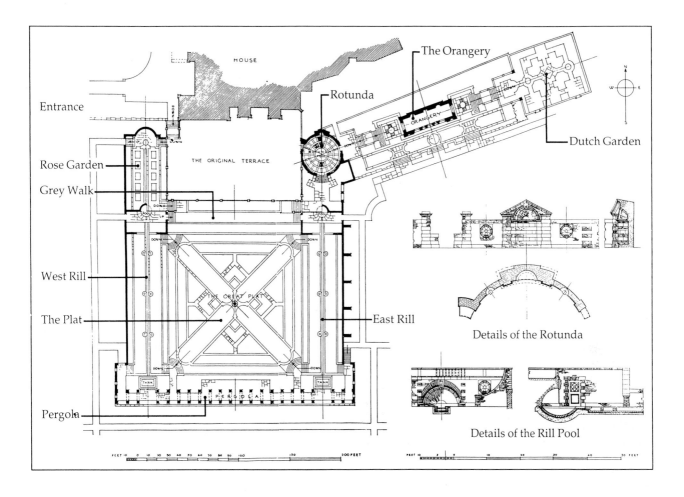

approved grant-aid for the restoration of stone-work, but not its maintenance.

The costed report covered a six-year programme in order to complete the stonework restoration, and it was essential that the highest standards of craftsmanship were achieved. As Lutyens liked to use local materials, the stone for the walls and paving was quarried from behind the house. It was reasonably durable but the quarry is now closed, having been worked out, and therefore existing stone has to be carefully reused. The dressed stone of the balustrades, quoins and as used in the Orangery, is Ham Hill stone and fortunately this is once again available in small quantities from the quarries near Yeovil.

The garden is being completed in a series of compartments and the planting following in the same manner. The Grey Walk was the first area to be chosen because many of the original species were in the garden and were available. It was probably the most typical of Miss Jekyll's planting schemes in the garden.

Hestercombe Gardens. The Plat looking south east towards the Pergola Walk. (Reproduced with kind permission of Somerset County Council.)

The most difficult element to restore in the gardens has been the water, the essential feature that so enthralled Lutyens in his designs. The original supply was via a stream into a reservoir behind the house. However, this reservoir no longer retains water and restoration costs would be prohibitive. Much of the original pipework was also defunct, but another supply has recently been constructed from an adjacent stream which appears to be providing a regular supply. Water is now available to all points of the garden. The water channels, called rills, are a major feature of the gardens, and these have recently been completely repaired, as have the gargoyle spouts from the head walls and the semicircular pools.

The restoration is now in its sixteenth year; it is worth remembering that it took five years to build it in 1908. The gardens at Hestercombe are open to the public all the year, and there are free car-parking facilities, toilets and disabled access available. The house is not open to the public as it is the administrative headquarters of the Somerset Fire Brigade, which maintains the historic gardens, whilst the buildings are maintained by the County Council's Property Services Department.

Much of the information has been provided by Andrew Paul, landscape architects, formerly of the Somerset County Council Architects Department.

(See Plates 26 and 27.)

HASKELL '91

END OF THE PERGOLA WALK

REFERENCE

1. Nicholson, H. (1944). *Friday Mornings*, p. 213.

SURREY

PROJECT 6.11, Painshill Park

Painshill was laid out by the Honourable Charles Hamilton (1704–1786), a gifted and imaginative designer, painter and plantsman, who created the garden from barren heathland and turned it into a fine example of an emerging art form, the landscape garden. The garden was developed between 1738 and 1773. Originally over 101 hectares (250 acres), the estate is now 64 hectares (158 acres) in size, of which 5.7 hectares (14 acres) are taken up by the lake, the centrepiece of Hamilton's design (Site plan: Project 6.11). The visitor was invited to follow a single circuit of the park during which a number of picturesque scenes were revealed and, as was usual at this time, various moods were evoked.

Notable features of the garden included the amphitheatre, created from evergreens, many of which were new introductions from North America and in the centre of which stood a lead copy of the statue of 'The Rape of the Sabine' by Giambologna; the Gothic temple; the ruined abbey, built on the site of Hamilton's brick and tile works; the grotto, a magnificent creation, beside an inlet of the lake, the water reflecting on the sparkling 'stalactites' above; the mausoleum which created a mood of gloomy contemplation, thoughts of death, and echoes of Italy and the Grand Tour; the water-wheel, which raised water from the River Mole to the lake; the hermitage (the hermit only lasted 3 weeks before being found drunk in a public house in Cobham); the Gothic tower; the Chinese bridge; the Turkish tent and the temple of Bacchus, which in contrast to the Mausoleum, was a light-hearted area – the temple contained a large statue of Bacchus said to have been brought back from Italy by Hamilton, as well as busts of Roman Emperors.

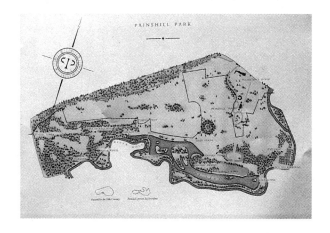

Hamilton was eventually forced to sell Painshill through lack of funds. The next owner, Benjamin Bond-Hopkins, erected the present mansion in the park. Painshill then passed through a number of changes of ownership until 1948, when it was purchased for land speculation and sold off in separate lots. Fortunately, the Garden History Society and a small but determined local pressure group prevailed on Elmbridge Borough Council to buy back what remained of the land. The original purchase price of £195 000 for 64 hectares (158 acres) in 1980 was made up from Elmbridge Borough Council, £125 000; Surrey County Council, £25 000; Countryside Commission, £45 000.

The Painshill Park Trust (an independent Trust) was established in 1981, with the aims of financing, planning and carrying out the restoration of the park, and opening it to the general

Painshill Park. View of Ruined Abbey and vineyard. (Photograph by Janie Bursford. Reproduced with kind permission of Surrey County Council.)

Painshill Park. The Chinese Bridge. (Photograph by Janie Bursford. Reproduced with kind permission of Surrey County Council.)

public. The Trust is endeavouring to restore the garden as it was in Hamilton's time. This has involved continuing research by historians into archival records, as well as on-site archaeology, to ascertain the precise sites of structures. Land Use Consultants produced a masterplan, not only for the restoration of the garden but also for the feasibility of the long-term future of the park.

A small team was established with a landscape architect as Director. Much of the landscape work at the park has been carried out under Manpower Services Commission Job Creation schemes. This has served a dual purpose of creating jobs and giving training skills to many unemployed people. From such schemes have emerged some of the present staff now in full-time employment. The Manpower Services Commission changed to the Training Commission in September 1988, and the

Community Programme Scheme was replaced by Employment Training. For the last 18 months of its existence, a Manpower Services Commission Community Programme Scheme was administered by Surrey County Council. The wages of the workers were claimed back from the Commission but the administrative costs were part of Surrey County Council's contribution to Painshill. Great assistance is given by Merrist Wood Agricultural College, for which Painshill is a principal training location for students.

Elmbridge Borough Council owns Painshill, but a long-term lease of the park has been granted to the Trust, which is responsible for raising all its own funds. Because of the national importance of the site, the principal financial backer of the project is the National Heritage Memorial Fund, which funded the original masterplan compiled by Land Use Consultants. The Heritage Fund agreed to give continuing support in 1984 to the extent of £1 million over a three-year period. As at March 1990, they have given (and promised) a total of £1 935 000.

The Countryside Commission and English Heritage have also contributed on a percentage-of-costs basis (as at March 1990, the Countryside Commission have given £60 000 and English Heritage, £346 000). The garden is 'outstanding' on the English Heritage Register of Parks and Gardens, and thus qualifies for financial assistance following the storms of 1987 and 1990 which caused so much damage to the landscape.

As well as their initial assistance with the purchase of the site, Surrey County Council has given financial and professional help with Painshill since 1980. As different buildings have been restored, grants have been given under the then appropriate legislation, the Local Authorities (Historic Buildings) Act 1962. The Restoration of the Aqueduct and Cascade was given £15 000 from the Countryside Block Sum (money available for work on countryside projects). As at March 1990, Surrey County Council has given or promised £81 000.

The Painshill Park Education Trust was incorporated on 24 January 1989, and its aim is to develop and promote Painshill as an educational resource and amenity for adults and children, both locally and nationally. Surrey County Council provided a classroom, and the funds to equip it, and has now seconded a teacher to work in the park on a three-year full-time contract. This support is the foundation of the Education Trust. A further private contribution of £2500 was made towards promotional material.

The most recent, and costly, restoration has been the Gothic Tower for which Architectural Heritage Fund provided a loan of £150 000.

Donations to the restoration of the Park have come from grant-making Trusts, some commercial contributions and from private donors. The value of Manpower Services Commission-sponsored job schemes at Painshill over seven years, amounted to some £600 000. Voluntary help, upon which the Painshill Park Trust depends for its visitor management and numerous other activities, represents a huge value in terms of support and staff. Many of the Trust's publications are fully sponsored and many building materials, supplies and equipment are donated. Elmbridge Borough Council provided accommodation and support services to the Trust from 1981 to the end of 1988.

WEST GLAMORGAN
PROJECT 6.12, Margam Park

Margam Park is situated some 5 km (3 miles) inland from Port Talbot, and 24 km (15 miles) south east of Swansea. Covering an area of just under 332 hectares (820 acres), this historic estate provides within its boundaries a landscape considered by many to be unique amongst the South Wales valleys. The wooded uplands in the northern part of the Park contrast with the flatter coastal belt in the south with its copses and lakes, more reminiscent of the parkland of lowland England.

The estate possesses evidence of very early occupation, including an Iron Age hill-fort, and became an important religious centre long before Cistercian monks built Margam Abbey, parts of which still stand. The Abbey became the largest and wealthiest in Wales during the twelfth century, but was one of many religious houses of England and Wales dissolved by Henry VIII in 1536.

The estate was subsequently acquired by the Mansel family, who already had extensive land holdings in other parts of Glamorgan. Sir Rice Mansel built a large house incorporating parts of the earlier Abbey, and in its day this mansion and the landscaped park around it were considered to be one of the greatest estates in the county. By the mid-eighteenth century the then owner of Margam, Thomas Mansel Talbot, decided that the house did not reflect the tastes of the period, was too old-fashioned and compared unfavourably with new mansions being built elsewhere. He built a villa as his new residence on another estate nearby, and demolished the old Margam House. On its site he decided to build a large structure to house his great collection of orange, lemon and citrus trees which the Talbots had inherited from their Mansel forebears. At this time, the collection contained about one hundred trees housed in several greenhouses about the Estate.

Thus began an enterprise that was to give to the Park its most magnificent building – the Orangery. Designed by a Gloucestershire architect, Anthony Keck, the Orangery is the longest in Britain, at 100 m (327 ft) – over twice that of the Orangery at the Royal Botanic Gardens at Kew. Of a bold, classical design, its simple and elegant appearance makes it, quite possibly, also the most beautiful in Britain. The repetitive arcading along its great length, contained within pedimented pavilions at each end has been handled with great skill, and at the time it was built, between 1786–1790, provided Wales with one of its first buildings in the Classical style.

Nearly 40 years after the demolition of the old mansion, a further descendant of the family resolved to build a new residence on higher ground at Margam, overlooking the lake. He commissioned Thomas Hopper, who had previously worked on Windsor and Penrhyn Castles, to design an imposing structure. In 1827, and again wishing to conform to the tastes of the times, a Tudor Gothic design was proposed. This was the time when many great houses were being constructed in Britain, and following on from the Classical influences of the preceding decades, designers were evolving a more 'romantic' approach borrowing heavily from earlier styles both in Britain and in Europe. This new mansion was to have an array of turrets, gables and clustered chimneys, bays and oriels, a castellated roof line and – surmounting the whole – a massive

(a)

(b)

Margam Park. The Orangery. Exterior view before (a) and interior view during (b) restoration. (Reproduced with kind permission of West Glamorgan County Council.)

tower. It was indeed the perfect foil to the strictly classical Orangery a short distance to its west. The building was completed in 1840, and Margam thus acquired another fine and majestic structure, Margam Castle. It remained a residence until World War II, when it was requisitioned by the Army. Sadly, after the War, both Margam Castle and the Orangery became derelict, the Castle itself becoming a roofless shell, stripped of all its fine interior work.

In 1973, the Glamorgan County Council acquired Margam Park and commenced a programme of restoration. In 1974, this responsibility passed to the West Glamorgan County Council who immediately undertook the task of restoring the Orangery. This involved completely repairing and relaying the stone floor, re-roofing the structure and renewing and repairing the elaborate fenestration, external stonework and internal plaster decorations. Wherever possible the work was carried out reusing original materials and following closely the original design. The work took four years to complete and was opened by Her Majesty the Queen in her Jubilee year. Today the building is used daily for exhibitions and functions of all kinds, including lectures and conferences and provides a valuable assembly facility for the region. It is listed Grade I.

Work has also been carried out within the Estate itself, which has been designated a Country Park.

Lakes have been cleared, extensive areas have been replanted, the deer herd is thriving and many wildlife habitats have been fostered to encourage a diverse and abundant fauna.

The ruins of the Cistercian Abbey are open to the public as are parts of the formal grounds around the Castle. The County Council has been very careful, in restoring and remodelling the parkland areas, that commercial motivation should not exploit the fine and tranquil setting of Margam. It has been an expensive undertaking, but the County Council is anxious to adhere to its programme of progressive restoration over the coming years.

Since 1974, the expenditure incurred at Margam has exceeded £7 500 000, including £1 160 000 on the restoration of the Orangery. This was offset by grant-aid from a number of sources including the Historic Buildings Council for Wales, the Wales Tourist Board and the Countryside Commission.

The future programme of work requires that attention is given to the need to consolidate the ruins of Margam Castle, until such time as a phased restoration can be contemplated. There is no doubt that the dramatic silhouette and skyline of this building makes a vivid and lasting impression on the many who visit this magnificent Park each year.

(See Plates 28 and 29.)

7

PUBLICITY AND PROMOTION

PROJECTS

INTRODUCTION

Previous chapters in this book have looked at the range of conservation works that have been and are being carried out by County Councils and National Park Authorities in caring for our Built Heritage. But there comes a point where we must ask ourselves 'how do these examples achieve a wider audience, and how do the lessons that have been learnt lead to a greater public awareness?'

Successful promotion requires successful publicity. Almost all the County Councils engage in some sort of heritage promotion and the following pages illustrate the many ways in which some have chosen to promote their work. These include newspaper features, promotional leaflets, videos, exhibitions, broadsheets on good repair practice and the promotion of completed restoration projects. Local award schemes and town trails are also a rewarding source of promotion, as are, of course, the heavy demands made upon County conservation staff in giving public lectures.

Caring for our Built Heritage is very much a matter of education and awareness. Publicity is one of many ways of achieving this, with the use of local newspaper circulation, where possible. The Pembrokeshire Coast National Park Authority publish their own informative newspaper, *Coast To Coast*, setting out both the work the Authority is carrying out, and coming visitor events. In Essex the Archaeological section of the County Council's planning department insert a 'state of the year message' in the local newspaper, describing the archaeological work that has been done during the previous twelve months. Archaeology has for many years had a significant public interest, although it is not every day that exciting discoveries are made that are destined to make headlines. The usual workload for a County Council archaeologist is at a more methodical and low key level of control, rescue and recording, and it is precisely this that the newsletter publicises. Derbyshire County Council in 1991, for the first time, produced an Annual Report on grant assisted archaeological work, written and presented in such a way as to demystify the subject to the layman.

The restoration of historic buildings is such an important aspect of the work of protecting our heritage, that very many County Councils, in conjunction with their District Council colleagues, have produced attractive and useful booklets and leaflets on exactly what to do in particular cases.

Hertfordshire, Surrey and Durham County Councils, for example, have produced excellent broadsheets for distribution to the public on almost any topic of repair that a historic building owner, agent and builder would need. The 'do's and don'ts' are clearly set out, with the intention that in some cases these advice notes will be attached to listed building consent permissions to ensure that any restoration and repair are carried out correctly. In Somerset, again in collaboration with the five District Councils in the county, a well illustrated booklet has been produced to give information on the measures which can be taken to preserve and enhance the historic environment of the county.

Lancashire County Council, through their County Planning Department, have published a fully illustrated book on Lancashire's Architectural Heritage, written by their conservation officer, John Champness. In about 170 pages it gives scholarly comment on many buildings and structures and is a valuable introduction to the architecture of the county. Similarly, Devon County Council have produced a number of informative and beautifully illustrated books. *Devon Roads* by Michael Hawkins, OBE, County Engineer, offers a fascinating account of the history of road making in Devon, whilst their Archaeologist, Frances Griffith, has written *Devon's Past – An aerial view*, which gives the reader a spectacular view, quite literally, of the archaeological treasures of the county. As for their buildings, Peter Beacham has edited *Devon Building – An introduction to local traditions*, an immensely valuable reference to the many and varied styles and textures of Devon buildings.

Cheshire County Council have produced an impressive book, which owes its origins to a 'handover statement' for the new County Council in 1974, entitled *Man's Imprint on Cheshire*. Written by their conservation officer, Oliver Bott, and the Principal Archaeologist, Rhys Williams, it describes in a most readable way the evolution of the man-made landscapes and the built environment in the county. Together with a gazetteer, which has subsequently proved popular with the general public and schools alike, this is a valuable reference book for all scholars studying the historic environment of that county.

Almost all County Councils and National Park Authorities have produced similar publications to those mentioned, but it would be impossible in this chapter to mention them all. However, there are enough to show the diversity of subjects that have been covered, which, at the end of the day, surely reflects the growing public interest that has been achieved and is now being catered for.

Whilst the printed word is often the easiest and most convenient way to get a message across, the promotion of our historic heritage in all its aspects can also be demonstrated in a variety of practical ways on the ground. Derbyshire County Council, for example, has chosen to use actual building restoration schemes as a means of promoting historic building conservation, with displays and exhibitions, whilst Kent County Council promote a 3-day Conservation Show, at which displays of appropriate products and suppliers, together with an exhibition, are the chief means of presentation.

Over the past fifty years or so we have enjoyed a degree of mobility, together with increased leisure time, undreamt of by earlier generations. Travel by car or coach means that access to almost any corner of the land is now relatively easy. Tourism initiatives rely heavily on promoting the particular historic aspects of an area, and the growth in membership of Trusts and Preservation Societies has meant that we are able to enjoy an almost limitless range of restoration projects from historic towns, houses, parks and gardens, archaeological sites and industrial structures.

Most of us respond to praise and recognition. Some counties have introduced, over the last few years, their own Award schemes which not only recognize and record the participants, but also bring the scheme to public prominence with, often, local newspapers taking an interest in these successes. The Civic Trust scheme has been running now for over 20 years; its accolade of an Award or a Commendation is highly valued, and its success in bringing to the public's attention the need for good and sensitive design is now well known. There are, of course, many other national and local Award schemes, by professional institutions and commercial firms, but this chapter reviews just a few of those operated and sponsored by County Councils, each promoting their own Award scheme aimed at encouraging good design in all aspects in the built and natural environment; awards usually taking the form of a plaque and certificate. Devon promotes the Arnold Sayers Award. A former Chairman of Devon County Council, he originated the idea for an annual award to mark European Heritage Year in 1975, and was originally restricted to awards for single houses and groups of houses, but the scheme now includes restored buildings. The Arthur Brown Trophy sponsored by Staffordshire County Council is concerned mainly with the restoration of historic buildings, and a recent award winner has been the scheme at Carter Lane, Uttoxeter, described in this chapter. Also illustrated is a scheme at Chichester which received an award from West Sussex County Council for the successful restoration of a group of Georgian houses in the older part of the city. The Derbyshire Awards for conservation of the Built Environment are part of a wider Award Scheme which encompasses the conservation of the natural environment. Derbyshire also provides an occasional newspaper publication, *Derbyshire Green Watch*, dealing with a broad range of environmental issues. By this means it is possible to reach a wider audience than the existing committed Civic Society member. County Durham also sponsors an Annual Environment Award for schemes that improve the built and natural environment of the county, and demonstrate good guardianship.

Schools and colleges have also recognized the importance of a knowledge of our built heritage in studies of our social and national history. The media, including the television companies, are able to demonstrate that historic building and heritage programmes achieve successful audience ratings, and recent programmes on the national networks have been popular. Clwyd County Council have produced their own video on their historic heritage, and many other Counties are following suit. Durham have produced attractive, pocket-sized, leaflets on walkabouts in a number of historic towns and villages in the County, laid out with informative texts, line drawings and maps. This is a theme Nottinghamshire have used with great success in their informative village guides, such as the Laxton Trail.

An indication of the interest shown in this subject by the public can be gauged by the demands placed upon the professional County and District conservation officers to give talks and lectures to a variety of audiences on almost every conservation topic. This is always seen as a valuable way of illustrating the latest work of Councils, and it is known that these talks are greatly appreciated.

On the local level, one must not overlook the enormous efforts that local groups go to in publicising and illustrating their town. Promotional leaflets, and the instigation of their own town walks are, indeed, valuable and rewarding ways of complementing the efforts of the local authorities.

CHESHIRE

PROJECT 7.1, *The Gazetteer: Man's Imprint on Cheshire*

Originating as a report to the new County Council following Local Government reorganization in 1974, this gazetteer reviewed the man-made heritage in Cheshire, and subsequently provided the basis for the development of County Council conservation policies. It has been available for sale and has sold out two printings, each of 3000 copies. It is popular with visitors, with those living in the county and with the schools. It is an impressive document, running to nearly 70 pages, by Oliver Bott and Rhys Williams, and reviews (with photographs) town plans and sketches, the wealth of examples in Cheshire where man has left his mark. As the introduction says 'almost the whole surface of lowland Britain bears the marks of man's long occupation and of the changes in his way of life and pattern of settlement which have taken place since prehistoric times. The evidence, above and below ground, can cast light on many aspects of past life – and of death; habitation; agriculture; industry; handiwork and arts; recreation; trade; travel and transport; worship; burial and communication.'

24

Cheshire from 1540 to 1750

From the dissolution of the Monasteries to the Canal Age

Two events which radically changed the flow of life in Cheshire were the dissolution of the monasteries in the 1540's and the genesis of economic heavy inland transport which came with the cutting of the artificial canals during the second half of the 18th century.

The dissolution of the monasteries caused the destruction of three of the largest and finest medieval building groups in the county — Norton Priory, Vale Royal Abbey and Combermere Abbey — together with their dependencies. More fundamentally it changed the whole pattern of land ownership, destroyed an important agency of road repair and maintenance and, together with Henry VIII's break with Rome, encouraged the growing emphasis on secular objectives in society, thought and the economy.

From the dissolution to the Civil War: 1540 to 1642

Oak framed "black-and-white" houses begin to give way to early classical designs in stone and brick.

The first fruit of this new growth was the proliferation of oak-framed houses. A good deal survives; new large houses in the countryside, extensions to old halls and manors and a number of buildings in the streets of old towns and villages (sometimes hidden behind later brick fronts). Henry VIII sold the monastic lands which the Crown had acquired to the peaceful rural landowners whose interest has been the progressive consolidation and improvement of their estates. They seem to have set to with vigour to improve countryside and towns as soon as the land was theirs.

The oak-framed houses — similar in all but detail and greater opulence to those which had been built before the Dissolution — are essentially late medieval country houses, friendly, informal and unsophisticated. Parallel with the continuance of the tradition of timber-framed building (common to the Border counties from Chester to Chepstow, where oak trees provided the readiest building material to hand), imposing brick and stone houses, showing the first faltering attempts at classicism, began to appear – Brereton Hall south of Holmes Chapel and, more ambitiously, Lyme Park. A little later, at the beginning of the 17th century, brick was used impressively in the fine Jacobean Halls of Crewe and Dorfold.

In Chester and Nantwich, and to a lesser extent elsewhere, a number of good half-timbered town houses from the late 16th and the 17th century survive, side by side with the brick which superseded timber framing, as a rule, by 1700.

Inns, schools, almshouses, windmills and water mills.

A greater variety of building began to emerge in the 17th century; for instance inns recognisably such as today, schools and almshouses. The old Grammar School at Audlem (1652) is an excellent example.

Wind and water mills were common in the Middle Ages, usually for grinding corn. Transport of heavy produce over long distances was laborious and expensive, except by sea or navigable rivers, so that corn mills had to be local, and consequently small. Chester, the biggest town in the region and a main port and centre of communications, at least since Norman times, had a larger mill on the north side of the Dee by the weir. Examples of water mill buildings survive from the 16th century onward. Nether Alderley Mill (restored by the National Trust) in east Cheshire and Stretton Mill in west Cheshire (in course of restoration by Cheshire County Council) are among the best examples. The oldest surviving mill machinery, at Stretton Mill, south east of Farndon, dates from the 18th century.

Farming and the countryside.

Of farming and the countryside, information is scanty, but, to judge from the record of complaints by cavalry commanders during the Civil War, Cheshire's farmland was fairly commonly enclosed by 1640, and divided by hedges which the horses could not jump. In the grounds of the great houses like Lyme Park, the deliberate creation of ornamental landscape was to come later. During the 16th and 17th century they appear to have been valued by their owners chiefly as deer-parks, good venues for hunting.

Oak-framed Jacobethan house, Prestbury, now the National Westminster Bank.

Hospital Street, Nantwich — 17th century doorway and windows embellish an earlier house.

Monument to Dame Alice Fitton, Gawsworth Church, 1627.

Lyme Park; the Elizabethan north front attempting classical composition, 1570.

Lyme Cage, Lyme Park — an Elizabethan hunt observation tower.

Cromwell's statue, Warrington, 1899, by John Bell of Kensington.

Detail of Wright's Almshouses, Nantwich, 1638.

School in Nether Alderley churchyard, 1693.

Queen Anne doorway, Chestergate, Macclesfield, the home of Charles Roe, founder of the local silk industry.

The Civil War

25

The Civil War must have brought development in Cheshire to a halt for more than ten years, with constant military activity in the countryside, a few pitched battles (notably Rowton Moor and Nantwich, where the field was by Acton), and the long siege of Chester. It was the last time that medieval fortifications were used in England. The walls of Chester were evidently an effective defence, but the garrison of Beeston Castle were surprised and overcome by a group of the enemy who climbed the rock and got in through the kitchens.

Military activity; civil stagnation; destruction.

Where new defences were needed (as at Nantwich), earthworks were thrown up, rather than stone walls. But the destruction to our heritage brought on by the war was to the medieval buildings and paintings on and in the churches, rather than to secular buildings. Indeed, there are links between the religious disputes which contributed to the 17th century Civil War and the sectarian aspect of the violence in 20th century Ulster.

Roads and bridges fell into serious disrepair for no one had replaced the monasteries as an effective agency for their management and maintenance, and the wars stopped such work as the parishes had undertaken.

The late 17th and early 18th Centuries

There are few individually noteworthy remains from the last decades of the 17th century or from the early 18th century. The Unitarian Chapels at Knutsford, Dean Row and Macclesfield — the first Non-Conformist churches in Cheshire — of around 1690 were Jacobean in character. On a grand scale, Leoni's substantial work at Lyme Park (1720's) was Cheshire's first major taste of the classical style, but even here more with a 17th than an 18th century character. The Bluecoat School at Chester (1717) is important as a mark of the growing use of private charitable funds for social purposes, here an orphanage as well as a school, not only for its architectural quality.

Chapels, country houses, schools, almshouses, orphanages.

The most widespread characteristic of the late 17th and early 18th century, on the evidence of remaining buildings, was the development and improvement of farms and farmland. Surviving farmhouses and farm buildings from this period in Cheshire can be measured by hundreds; and it is the first period to leave a substantial legacy of cottages in the countryside and villages.

Farms and farmland.

Chester steadily sank in importance as a port; Parkgate took its place for the Irish trade, and Liverpool began to grow as a major port. But this meant change of emphasis rather than eclipse for Chester. Its importance as a market centre for West Cheshire and North Wales, as a garrison town and as an ecclesiastical, administrative and judicial centre remained.

Chester's changing role.

Button-making was an organised industry in Macclesfield from the 17th century, but organised by contractors who farmed out the work to craftsmen who had their workshops in their own homes.* But on this domestic basis, the making of copper buttons and the covering of them with silk, the beginning of the silk industry in Cheshire developed. In the early 18th century machinery which could be operated in series by the power of water wheels was developed for the thread-making processes of the textile industry. This, the birth of the factory system, was introduced to Cheshire by Charles Roe, who opened his first silk mill in Macclesfield in 1743.

Macclesfield and the birth of the modern silk industry.

*Now the Japanese are making zips at Runcorn; world-wide distribution of light articles has become possible.

Two typical pages from *The Gazetteer*.

DERBYSHIRE

PROJECT 7.2, *Derbyshire Greenwatch*

Responding to the considerable groundswell of concern for 'green' issues, in 1989 Derbyshire County Council began publishing its own environmental newspaper. Produced as a high-quality full colour publication, *Derbyshire Greenwatch* has been very well received by both Derbyshire residents and visitors to the county, and has clearly filled a need as a means of communication in this specialist area.

The County Council has recently published the third in the series of twice-yearly newspapers for which an annual budget of £28 000 has been provided. The first *Greenwatch* ran to eight pages, but such was the popularity of the newspaper that the second and third issues both contained twelve pages. With 20 000 copies of each issue printed *Greenwatch* is circulated to other local authorities and organizations with an interest in the environment and is distributed to all County educa-

tional establishments throughout Derbyshire. It is also made available to the public who can pick up copies from countryside sites and visitor centres, and has been widely praised for its quality, content, design and layout.

Building conservation issues can be presented as part of the wider environmental movement and this is beneficial because too often heritage issues are presented and perceived as an esoteric minority concern. Within the first three issues, heritage subjects such as threatened buildings, unsympathetic repair, and conservation awards have been presented side-by-side with articles on water pollution, access to the countryside, and tree planting.

The newspaper is also proving to be a valuable medium to publicise the pioneering work of the County Council in the field of environmental education.

DERBYSHIRE GREEN WATCH

DERBYSHIRE COUNTY COUNCIL
CARING FOR — THE — ENVIRONMENT

The Environmental Newspaper of Derbyshire County Council

Issue No. 3 Summer 1990

Environment brings everyone together

MORE people from the ethnic minority communities are being encouraged to visit Derbyshire's popular country parks.

A leaflet highlighting the attractions of both Elvaston Castle and Shipley Park has just been published in Punjabi and Urdu.

And a follow-up pamphlet will be translated into Hindi, Gujarati and Chinese.

The leaflets are to be circulated to community centres and groups not only in Derby but also in Nottingham, Leicester and Sheffield.

Action team to direct county green crusade

Highly tropical subject

DERBYSHIRE County Council
We're **proud** of Derbyshire.

YOUNGSTERS at a Derby school didn't need to travel very far to experience the sights and sounds of the rain forest — they simply built their own!

Pupils of Lees Brook Community School created a colourful haven of trees, plants and animals as part of a project to raise awareness about the plight of the rain forests.

Find out more about their adventures — and what it's like to visit a REAL rain forest — on the centre pages.

AN INFLUENTIAL 'cabinet' of leading councillors has been formed to forge ahead with Derbyshire's trailblazing environmental work.

The County Council's new environment panel will ensure that the authority's high-profile approach to 'green' issues extends across all its policies.

In the last few years the council has led the field in taking environmental action — providing a model for many other authorities to follow.

It made history when it successfully prosecuted local water authorities for river pollution offences, its nature conservation policies have scooped a major national award and its work to promote environmental education has won countrywide acclaim.

Chair of the panel, Cllr Joe Heathcote, said: "Initiatives launched by Derbyshire County Council over recent years have had a major impact on the national environment debate.

"We hope that this new panel will consolidate and build on our work in what is becoming an increasingly crucial field."

The panel's brief is to:

● Draw up a major new environmental strategy to examine and review existing county policies.

● Involve the community — along with national environmental groups and agencies — in the preparation of the strategy.

● Launch and monitor new environmental projects.

● Promote the County Council as an environment-friendly organisation.

● Encourage a positive attitude towards the Derbyshire environment from residents, voluntary groups and other organisations.

● Campaign on national and global environmental issues.

Danger list of buildings in decay

THIS crumbling cottage at Glapwell has been placed on a new 'danger list' drawn up by Derbyshire County Council.

Isolated by farmland, the cottage — probably once used as the garden house for the old Glapwell Hall — is one of many historic Derbyshire buildings facing dereliction and decay.

And without urgent action, it is feared that some of these county landmarks could be lost forever . . .

● For full story — see page four.

GREENWATCH AWARDS: THE NATURAL CHOICES — BACK PAGE

Front page from a copy of the *Derbyshire Greenwatch* newspaper.

DURHAM

PROJECT 7.3, Caring for our Heritage

Durham County Council published the *Durham Book* in 1974 which has been revised and updated in both hard- and paperback. It is an attractive and well presented book introducing and promoting the county to visitors and contains sections on the history and character of the built heritage of the county. The book has been very popular ever since it was first published.

Durham's Environment Department has produced a pack containing a series of leaflets which, with the aid of clear line drawings and sketches, give information to all those involved in work on listed buildings. These leaflets, produced in conjunction with Wear Valley District Council, Teesdale District Council and English Heritage, include subjects such as general information on listed buildings, how they are chosen, what is the effect of listing a building, and a summary of the current listed building legislation. To keep an old building in good repair, careful maintenance is essential, and a series of guides give advice on the many aspects that an owner might encounter. Grants may be given for the repair of historic buildings; a leaflet with particular reference to Town Schemes in Barnard Castle and Bishops Auckland, gives helpful advice to owners contemplating involvement in such a scheme.

Also contained in the pack are a number of 'walkabouts' – guides to walks around the conservation areas pointing out historical and architectural features.

Repointing

Over a hundred years or so the joints in a wall will fail, simply through old age. When they do, rainwater will soak into the wall instead of running down it and when that happens, repointing — replacing the outer parts of the joints — becomes necessary.

Rainwater falling on a wall can either run off or soak in. If it soaks in, then it will either keep on moving inwards and evaporate out when dry weather comes. Once in, water will start breaking up a wall by either frost or chemical action. Either way, the effect is the same — the mortar softens or cracks and drops out or the face of the stone flakes off. It may be a long time before the wall falls down but it will not be long before its inside face becomes damp.

It is important to do everything possible to make sure that water runs off a wall or, if it gets in, evaporates straight back out again.

Our older stone houses were built to do just that.

Firstly, the builders made sure there was nowhere on the outside face of the wall where water could collect. Joints were finished flush with the edges of the stones, sometimes very slightly recessed — but never projecting because that might allow water to collect and find its way in between the mortar and the stones where the frost or chemical action would start damaging the wall.

Secondly, the mortar was generally a mixture of sand and lime, which is porous, flexible and weaker than the stones it is bonding together. Because it is porous, any water getting into the wall can evaporate out through the joints as well as the stone instead of concentrating only on the stone. Because it is weaker and more flexible than the stone, sand-lime mortar resists any small movements in the wall without itself cracking and without damaging the stones. And, because these factors reduce the risks of decay, the wall will last longer without major maintenance or repair.

Not only do walls built like this function properly, they also look right — and good pointing is as important to the appearance of a building as the right doors and windows. Repointing should therefore, try to match the original pointing as closely as possible.

Modern practices have changed from the old ways but are not necessarily as well suited to repairing old buildings as they are to building new.

Standard mortar mixes, especially those sold ready-mixed, are often just sand and cement, which is too hard and too strong for an old stone wall. The mortar is not flexible enough to absorb any movement in the wall, for example, from expansion and contraction, which means that the stones may crack, and it is not porous, which means water can only evaporate out through the stone, adding to the risk of cracking.

The modern trend is also to spread mortar beyond the actual joints and over all the little irregularities that are found in old stone walls, covering up some of the stone to give a smooth finish. Although this sounds sensible, it is likely to leave many more places where water can collect, cause cracks between mortar and the stone and seep into the wall.

Another recent trend which is also damaging both visually and practically is the use of raised or 'ribbon pointing' which emphasizes the pointing rather than the stonework.

In practice, there is a suitable compromise between the old methods and the new. Some cement can be used in the mortar mix, but it should be kept to a minimum, and some lime should be added too, giving flexibility and also helping to match the colour of the original mortar. It is also a good idea to use sand which is not pure in colour, or to add in some stone grit, as this helps the colour and texture of the repointing.

If you can try a small sample area first, then do so. You can then vary the mix quite easily, if need be, in order to get a better colour match. To get a good repair, matching the old pointing as far as possible, repointing means going through the steps described on the back page.

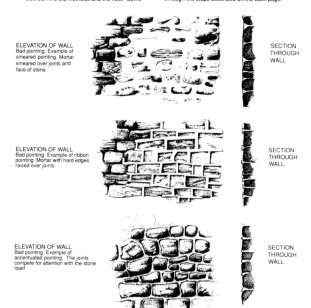

TYPICAL ELEVATION/SECTION OF STONE RUBBLE WALL IN NEED OF REPOINTING

Good pointing

Old mortar has fallen out of joints, now in need of repointing.

Bad pointing: Old flush pointing smeared over the edge of the stone tends to pull away from the stone, allowing water to penetrate. It also looks unsightly.

ELEVATION OF WALL
Bad pointing: Example of smeared pointing. Mortar smeared over joints and face of stone.

SECTION THROUGH WALL

ELEVATION OF WALL
Bad pointing: Example of ribbon pointing. Mortar with hard edges raised over joints.

SECTION THROUGH WALL

ELEVATION OF WALL
Bad pointing: Example of accentuated pointing. The joints compete for attention with the stone itself.

SECTION THROUGH WALL

Sample pages from a recent report.

Gainford, midway between Barnard Castle and Darlington, is one of Teesdale's most attractive villages. In 1971 the oldest part of the village was designated a Conservation Area to secure its protection and improvement. This leaflet is a guide to a 30 minute walk around the Conservation Area, pointing out the most interesting historical and architectural features along the way.

On the lower side of the Green some of the houses have recently been renovated with traditional materials. The row of new houses, although pleasant enough in themselves, do not fit comfortably among the older houses. This is because they are detached, leaving gaps between them and because they are sideways onto the green with a very shallow roof pitch. At the corner of the green some new bungalows have been hidden away behind the older houses.

West House

The walk starts on the VILLAGE GREEN

1.   Nearly all the houses that can be seen date from the eighteenth century, the village's boom period, but its history goes back much further. The first church was built in Saxon times, at the beginning of the ninth century, by Egred, Bishop of Lindisfarne. The place was then called Geginford and was built in a square around the green so that cattle and sheep could be driven into this compound and there defended against raiders from the Scottish borders.

2.   *Turn towards SOUTH TERRACE* past a terrace of eighteenth century cottages, typical of the villages in this part of Durham. Climb the steps to the upper green. The three storey buildings here testify to Gainford's prosperity in Georgian times. The white building to the west of the Co-operative shop was formerly St. Colette's School House and was built in 1712. The original bay windows remain on the ground floor but the facade has been changed by the addition of a nineteenth century wooden bay window and the resashing of the upper storey windows without glazing bars. The eighteenth century glassblowers could not produce panes of glass much larger than 18 inches square. When it became possible to make larger panes the glazing bars were taken out of many windows, which transformed the original design of the buildings.

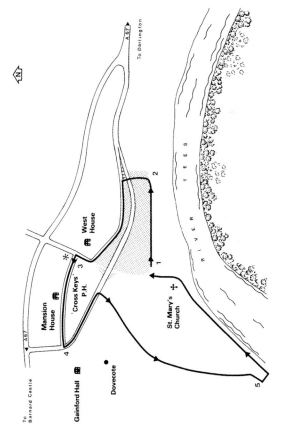

Sample pages from *Walkabout*, *No. 3 – Gainford*.

ESSEX

PROJECT 7.4, *Essex Archaeology*

Early in 1984, the County Planning Department's Archaeology Section approached a local weekly newspaper, the *Essex Chronicle*, with the idea of producing an archaeological supplement. This was to be a digest, written at a popular level, presenting all aspects of recent archaeological activity in the county. The response of the *Essex Chronicle* management was both prompt and enthusiastic, and so the first issue of *Essex Archaeology* appeared as an eight-page pull-out in September 1984. The response of the general public was so good that it has now become an annual event.

The supplement's aim is a simple one: it is to publicise and promote archaeology within the county. Although it is collated and edited by one of the archaeology section staff, the contents cover a wide range of discoveries and initiatives undertaken by a variety of organizations. These include the many active local societies, museums, and other professional organizations (both local and national). A typical issue contains articles on excavation, field survey, historic buildings, museum displays and other exhibitions, industrial archaeology, aerial photography, local events, and artist's reconstructions of archaeological sites and landscapes.

Because of the high level of interest generated, the circulation of the supplement has risen considerably. The first issue, in 1984, had a circulation of around 37 000 through the *Essex Chronicle* alone, plus a reprint of 10 000 for distribution to schools, libraries, museums and tourist outlets. By 1990 (Issue no. 7) the circulation had gone up to 65 000, through the *Essex Chronicle* and its sister newspapers, plus a reprint of 15 000. A substantial mailing list has been built up with addresses throughout the UK, and even a scattering of Essex exiles in North America and Australia. The size has also gone up from eight to twelve pages.

The supplement has also had two unexpected side-effects, both positive. First, when officers of the Archaeology Section are negotiating with developers for access to, and funding for, sites threatened by development, it has proved enormously helpful to send them copies of the supplement. Developers can then quickly see just how much rescue archaeology is going on in the county, how it is integrated into the planning process, and how exciting the results can be. For those with an eye for good public relations, the benefits of linking their company's name with an archaeological project featured in a publication with a circulation of approaching 80 000 are obvious. Secondly, there has been a great deal of interest and favourable comment from the archaeological profession. Enquiries have been received from every part of the country, especially from local government-based archaeologists, about how the supplement is put together and how much it costs.

Essex County Council Supplement—1

ESSEX ARCHAEOLOGY

ISSUE No. 6

FROM PIT TO PAINTING

The County Council's Archaeology Section has been working continuously at Stansted Airport for almost four years, in conditions varying from minus 17°c during the winter of 1985/86, to the baking heat of this summer. Occasionally, urgent contractors' deadlines have meant working seven days a week, and sometimes well into the nights under the beams of car headlamps.

Many of the discoveries have been spectacular, and none more so than the remains of a complete Iron Age village. This site was called the Airport Catering Site (or ACS for short), because it was next to the former catering service building providing in-flight meals for airline passengers. It took 12 months to investigate the site, which turned out to be unlike any other in the county for that date.

Excavation revealed an enclosure about 80 metres across, defined by a substantial ditch up to 1.5 metres deep and averaging four metres wide at the top. Originally, there was a bank inside the ditch, but this had weathered down and been ploughed away over the years. Traces of 11 wooden round houses were found in the form of circular gulleys, although the pottery suggests that no more than six or seven were contemporary, implying six or seven households at any one time. The houses would have had timber uprights, with wattle and daub infilling and thatched roofs.

The lay-out of the settlement indicates a strong element of planning. The round houses (and some equally well-defined semi-circular structures which may have been workshops) were all built just inside the enclosure bank, which may have sheltered them from the prevailing wind. The centre of the enclosure was relatively empty, apart from traces of a square building, quite different from the many round houses.

The finds were remarkable. There were nearly 40 bronze brooches, and an intaglio (a carved semi-precious stone) from a finger ring. The intaglio and a number of the brooches came from a pit adjacent to the central square building, which has been interpreted as a shrine or place of worship. There were enormous amounts of pottery and animal bone. The former included fragments of vessels from southern Italy, originally containers for wine. The latter hinted at an economy based largely on cattle-raising. Finally, on the last afternoon of a year-long excavation, the most dramatic find of all - a hoard of 50 superbly preserved potin coins. These were Iron Age "small change," made of an alloy of copper, zinc, lead and tin.

In spite of all these extraordinary finds, the site was not an easy one to excavate properly during the excavation. For one thing, because of contractors' timetables, the whole site was never open at any one time, but in bits. Secondly, the site was on sticky grey boulder clay. Archaeological features were visible only as slight variations in the greyness. Thirdly, most of the

site had inadvertently been covered by a huge dump of boulder clay from earth-moving operations elsewhere in the airport, before excavation began. When this dump was removed, it left huge spoil heaps up to 12 feet high all round the edge of the excavation. In wet weather it was a feat of endurance merely to reach the site, let alone understand what was going on.

Similar practical problems have been met on many sites, and so the County Council has over recent years maintained a policy of producing detailed reconstructions of major sites, so that their full significance may be appreciated by everyone, not just the specialist. The illustrations on this page tell the story which led to the most recent painting in this series, the reconstruction of the Iron Age village at Stansted Airport.

Stage 1. Detailed drawings are made to cover the entire site. The draughtsman has laid out a gridded metal planning frame over an archaeological feature. The frame provides an accurate square grid which matches the graph paper grid on the drawing board at a 1:20 reduction. For a site as large as ACS, many such plans are produced.

STANSTED PROJECT
AIRPORT CATERING SITE
Provisional July 1987

Stage 2. The site plans are put together to produce an overall lay-out, which shows a ditched enclosure, about 80 metres across. There is evidence of "town planning" here, as all the round houses are zoned just inside the former bank (the presence of which is inferred from the gap between the edge of the ditch and the round houses).

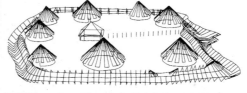

Stage 3. This is a computer-generated perspective view of the site from the west, using the Stage 2 plan. The "annexe" in the bottom right hand corner of the Stage 2 plan has been omitted. The pottery suggests it was of a slightly different date to the main enclosure. In the County Council's Planning Department, the computer programme which produced this view is normally used in assessing the appearance of housing schemes at the planning application stage. (It has been particularly used in connection with the new town of South Woodham Ferrers). The programme needs a ground plan and details of the elevation, and can then provide accurate perspectives from any angle and any height. This is the first time it has been used for an archaeological site in Essex.

Stage 4. The artist, Frank Gardiner, nearing completion of his watercolour painting of the late Iron Age village. The perspective finally chosen was a view from the north-east, which gave a slightly clearer impression of the central square structure (thought to be a shrine), than the view from the west shown in Stage 3. Various details, such as the fenced paddocks, were added after discussion with the excavators.

Stage 5. The finished product. The painting shows the enclosure in its setting during the first century BC. There was no sign of fields laid out around the enclosure, suggesting that the land was mainly pasture, for rearing the cattle which are thought to provide the economic basis of the settlement. The reconstruction of the gateway is conjectural, because no trace of an entrance was found within the excavated area.

PUBLISHED BY ESSEX COUNTY COUNCIL 1989
Prepared within the Planning Dept. for the Environment Committee

Sample pages from *Essex Archaeology*, Supplement.

HERTFORDSHIRE

PROJECT 7.5, *Hertfordshire Conservation File*

The County Planning and Estates Department has produced, through their Design and Conservation Consultancy, a set of leaflets which form the *Hertfordshire Conservation File*. These have been devised to assist owners of properties, architects, surveyors and others involved in good conservation practice. These leaflets are a source of information and guidance and provide a sound basis for those involved in advising on historic building repair, at both the County and District Offices, and those working in the private sector.

Subjects covered include thatching, cleaning old brickwork, pargetting, repair of historic windows, and fact sheets on grants and loans, listing procedures and the law.

The leaflets are colour coded into separate categories: Information and Advice, Fact Sheets, Crafts and Skills, and Materials; and can be collected together to form an updatable loose-leaf file, to facilitate keeping abreast with current legislation and procedures.

HISTORIC WINDOWS

HISTORY AND CONSERVATION

The essential character of many unlisted buildings such as this Victorian terrace, is being slowly eroded by badly designed window replacements. On the right are original windows, on the left are replacement windows. Historically correct joinery should be repaired as it usually looks better, lasts longer and is cheaper in the long run.

INTRODUCTION

Many people have 'improved' their homes by replacing original joinery. In fact, there is no easier and quicker way to destroy the genuine character of an historic building, than to replace joinery inappropriately. New structural problems may be created. New materials such as uPVC and poor design simply do not belong in historic buildings for which they were not intended. It is important to know that there is often little difference between the cost of repair and replacement.

This leaflet is aimed chiefly at those who are considering repairing or replacing original windows in historic buildings. The leaflet encourages sympathetic conservation, and does not discourage modern materials in modern buildings. For information and advice in the history and repair of historic doors, please refer to leaflet 9, 'Historic doors: History and Conservation'.

The Law

Proposals to alter joinery in listed buildings requires listed building consent, and it is unlikely that consent would be given for inappropriate replacements. Failure to observe the law may result in an enforcement notice being served, and replacements having to be replaced. (See information sheet no. 5:1. A listed building is a building or structure protected by law, for which alterations, demolition and extensions require listed building consent.) Alterations in conservation areas should be referred to the relevant District Council Planning department for advice. (A conservation area is a legally designated area with tighter planning control than elsewhere, an area of 'special architectural or historic interest, the character or appearance of which is desirable to preserve or enhance'.) There have been a number of cases concerning listed buildings, where the owner did not know the legal position, and was wrongly informed that it was impossible to replace the joinery with timber copies. Grant aid may be available for sympathetic repair to a listed building using traditional methods. For further information, please see fact sheet no. 5:2, 'Grants and Loans for Historic Buildings.'

The street scene

It has been the fashion to replace windows, partly because other houses in the street have been altered. But if the outside of all the houses in a street were inappropriately altered, the street would be a mixture of jarring forms, rather than a harmonious whole. This is particularly the case with terrace houses. All the buildings – and all their exterior joinery – play an important part in the 'picture' of the whole. Sadly, many of our streets are now effectively being altered according to the availability of ready-made goods. If replacement is being considered, it is worthwhile to look at, and possibly photograph, historic examples nearby to be aware of the subtle but

of a historical building. They break up the design and create interest. Because they are moulded (are cut in different forms in cross-section), an interesting effect of light and shade is given.

Large areas of plate glass can have a blank, soulless appearance, especially in small houses. (Many people have net curtains for privacy anyway, so the effect is lost.)

It is often thought that because a replacement window has glazing bars, or an echo of history, that it is correct for a historic building. However, a main advantage of original windows over bad replacements are the actual mouldings of the glazing bars (also known as astragals). As shown in the illustration, these were made in different forms, each giving their own attractive quality. Mouldings give an effect of light and shade, and of elegance which is not possible with modern flat, block-like glazing bars. Often the mouldings on the inside of the window would be plainer than the outside. These details were made for a purpose: as with many details on historic buildings, the subtleties of specific areas of design are essential to the quality of the whole.

WINDOW GLAZING BARS: STYLES AND DATES

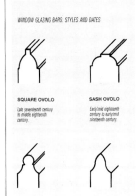

SQUARE OVOLO

Late seventeenth century to middle eighteenth century.

SASH OVOLO

Early/mid eighteenth century to early/mid nineteenth century.

ASTRAGAL AND HOLLOW

Early/mid eighteenth century to twentieth century.

LAMB'S TONGUE

Mid eighteenth century to twentieth century.

Late seventeenth century and early eighteenth century glazing bars were fairly thick, and later were made narrower. By 1820, bars sometimes were as slim as half an inch. Many people make the mistake, when painting the bars, of painting too far onto the surrounding glass. Glazing bars are also often re-painted carelessly, with an uneven line showing on the glass. Painting too far onto the glass makes the bars look thicker than they really are. Original iron-framed casements should be kept and repaired properly.

The widespread fashion for sash windows was impressive considering that a window tax was imposed from 1696 for houses worth more than five pounds per annum; according to the number of windows. Windows were bricked up and painted, to avoid paying tax; some remain thus today. The window tax was reduced in 1825 and finally repealed in 1851. Excise duty on glass was imposed in 1746 and abolished in 1840.

Two London Building Acts intended to reduce fire risk by limiting the amount of exposed timber, influenced window design nationwide. The Act of 1709 required wooden frames in London to be set four inches behind the front of the wall, instead of being flush with it. The Act of 1774 required windows to have their sash boxes concealed by the wall, instead of being exposed.

'Gothick' windows with Y-shaped glazing bars at the top, and round-headed windows, were introduced in the late eighteenth and early nineteenth centuries.

Unfortunately, Georgian windows sometimes have had sheet glass installed, and the correct number of glazing bars removed. In some buildings, the correct form has been reinstated, greatly to the advantage of the appearance.

Bow windows

Many people have installed bow windows in houses, without considering how this destroys the symmetry of the front elevation. Bow windows were an eighteenth century innovation, used mostly as shop fronts in urban locations.

Victorian windows

The design of Victorian windows was largely determined by improved glass-making technology, from 1838, which enabled larger areas of glass to be made. The number of panes in each sash half was progressively 'four over four', 'two over two' then 'one over one'. One design answer to the blank appearance of sheet glass and no glazing bars was the tripartite window (a sash window with a narrow sash on either side), which was more interesting visually. Another design, from the late 1830s, had narrower panes to the sides, known as margin-lights. As part of the revival of interest in the Queen Anne style and classicism, smaller panes and thicker glazing bars were re-introduced at the end of the nineteenth century.

Victorian sash windows needed additional strength and support for the increased amount of glass: this was provided by including horns under the top sash. It is a mistake, therefore, to include horns in replacement Georgian windows.

Sample pages from *Conservation File 8*.

KENT

PROJECT 7.6, Conservation Show

In 1989 the County promoted a Conservation Show displaying craft skills and products for building renovation. This was a three-day exhibition, held at the Museum of Kent Rural Life, Maidstone, and promoted the use of appropriate materials, techniques and products for the maintenance and repair of traditional buildings. On this occasion over 5300 people visited the show, which was opened by Lord Montague, then Chairman of English Heritage. The Conservation Show was aimed at those who owned a listed building, or lived in a conservation area, or were professionally involved in the business of conservation.

In order to care properly for old buildings it is necessary to understand their methods of construction and the nature of the materials used. Sometimes modern technology can play its part in their repair, but all too often the character of the building can be spoilt by inappropriate design or materials. The show included companies and organizations offering suitable products, or services, which could be appropriate for conservation purposes.

Following the success of the show, future events are planned, where the conservation theme embraced countryside issues, archaeology and museum-based conservation, as well as architectural conservation.

**Craft skills and
products for building renovation**

•**CATALOGUE**•

NOTTINGHAMSHIRE

PROJECT 7.7, Village trail

Many counties have produced attractive guides to particular parts of their county, often in association with the respective District Council. Well presented and informative, they offer an opportunity to promote an area and with the assistance of historical information and attractive illustrations and plans, they are probably one of the best methods of explaining this to be public.

Nottinghamshire County Council have produced a 'walk-about' guide to the village of Laxton: its handy pocket size, its clean and logical display, accompanied by an interesting range of information and graphics, make it a model for others to follow.

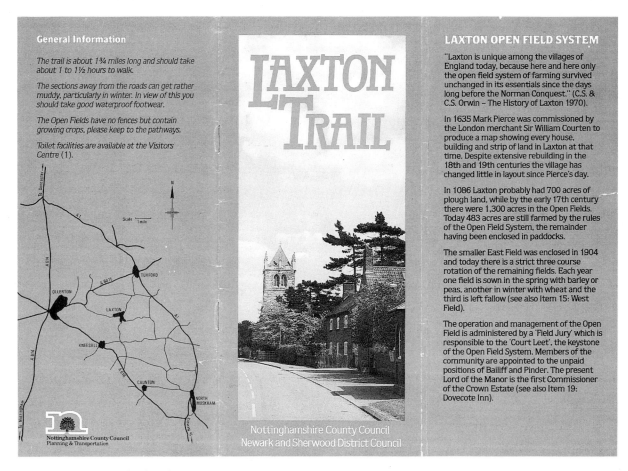

Extracts from *Laxton Trail* leaflet.

SOMERSET

PROJECT 7.8, *Protecting the Historic and Architectural Heritage of Somerset*

A publication entitled *Protecting the Historic and Architectural Heritage of Somerset* has been produced by the County Planning Department in conjunction with all the District Councils in the county, to provide general advice and information on the various measures which exist for the preservation and enhancement of the historic environment of the County. The subject has been divided into four parts; namely archaeology, historic buildings, conservation areas, and historic parks and gardens. Guidance on legal aspects is included and references are made to current legislation and circulars. With the aid of photographs, sketches and line drawings, the publication provides a clear indication of policy and procedures being followed in the county.

To any reader involved in this subject, the explanations in the publication are clear and concise, and the illustrated examples within each section provide ample advice to those contemplating works to historic buildings.

Protecting the Historic and Architectural Heritage of Somerset

Somerset possesses a rich architectural and historic environment derived from the variety of buildings, its landscape and its archaeology. Collectively they constitute a valuable resource, particularly in terms of recreation, tourism, and education.

This heritage is a real capital asset which must be protected for this and future generations.

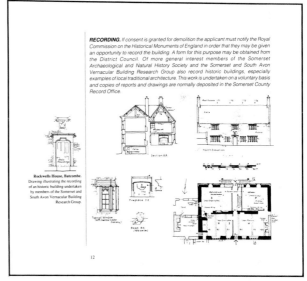

RECORDING. If consent is granted for demolition the applicant must notify the Royal Commission on the Historical Monuments of England in order that they may be given an opportunity to record the building. A form for this purpose may be obtained from the District Council. Of more general interest members of the Somerset Archaeological and Natural History Society and the Somerset and South Avon Vernacular Building Research Group also record historic buildings, especially examples of local traditional architecture. This work is undertaken on a voluntary basis and copies of reports and drawings are normally deposited in the Somerset County Record Office.

Rockwells House, Batcombe. Drawing illustrating the recording of an historic building undertaken by members of the Somerset and South Avon Vernacular Building Research Group.

The cover and an extract from *Protecting the Historic and Architectural Heritage of Somerset*.

357

STAFFORDSHIRE

PROJECT 7.9, The Arthur Brown Trophy

Shortly before his death in 1988 Arthur Brown, a member of Staffordshire County Council since 1973, presented a trophy to be awarded annually for projects illustrating the theme 'Caring for Staffordshire's Buildings'. Arthur Brown had himself been active in architecture in Staffordshire since moving to the County from his native Yorkshire in 1944.

The scheme is open to individuals, parish councils, amenity bodies, small businesses, etc. Larger organizations were deliberately excluded from the outset. The trophy is a ceramic cup depicting various historic buildings in Staffordshire.

It has now been presented twice. In its first year the Uttoxeter Town Council's restoration of a range of timber framed and brick buildings at 32–42 Carter Street on the edge of the town centre conservation area was chosen by judges representing the County Council and the Staffordshire Historic Buildings Trust. Incorporated in the project is the Uttoxeter Heritage Centre.

(a)

(b)

(c)

32–42 Carter Street. (a) Shows Uttoxeter Heritage Centre, and (b) and (c) the street frontage.

SURREY

PROJECT 7.10, Advisory Leaflets

It is, perhaps, inevitable that the Home Counties have endured tremendous development pressures over the past decades, and therefore measures to protect their historic environment need to be wide-ranging and effective. Surrey has an enviable heritage of archaeological sites, historic towns and villages and fine buildings and gardens.

As with other counties, they have seen the value of advisory leaflets in promoting an understanding of this heritage, which contains some 8000 historic buildings alone, apart from archae-ological sites. A series of leaflets is available, being produced jointly by the Surrey County Council and the eleven District Councils to provide advice, without prejudice, for the owners of – and those working with – historic buildings. The subjects of the four already available are: Historic Buildings – An owner's guide; The Preservation and Repair of Timber-framed Buildings; The Repointing of Brick and Stonework; and Windows in Historic Buildings.

WHAT HAPPENS IF YOU FAIL TO MAINTAIN A LISTED BUILDING ?.

If your Local Authority consider that a listed building is not being maintained in a reasonable condition, or that it is deliberately being neglected, they have the power to serve a repairs notice. This will specify the works the council consider reasonable to ensure the proper preservation of the building. The notice will indicate that if these works are not carried out the council may decide to seek a compulsory purchase, (sections 114-117 of the 1971 Act). Local Authorities may also carry out urgent repairs to a vacant or partially vacant listed building and the cost can be recovered from the owner. Where a building is deliberately being neglected the Local Authority may make an application to the Secretary of State for a direction for minimum compensation to be included in the compulsory purchase order. With all of the above measures there is a right of appeal, but it is hoped that it will not prove necessary to use these powers and that owners of historic buildings will take the necessary action to preserve their properties.

St. Martins Church, Dorking.

The Gibbet Stone, Hindhead.

CAN YOU GET HELP WITH THE COSTS OF MAINTAINING A BUILDING?.

Most Local Authorities and the County Council are able to make small discretionary grants towards the costs of structural repairs to historic buildings. These grants are a recognition of the extra costs incurred in keeping repairs in character with the historic fabric. Grants are not intended for standard maintenance or improvements such as re-painting internal walls or fitting new kitchen or bathroom equipment. They are intended to assist with works such as re-roofing, re-pointing, damp-proofing and timber treatment. Grants are not given automatically on application, but are offered only, if after consideration, the works proposed are suitable and funds are available. Works which have been started before an application is made will not normally be considered. Contact your local authority for further information and advice.

If you own a Grade II* or Grade I building, financial assistance may also be available from English Heritage.

Some Local Authorities offer Home Improvement Grants towards the costs of providing basic amenities. They may also offer Housing Repair Grants for major structural works. Both these grants are discretionary and you should contact your local authority to find out if you are eligible for them.

In addition, certain 'approved alterations' for which Listed Building Consent has been obtained may, at present, be 'zero rated' for VAT.

Further information is given in VAT leaflet No 708/1/85, available from HM Customs and Excise.

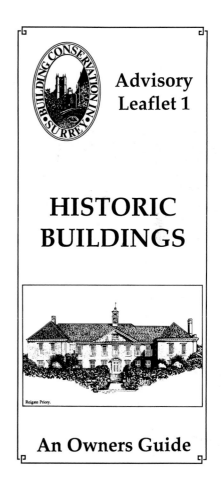

Advisory Leaflet 1

HISTORIC BUILDINGS

Reigate Priory.

An Owners Guide

Advisory Leaflet 1: Historic Buildings – An Owners Guide.

The county of Surrey enjoys a wealth of historic buildings, some 8,000 of which are "listed" in the Department of the Environment Lists of Buildings of Special Architectural or Historic Interest. These buildings cover a wide range of architectural styles and types of construction, as well as being of historic importance. Many of the buildings represent significant events in Surrey's history or illustrate the use of local building materials.

Pressure for development can still pose a threat to the survival of these buildings. However, the greatest danger is from the damage caused by crude or ill-advised improvements or alterations. Carried out without proper consideration, such changes can ruin the structure and integrity of an historic building.

This leaflet explains how and why buildings are listed and what such listing means in practice for owners. The leaflet is also one of a series being produced jointly by the Local Planning Authorities and Surrey County Council to provide advice, without prejudice, to the owners of, and those working with, historic buildings.

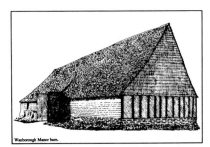

Wanborough Manor barn.

WHY ARE BUILDINGS LISTED?.

Historic buildings in towns and the countryside are part of our heritage. They provide an historical perspective on the development of these areas as well as adding charm and character to the environment. Such buildings may represent significant events, changes in technology, the work of notable architects, be associated with a well-known person, or make a contribution to the overall appearance of an area. Listing ensures that proposals to alter or demolish these structures can be given full consideration and assessed for possible detrimental effects.

WHAT IS A LISTED BUILDING?.

In simple terms, the whole building, both interior and exterior, is covered by the listing. This also includes any object or structure fixed to the building and any object or structure within the curtilage which is not fixed to the building but which forms part of the land and has done so since before 1 July 1948. This would include for example boundary walls, outbuildings (pre 1948), cobbles in a courtyard or any signs attached to the building.

Advisory Leaflet 1: continued.

HOW ARE LISTED BUILDINGS CHOSEN?.

The responsibility for listing buildings rests with the Secretary of State for the Environment. The buildings are selected according to the criteria laid down by the Department of the Environment. All buildings built before 1700 surviving in anything like their original condition are listed. Buildings dating from between 1700 - 1840 are listed, although some selection is necessary. Buildings from 1840 - 1914 are selected where they demonstrate new technological advances, are the principal works of notable architects or are otherwise important examples of civic building. More recent interwar and post war buildings are now also being considered for listing. Listed buildings are not just houses but include a variety of structures such as barns, bridges and statues.

There are three grades of statutory listed buildings and these are classified according to their relative importance:

Grade I : these are buildings of outstanding national importance which should on no account be destroyed. These account for about 4% of all listed buildings.

Grade II* : these are buildings of particular importance and of more than special interest. These account for about 5% of all listed buildings.

Grade II : these are buildings of special interest which warrant every effort being made to preserve them. These account for about 91% of all listed buildings.

In addition, some district councils also maintain a list of buildings of local interest. In general, these are buildings which are not of sufficient quality to warrant statutory listing but which are nonetheless considered to have some merit. Such buildings are not covered by any form of statutory protection but local list status is important in the consideration of a planning application. For information on the status of the local list in your area, you should contact your local planning authority.

Goldsworth Bridge, Basingstoke Canal.

HOW CAN YOU FIND OUT IF YOUR BUILDING IS LISTED ?.

When a building is listed, the owners or occupiers have to be notified by their local authority as soon as possible following the building's inclusion in the statutory list. When purchasing a building, if it is statutorily listed this should be disclosed when the land charge search is made. In addition, copies of the statutory lists are available for inspection at your local authority offices, the County Council, County Library and the National Monument Record at Fortress House, Savile Row, London.

Pollard House, Lingfield.

WHAT IS LISTED BUILDING CONSENT?.

Owners of listed buildings have a responsibility to keep their building in good repair. General maintenance or repair to the building, provided it does not interfere with important features (e.g. panelling) or historic fabric do not normally require consent. However, repairs which require the partial demolition of the building (e.g. roof repairs involving replacement rafters) or maintenance that includes painting may need Listed Building Consent. If in doubt, contact your Local Planning Authority. Listed Building Consent must be obtained if you wish to demolish, alter or extend the building in any way which affects the character or setting.

The consent is similar to planning permission but there are no fees involved. Failure to obtain a consent before altering a listed building is an offence which may result in a fine or a term of imprisonment. The local authority can also serve an enforcement notice in respect of unauthorised works specifying the alleged contravention and detailing the steps required to restore the building to its former state.

If you are granted permission to demolish you are required to notify The Royal Commission on Historic Monuments. Following the granting of Listed Building Consent, at least one month must be allowed for the Commission to either record the building, or state that they have no wish to record it. Only then can demolition work begin.

You may also need planning permission and building regulations approval and in certain instances English Heritage will have to be consulted. These separate requirements would normally be expected to run parallel to the Listed Building Consent.

Works to a listed building can often involve specialist skills. It is therefore adviseable to obtain the services of a reputable and experienced architect, surveyor or builder at an early stage. You should also contact your Local Planning Authority who should be able to help with specialist advice.

WEST SUSSEX

PROJECT 7.11, Biennial Design Awards Scheme

The retention of historic buildings sometimes requires extensions or alterations and often necessitates a new use being found. Successful examples stimulate others to undertake similar work. The County Council promotes and administers a biennial Design Award Scheme for outstanding conservation projects. The conversion of redundant buildings, extensions to and the restoration of Listed Buildings are eligible for entry.

A panel of judges is drawn from the architectural profession and the building industry, and the award takes the form of a metal plaque to be affixed to the building, or a commendation certificate. The publicity given to the award presentation in the local press is welcomed by the winners and the County Council alike. Awards are considered under the categories: restoration; new uses and conversions; extensions; shopfronts; and new buildings in historic settings.

A recent award winner has been the Theological College buildings at the Georgian Priory, Westgate, Chichester. Here the old buildings were sympathetically adapted to form five town houses and six apartments. The work involved the restoration of disused historic buildings, which with their traditional Georgian facades played a vital role in the streetscape of this part of Chichester.

Georgian Priory, Westgate, Chichester.

APPENDICES

Appendix 1
Chief Planning Officers

M.C. Gwilliam
County Planning Officer
Bedfordshire County Council
County Hall
Bedford MK42 9AP
Tel 0234 63222
Fax 0234 228619

R.H. Clarke
Director of Highways and Planning
Berkshire County Council
Shire Hall
Shinfield Park
Reading RG2 9XG
Tel 0734 875444
Fax 0734 310268

G.E. Schoon
County Planning Officer
Buckinghamshire County Council
County Offices
Aylesbury HP20 1UX
Tel 0296 395000
Fax 0296 328848

I. Gilfoyle
County Planning Officer
Cheshire County Council
Commerce House
Hunter Street
Chester CH1 1SN
Tel 0244 603101
Fax 0244 603802

W. Ault
Director of Economic Development and Planning
Cleveland County Council
Gurney House
Gurney Street
Middlesborough TS1 1JJ
Tel 0642 248155
Fax 0642 248314

P. Eyton-Jones
Director of Architecture, Planning and Estates
Clwyd County Council
Shire Hall
Mold CH7 6NH
Tel 0352 2121
Fax 0352 57799

C.G. Griffin
County Planning Officer
Cornwall County Council
County Hall
Truro TR1 3BB
Tel 0872 74282
Fax 0872 70340

W.D. Biggs
County Planning Officer
Cumbria County Council
County Offices
Kendal LA9 4RQ
Tel 0539 721000
Fax 0539 726276

P. Clark
County Planning Officer
Derbyshire County Council
County Offices
Matlock DE4 3AG
Tel 0629 580000
Fax 0629 580121

E. Chorlton
County Engineer and Planning Officer
Devon County Council
County Hall
Exeter EX2 4QH
Tel 0392 382000
Fax 0392 272135

R.T. Townley
County Planning Officer
Dorset County Council
County Hall
Dorchester DT1 1XJ
Tel 0305 251000
Fax 0305 204839

J.E. Nearmouth
Director of Environment
Durham County Council
County Hall
Durham DH1 5UQ
Tel 091 3864411
Fax 091 3865801

D.P. Bown
County Planning Officer
County Planning Department
Dyfed County Council
40 Spilman Street
Carmarthan
Tel 0267 233333
Fax 0267 238603

N. Wheeler
National Park Officer
Pembrokeshire Coast National Park
County Offices
St Thomas' Green
Haverford West
Pembrokeshire
Dyfed SA61 1QZ

C.M. Williams
County Planning Officer
East Sussex County Council
Southover House
Southover Road
Lewes BN7 1YA
Tel 0273 481651
Fax 0273 479040

P.O. Milton
County Planner
Essex County Council
Planning Department
County Hall
Chelmsford
Essex CM1 1LF
Tel 0245 492211
Fax 0245 491189

M. Cook
County Planning Officer
Gwent County Council
County Hall
Cwmbran NP44 2XF
Tel 0633 838838
Fax 0633 838225

J.O. Lazarus
County Planning Officer
Gwynedd County Council
County Offices
Caernarfon LL55 1SL
Tel 0286 672255
Fax 0286 673324

R. Savage
County Planning Officer
Hampshire County Council
The Castle
Winchester SO23 8UE
Tel 0962 846800
Fax 0962 846776

Dr M.P. Hayes
County Engineer and Planning Officer
Hereford and Worcester County Council
County Hall
Spetchley Road
Worcester WR5 2NP
Tel 0905 763763
Fax 0905 763000

B. Merrick
County of Herefordshire and Worcester Building
  Preservation Trust
'Pilgrims'
Cradley
Malvern WR13 5LQ

G.C. Steeley
County Planning and Estates Officer
Hertfordshire County Council
County Hall
Hertford SG13 8DN
Tel 0992 555200
Fax 0992 555648

R. Thompson
County Planning Officer
Kent County Council
Springfield
Maidstone ME14 2LX
Tel 0622 671411
Fax 0622 687620

J.M. Pattison
Chief Planning Officer
Lake District National Park
National Park Offices
Busher Walk
Kendal LA9 4RH
Tel 0539 724555

D. Tattersall
County Planning Officer
Lancashire County Council
East Cliff County Offices
PO Box 160
Preston PR1 3EX
Tel 0772 264111
Fax 0772 264201

T.W. Thompson
Director of Planning and Transport
Leicestershire County Council
County Hall
Glenfield
Leicester LE3 8RJ
Tel 0533 323232
Fax 0533 314186

J.M. Shaw
Director of Planning and Property
Norfolk County Council
County Hall
Martineau Lane
Norwich NR1 2DH
Tel 0603 222500
Fax 0603 222970

M.J. Kendrick
Director of Planning and Transportation
Northamptonshire County Council
Northampton House
Northampton NN1 2HZ
Tel 0604 236650
Fax 0604 236644

P.J. Johnson
Director of Planning and Economic Development
Northumberland County Council
County Hall
Morpeth NE61 2EF
Tel 0670 514343
Fax 0670 515615

J.D. Rennilson
County Planning Officer
North Yorkshire County Council
County Hall
Northallerton DL7 8AQ
Tel 0609 780780
Fax 0609 780447

H. Jackson
Director of Planning and Transportation
Nottinghamshire County Council
Trent Bridge House
Fox Road
West Bridgford
Nottingham NG2 6BJ
Tel 0602 824260
Fax 0602 455113

J.R. Anfield
National Park Officer
Peak District National Park
Aldern House
Baslow Road
Bakewell DE4 1SD
Tel 0629 814321
Fax 0629 812659

D. Keast
County Planning Officer
Powys County Council
Powys County Hall
Llandrindod Wells LD1 5LE
Tel 0597 3711
Fax 0597 2439

R.J. Chapman
Director for the Environment
Somerset County Council
County Hall
Taunton TA1 4DY
Tel 0823 333451
Fax 0823 255288

P. Cope
County Planning Officer
Director of the Environment
South Glamorgan County Council
County Hall
Atlantic Wharf
Cardiff CF1 5UW
Tel 0222 873100
Fax 0222 873161

J. Shryane
Director of Planning and Economic Development
Staffordshire County Council
County Buildings
Martin Street
Stafford ST16 2LE
Tel 0785 223121
Fax 0785 223316

E.E. Barritt
County Planning Officer
Suffolk County Council
St Edmund House
County Hall
Ipswich IP4 1LZ
Tel 0473 265123
Fax 0473 288221

J.W. Bailey
County Planning Officer
Surrey County Council
County Hall
Penrhyn Road
Kingston upon Thames KT1 2DT
Tel 081 541 9400
Fax 081 541 9447

L.W.A. Rendell
Director of Planning and Transportation
Warwickshire County Council
Shire Hall
Warwick CV34 4SX
Tel 0926 410410
Fax 0926 491665

D.M. Morgan
Director of Environment and Highways
West Glamorgan County Council
County Hall
Swansea SA1 3SN
Tel 0792 471111
Fax 0792 471340

P. Bryant
County Planning Officer
West Sussex County Council
County Hall
Chichester PO19 1RL
Tel 0243 777100
Fax 0243 777952

D. Gardner
Director of Planning and Highways
Wiltshire County Council
County Hall
Bythesea Road
Trowbridge BA14 8JN
Tel 0225 753641
Fax 0225 765196

R. Harvey
National Park Officer
Yorkshire Dales National Park
Yorebridge House
Bainbridge
Leyburn
North Yorkshire DL8 3BP

K. Bungay
National Park Officer
Exmoor National Park
Exmoor House
Dulverton
Somerset TA22 9HL

Appendix 2
Useful Addresses

Ancient Monuments Board for Wales
Brunel House
2 Fitzalan Road
Cardiff CF2 1UY
Tel 0222 465511

Ancient Monuments Society (AMS)
St Andrew-by-the-Wardrobe
Queen Victoria Street
London EC4V 5DE
Tel 071-236 3934

Architectural Heritage Fund (AHF)
17 Carlton House Terrace
London SW1Y 5AW
Tel 071-925 0199
Fax 071-321 0180

Arts Council of Great Britain (Arts Council)
14 Great Peter Street
London SW1P 3NQ
Tel 071-333 0100

Welsh Arts Council
9 Museum Place
Cardiff CF1 3NX
Tel 0222 394711

Association of County Councils
Eaton House
66A Eaton Square
London SW1W 9BH
Tel 071 235 1200
Fax 071 235 9549

Association for Industrial Archaeology (AIA)
Ironbridge Gorge Museum
The Wharfage
Ironbridge
Telford
Shropshire TF8 7AW
Tel 0952 45 3522

Association for Studies in the Conservation of Historic Buildings (ASCHB)
c/o Institute of Archaeology
31–34 Gordon Square
London WC1H 0PT

Association of Conservation Officers (ACO)
25 Willington Road
Cople
Bedford MK44 3TH
Tel 0462 686500, ext. 2411
Fax 0462 480043

Association of Preservation Trusts (APT)
c/o Architectural Heritage Fund
Environmental Institute
Greaves School
Bolton Road
Swinton
Manchester M27 2UX
Tel 061-794 8035
Fax 061-794 8072

British Archaeology Association
c/o Society of Antiquaries of London
Burlington House
Piccadilly
London W1V 0HS

British Brick Society
c/o Brick Development Association
Winkfield
Windsor
Berkshire SL4 2DX
Tel 0344 885651
Fax 0344 890129

British Heritage Committee
c/o Sue Garland
The British Tourist Authority
24 Grosvenor Gardens
London SW1W 0ET
Tel 081-846 9000, ext. 4439

The Building Conservation Trust (BCT)
Apartment 39
Hampton Court Palace
East Molesey
Surrey KT8 9BS
Tel 081-943 2277

Cadw (Welsh Historic Monuments)
9th Floor
Brunel House
2 Fitzalan Road
Cardiff CF2 1UY
Tel 0222 465511
Fax 0222 465511

Capel, the Chapels Heritage Society
c/o Department of Pictures & Maps
The National Library of Wales
Aberystwyth
Dyfed SY23 3BU
Tel 0970 623816
Fax 0970 615709

Centre for the Conservation of Historic Parks and Gardens
Institute of Advanced Architectural Studies
University of York
The King's Manor
York YO1 2EP
Tel 0904 433963
Fax 0904 433949

Centre for Conservation Studies, University of York (CCS)
Institute of Advanced Architectural Studies
University of York
The King's Manor
York YO1 2EP
Tel 0904 433963
Fax 0904 433949

The Chapels Society
c/o Hon. Secretary
Frognal
25 Berks Hill
Chorleywood
Hertfordshire WD3 5AG
Tel 09278 2044

The Chartered Institute of Building (CIOB)
Englemere
Kings Ride
Ascot
Berkshire SL5 8BJ
Tel 0344 23355
Fax 0344 23467

Church Commissioners for England (Church Commissioners)
1 Millbank
Westminster
London SW1P 3JZ
Tel 071-222 7010
Fax 071-233 0171

Civic Trust
17 Carlton House Terrace
London SW1Y 5AW
Tel 071-930 0914
Fax 071-321 0180

Civil Trust for Wales
4th Floor
Empire House
Mount Stewart Square
The Docks
Cardiff CF1 6DN
Tel 0222 484606

The Concrete Society
Framewood Road
Wexham
Slough SL3 6RJ
Tel 0753 662226

Conference on Training Architects in Conservation (COTAC)
Keysign House
429 Oxford Street
London W1R 2HD
Tel 071-973 3486
Fax 071-973 3430

The Conservation Unit
Museums & Gallieries Commission
16 Queen Anne's Gate
London SW1H 9AA
Tel 071-233 3683
Fax 071-233 3686

Council for British Archaeology (CBA)
112 Kennington Road
London SE11 6RE
Tel 071-582 0494
Fax 071-587 5152

The Council for the Care of Churches (CCC)
83 London Wall
London EC2M 5NA
Tel 071-638 0971/2

Council for the Protection of Rural England
   (CPRE)
Warwick House
25 Buckingham Palace Road
London SW1W 0PP
Tel 071-976 6433

Council for the Protection of Rural
   Wales/Cymdeithas Diogelu Cymru Wledig
   (CPRW/CDCW)
Ty Gwyn
31 High Street
Welshpool
Powys SY21 7JP
Tel 0938 522525/556212

The Country Landowners Association (CLA)
16 Belgrave Square
London SW1X 8PQ
Tel 071-235 0511

Countryside Commission
John Dower House
Crescent Place
Cheltenham
Gloucestershire GL50 3RA
Tel 0242 521381

Countryside Commission (Wales)
Ladywell House
New Town
Powys SY16 1RD
Tel 0686 626799

Crafts Council (CC)
12 Waterloo Place
London SW1Y 4AU
Tel 071-930 4811
Fax 071-930 4810

Dry Stone Walling Association of Great Britain
   (DSWA)
c/o YFC Centre
National Agricultural Centre
Kenilworth
Warwickshire CV8 2LG
Tel 021-378 0493

Ecclesiastical Architects' and Surveyors'
   Association (EASA)
Scan House
29 Radnor Cliff
Folkestone
Kent CT20 2JJ
Tel 0227 459401 (day)
   0303 54008 (eve)
Fax 0227 450964

English Heritage
Fortress House
23 Savile Row
London W1X 2HE
Tel 071-973 3000
Fax 071-973 3001

Finds Research Group 700–1700
c/o Castle Museum
Norwich NR1 3JU
Tel 0603 611277

The Folly Fellowship
Woodstock House
Winterhill Way
Burpham
Surrey GU4 7JX
Tel 0483 65634/0636 42864

Fortress Study Group (FSG)
Blackwater Forge House
Blackwater
Newport
Isle of Wight PO30 3BJ
Tel 0983 526207

Friends of Friendless Churches
12 Edwardes Square
London W8 6HG
Tel 071-602 6267

Garden History Society
5 The Knoll
Hereford HR1 1RU
Tel 0432 354479

The Georgian Group
37 Spital Square
London E1 6DY
Tel 071-377 1722
Fax 071-247 3441

The Guild of Master Craftsmen
166 High Street
Lewes
East Sussex BN7 1XU
Tel 0273 478449
Fax 0273 478606

Heritage Co-ordination Group (HCG)
Conewood House
Crawley Ridge
Camberley
Surrey GU15 2AN
Tel 0276 22034

Heritage Education Trust (HET)
St Mary's College
Strawberry Hill
Middlesex TW1 4SX
Tel 081-892 0051, ext. 202
Fax 081-744 2080

Historic Churches Preservation Trust (HCPT)
Fulham Palace
London SW6 6EA
Tel 071-736 3054

Historic Farm Buildings Group
c/o Museum of English Rural Life
University of Reading
Whiteknights
PO Box 229
Reading
Berkshire RG6 2AG
Tel 0734 318663

Historic Houses Association (HHA)
2 Chester Street
London SW1X 7RB
Tel 071-259 5688
Fax 071-259 5590

The Inland Waterways Association (IWA)
114 Regent's Park Road
London NW1 8UQ
Tel 071-586 2510/2556

Institute of Field Archaeologists (IFA)
Minerals Engineering Building
The University
PO Box 363
Birmingham B15 2TT
Tel 021-471 2788

Institution of Civil Engineers (ICE)
1–7 Great George Street
London SW1P 3AA
Tel 071-222 7722
Fax 071-222 7500

Institution of Structural Engineers (IStructE)
11 Upper Belgrave Street
London SW1X 8BH
Tel 071-235 4535
Fax 071-235 4294

International Council on Monuments and Sites UK (ICOMOS UK)
10 Barley Mow Passage
Chiswick
London W4 4PH
Tel 081-994 6477

The Ironbridge Institute
Ironbridge Gorge Museum
Ironbridge
Telford
Shropshire TF8 7AW
Tel 0952 45 2751

The Landmark Trust
Shottesbrooke
Maidenhead
Berkshire SL6 3SW
Tel 0628 82 5925
Fax 0628 82 5417

Master Carvers' Association
23 Fisher Gate
York YO1 4AE
Tel 0904 659121
Fax 0904 640018

Medieval Settlement Research Group (MSRG)
c/o National Archaeological Record
Fortress House
23 Savile Row
London W1X 2HE

Men of the Stones
The Rutland Studio
Tinwell
Stamford
Lincolnshire PE9 3UD
Tel 0780 63372

National Heritage Memorial Fund (NHMF)
10 St James's Street
London SW1A 1EF
Tel 071-930 0893
Fax 071-930 0968

National Trust (NT)
36 Queen Anne's Gate
London SW1H 9AS
Tel 071-222 9251
Fax 071-222 5097

Pilgrim Trust
Fielden House
Little College Street
London SW1P 3SH
Tel 071-222 4723

Public Record Office (PRO)
(Medieval and early modern records, nineteenth-century census microfilm reading room)
Chancery Lane
London WC2A 1LR
Tel 071-405 3488
Fax 071-878 7231

Railway and Canal Historical Society (RCHS)
17 Clumber Crescent North
The Park
Nottingham NG7 1EY
Tel 0602 414844

Railway Heritage Trust
Melton House
65 Clarendon Road
Watford
Hertfordshire WD1 1DP
Tel 0923 240250/240288
Fax 071-922 6800

Redundant Churches Fund (RCF)
St Andrew-by-the-Wardrobe
Queen Victoria Street
London EC4V 5DE
Tel 071-248 7461

The Refurbishment Register
Cleave Farm
Burrington
Umberleigh
Devon EX37 9JW
Tel 07693 239

Rescue: The British Archaeological Trust
15a Bull Plain
Hertford
Hertfordshire SG14 1DX
Tel 0992 553377

Royal Archaeological Institute (RAI)
c/o Society of Antiquaries
Burlington House
Piccadilly
London W1V 0HS

Royal Commission on Ancient and Historical Monuments in Wales/National Monuments Record for Wales (RCAHMW/NMRW)
Crown Buildings
Plas Crug
Aberystwyth
Dyfed SY23 2HP
Tel 0970 624381

Royal Commission on the Historical Monuments of England/National Monuments Record (RCHME/NMR)
Fortress House
23 Savile Row
London W1X 2JQ
Tel 071-973 3500
Fax 071-494 3998

Royal Fine Art Commission (RFAC)
7 St James's Square
London SW1Y 4JU
Tel 071-839 6537
Fax 071-839 8475

Royal Institute of British Architects (RIBA)
66 Portland Place
London W1N 4AD
Tel 071-580 5533
Fax 071-255 1541

**Royal Institution of Chartered Surveyors
(Building Conservation Committee)** (RICS)
Building Surveyors Division
12 Great George Street
Parliament Square
London SW1P 3AD
Tel 071-222 7000
Fax 071-222 9430

The Royal Town Planning Institute (RTPI)
26 Portland Place
London W1N 4BE
Tel 071-636 9107
Fax 071-323 1582

Rural Development Commission
141 Castle Street
Salisbury
Wiltshire SP1 3TP
Tel 0722 336255
Fax 0722 332769

Save Britain's Heritage (SAVE)
68 Battersea High Street
London SW11 3HX
Tel 071-228 3336
Fax 071-223 2714

**Society of Architectural Historians of Great
Britain** (SAHGB)
55 Blakeney Road
Sheffield
South Yorkshire S10 1FD

Society for Medieval Archaeology
c/o CLAU
Charlotte House
The Lawn
Union Road
Lincoln LN1 3BG
Tel 0522 545326

Society for Post Medieval Archaeology (Ltd)
(SPMA)
c/o Council for British Archaeology
112 Kennington Road
London SE11 6RE
Tel 071-600 3699
Fax 071-600 1058

Society for the Protection of Ancient Buildings
(SPAB)
37 Spital Square
London E1 6DY
Tel 071-377 1644

The Thirties Society
58 Crescent Lane
London SW4 9PU
Tel 071-738 8480

The Transport Trust
c/o BP International
Britannic House
Moor Lane
London EC2Y 9BU
Tel 071-920 8658

**United Kingdom Institute for Conservation of
Historic and Artistic Works** (UKIC)
37 Upper Addison Gardens
London W14 8AJ
Tel 071-603 5643
Fax 071-603 5643

Vernacular Architecture Group (VAG)
16 Falna Crescent
Coton Green
Tamworth
Staffordshire B79 8JS
Tel 0827 69434

The Victorian Society
1 Priory Gardens
Bedford Park
London W4 1TT
Tel 081-994 1019

Waterway Recovery Group Ltd (WRG)
114 Regents Park Road
London NW1 8UQ
Tel 071-722 7217/071-586 2510
Fax 071-722 7213

Weald and Downland Open Air Museum Library
Singleton
Chichester
West Sussex PO18 0EU
Tel 0243 63348
Fax 0243 63475

Welsh Mills Society/Cymdeithas Melinau Cymru
c/o 269 St Fagans Road
Fairwater
Cardiff CF5 3DW
Tel 0222 569441 (work), 0222 567418 (home)
Fax 0222 578413

Wetland Archaeology Rescue Project (WARP)
c/o Mrs Bryony Coles
Department of History and Archaeology
The University
Exeter EX4 4QH
Tel 0392 77911

The William Morris Society
Kelmscott House
26 Upper Mall
Hammersmith
London W6 9TA
Tel 081-741 3735

BIBLIOGRAPHY

I have found the following books helpful in preparing the Introductions to the various chapters of this book, although there are a great many more books and reports available that cover each subject exhaustively.

L.E.R. Adkins (1989) *An Introduction to Archaeology*, The Apple Press, London.

Michael Aston and Trevor Rowley (1974) *Landscape Archaeology – an introduction to fieldwork techniques on post-Roman landscapes*, David and Charles, Newton Abbot and London.

Michael Aston and James Bond (1976) *The Landscape of Towns*, J.M. Dent and Sons, London.

Marcus Binney, Francis Machin and Ken Powell (1990) *Bright Future – the re-use of industrial buildings*, SAVE Britains Heritage.

Christopher Brereton (1991) *The Repair of Historic Buildings*, English Heritage, London.

Britains Historic Buildings: A policy for their future use (1980), a British Tourist Authority Publication.

The Conversion of Historic Farm Buildings (1990) A guidance pamphlet prepared by English Heritage, London.

N. Cosson (1987) *BP Book of Industrial Archaeology* (2nd edition), David E. Charles, Newton Abbot and London.

Timothy Darvill (1987) *Ancient Monuments in the Countryside – An archaeological management review*, English Heritage, London.

Department of the Environment Policy Planning Guidance Note 16 on Archaeology and Planning (1990) Department of the Environment, London.

Directory of Public Sources of Grant for the Repair and Conservation of Historic Buildings (1990) A conservation publication by English Heritage, London.

Eleanor Michell (1988) *Emergency Repairs to Historic Buildings*, English Heritage, London.

Keith Falconer (series editor) (1977) *Batsford Guide to the Industrial Archaeology of the British Isles*.

New Directions for County Government (1989) (ed. Ken Young), published by the Association of County Councils in association with the Institute of Local Government Studies.

Recording Historic Buildings: A description specification (1990), published by the Royal Commission on the Historical Monuments of England.

Michael Ross (1991) *Planning and the Heritage, Policy and Procedures*, Chapman & Hall, London.

David Smith (1979) *Amenity and Urban Planning*, Crosby Lockwood Stapley, London.

G.J. Wainwright (1990) *The Management of Change – archaeology in historic towns* and Paula Griffith (1990) *Constraint or Opportunity*, papers prepared for the English Historic Town Forum, Lincoln.

A.A. Wood (1969) *Norwich. The Creation of a Foot Street*, Norfolk Corporation, Norwich.

Many County Councils have produced their own 'heritage' books, and, indeed, in 1989, published 'County Centenary Books', which are a mine of information for those studying the work and achievements of an individual county during the past one hundred years. The following have been referred to in preparing this book.

Cheshire. *Man's Imprint on Cheshire* (1975), Oliver Bott and Rhys Williams, published by Cheshire County Council.

Durham. *The Durham Book* (1983), James Wilson, former County Planning Officer, published by Durham County Council.

Hampshire. *Hampshire County Council. 100 years of Progress 1889–1989* (1989), Gillian A Rushton, Hampshire Record Office, published by Hampshire County Council.

Kent. *A Celebration of Kent's Architectural Heritage* (1989), Tony Wimble, published by Kent County Council.

Lancashire. *Lancashire's Architectural Heritage* (1989), John Champness, published by the Lancashire County Council, Planning Department.

Norfolk. *Norfolk County Council: Centenary. A Hundred Years of County Government in Norfolk* (1989), (ed. Clive Wilkins-Jones), published by the Norfolk County Council Library and Information Service.

Northamptonshire. *Northamptonshire County Council, 1889–1989 – Government and County; A history of Northamptonshire County Council* (1989), Jonathan Bradbury, published by the University of Bristol Press.

Shropshire. *Shropshire County Council – A centenary history* (1989), D.C. Cox, published by Shropshire County Council.

Somerset. *The Archaeology of Somerset* (1984), (ed. Michael Aston and Ian Burrow), published by Somerset County Council.

Surrey. *Surrey County Council. Surrey through the Century 1889–1989* (1989), Dr David Robinson, County Archivist, published by the Surrey County Council.

West Sussex. *West Sussex County Council: The first hundred years* (1988), John Godfrey, Kim Leslie and Diana Zeuner, published by West Sussex County Council.

A great number of Reports and booklets from Societies and Trusts, together with copies of the Annual Reports from English Heritage, the Historic Buildings Council for Wales (Cadw), and the recent Civic Trust Awards report have also been referred to in compiling this book, and may be of interest to readers.

For all students of the subject, English Heritage's four monthly *Conservation Bulletin* must be commended. It is a most readable, informative and invaluable document covering the very latest developments carried out by the Commission in the field of the conservation of our built heritage.

COUNTY INDEX

SUBJECT INDEX

Numbers in *italics* refer to illustrations.